Lecture Notes in Computer Sci

Commenced Publication in 1973
Founding and Former Series Editors:
Gerhard Goos, Juris Hartmanis, and Jan van Leeuwen

Frank S. de Boer   Marcello M. Bonsangue
Eric Madelaine (Eds.)

Formal Methods for Components and Objects

7th International Symposium, FMCO 2008
Sophia Antipolis, France, October 21-23, 2008
Revised Lectures

 Springer

Volume Editors

Frank S. de Boer
Centre for Mathematics and Computer Science, CWI
Science Park 123, 1098 XG Amsterdam, The Netherlands
E-mail: F.S.de.Boer@cwi.nl

Marcello M. Bonsangue
Leiden Institute of Advanced Computer Science, Leiden University
P.O. Box 9512, 2300 RA Leiden, The Netherlands
E-mail: marcello@liacs.nl

Eric Madelaine
INRIA, Centre Sophia Antipolis
2004 route des Lucioles, B.P. 93, 06902 Sophia Antipolis, France
E-mail: eric.madelaine@sophia.inria.fr

Library of Congress Control Number: 2009933501

CR Subject Classification (1998): D.2, D.3, F.3, D.4, D.1

LNCS Sublibrary: SL 2 – Programming and Software Engineering

ISSN   0302-9743
ISBN-10   3-642-04166-3 Springer Berlin Heidelberg New York
ISBN-13   978-3-642-04166-2 Springer Berlin Heidelberg New York

springer.com

© Springer-Verlag Berlin Heidelberg 2009
Printed in Germany

Typesetting: Camera-ready by author, data conversion by Scientific Publishing Services, Chennai, India
Printed on acid-free paper   SPIN: 12742981   06/3180   5 4 3 2 1 0

Preface

Large and complex software systems provide the necessary infrastructure in all industries today. In order to construct such large systems in a systematic manner, the focus in development methodologies has switched in the last two decades from functional issues to structural issues: both data and functions are encapsulated into software units which are integrated into large systems by means of various techniques supporting reusability and modifiability. This encapsulation principle is essential to both the object-oriented and the more recent component-based software engineering paradigms.

Formal methods have been applied successfully to the verification of medium-sized programs in protocol and hardware design. However, their application to the development of large systems requires more emphasis on specification, modeling and validation techniques supporting the concepts of reusability and modifiability, and their implementation in new extensions of existing programming languages like Java.

The 7th Symposium on Formal Methods for Components and Objects was held in Sophia Antipolis, France, during October 21–23, 2008. It was realized as a concertation meeting of European projects focussing on formal methods for components and objects. This volume contains the contributions submitted after the symposium by the speakers of each of the following European IST projects involved in the organization of the program:

- The IST-FP7 project COMPAS on compliance-driven models, languages, and architectures for services. The contact person is Schahram Dustdar (Technical University of Vienna, Austria)
- The IST-FP6 project CREDO on modelling and analysis of evolutionary structures for distributed services. The contact person is Frank de Boer (CWI, The Netherlands).
- The IST-FP7 DEPLOY on industrial deployment of advanced system engineering methods for high productivity and dependability. The contact person is Alexander Romanovsky (Newcastle University, UK).
- The IST-FP6 project GridComp on grid programming with components. The contact person is Denis Caromel (INRIA Sophia-Antipolis, France).
- The IST-FP6 project MOBIUS aiming at developing the technology for establishing trust and security for the next generation of global computers, using the proof carrying code paradigm. The contact person is Gilles Barthe (IMDEA Software, Spain).

The proceedings of the previous editions of FMCO have been published as volumes 2852, 3188, 3657, 4111, 4709 and 5382 of Springer's *Lecture Notes in Computer Science*. We believe that these proceedings provide a unique combination of ideas on software engineering and formal methods which reflect the expanding body of knowledge on modern software systems.

Finally, we thank all authors for the high quality of their contributions, and the reviewers for their help in improving the papers for this volume.

June 2009   Frank de Boer
                                                                      Marcello Bonsangue
                                                                          Eric Madelaine

Organization

.

FMCO 2008 was part of the 5th Grids@Work event, co-organized by ERCIM, ETSI, INRIA, I3S, and CNRS. The 5th Grids@Work event was composed of:

The 5th Grid Plugtest, including the *Grids for Finance and Telecommunication Contest*
The GridCOMP conference
The FMCO symposium
The European technical concertation meeting *From Components to Services to Utilities* by the European units D3, *Software, Service Architectures and Infrastructures*, and F3, *eInfrastructures*
ProActive and GCM user groups and tutorials

The FMCO symposia are organized in the context of the project Mobi-J, a project founded by a bilateral research program of The Dutch Organization for Scientific Research (NWO) and the Central Public Funding Organization for Academic Research in Germany (DFG). The partners of the Mobi-J projects are: the Centrum voor Wiskunde en Informatica, the Leiden Institute of Advanced Computer Science, and the Christian-Albrechts-Universität Kiel.

This project aims at the development of a programming environment which supports component-based design and verification of Java programs annotated with assertions. The overall approach is based on an extension of the Java language with a notion of component that provides for the encapsulation of its internal processing of data and composition in a network by means of mobile asynchronous channels.

Sponsoring Institutions

The Dutch Organization for Scientific Research (NWO)

L'Institut National de Recherche en Informatique et Automatique (INRIA)

Le Laboratoire d'Informatique, Signaux et Systèmes de Sophia-Antipolis (I3S, Université de Nice Sophia-Antipolis et CNRS)

Table of Contents

The COMPAS Project

Reusable Architectural Decision Model for Model and Metadata
Repositories 1
    Christine Mayr, Uwe Zdun, and Schahram Dustdar

Formal Behavioral Modeling and Compliance Analysis for
Service-Oriented Systems 21
    Natallia Kokash and Farhad Arbab

The CREDO Project

A Real-Time Extension of Creol for Modelling Biomedical Sensors 42
    Marcel Kyas and Einar Broch Johnsen

Conformance Testing of Distributed Concurrent Systems with
Executable Designs.. 61
    Bernhard K. Aichernig, Andreas Griesmayer, Einar Broch Johnsen,
    Rudolf Schlatte, and Andries Stam

Formal Verification for Components and Connectors.................. 82
    Christel Baier, Tobias Blechmann, Joachim Klein, and
    Sascha Klüppelholz

The DEPLOY Project

Formal Modular Modelling of Context-Awareness 102
    Mats Neovius and Kaisa Sere

Towards Demonstrably Correct Compilation of Java Byte Code 119
    Michael Leuschel

Incremental System Modelling in Event-B 139
    Stefan Hallerstede

The GRIDCOMP Project

An Asynchronous Distributed Component Model and Its Semantics 159
    Ludovic Henrio, Florian Kammüller, and Marcela Rivera

Specification and Verification for Grid Component-Based Applications:
From Models to Tools 180
    Antonio Cansado and Eric Madelaine

Semi-formal Models to Support Program Development: Autonomic
Management within Component Based Parallel and Distributed
Programming.. 204
    M. Aldinucci, M. Danelutto, and P. Kilpatrick

The MOBIUS Project

Session-Based Compilation Framework for Multicore Programming 226
    *Nobuko Yoshida, Vasco Vasconcelos, Hervé Paulino, and
    Kohei Honda*

Abstract Interpretation of Symbolic Execution with Explicit State
Updates 247
    Richard Bubel, Reiner Hähnle, and Benjamin Weiß

BML and Related Tools 278
    Jacek Chrząszcz, Marieke Huisman, and Aleksy Schubert

Author Index... 299

Reusable Architectural Decision Model for Model and Metadata Repositories

Christine Mayr, Uwe Zdun, and Schahram Dustdar

Distributed Systems Group
Information System Institute
Vienna University of Technology, Austria
christine.mayr@inode.at, {zdun,dustdar}@infosys.tuwien.ac.at

Abstract. Models are gaining importance in software development, for instance in the MDD field, as well as in other disciplines such as biology and physics. Hence, tool support is needed to manage these models and metadata about the models. Model repositories support this trend by managing these model artifacts. While setting up model and metadata repositories, architects have to make several fundamental design decisions and balance various forces. In this paper we describe reusable knowledge in form of reusable architectural decisions for IT-architects in setting-up, planning, and developing model and metadata repositories, as well as the main decision drivers. Our decisions are documented in a reusable architectural decision model that can be instantiated for a concrete system. It also supports a lightweight approach to architecture documentation. A case study illustrates the decisions made when setting up our own data access object model repository by walking through the reusable architectural decision model.

1   Introduction

Today many systems are modeled with precisely specified and detailed models. Reasons are among others the increasing support for model interoperability between modeling tools [1] and the increasing use of model-driven development (MDD) [2, 3]. In MDD many tools in a tool chain must work on a set of models, and they must be able to import models developed with external modeling tools.

Model repositories [4, 5, 6, 7] support this trend by managing modeling artifacts, such as models, model instances, model relationships, and so on. A model repository enables modelers to create, retrieve, update, and delete modeling artifacts, and to query for them. Usually additional metadata about the modeling artifacts can be stored and used in the queries. Some repositories are even pure metadata repositories. In addition, model repositories can support extra functionality, such as versioning support, security functions, or storing of related source code artifacts.

Model repositories should often be optimized for the kind of modeling artifacts they store and the task they should fulfill. For instance, usually custom, model-aware queries should be provided that are simplified or more powerful compared to standard queries, such as SQL queries, because they can make use of the information in the modeling artifacts. Model repositories are often realized on top of existing basic technology such

F.S. de Boer et al. (Eds.): FMCO 2008, LNCS 5751, pp. 1–20, 2009.

as databases, but it is not enough to simply store the models in and retrieve them from such a basic technology. In this context, a number of recurring design decisions must be made. In this paper, we propose a reusable architectural decision model that describes these design decisions in a reusable fashion, so that they can be applied step-by-step for new model repository projects. Our research results are based on field notes and observations from our own model repository projects, a detailed analysis of existing model repository projects (both open source and commercial), and interviews and discussions with other model repository developers.

In this paper we provide architectural decision-support for architects in finding a suitable solution to resolve fundamental design problems arising when planning and setting-up model and metadata repositories. For each decision we present recommendations which alternative to choose depending on certain requirements and boundary conditions. Some of our decisions might be intuitively decided in a suitable way by architects. However, other decisions might be skipped or decided in a non-optimal way because of missing knowledge of alternatives and consequences. Our approach mainly aims at decreasing the costs and impact of making wrong decisions related to setting-up model and metadata repositories. In addition, our approach can be used as a lightweight approach to architecture documentation: If the reusable architectural decision model is used to make decisions, only a reference to the decision model is needed to document an architectural decision instead of documenting the whole decision as well as the rationale.

Our paper is structured as follows: First, we define the terms repository, metadata repository, and model repository in Section 2. In Section 3 we introduce reusable architectural decision models as the background of our work. Section 4 provides detailed specifications of the architectural decisions and describes the dependencies between them. We illustrate the applicability of our approach through a case study in the area of modeling jurisdictional provisions in the context of a district court, described in Section 5. Section 6 discusses related work, and finally Section 7 concludes this paper.

2   Repository, Metadata Repository, and Model Repository

Before we go deeper into modeling architectural decisions of a model repository or metadata repository, we would like to define the terms *repository*, *metadata repository*, *model repository* and *model and metadata repository*, as these are forming the basis for our work. The field of repositories is currently a popular area of research. Therefore the following definitions are not exhaustive with regard to a full functional and non-functional requirements specification of a repository. These nominal provisions rather point out those characteristics of a repository we in particular focus on in this paper.

We define a *repository* as a central accessible component storing information about reusable artifacts [8]. Examples of these artifacts are source code, documents, and special-purpose models such as data models for defining the relationships between objects in object-oriented environments, models for MDD [2], biology models [9], and so on. Furthermore, a repository has to provide the means to query these information artifacts and metadata about these information artifacts respectively according to certain search criteria. In many cases, querying is performed using some query language.

When setting-up a repository, architects can choose between two alternatives. The repository can either provide this information by storing the artifacts themselves, or it stores metadata about where and how a specific artifacts can be accessed, reached, or invoked. We refer to a repository that stores arbitrary or user-defined metadata on artifacts as a *metadata repository*. Typical examples of (categorized) information many metadata repositories use is information about users, versions, affiliations, etc.

When a repository provides models and/or model instances such that it either stores models and/or model instances as its artifacts or provides these models and/or model instances stored at other locations, we refer to a repository as a *model repository*. Usually, a model repository additionally provides metadata of models or model instances. Hence, we refer to a repository that provides meta-data of models and/or model instances as a *model and metadata repository*.

3 Reusable Architectural Decision Models

According to Taylor and van der Hoek [10], as well as Jansen and Bosch [11], software architecture is a set of principal design decisions governing a system. During a software system's design phase, architects have to make numerous decisions for organizational and business issues, for matters of broad and detailed design, and for technologies [12]. We refer to a design decision using the term *architectural decision*, if firstly it affects either the architecture of a system or the role of the architect. Secondly, the architects of the system see those decisions as *principal* decisions. The main argument for using architectural decision modeling is that such principal decisions should not get lost.

Architectural decision models are used to document architectural decisions [11, 13, 14]. These architectural models capture selected decision options and justifications for these decisions. In industry, architects often do not attach great value to decision modeling, and, if it is performed at all, architectural decision modeling is usually done in retrospect. Thus, architectural decision models cannot solve all problems of lacking documentation [15, 14]. Many techniques such as text templates and tool support have been proposed, but until now they have not become broadly adopted in practice [12].

Reusable architectural decision models proposed by Zimmermann et al. [16, 12] focus on solving these problems. A *reusable architectural decision model* enhances the basic decision model by steering the architectural decision making activities [12]. Reusable decision models are closely related to software pattern concepts (see [15]). For instance, Zimmermann et al.'s approach uses the resuable decision models for pattern selection. The advantage of this approach is that a decision model that is based on patterns does not have to copy the pattern text and hence is easier to create than a self-contained decision model.

In this paper, we describe a reusable architectural decision model for model and metadata repositories. Each *architectural decision* is characterized by a *decision name*. In our model, the decisions either have a number of *alternatives* or *options* for which the architect can decide. Some alternatives or options have *variants*, which can be selected, too. For each decision, we describe the *forces* or *decision drivers* that must be considered when selecting an alternative or option. Usually, the different alternatives and options have different *consequences* with regard to the forces. To illustrate the alternatives or options, we describe a few *known uses*. Finally, decisions have *relationships* to

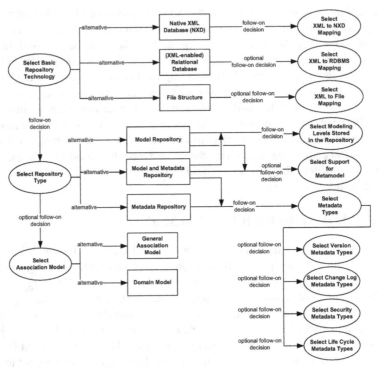

Fig. 1. Dependencies between architectural decisions

other decisions. For instance, a decision can be a follow-on decision to another decision, if a specific alternative or option is chosen.

4   Architectural Decisions

In this section, we describe architectural decisions architects must make for planning, setting-up, developing, and installing a model repository. In particular, we focus on the underlying data model design – the core of a model repository. At first, we give a short overview over these decisions and the dependencies between them (see Figure 1). Subsequently, we present each of these decisions in detail.

The decision model is distilled from our experiences, our study of other projects (both open source and commercial), as well as the documented experiences of others. Please note that the decisions and their alternatives are for this reason not exhaustive.

- *Select Basic Repository Technology*: Usually, one of the first decisions is which basic technology should be used for the repository. Depending on the types and amounts of models or metadata to be stored, either an XML database, a specific file structure, or a standard relational database are alternatives.
- *Select XML to NXD Mapping*: When architects decide for an XML database, they can select between two basic mapping alternatives, namely an XSD model-based and a text-based approach.

- *Select XML to RDBMS Mapping*: When architects choose an RDMBS, an important follow-on decision is how to map the XML documents to the database, namely by a domain model mapping or an XSD model mapping.
- *Select XML to File Mapping*: When architects decide for a file storage solution, they can select between three basic mapping alternatives, namely a XSD model-based, a domain model-based and a simple text-based approach.
- *Select Repository Type*: Depending on important decision drivers such as searching capabilities and data categorization, architects can decide for a Model Repository, a Metadata Repository, or a Model and Metadata Repository.
- *Select Support for Metamodel*: When architects decide for storing models by selecting the Model Repository and Model and Metadata Repository respectively, they optionally can choose a Metamodel that specifies the elements of the stored models.
- *Select Modeling Levels Stored in the Repository*: Architects have to select the modeling levels such as models, model instances, source code, and runnable code to be stored in a Model Repository or a Model and Metadata Repository.
- *Select Metadata Types*: In case a Metadata Repository or a Model and Metadata Repository is used, architects can select model-independent metadata such as version information, ownership, affiliations, and security data.
- *Select Version Metadata Types*: An optional follow-on decision of selecting necessary metadata types is choosing an adequate version granularity. Versioning can be either settled on the model or model element level.
- *Select Change Log Metadata Types*: According to the decision of selecting version metadata, architects have to decide whether to add change log metadata to either the model or model element level.
- *Select Security Metadata Types*: Architects can choose among several security metadata options. Unlike the decisions described before, security metadata does not solely focus on several artifacts, but on mechanisms to secure the whole repository.
- *Select Life Cyle Metadata Types*: Architects can opt for a life cycle manager, that can determine if a requested action is allowed dependent on the current state.
- *Select Association Model*: This decision deals with whether to model relationships in the domain models themselves or using a general association model [17].

4.1 Architectural Decision: Select Basic Repository Technology

A fundamental task of a model repository architect is to choose a basic storage technology for the repository. As illustrated in Figure 2, there are three basic alternatives for storing artifacts: Native XML Databases (NXD), (XML-enabled) RDMBS, and a File System using a specific file structure. RDF triple stores are a popular variant of NXD.

Important decision drivers for this decision are the *amount of data* to be stored in the repository and the expected *performance/throughput* the repository should provide. For developers and administrators it is important to know which *technology know-how* is needed in order to set-up and run the repository technology. One important aspect of the repository technology are the *searching capabilities* provided. When a partner or a customer should be enabled to search for a model or model instance, it is helpful

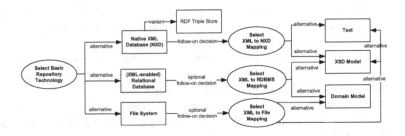

Fig. 2. Architectural Decision: Select basic Repository Technology

to use a repository based on *standard technology*, as standard interfaces often ease the integration. For standard technologies, often a number of tools and IDE plugins exist, which help developers and partners to work with the repository.

There are a number of follow-on decisions related to mapping XML to one of these storage alternatives. Although we mention alternative exchange formats such as objects of a programming language (e.g., as possible in EMF [18]), because XML is the common model data exchange format, in the following we focus only on an in-detail description on XML model exchange format mappings.

Each of these approaches has its own advantages and limitations [19]. Particularly with regard to throughput and huge amount of data, a NXF system may work best, because no mapping process from XML files to database schemes is required [19]. Furthermore most native XML databases support sophisticated full-text searches. However, due to the document-centric approach, complex queries can have longer response times compared to (XML-enabled) RDBMS systems [20]. One known use is XTC, the XML Transformation Coordinator for XML Document Transformation Technologies [21].

Relational databases provide both maturity, scalability, portability, and stability [19, 22], and they are the RDBMS that are probably most widely used today [19]. Known uses of model repositories based on RDMBS are the SWISS–MODEL Repository [23] for three-dimensional comparative protein structure models and the BrainML Model Repository [24] storing neuroscience data.

Alternatively, especially for small amounts of data, architects could choose a simple file structure as repository storage. For this, one of many known uses is the CellML Model Repository [9] for storing and exchanging computer-based mathematical models. Of course, when using a file storage, searching a large amount of data, could be rather inefficient in comparison to using either a NXD system or RDBMS. However, for repositories with only small amount of data, this might be the simplest and most appropriate solution. In particular when using proprietary file formats, the repository can be set-up quickly, because no data mapping is required.

4.2 Architectural Decision: Select XML to NXD Mapping

Provided that architects opt to use a Native XML database, they can decide between two basic storing alternatives (see Figure 2). Either the entire XML document can be stored in *Text* format or the XML document can be modeled as DOM and mapped to *XSD*

Model objects such as Elements, Values, etc. [19]. In the former case the database or file managing component has to manage indexes to improve performance on its own. In the latter case, XML documents can be stored as type-annotated trees on disk pages [25]. These database trees are indexed with path-specific indexes, and can be queried with XQuery and SQL/XML [25].

Whether to use a text-based or an XSD model-based mapping depends on the required *performance* and on the *effort* to establish the system. There are many NXD systems both commercial and open-source. Most XML databases such as DB2 [25] support the *XSD Model* for Mapping XML to corresponding tree structures in NXD [20].

4.3   Architectural Decision: Select XML to RDBMS Mapping

Provided an RDMBS database is selected as the basic repository technology and the raw models are provided in XML format, an important follow-on decision is how to resolve the conflict between the hierarchical nature of an XML data model and the row and column nature of a relational data model [19, 20]. Architects can mainly choose between two alternatives: They can either decide to map the *Domain Model* elements to a database schema or use an *XSD model* approach by mapping standard *XML model* elements to RDBMS. By using the *Domain Model* mapping approach, a separate table is generated for each domain model element. In contrast, the *XSD Model* mapping approach is characterized by a lesser number of resulting tables and columns, because unlike the *Domain Model* approach, several XML elements are combined into a single table. Moreover, the resulting RDBMS schema, here, can either be generated from an XSD or from a DTD. Algorithms for mapping XML data to relational data can be found in [20]. See [26] for a comparison of the most cited and DTD-independent methods in terms of resource usage and query response times.

Many commercial XML-enabled database systems such as SQL Server and Oracle support both the *XSD Model* and the *Domain Model* mapping. In the latter approach the existing data model is extended to an additional XML data type [20].

Decision drivers are both *performance* and the *effort* to accomplish the mapping. In case neither an XSD nor a DTD exists, architects should decide to use the *XSD Model* mapping approach. Additionally, this approach can reduce the number of join operations incurred during query operations [19]. Florescu's and Kossmann's work [27] shows that even the simplest and most obvious approaches provide a good performance. Thus, in most cases, we would clearly recommend to use the *XSD model* mapping approach, especially if performance is the most important decision driver.

4.4   Architectural Decision: Select XML to File Mapping

In case architects decide to use an appropriate file system structure and the models are stored as XML documents, they can select among three basic storing alternatives (see Figure 2). The file itself can contain the entire XML document as *Text*, the XML document can be separated according to the *XSD* model, or the document can be split into several files according to its *Domain Model*.

The advantages and disadvantages for using the XSD model-based or the Domain model-based approach were already discussed in Section 4.2 and Section 4.3

respectively. The obvious advantages of the text-based alternative are simplicity and the low effort to establish the system. Thus which alternative to use depends on the required *performance* and on the *effort* to establish the file system storage.

4.5   Architectural Decision: Select Repository Type

Depending on the repository's functional requirements, models, model instances, and/or metadata must be stored in a model repository. As already defined in Section 2, we can distinguish three alternative repository types: *Model Repository, Metadata Repository*, and *Model and Metadata Repository*. Figure 1 depicts these alternatives. Most repositories use metadata to describe general characteristics such as version information, user information, and security data. In contrast to metadata, models contain domain-specific elements. Some metadata, such as version information, is linked to specific models as add-on data, other metadata, such as user authorization data, can be considered as general repository data that is not linked to specific model data. In Section 4.8 we focus on selecting adequate metadata types.

The decision drivers for storing models in the repository are mainly *functional requirements*. Examples are: An important decision for architects is if the MDD paradigm [2] should be supported using the repository architecture. When using MDD, the source code is generated from the underlying models and these models must be accessible from the repository. In Section 2 we stated that a repository should provide *query mechanisms* to search for repository artifacts according to certain search criteria. These query mechanisms are based on categorized data such as domain specific model data and repository metadata.If architects want to store non-model artifacts, in order to provide appropriate searching mechanisms, they should at least provide these artifacts with some add-on metadata. Accordingly, in case solely non-model artifacts are stored in the repository and provided with add-on metadata, architects decide in favor of a *Metadata Repository*.

Architects choose a *Model Repository* if they intend to store models in the repository and do not require additional metadata, because the domain models possibly contain part of this information. Moreover, adding special-purpose metadata such as ownership and affiliation information to repositories in small companies may not be necessary.

If more sophisticated queries about the repository artifacts are required, architects should consider storing categorized model data and thus select the *Model and Metadata Repository* alternative. A known use of a *Model and Metadata Repository* is the Data Access Object (DAO) Repository that we developed during our studies. In our case study (see Section 5) we give more details about the DAO repository by applying it to our reusable architecture decision model.

Once this decision has been made and if we have decided for one of the alternatives that include metadata, we need to make a follow-on design decision, selecting the types of metadata that are represented in the repository. Accordingly, if we have decided for one of the alternatives that include modeling data, we need to make one or two follow-on decisions: An optional follow-on decision is selecting support for metamodels, and an mandatory decision is selecting the modeling levels stored in the repository.

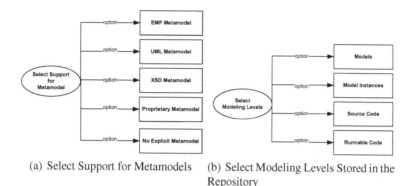

(a) Select Support for Metamodels   (b) Select Modeling Levels Stored in the Repository

Fig. 3. Architectural Decisions

4.6 Architectural Decision: Select Support for Metamodel

Provided that architects decide for a *Model Repository* or a *Model and Metadata Repository*, they can select a metamodel for the domain models to be stored. A metamodel describes models and thus is the basis for model validation by tools. Eessaar illustrates the advantages of using metamodels [28]: Metamodels are a clear and useful supplement to textual specifications. Compared to a purely textual specifications, metamodels enable a much more compact and clear overview of the model. In addition, metamodels such as UML and EMF [18] can support visualizing models and thus ease model readability and understandability. It has also been demonstrated that a metamodel could be used to compare heterogeneous models. In the literature there are various approaches addressing the problem of integrating heterogeneous models [29, 30].

Decision drivers are both the *functional* and *technical requirements*. Firstly, architects might use an explicit metamodel if they wish to benefit from one or more of the properties described above. Secondly, technology reasons such as using MDD [2] can be a determining factor for using a metamodel. In case of MDD [2], architects profit from tool support. For instance, they can use a metamodel-based generator, such as openArchitectureWare [31], to generate source code from models specified by a corresponding metamodel such as EMF [18]. If architects do not want to profit from these functional and technical features, they can make use of a simple, but much less flexible approach: To support no explicit meta-model. That means, to hard-code the metamodel information and thus specifying a model without an underlying metamodel.

In addition to that option, in Figure 3(a) we illustrate several metamodel options among which architects can select: EMF [18], UML, XSD, and a proprietary domain meta model (see Figure 3(a)). They should choose a proprietary domain metamodel, if standard metamodels such as UML and EMF [18] do not fulfill the requirements.

A known use of using EMF [18] metamodels, is our VbMF [32] repository that we developed during our studies. A known use for a model repository that loads UML2 models into EMF is the AndroMDA's EMF UML2 Repository [33]. In contrast, the BrainML Model Repository [24] consists of a standard XML Schema, defining XML elements, and referencing other schema definitions using standard mechanisms.

4.7   Architectural Decision: Select Modeling Levels Stored in the Repository

Provided that architects choose a *Model Repository* or a *Model and Metadata Repository*, an important follow-on decision is to select the modeling levels stored in the repository: Models, model instances, source code, runnable (byte) code, or all of them.

Figure 3(b) depicts this architectural decision and its four modeling layer options. In the following we specify important decision drivers for each of these layers.

At first, architects should face the question whether to store models or not. In this context an important decision driver is *automatic validation* of new models and model instances. When storing models in addition to model instances, the model instances can be validated using their models. In order to accomplish this validation, the model instances have to be linked with their specific models. Accordingly, if an automatic syntax-check fails, the publishing request can be rejected by the repository. Furthermore, in an extended version the repository could try to *automatically adapt* existing model instances when the underlying model changes. When architects do not want to profit by the advantages of automatic syntax checking and automatic adaption of source code, they can ignore the model layer in favor of saving *storage space* and *effort*.

The next decision is whether architects should store model instances in the repository. This decision is closely related to the required *search capabilities*. Besides the desired search capabilities, another decision driver is whether to support MDD or not. In case MDD is supported, model instances rather than source code are stored by the repository because the generator can use transformations to generate the source code. In some cases, this means that the transformations for the generator should also be placed in the repository . However, even for non-model-driven projects, we recommend storing model instances, if at least simple queries to find certain source code are required.

There is also the option to store the model instances but not the models. An example of a known use that stores model instances, but no models is the Eclipse CDO Project [6]. In contrast, another known use, the Netbeans Metadata Repository (MDR) [7], stores both models and model instances.

Whether the repository should provide source code, depends both on the *technical requirements*, such as using MDD [2], and on the *development environment* and *platform* of repository users. When MDD is used, commonly *technology- and platform-independent* model instances are stored in the repository. Accordingly, on the client side, repository users can generate source code from these model instances according to their specific platform- and technology requirements. Thus, if more than one technology or platform should be supported, source code should not be stored in the repository, but generated by the repository users. Otherwise, if no technology- and platform-dependent source code generators are required, architects can decide to store the source code in the repository. In this case, generated source code can also be stored in the repository, e.g., to archive it. Alternatively, the source code can be stored in an external repository specified by references in the models (if the model instances should be aware of the source code artifacts) or appropriate metadata information (for more information about selecting metadata types please refer to Section 4.8).

The next decision architects should make is whether the repository should supply runnable byte code and how. In the following we present three alternatives: The first alternative proposes to build the source code on the client side. This alternative primarily depends on the users' *source code build environment* that has to fulfill the *technical requirements* to build the source code. The second alternative discusses storing the byte code in the repository itself. A disadvantage of this alternative are the associated *storage costs*. An advantage is that *building the source code* on the client side is not necessary. The third alternative only provides metadata about where and how to locate a runnable software component. From the users' point of view, this alternative is probably the simplest one. However, for technical reasons, such as performance issues, architects could reject this alternative and decide in favor of storing or building the byte code.

4.8   Architectural Decision: Select Metadata Types

Common repositories include metadata to provide additional, model-independent information of repository artifacts. Figure 4 shows a few options: Metadata can include versioning information; change log data; ownership and/or affiliation information; security data such as information on role-based access control and identity management; location information; life cycle data and data for internationalization features (see Section 4.8). In the following we give a detailed overview of each of these metadata options commonly used in repositories. Architects can use this checklist to decide whether to apply a certain metadata type or not. We have developed this checklist by studying common repositories to the best of our knowledge. However, due to the diversity of possible metadata types, the list is not exhaustive. After illustrating the checklist, in the proceeding sections (4.9, 4.10, 4.11, 4.12) we particularly focus on the follow-on decisions as well as resulting options and alternatives depicted in Figure 4.

Version Information Metadata. Architects have to decide whether to add version metadata or not. In the simple case, architects can opt for using no versioning. For this purpose, they solely need to provide the *most recent version* of repository artifacts.

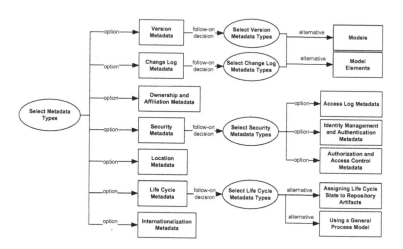

Fig. 4. Architectural Decisions: Select Metadata Types

Otherwise, if the repository shall support version management, the have to make the follow-on decision illustrated in Section 4.9.

Change Log Metadata Change log metadata can include information about which user inserted or updated a certain repository artifact. The decision whether to add change log data is based on the previous decision of adding *version information metadata*. Thus, architects can not opt for providing change log metadata, not until they decide in favor of using version metadata. In Section 4.10, we present the follow-on decision of selecting different change log metadata types.

Ownership and Affiliation Metadata. Architects can decide to tag repository artifacts with ownership and affiliation metadata. This information can contain name, contact details, and affiliation information of repository artifact owners. By using this metadata, architects can enhance *reuse* of stored artifacts such as models, model instances and source code. Adding this metadata and thus being able to search for specific artifacts, is especially essential in *large and medium-sized companies*. If, however, stored repository artifacts are intended to be solely used by a *small team* of developers anyway, architects could determine to omit this type of metadata.

Security Metadata. According to their security requirements, architects can choose one or more types of security metadata (see ebXML Registry Services and Protocols [17]). Please note that unlike other types of metadata, security metadata does not solely focus on several artifacts, but on mechanisms to secure the whole repository. In Section 4.11 we present some basic security options architects can install.

Location Metadata. Another type of metadata architects can choose is location metadata. As already mentioned in Section 4.7, source code and runnable code can be linked to models and model instances stored in other repositories. The decision drivers for deciding whether source code and runnable (byte) code should be stored in the repository itself or in an external repository are the same as those describd in Section 4.7. Besides source code and runnable code, location metadata can be important, e.g., for linking model instances or source code to specific documentation on document servers. In order to *save storage cost* and *maintainance efforts*, we recommend to decide in favor of referring to existing documentation instead of storing this information redundantly.

Life Cycle Metadata. A repository incorporating life cycle metadata manages all life cycle actions such as inserting, updating, deleting, and deprecating repository artifacts. Besides these basic actions, the life cycle manager can oversee further actions such as validating model instances and finally publishing changes to repository users. Depending on the current life cycle state, the life cycle manager determines if the requested action is allowed and consequently performs or rejects the action. In Section 4.12 we present the follow-on decision of selecting a suitable life cycle metadata type.

Internationalization Metadata. Internationalization metadata can be used for storing location-specific settings, such as different languages and coding sets. In the EBXML standard [17] internationalization metadata is defined as attributes that are I18N capable and may be localized into multiple native languages. Architects may choose internationalization metadata, if e.g. *international project members* shall access the repository or *different coding sets* shall be supported.

4.9   Architectural Decision: Select Version Metadata Types

When storing models, architects can decide to either add version information meta-data to the whole model or to each model element. The CellML Model Repository [9] is a known use of a repository, that stores version information at the model level. If a CellML model is modified, the new updated version(s) are added to the repository and they are automatically allocated a new version number [9]. The BrainML Model Repository [24] is another known use that adds version information metadata at the model level. Version numbers start at 1 and are incremented whenever an augmented or modified version of the model is submitted. Earlier versions remain available in the repository and can be referenced by their version number to support data using them.

Standards such as UDDI [34], EbXML [17], and the Content Repository API for Java Technology of Java Specification Request (JSR) 170 [35] support adding version information to model elements. JCR consists of one or more workspaces that each consist of a tree of items representing either nodes or properties. A content repository [35] workspace that supports versioning may contain both versionable and nonversionable nodes. A known use open-source implementation variant of a Java Content Repository is eXo JCR [36]. According to the JCR, eXo JCR supports separate versioning of repository artifacts such as model elements.

The decision, which of the alternative to select, depends on the type of update-strategy in case of changes. If selective updates are desirable, we recommend using versioning for *Model Elements*. If artifacts such as models should be updated as a whole, the alternative of versioning *Models* rather than *Model Elements* should be chosen.

4.10   Architectural Decision: Select Change Log Metadata Types

The decision whether to set-up versioning on the model or model element level is closely related to the question how fine-grained changes need to be traced and monitored. When choosing the alternative to version *Model Elements* a specific event log of changes for each model element is stored. An alternative is versioning of *Models* where an event log of changes is only available on the model level.

If architects want to provide change log data on the model element level, the corresponding change log information on the model level can be a view of all related model element change log data. Moreover, when architects only need change logging on the model level, they save *effort* compared to storing logs on the model element level. However, if architects already decided in favor of *versioning*, the change log information should be set-up on the same model and model element respectively as selected for the previous version management decision.

4.11   Architectural Decision: Select Security Metadata Types

Provided that architects settled for storing security metadata, they can decide in favor of one or more of the following options.

The first option is to provide *access log metadata*. Hereby, the repository keeps a journal of all significant actions performed by repository requesters on repository resources. Another option is to establish *identity management and authentication*.

Choosing this option means, the repository manages the identity and credentials associated with authorized users and services. Finally, architects can enable authorized users to perform specific actions or to access specific resources by establishing the *authorization and access control* option. The repository provides a mechanism to protect its resources from unauthorized access. In this context, architects can augment a role based access control solution with well-defined authorizations for each role.

4.12   Architectural Decision: Select Life Cycle Metadata Types

In this decision, architects have two basic alternatives: They can either *assign a life cycle state to each repository artifact* or implement a *general process model* containing flows of activities. In the latter case, a process engine is needed to drive the execution of activities [8]. When deciding for the first alternative, the *complexity* of the life cycle grows much more than proportional by the number of life cycle states. Thus, if architects intend to use only *basic life cycle actions* such as insert, update, and delete, this alternative is a very effective one.

A known use implementation incorporating life cycle metadata is the ebXML Registry Reference Implementation Project [37]. The exXMLRR project aims at delivering a functionally complete reference implementation for the OASIS ebXML specification [17]. According to the ebXML standard, each RegistryObject instance must have a life cycle status indicator that is assigned by the registry. In contrast, the alternative of using a general process model should be used if there are potentially new actions that will be developed in future. Accordingly, if architects attach a great value on *life cycle scalability*, they should decide in favor of a general life cycle model.

4.13   Architectural Decision: Select Association Model

Modeling associations among models and model instances is a commonly addressed problem today. As described in [38] a current problem in process-driven SOAs is to retrieve the relationships between different components, such as which service operations can be invoked from which process activity and which services access which data. Furthermore components that are not depending on any component can be seen as obsolete and thus can be deleted [38]. Another benefit of modeling dependencies between different components is to visualize these dependencies to better support understandability of the models. For this purpose, graphical tools can be designed because the tools are what give value to a repository [39].

As seen in Figure 1 there are two basic alternatives among which architects can choose: As described in our previous work [38], general models can specify associations between certain special-purpose models. In the example, our view-based models of the View-based Data Modeling Framework describe the associations between processes, services, and DAOs [38]. If domain models do not specify associations between them, the repository should handle these associations by defining a general Association Model as specified in the EbXML standard [17]. EbXML's Association Information Model defines classes that enable artifact instances to be associated with each other.

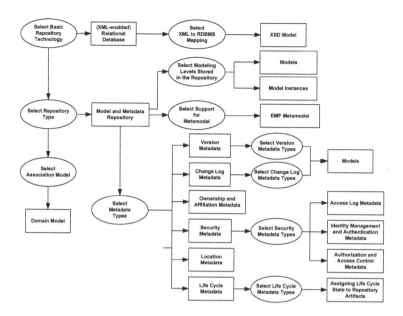

Fig. 5. Case Study: Selected Architecture Decisions of the DAO Repository

5   Case Study

In this case study we illustrate major design decisions that we made when setting-up our own Data Access Object (DAO) Model Repository. During the design process of the repository we were faced with several fundamental architectural decisions. In this case study we reflect the decisions made to set-up our DAO Model Repository by walking through the reusable architectural decision model presented in the section before (see Figure 5).

Before we walk step by step through our reusable architecture decision model we would like to shortly motivate the use of a Data Access Object (DAO) Model Repository: Developers typically store DAOs in local file systems and concurrent versioning systems, such as CVS or SVN. However, especially as the number of DAOs grows, finding a particular DAO on a concurrent versioning system, in order to reuse the DAO, can become rather time-consuming. Thus, developers need more sophisticated query mechanisms to quickly locate existing database operations in order to increase DAO reuse. The DAO Model Repository supports queries for retrieving desired DAOs by diverse search criteria, such as finding all DAOs accessing a particular database, all DAO operations inserting data into a particular table, or all DAO operations updating a certain column of a table. Moreover, DAO developers are able to query ownership information about a certain DAO and thus look for all DAOs registered by a certain user or department. Furthermore we use a model-driven approach so that DAO developers do not have to deal with various Object Relational Mapping (ORM) technologies. The goal was that developers simply need to generate source code from a chosen model instance persistently stored in the DAO Model Repository or from a newly defined model respectively to create a DAO for a specific ORM technology.

1. *Select Basic Repository Technology*: When setting-up our DAO repository, we decided in favor of the *(XML-enabled) Relational Database* alternative. Our main decision driver was that RDBMS are very common and hence, we can benefit from tool support. We decided against using a *NXD* system, because our DAO repository models have many associations between them and thus many joins are necessary when querying DAO data. Accordingly, they are the joins in *NXD* storages, that can have longer response times compared to RDBMS. As searching a large number of DAOs could be rather inefficient, for us, a *File System* storage, was out of question.

2. *Select XML to RDBMS Mapping*: We decided in favor of the *XSD Mapping Model* alternative because this approach requires less tables to join and thus results in quicker response times than the *Domain Model* approach.

3. *Select Repository Type*: Our DAO Model Repository should primarily store models, but also to be defined metadata. As a consequence we opted for the *Model and Metadata Repository* alternative.

4. *Select Support for Metamodel*: We chose *EMF* [40] as an explicit metamodel to specify our models of Viewbased Data Modeling Framework [38]. Thus, we can benefit from existing tool support such as openArchitectureWare [31] to generate code from existing model instances.

5. *Select Modeling Levels Stored in the Repository*: Our generated DAO source should be dependent on the specific Object Relational Mapping (ORM) technology such as HIBERNATE [41] or IBATIS [42]. For this purpose our DAO Repository stores technology- and platform-independent *model instances*, that are used for source code generation on the client side. Another requirement was to automatically validate checked-in model instances. In order meet this requirement, we settled for storing *models* in addition to model instances. As they are the repository users that have to generate the source code, they need to integrate required source code generation tools into their development environment. Accordingly, repository users generate *runnable code* by compiling the generated source code. Thus our repository does neither store source code nor runnable code.

6. *Select Metadata Types*: According to the decision of selecting the Model and Metadata Repository as repository type, we decide to add metadata to our repository. In the following we focus on those decisions that are not covered by follow-on decisions: We settled for adding *ownership and affiliation* metadata to being able to efficiently set-up our prototype in medium-sized and large companies. Up-to-now, we do not relate to documentation or source code stored on other repository. Thus we do not store *location metadata* in our repository. As our Repository still is a prototype solution, at the moment, we do not provide *internationalization* metadata.

7. *Select Version Metadata Types*: Our DAO repository requires *versioning* artifacts. However, we wanted to save extra efforts related to *versioning model elements*. Thus, we decided in favor of adding version information metadata to *whole models and model instances*.

8. *Select Change Log Metadata Types*: As this decision is based on the decision of selecting version metadata types, we opted for adding *change log metadata to models and model instances* rather than to *model and model instance elements*.

9. *Select Security Metadata Types*: As we intend to provide our repository to industry, we added basic *security* metadata for all three security options illustrated before, namely *access log metadata*, *identity management and authentication metadata* and *authorization and access control metadata*.

10. *Select Life Cycle Metadata Types*: Our repository incorporates a basic *life cycle manager*, that manages basic actions such as insert, update, delete and validate. As we required both a simple solution and the life cycle manager not necessarily to be scalable related to new actions and states, we opted for *assigning a life cycle state to repository artifacts*. We have decided against using a *general process model*, because this solution seems a bit oversized for our prototype repository solution.

11. *Select Association Model*: Our DAO models incorporate relationships between *domain model instances*. Thus, we use our own *domain models* to specify associations between DAO model instances instead of using a *general association model*.

6   Related Work

To be able to accomplish this work we were inspired of repositories in general. In [8], Bernstein and Dayal give a fundamental overview of repository technology as well as functional requirements of a repository. Afterwards, we focused on repositories incorporating metadata. A common representative of Metadata Repositories are service repositories that contain metadata about location information such as service bindings according to the Web Service Description Language (WSDL). Here, there exist various standards such as [34], ebXML [17] and related implementations such as the ebXML Repository Reference implementation [37] and the WebSphere Service Registry and Repository that is based on UDDI.

Furthermore we focused on current model repository standards and implementations. As illustrated in this paper, there are many known model repository implementations such as Netbeans MDR [7] that stores models and model instances and Eclipse CDO [6] that stores models, but no XMI model instances. In [43] France et.al.'s interesting approach introduces a development plan for setting up model repositories storing MDD artifacts. In contrast to our paper, the authors of the ReMoDD project in particular focus on the types of interactions that are most useful for repository users. Besides, the ReMoDD project's scope of research does not include storing metadata.

Finally, there are many articles that focus on each of the illustrated decisions for their own. For example, several work [19,20] focus on algorithms of mapping XML model instances to a certain Repository storage type. However, for the best of our knowledge there is no work that connects all these illustrated architecture decisions with each other. In [44] Milanovic et.al. presents an approach of designing and implementing a repository that supports storing and managing of artifacts such as metamodels, models, code, and their metadata. As our approach, the illustrated repository stores metadata such as versioning information. However they do not provide an overview about different types of metadata such as those presented in our work. They exemplary illustrate the design of the BIZY-CLE repository architecture without identifying architecture decisions to select different alternatives and options. Instead of involving management issues such as project management and user control, our decisions primarily deal with the question which artifacts should be stored in a repository and how to model the associations between them.

7 Conclusion and Outlook

In this paper we introduced a Reusable Architecture Decision Model (RADM) for setting-up Model and Metadata Repositories. These decisions in particular aim at data design for Model and Metadata Repositories. We provided a decision basis for fundamental choices such as selecting a basic repository technology, choosing appropriate repository metadata, and selecting suitable modeling levels of the model information stored in the repository. Our experiences result from developing our own Model Repositories, from researching on other works, discussions with other people involved in repository projects, and applying our RADM in a case study.

Part of our future work could be a more precise evaluation of our decisions based on using quality management methods such as Quality Function Deployment (QFD). QFD could capture the repository's requirements and thus selectively deploying the activities for each decision alternative. Besides specifying reusable architecture decisions for setting-up Model and Metadata Repositories we increasingly concentrate on server-client interactions and repository client tools, that give value to the repositories. Finally, using ontologies for querying repository artifacts could improve the quality of the retrieved result sets.

Acknowledgement. This work was supported by the European Union FP7 project COMPAS, grant no. 215175.

References

1. Riggio, R., Ursino, D., Kühn, H., Karagiannis, D.: Interoperability in meta-environments: An XMI-based approach. In: Pastor, Ó., Falcão e Cunha, J. (eds.) CAiSE 2005. LNCS, vol. 3520, pp. 77–89. Springer, Heidelberg (2005)
2. Völter, M., Stahl, T.: Model-Driven Software Development: Technology, Engineering, Management. Wiley, Chichester (2006)
3. Greenfield, J., Short, K., Cook, S., Kent, S.: Software Factories: Assembling Applications with Patterns, Models, Frameworks, and Tools. John Wiley & Sons, Chichester (2004)
4. Sriplakich, P., Blanc, X., Gervais, M.P.: Supporting transparent model update in distributed case tool integration. In: SAC 2006: Proceedings of the, ACM Symposium on Applied Computing, pp. 1759–1766. ACM, New York (2006)
5. Kramler, G., Kappel, G., Reiter, T., Kapsammer, E., Retschitzegger, W., Schwinger, W.: Towards a semantic infrastructure supporting model-based tool integration. In: GaMMa 2006: Proceedings of the 2006 international workshop on Global integrated model management, pp. 43–46. ACM, New York (2006)
6. Eclipse: Eclipse CDO, http://wiki.eclipse.org/CDO (CCopyright2009)
7. NetBeans Community: Metadata repository (MDR), http://mdr.netbeans.org/ (retrieved January, 2009)
8. Bernstein, P.A., Dayal, U.: An overview of repository technology. In: VLDB 1994: Proceedings of the 20th International Conference on Very Large Data Bases, San Francisco, CA, USA, pp. 705–713. Morgan Kaufmann Publishers Inc., San Francisco (1994)
9. Lloyd, C.M., Lawson, J.R., Hunter, P.J., Nielsen, P.F.: The cellml model repository. Bioinformatics 24(18), 2122–2123 (2008)

10. Taylor, R.N., van der Hoek, A.: Software design and architecture: The once and future focus of software engineering. In: Future of Software Engineering (FOSE 2007), pp. 226–243 (2007)
11. Jansen, A., Bosch, J.: Software architecture as a set of architectural design decisions. In: Proceedings of the 5th Working IEE/IFP Conference on Software Architecture, WICSA (2005)
12. Zimmermann, O., Zdun, U., Gschwind, T., Leymann, F.: Combining pattern languages and reusable architectural decision models into a comprehensive and comprehensible design method. In: WICSA 2008: Proceedings of the Seventh Working IEEE/IFIP Conference on Software Architecture (WICSA 2008), Washington, DC, USA, pp. 157–166 (2008)
13. Kruchten, P., Lago, P., van Vliet, H.: Building up and reasoning about architectural knowledge. In: Hofmeister, C., Crnković, I., Reussner, R. (eds.) QoSA 2006. LNCS, vol. 4214, pp. 43–58. Springer, Heidelberg (2006)
14. Tyree, J., Ackerman, A.: Architecture decisions: Demystifying architecture. IEEE Software 22(19-27) (2005)
15. Harrison, N., Avgeriou, P., Zdun, U.: Using patterns to capture architectural decisions. IEEE Software, 38–45 (July/August 2007)
16. Zimmermann, O., Gschwind, T., Kuester, J., Leymann, F., Schuster, N.: Reusable architectural decision models for enterprise application development. In: Overhage, S., Szyperski, C., Reussner, R., Stafford, J.A. (eds.) QoSA 2007. LNCS, vol. 4880, pp. 15–32. Springer, Heidelberg (2008)
17. OASIS/ ebXML Registry Technical Committee: Registry Services Specification v2.0 (December 2001), http://www.ebxml.org/specs/ebrs2.pdf
18. Eclipse: Eclipse Modeling Framework Project, http://www.eclipse.org/modeling/emf/ (retrieved December 2008)
19. Haw, S., Rao, G.R.K.: Query optimization techniques for xml databases. International Journal of Information Technology 2(1), 97–104 (2005)
20. Atay, M., Sun, Y., Liu, D., Lu, S., Fotouhi, F.: Mapping xml data to relational data: A dom-based approach. In: Eighth IASTED International Conference on Internet and Multimedia Systems and Applications, Kauai, pp. 59–64 (2004)
21. Fotsch, D., Speck, A.: XTC – The XML Transformation Coordinator for XML Document Transformation Technologies. In: DEXA 2006: Proceedings of the 17th International Conference on Database and Expert Systems Applications, pp. 507–511. IEEE Computer Society, Los Alamitos (2006)
22. Khan, L., Rao, Y.: A performance evaluation of storing XML data in relational database management systems. In: WIDM 2001: Proceedings of the 3rd international workshop on Web information and data management, pp. 31–38. ACM, New York (2001)
23. Schwede, T., Kopp, J., Guex, N., Peitsch, M.C.: Swiss-model: An automated protein homology-modeling server. Nucleic Acids Res. 31(13), 3381–3385 (2003)
24. BrainML: Neurodatabase construction kit, repository server, http://brainml.org (retrieved January, 2009)
25. Nicola, M., van der Linden, B.: Native xml support in db2 universal database. In: VLDB 2005: Proceedings of the 31st international conference on Very large data bases, VLDB Endowment, pp. 1164–1174 (2005)
26. Emadi, M., Rahgozar, M., Ardalan, A., Kazerani, A., Ariyan, M.M.: Approaches and schemes for storing dtd-independent xml data in relational databases. Trans. on Engineering, Computing and Technology 13 (May 2006)
27. Florescu, D., Kossmann, D.: Storing and querying xml data using an rdbms. IEEE Data Eng. Bull. 22(3), 27–34 (1999)

28. Eessaar, E.: Using metamodeling in order to evaluate data models. In: AIKED 2007: Proceedings of the 6th Conference on 6th WSEAS Int. Conf. on Artificial Intelligence, Knowledge Engineering and Data Bases, Stevens Point, Wisconsin, USA, pp. 181–186. World Scientific and Engineering Academy and Society, WSEAS (2007)

29. Nayak, R., Xia, F.B.: Automatic integration of heterogenous xml-schemas. In: iiWAS (2004)

30. Castano, S., Ferrara, A., Ottathycal, G.S.K., Antonellis, V.D.: A disciplined approach for the integration of heterogeneous xml datasources. In: DEXA 2002: Proceedings of the 13th International Workshop on Database and Expert Systems Applications, pp. 103–110. IEEE Computer Society, Los Alamitos (2002)

31. openArchitectureWare: oaw (August 2002),
    `http://www.openarchitectureware.org`

32. Tran, H., Zdun, U., Dustdar, S.: View-based and model-driven approach for reducing the development complexity in process-driven SOA. In: In Abramowicz, W., Maciaszek, L.A. (eds.) Business Process and Services Computing: 1st International Conference on Business Process and Services Computing (BPSC 2007), Leipzig, Germany, September 25-26. LNI, vol. 116, pp. 105–124. GI (2007)

33. AndroMDA: Emf uml2 repository (November 2006), `http://galaxy.andromda.org/docs-3.2/andromda-repository-emf-uml2/index.html`

34. Clement, L., Hately, A., von Riegen, C., Rogers, T.: UDDI Version 3.0.2, UDDI Spec Technical Committee Draft. (October 2004), `http://www.uddi.org/pubs/uddi_v3.htm`

35. Nuescheler, D., Piegaze, P.: Other members of the JSR 170 expert group: Content Repository API for Java Technology Specification, Java Specification Request 170 (May 2005), `http://www.jcp.org/en/jsr/all`

36. eXo: Java content repository (jcr - jsr 170),
    `http://www.exoplatform.org/portal/public/en/product/oemisv`
    (retrieved December, 2008)

37. freebXML: Oasis ebxml registry reference implementation project (July 2007), `http://ebxmlrr.sourceforge.net/`

38. Mayr, C., Zdun, U., Dustdar, S.: Model-driven integration and management of data access objects in process-driven sOAs. In: Mähönen, P., Pohl, K., Priol, T. (eds.) ServiceWave 2008. LNCS, vol. 5377, pp. 62–73. Springer, Heidelberg (2008)

39. Bernstein, P.A.: Repositories and object oriented databases. In: BTW, pp. 34–46 (1997)

40. Eclipse: Eclipse modeling framework (emf) (2006), `http://www.eclipse.org/emf/`

41. Hibernate: Hibernate (2006), `http://www.hibernate.org`

42. Ibatis: Ibatis (2006-2007), `http://www.ibatis.org`

43. France, R.B., Bieman, J., Cheng, B.H.C.: Repository for model driven development (ReMoDD). In: Kühne, T. (ed.) MoDELS 2006. LNCS, vol. 4364, pp. 311–317. Springer, Heidelberg (2007)

44. Milanovic, N., Kutsche, R.-D., Baum, T., Cartsburg, M., Elmasgünes, H., Pohl, M., Widiker, J.: Model&Metamodel, metadata and document repository for software and data integration. In: Czarnecki, K., Ober, I., Bruel, J.-M., Uhl, A., Völter, M. (eds.) MODELS 2008. LNCS, vol. 5301, pp. 416–430. Springer, Heidelberg (2008)

Formal Behavioral Modeling and Compliance Analysis for Service-Oriented Systems

Natallia Kokash and Farhad Arbab

CWI, Science Park 123, Amsterdam, The Netherlands
firstName.lastName@cwi.nl

Abstract. In this paper, we present a framework for formal modeling and verification of service-based business processes with focus on their compliance to external regulations such as Segregation of Duties (SoD) or privacy protection policies. In our framework, control/data flow is modeled using the exogenous coordination language Reo. Reo process models are designed from scratch or (semi-)automatically obtained from BPMN, UML or WS-BPEL specifications. Constraint automata (CA), a semantic model for Reo, provide state-based representations of process workflows and enable their verification by means of model checking technology. Various extensions of CA make it possible to analyze time-, resource- and Quality-of-Service (QoS) process models.

1 Introduction

One if the key ideas of Service-Oriented Computing (SOC) is to enable the development of cross-organizational software systems by composing pre-existing services. Services are self-contained and loosely-coupled applications that advertise their interfaces and/or observable behavior specifications. Given such specifications, one can compose appropriate services to realize a certain business logic. This paradigm helps designers to abstract from low-level details and implementation issues, reduces time and cost of software development and increases its reusability and adaptability to changing process requirements.

Despite this promise, implementation of business processes by composing services remains a challenging task. The problem of ensuring that the composed behavior is compliant to the process specification and related business requirements is one of the key issues here. Formal approaches to process behavior specification such as Petri-nets, automata-based models or process algebras together with logic-based formalisms for specifying system properties provide rigorous tools for compliance analysis. However, complexity, the absence of visual notations and difficulties to obtain these models from widely-recognized high-level specification formats such as Unified Modeling Language (UML) or Business Process Modeling Notation (BPMN) limit their utility in practice. Another problem is the absence of actually implemented software tools that use theoretical approaches in this area to support automated process analysis and generate executable code to run corresponding service compositions. Finally, business requirements may affect various aspects of the corresponding process

F.S. de Boer et al. (Eds.): FMCO 2008, LNCS 5751, pp. 21–41, 2009.

model such as its control, data or time- flow, impose constraints on access control or performance. All these issues entail the need for an extensible formal model for service-based business process design suitable for reasoning about various types of functional and non-functional properties.

In this paper, we introduce a framework to benefit compliance-aware business process development with formal analysis and automated code generation. This work is part of the EU project COMPAS (Compliance-driven Models, Languages, and Architectures for Services) which aims at designing and implementing novel models, languages, and an architectural framework to ensure dynamic and on-going compliance of software services to business regulations and stated user-service requirements. We understand *compliance* as any explicitly stated rule or regulation that prescribes any aspect of an internal or cross-organizational business process. Such compliance rules come from internal sources, e.g., technical instructions, regulations aimed at improving Quality-of-Service (QoS) delivered to end users, Service-level Agreements (SLAs), or external sources such as user privacy protection policies, fraud prevention regulations and laws. *Compliance policy* is a logical grouping of a set of coherent rules that realizes a specific goal, e.g., fraud prevention by limiting access to vulnerable data. By context-aware analysis and stepwise decomposition of organizational high-level goals such as "comply to Sarbanes-Oxley Act or Basel II" to a set of relevant policies and, finally, to concrete compliance rules, we can come up with a number of formally-expressed constraints that must be satisfied to guarantee the compliance of a particular process to the initial requirements. We aim at developing a unified extensible behavioral model that is able to incorporate various types of information relevant to automated design-time compliance analysis. Our solution is based on Constraint Automata (CA) which offers an operational model for specifying composite service behavior. CA are essentially a variant of a labeled transition system where transitions are augmented with pairs of synchronization and data constraints. The states of a CA stand for the process configurations while transition labels can be viewed as input/output operations performed in parallel (more precisely, sets of nodes where data flow is observed in parallel and boolean conditions on the data items observed on those models). This model is fully compositional, and can express arbitrary mixes of synchronous and asynchronous communication. CA were developed as a semantic model for the coordination language Reo [1] (although several other semantic models for Reo are available) and later have been extended to express time dependent behavior, probabilistic, and stochastic systems.

There are several reasons that motivate our choice of Reo and CA for specifying the behavioral composition of business processes and web services. First, Reo has a simple graphical notation which makes it easy to use in practical applications by process designers without any prior experience in formal methods. A small number of Reo modeling primitives (channels) are sufficient for representing rather complex behavioral protocols. Second, precise semantics of Reo in terms of CA enables automated process verification. Reo process models can be automatically translated into CA which are suitable for representing service compositions with QoS guarantees [2], and time- and resource-aware processes [3,4]. Moreover, there is a solid set of software tools supporting process modeling, verification and code generation based on Reo process models.

The rest of this paper is organized as follows: Section 2 contains an overview of domain-level compliance-aware business process design. In Section 3, we introduce the coordination language Reo and illustrates its application to business process modeling. In Section 4, we discuss several extensions of constraint automata used for automated workflow analysis. Section 5 exemplifies the application of Reo/CA for detecting errors in process workflow. Section 6 illustrates how our framework can be applied to deal with advanced process requirements such as separation-of-duty and privacy constraints. Section 7 is a survey of related work. Finally, Section 8 provides our conclusions and an outline of our future work.

2   Business Process Modeling

In SOC, *business process* is defined as a collaborative service that is closely linked to a business purpose[1]. A collaborative service is a service implemented through the composition of other services. This definition poses no restrictions on the nature of the composed services. We can distinguish *functional services* which perform self-contained business operations, and *coordination services*, which implement so called "glue code". In our approach, we assume that observable behavior of functional services is described using CA, while "glue code" is modeled by means of the Reo coordination language.

Traditional graphical notations for business process modeling such as BPMN and UML Activity Diagrams (ADs) represent business processes in the form of abstract tasks (activities) with a control flow over them. Additionally, BPMN provides modeling primitives for specifying important events occurring in the system, exception handling, compensation associations and transactional sub-processes, which make it possible to depict most common features of real-world business processes. However, the specification of this notation does not assume a formal semantics. As a result, BPMN process diagrams can be misunderstood and require preprocessing and refinement before they become suitable for rigorous analysis or software implementation.

Figure 1 shows a BPMN diagram for a sample purchase order process that appeared in [5]. It consists of three basic activities, *checkCreditCard*, *prepareProducts* and *shipItems*. When a purchase request is received, the client's credit card is checked and the requested products are prepared simultaneously. After that the prepared products are shipped to the customer.

UML Sequence Diagrams (SDs) present a conceptually different approach to system modeling. The goal of UML SDs is to model dynamic system behavior in terms of entities, components/services or objects that exchange messages or functional calls. The diagram conveys the information along the horizontal and vertical dimensions: the vertical dimension shows the time sequence of messages/calls as they occur, and the horizontal dimension shows with the help of

---

[1] http://www.nexof-ra.eu/?q=node/187

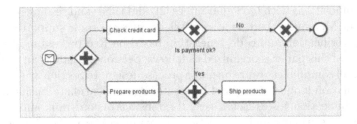

Fig. 1. BPMN diagram for the purchase order scenario [5]

lifelines, the object instances that the messages are sent to. In the context of business process modeling UML SDs are convenient to represent scenarios involving several interacting entities such as auctions or service contract negotiation.

WS-BPEL is a language for describing executable business processes on top of WSDL service specifications. Due to the lack of graphical notation and the need to deal with implementation-level details, WS-BPEL is not suitable for domain analysis and conceptual business process modeling, although some efforts exist to adopt WS-BPEL for this purpose. Nevertheless, modern business processes are rarely developed from scratch. We assume they can be composed from reusable business process fragments with existing behavioral specifications in WS-BPEL.

The aforementioned notations lack support for compliance. For example, they provide no standard ways to express Segregation of Duties (SoD) requirements, show link dependencies, or specify QoS constraints on sub-processes rather than using textual annotations or additional domain-specific languages. Both industry and academia have proposed numerous extensions for process compliance support on top of these notations. For instance, in [6] BPMN processes are annotated with QoS information, in [7] additional textual annotations expressing task authorization constraints are introduced, while in [8] a language for specifying regulatory compliance on top of WS-BPEL is proposed. Due to the higher level of expressiveness of Reo, we can explicitly model some of these requirements in a formal way. In Section 6, for instance, we demonstrate how SoD can be enforced using our framework.

3   Process Modeling with Eclipse Coordination Tools

In this section, we summarize the main concepts of Reo. Further details about Reo and its semantics can be found in [9,1,10].

Reo [1] is a channel-based exogenous coordination model wherein complex coordinators, called *connectors*, are compositionally constructed from simpler ones. Complex connectors in Reo are formed as a network of primitive connectors, called *channels*, that serve to provide the protocol which controls and organizes the communication, synchronization and cooperation among the services that they interconnect. Each channel has two channel ends which can be of two types: source or sink. A source end accepts data into its channel, and

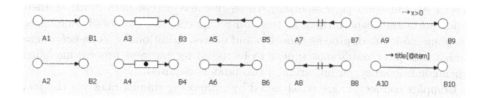

Fig. 2. Basic Reo channels

a sink end dispenses data out of its channel. It is possible for both ends of a channel to be either sinks or sources. Reo places no restriction on the behavior of a channel and thus allows an open-ended set of different channel types to be used simultaneously together.

Figure 2 shows the graphical representation of basic channel types in Reo. A *synchronous channel* SYNC(A1,B1) has a source and a sink end and no buffer. It accepts a data item through its source end iff it can simultaneously dispense it through its sink. A *lossy synchronous channel* LOSSY(A2,B2) is similar to synchronous channel except that it always accepts all data items through its source end. The data item is transferred if it is possible for the data item to be dispensed through the sink end, otherwise the data item is lost. A *FIFO1 channel* FIFO1(A3,B3) represents an asynchronous channel with one buffer cell which is empty if no data item is shown in the box. If a data element d is contained in the buffer of a FIFO1 channel, it looks like a channel FIFO1_FULL(A4, B4) in this figure.

A *synchronous drain* SYNC_DRAIN(A5,B5) has two source ends and no sink end. A synchronous drain can accept a data item through one of its ends iff a data item is also available for it to simultaneously accept through its other end as well, and all data accepted by this channel are lost. An *asynchronous drain* ASYNC_DRAIN(A7,B7) accepts data items through its source ends and loses them, but never simultaneously. *Synchronous* and *asynchronous spouts* SYNC_SPOUT(A6,B6) and ASYNC_SPOUT(A8,B8) are duals to the drain channels, as they have two sink ends. For a *filter channel* FILTER(A9,B9), its pattern $P \subseteq Data$ specifies the type of data items that can be transmitted through the channel. Any value $d \in P$ is accepted through its source end iff its sink end can simultaneously dispense d; all data items $d \notin P$ are always accepted through the source end but are immediately lost. Finally, a *transformer* channel TRANSFORMER(A10, B10) accepts a data item and rewrites it according to the transform expression of the channel (e.g., xPath expression), as the data item passes through.

The aforementioned channels are supported by Eclipse Coordination Tools (ECTs), a tool suite consisting of Eclipse plug-ins for designing, testing and verification of connectors, as well as runtime engines for executing coordination protocols on multiple platforms [11]. This set can be extended with new channels. For example, *timer* channels, namely, *t-timer*, *t-timer with off- and reset-option* and *t-timer with early expiration* have been introduced to deal with time-aware service coordination [3]. Essentially, these channels accept data items at their input ports and dispose them at their output ports after t units of time, thus, enabling modeling of process timeouts and delays. Additionally, *(a)synchronous drains with filter conditions* appear to be useful for business process modeling when conditional synchronization of two flows is required.

Complex connectors are constructed by composing simpler ones via the *join* and *hiding* operations. Join plugs two channel-ends together creating a node at the point of connection. To this node one can connect more channels via join afterwards. If more than one accepting channel end is connected to a node every incoming message is simultaneously written to all outgoing channels whenever all outgoing channels at the node are ready to accept data. Whenever more than one channel-end offers data at a node a non-deterministic choice decides which data item is taken and written to all outgoing channels. The hiding operation hides away one node which means that the data-flow occurring at this node cannot be observed from outside and no new channel-end can be connected to this node.

Figure 3 shows a Reo connector that simulates the purchase order scenario introduced in Figure 1. We represent BPMN activities as simple FIFO1 channels meaning that data flow in the source end of each channel corresponds to the start of the activity, data flow in the sink end of the channel corresponds to the end of the activity, while the data token residing in the channel buffer implies that the activity is being executed. Special components, *Writer* and *Reader*, are used to introduce and consume data flow at the beginning and the end of the process. Nodes obtained by joining both source and sink ends of Reo channels are called *mixed* and considered to be *internal* for the connector. In contrast, nodes where only source or only sink channel ends are merged are considered to be *external* and can be attached to writers or readers, respectively. The Reo editor in the ECT environment automatically highlights the internal nodes with grey color. Two parallel flows are initiated by joining a sink end of a Reo channel with start ends of two other channels (see, e.g., node *start*), and synchronized using a synchronous drain (see, e.g., SYNC_DRAIN(*paymentIsOk, paymentAck*) which requires tokens on both sides to fire). As explained in [12], data-driven conditional choice can be realized using Reo filter channels. However, in this model, for simplicity, we abstract from data issues and use a non-deterministic exclusive router connector to direct a token from the node *isPaymentOk* either to the node *paymentIsNotOk* or to the node *paymentIsOk*, thus, obtaining a process model with two possible execution paths.

Preliminary business process analysis and simulation can be accomplished using a tool that generates flash animated simulations of Reo connectors. The plug-in depicts the connector shown in the editor in the animation view and generates a list of possible execution scenarios. The parts of the connector highlighted blue represent synchronous data flow. Tokens move along these synchronous regions. Two simulation modes are supported: a *plain mode*, which demonstrates all possible execution alternatives for the whole process, and a *guided* or *stepwise mode*,

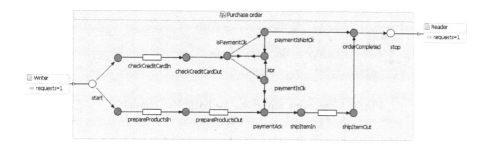

Fig. 3. Reo circuit for the purchase order scenario

which shows each execution step separately, including all possible alternatives for a current step.

Reo process models can be automatically obtained from BPMN diagrams using the *BPMN2Reo* converter available as part of ECT. In our previous work [12], we defined rules for mapping all major BPMN modeling primitives to Reo. In this way, we can also refine ambiguous BPMN diagrams by giving them precise semantics. The mapping of UML ADs to Reo is similar to the mapping of a subset of BPMN to Reo and will be integrated into ECT as well. The theoretical basis for the converter from UML SDs to Reo is given in [13]. Such conversion is automatically performed by the *UMLSDs2Reo* mapping tool which is currently being integrated into ECT. Finally, *BPEL2Reo* converter is a tool provided by the University of Tehran for converting BPEL process specifications to Reo [14].

4   Formal Behavioral Model for Service Composition: Extended Constrained Automata

There are several extensions of CA that can be useful for automated analysis of time-, resource- and QoS-aware Reo process models.

Let $\mathcal{N}$ be a finite set of nodes, *Data* a fixed, non-empty set of data that can be sent and received via Reo channels, and define a function $\delta : N \rightarrow Data, N \in \mathcal{N}$ as a data assignment. CA use a symbolic representation of data assignments by data constraints which are propositional formulas built from the atoms $d_A \in P$, $d_A = d_B$, and $d_A = d$ with standard boolean connectors, where $A, B \in \mathcal{N}, d_A$ is a symbol for the observed data item at node A and $d \in Data, P \in Data$. We write $DA(N)$ to refer to the set of all data assignments for the node-set N, $DC(N)$ to denote the set of data constraints that at most refer to the observed data items d_A at node $A \in N$, and DC for $DC(\mathcal{N})$.

Definition 1 (Constraint Automaton (CA) [10]). *A CA is a tuple* $\mathcal{A} = (S, S_0, \mathcal{N}, E)$ *where*

- S *is a finite set of control states,*
- S_0 *is is a set of initial states,*

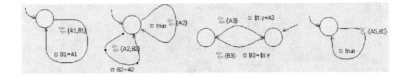

Fig. 4. Constraint automata for basic Reo channels

- $\mathcal{N}$ is a finite set of node names (e.g., I/O ports of components/services),
- E is a finite subset of $S \times 2^N \times DC \times S$ called the transition relation of $\mathcal{A}$,
- DC is a data constraint that plays the role of the guard for a transition.

Figure 4 shows the CA for the basic Reo channels. The behavior of any Reo process model can be obtained by computing the product of these automata.

Definition 2 (Product of CA [10]). *The product for two constraint automata $\mathcal{A}_1 = (S_1, S_{0,1}, \mathcal{N}_1, E_1)$ and $\mathcal{A}_2 = (S_2, S_{0,2}, \mathcal{N}_2, E_2)$ is defined as a constraint automaton $\mathcal{A}_1 \bowtie \mathcal{A}_2$ with the components $(S_1 \times S_2, S_{0,1} \times S_{0,2}, \mathcal{N}_1 \cup \mathcal{N}_2, E)$ where E is the set of transitions e given by the following rules, where $e_1 \in E_1$ and $e_2 \in E_2$:*

- *If $e_1 = (s_1, N_1, g_1, s_1')$, $e_2 = (s_2, N_2, g_2, s_2')$, $N_1 \cap \mathcal{N}_2 = N_2 \cap \mathcal{N}_1 = \emptyset$ and $g_1 \wedge g_2$ is satisfable, then $e = (\langle s_1, s_2 \rangle, N_1 \cup N_2, g_1 \wedge g_2, \langle s_1', s_2' \rangle)$.*
- *If $e_1 = (s_1, N, g, s_1')$ where $N \cap \mathcal{N}_2 = \emptyset$, then $e = (\langle s_1, s_2 \rangle, N, g, \langle s_1', s_2 \rangle)$.*
- *If $e_2 = (s_2, N, g, s_2')$ where $N \cap \mathcal{N}_1 = \emptyset$, then $e = (\langle s_1, s_2 \rangle, N, g, \langle s_1, s_2' \rangle)$.*

Figure 5(a) shows the CA for one instance of the purchase order scenario, that is, only states that are reachable from the initial state after a single reading operation. Such CA are automatically obtained from Reo process models. Intuitively, each state of a CA without hiding corresponds to a unique combination of empty/full buffers of the corresponding Reo circuit. We reflect this dependency in state names by writing 1 for a full FIFO1 channel and 0 for an empty FIFO1 channel assuming their top-down left-to-right order in Fig. 3. CA transition labels correspond to the names of Reo nodes where data flow is simultaneously observed during the transition. After hiding internal ports, CA control states represent process states observable by an external user. In this example, three logical states have been identified: the initial state s_1, state s_2 corresponding to the started process execution, and state s_3 that implies the presence of the deadlock in the process model due to the payment failure.

Reo timer channels can be exploited for time-aware analysis of business process models with ECT. In our case study, one may be interested to know how much time is required to process a single purchase order. The operational model for time-aware Reo connector circuits is given with the help of *Timed Constraint Automata (TCA)*, which can be defined as follows. Additionally to the notation introduced for CA, let $\mathcal{C}$ be a finite set of clocks. A clock assignment means a function $v : \mathcal{C} \to \mathbb{R}_{\geq 0}$. If $t \in \mathbb{R}_{\geq 0}$ then $v + t$ denotes the clock assignment that assigns the value $v(x) + t$ to every clock $x \in \mathcal{C}$. If $C \in \mathcal{C}$ then $v[C := 0]$ stands

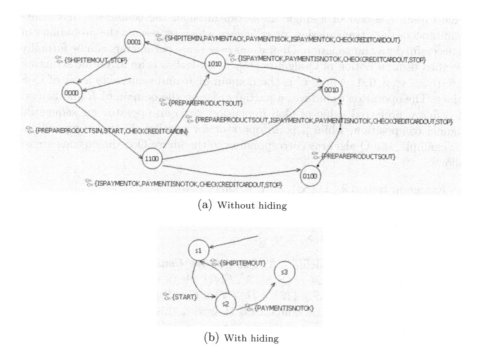

(a) Without hiding

(b) With hiding

Fig. 5. Constraint automata for the purchase order scenario

for the clock assignment that returns the value 0 for every clock $x \in C$ and the value $v(x)$ for every clock $x \in C \setminus C$. A clock constraint (denoted cc) for C is a conjunction of atoms of the form $x \bowtie n$ where $x \in C$, $N \in \{<, \leq, >, \geq, =\}$ and $n \in \mathbb{N}$. $CS(C)$ (or CS) denotes the set of all clock assignments and $CC(C)$ (or CC) the set of all clock constraints.

Definition 3 (Timed Constraint Automaton (TCA) [3]). *A TCA is an extended CA $\mathcal{A} = (S, S_0, \mathcal{N}, E, C, ic)$ where the transition relation E is a finite subset of $S \times 2^N \times DC \times CC \times 2^C \times S$ such that $dc \in DC(N)$ for any transition $e = (s, N, dc, cc, C, s') \in E$, C is a finite set of clocks, and $ic : S \to CC$ is a function that assigns to any state s an invariance condition $ic(s)$.*

The time required to perform certain actions in the process may depend on the availability of resources. For example, the time to deliver products in our case study may depend on the capacity of a purchase delivery service. Moreover, most of the systems have to change their states if an interaction has not occurred or an operation has not been completed within a certain timeout. For modeling such requirements in business processes, we extend Reo with time and resource-awareness information. The formal model for this extension relies on the notion of *Resource-aware Timed Constraint Automata (RSTCA)* [4].

It is possible to enable QoS analysis of Reo process models by assigning certain properties to Reo basic channels such as the *execution time* required to transmit a data item, the *cost* of a single data transmission, the *bandwidth* that limits simultaneous data transmission, or *reliability* which represents the probability of a successful data transmission. Operations over these parameters can be formally specified using a notion of Q-algebra [15]. A Q-algebra is an algebraic structure $R = (C, \oplus, \otimes, ||, \mathbf{0}, \mathbf{1})$ where C is the domain of R and represents a set of QoS values. The operation $\oplus$ induces a partial order on the domain of R and is used to define a preferred value of QoS dimension, $\otimes$ is an operator for sequential channel composition, while $||$ is an operator for parallel channel composition. For example, the Q-algebras corresponding to the above QoS dimensions are as follows:

- *Execution time*: $(\mathbb{R}_{\geq} \cup \{\infty\}, min, +, max, \infty, 0)$,
- *Cost*: $(\mathbb{R}_{\geq} \cup \{\infty\}, min, +, +, \infty, 0)$,
- *Bandwidth*: $(\mathbb{N} \cup \{\infty\}, max, min, +, 0, \infty)$,
- *Reliability*: $([0, 1], max, \times, \times, 0, 1)$.

Taking into account this definition, *Quantitative Constraint Automata (QCA)* [2] is as an extended CA $\mathcal{A} = (S, S_0, \mathcal{N}, E, R)$ where the transition relation E is a finite subset of $\cup_{N \in \mathcal{N}} S \times \{N\} \times DC(N) \times C \times S$ and $R = (C, \oplus, \otimes, ||, 0, 1)$ is a labeled Q-algebra with domain C. However, this model is not sufficient for practical applications as certain QoS (e.g., execution time) may change the intended behavior of Reo circuits. For example, consider a circuit consisting of two channels, SYNC(A, B) and ASYNC_DRAIN(A, B), whose execution times are t_1 and t_2, respectively. Assuming that the asynchronous drain accepts data at port A at time t_0 only if there is no data flow on port B within the time interval $[t_0, t_0 + t_1]$, while the synchronous channel accepts data at port A only if it can dispose it at time $t = t_0 + t_2$, the overall connector will accept data if $t_2 > t_1$, and get blocked, otherwise. Therefore, QoS-aware Reo models require more expressive formalisms to represent their behavior. Indeed, depending on whether delays are attributed to input/output operations on source/sink ends or to data transmission across the channel, the computation of a delay of data transmission across a composite connector may differ. Another type of automata, namely, *Quantitative Intentional Automata (QIA)*, have been introduced to specify the semantics of stochastic Reo: a version of Reo where one or more delays can be assigned to input/output operations on channel ends and transmission delays. QIA can be converted to Continuous-Time Markov Chains (CTMC) and used for process performance analysis using PRISM model checker[2]. More details about this work can be found in [16].

5   Verifying Business Process Specification

The main purpose of the formal models presented above is to enable automated verification of compliance-aware business processes and web service compositions. This can be accomplished with the help of the *Vereofy* model checking

---

[2] http://www.prismmodelchecker.org/

tool [17] developed at the University of Dresden. Vereofy is integrated into ECT, but also can be executed from a command shell. It uses two input languages, namely, Reo Scripting Language (RSL), and a guarded command language called Constraint Automata Reactive Module Language (CARML) which are textual versions of Reo and CA, respectively. Scripts in these languages are automatically generated from graphical Reo/CA models, however, they can be written manually as well, e.g., to specify connectors composed of a huge number of channels with repeating patterns.

Vereofy supports linear and branching-time model checking. Properties of the Reo circuits are specified either in Linear Temporal Logic (LTL) or Alternating-time Stream Logic (ASL). LTL allows designers to encode formulae about the future of execution paths such as that some condition will eventually be true or will be true until another condition remains true. Computation Tree Logic (CTL) is a branching-time logic which models time as a tree-like structure and allows designers to encode formulae about the future of possible execution paths. Branching Time Stream Logic (BTSL) is a logic specifically designed for Reo [18]. It extends CTL with the ability to express conditions on data flow in channel nodes using regular expressions. A standard Alternating-time temporal Logic (ATL) aims at reasoning about existence or absence of a coalition's strategy to achieve or avoid a specific temporal goal given the behavioral specification of each component. ASL is a CTL-like branching-time logic which combines features of BTSL and ATL.

For model checking, a constraint automaton needs to be associated with an arbitrary finite data domain (Data), which collects all possible data items transmitting through the corresponding Reo circuit or stored within the local variables of components. Data is a global data type, which can be Bool, int, or enum, depending on the user settings. The default data domain is int(0,1) and in our case it is used for control flow analysis.

There exist a number of studies on how system properties can be expressed using logical formalisms. COMPAS deliverable D2.2 [19] examines the suitability of Deontic logic, LTL, and XML-based approaches for formal specification of regulatory compliance requirements. It demonstrates that basic compliance requirements can be successfully expressed in all these languages, but advocates the use of LTL as the most comprehensible notation by end users. In our case study, the following LTL formula

$$\mathbf{G}(PrepareProductsOut \rightarrow \mathbf{F}\ ShipItemsIn)$$

states that whenever the data flow is observed in *PrepareProductsOut* port meaning that the activity *PrepareProducts* is finished, a data flow must be eventually observed in *ShipItemsIn* port corresponding to the invocation of the *ShipItems* activity. An ASL formula $\mathbf{AG}[\mathbf{EX}[true]]$ which literally means *"for all paths, it is globally true that there exists a next state"* can be used for deadlock detection. Both these formulae fail for the Reo process model presented in Figure 3. Indeed, in this scenario, if customer payment fails, the products remain prepared (e.g., packed), but will never be shipped. A proper model for this scenario is shown in Figure 6.

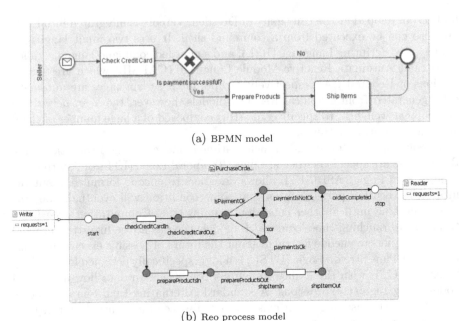

(a) BPMN model

(b) Reo process model

Fig. 6. Refined purchase order scenario

Once the process model is refined to satisfy all necessary conditions, it can be turned into an executable process. Figure 7 shows our scenario with Reo primitives called *components* attached to in/out ports of the FIFO1 channels which simulate activity invocations and replies. The observable behavior of real world services expressed by means of extended CA can be associated with these components. An executable code that realizes such a service composition is automatically generated by code generation tools of ECT.

Certain compliance requirements can be seen as informal descriptions of ideal business process fragments. Such process fragments in their turn can be modeled using Reo and/or CA. In this case, the compliance of software systems actually used in organizations with the ideal processes can be established by checking bisimulation equivalence of their corresponding CA models. Beforehand, one can abstract from unimportant details of an existing process by hiding data flow of the automata ports that are not relevant to a particular compliance policy. Algorithms for finding bisimilar states, and, thus, checking behavioral equivalence of CA or Reo circuits are presented in [20].

6   Compliance-Aware Process Modeling by Examples

One of the popular resource-aware constraints is a dual control or so-called four eyes principle. It is applied, for example, in investment banking, to segregate the duties of a trader from the duties of an internal auditor. In the corresponding

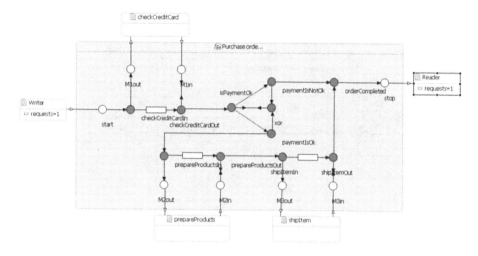

Fig. 7. Reo model of a service composition for the purchase order scenario

process model, it is important to ensure that generally each bank clerk can play both roles, but he/she cannot play both roles in a single instance of the process. Later, the term SoD was introduced for referring to a principle of information protection and fraud prevention by limiting user access to vulnerable data and/or operations. This category of compliance requirements is extensively discussed in [21,22].

Figure 8 shows a Reo process model which consists of sequential invocation of two activities, $T1$ (investment) and $T2$ (authorization), simulated using FIFO1 channels in separate Reo connectors. In this model, the activity $T1$ can be executed by three authorized clerks, *Alice*, *Bob* and *Clara*, while the activity $T2$ can be executed by *Alice*, *Bob* and *Frank*. These access control rights are modeled by means of filter channels FILTER(T1in, T1start) and FILTER(T2in, T2start) with conditions

$$\#T1in.clerkName \in D1 = \{Alice, Bob, Clara\}$$

and

$$\#T2in.clerkName \in D2 = \{Alice, Bob, Frank\},$$

respectively. Here we use "$\#X$" to refer to data observed at port X. Parts of the *Coordinator* circuit emphasized with dashed rectangles impose the dual control constraint in this scenario. The two *Writer* components connected to ports $U1$ and $U2$ correspond to two users, *trader* and *internal auditor*, who login to the system and perform the investment and authorization operations, respectively. The synchronous drain channel with filter FILTER_SYNC_DRAIN(U2, A5) uses a condition $\#U2 \neq \#A5.trador$ to ensure that the internal auditor differs from the trader who performed the investment operation in this process instance. This circuit uses two special join nodes $A2$ and $A6$ which merge the data items from

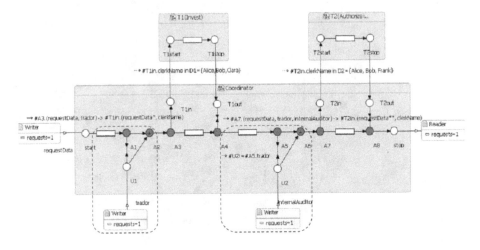

Fig. 8. Modeling a process with segregation of duties in Reo

the incoming channels. Transformer channels TRANSFORMER(A2, T1in) and TRANSFORMER(A6, T2in) are employed to transform data objects from the *Coordinator* circuit to the format used in circuits representing operations $T1$ and $T2$.

The compliance of this process model to the dual control principle can be checked using the ASL formula

$$\mathbf{A}[\#T1start.clerkName \neq \#T2.start.clerkName]true,$$

which requires clerk names executing the involved operations to be different.

Suppose now an organization providing a composite service needs to ensure compliance to a privacy policy stating that user personal data can be transferred to a third party only if the user explicitly authorized such a transfer. For example, in the above investment process, the trader may invest on behalf of a bank client who entrusts his/her personal data (name, passport number, organization, address, etc.) to the bank, but does not want them to be shared with other partners/services (e.g., trading organization). On the other hand, some of these data can be vital for involved services, and to complete the process the bank needs to get the client's permission to transfer particular data to particular services. Such permissions can be formalized by means of privacy rules and stored in the following format:

$$r_i = (ruleID,\ clientID,\ dataItem,\ recipientID,\ action,\ permission),$$

where *ruleID* is a rule identifier, *clientID* is a client identifier, *dataItem* is a data item that requires authorization, *recipientID* is a partner (service) to whom the data item will be transferred, *action* is an action on data item performed by the recipient (e.g., *use*, *retain*, *share*, etc.) *permission* is a boolean value that permits or prohibits the transfer of the specified data item to the specified partner for the particular purpose defined by the action. For example, *Alice* can authorize the transfer of her *passport number* to the *T1 (Investment)* service if it is needed for processing her request (*use*), but prohibit to *retain* this data after her request has been processed.

Although the majority of the publicly available service policies are published in plain natural languages, they usually provide sufficient information about the intended use of personal data. XML-based specifications such as WP-Policy and XARML allow designers to express privacy policies in a more structured manner. Recent approaches to privacy management suggest the transfer from static policies to customizable solutions which allow parties to negotiate the use of personalized data. This assumes a formalization of possible actions performed by each partner on these data. In our case, providers of composite services may store privacy policies of individual services in the form

$$p_j = (ruleID, serviceID, dataItem, action, purpose, necessity, disclosure),$$

where *ruleID* is a rule identifier, *serviceID* is a service used in the composition, *dataItem* is a private information concern, *action* is an action on data item performed by the service, *purpose* explains the intended use of this data item, *necessity* indicates whether this data item is vital for a service or optional, while *disclosure* specifies whether it can be shared with other partners.

The selection of permitted actions on protected data items regarding the invocation of a particular service by a particular client can be modeled using Reo transformer channels. Assuming that $R : r_i, i = \overline{1,n}$ is a table of client permissions, an SQL request

```
SELECT action FROM R
  WHERE clientID = %currentClientName
    AND dataItem = 'passport number'
    AND recipientID = 'T1'
    AND permission = 'true'
```

can be realized by a channel TRANSFORMER(A2, T1in) to select a set $\mathcal{P}$ of actions permitted for the service $T1$ over a client's passport number. Here the variable %currentClientName refers to a client name from the current investment request (Alice). Similarly, assuming that $P : p_j, j = \overline{1,m}$ is a table of rules formalizing service privacy policies, a set $\mathcal{R}$ of requested actions can be obtained using the following SQL request

```
SELECT action FROM P
  WHERE serviceID = 'T1'
    AND dataItem = 'passport number'
    AND necessity = 'vital'.
```

A constraint $\mathcal{R} \subseteq \mathcal{P}$ for the FILTER(T1in, T1start) channel will ensure that the data transition through this channel is possible only if the set of requested actions is included in the set of permitted actions. Checking an appropriate

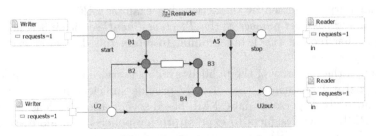

(a) Auditor notification

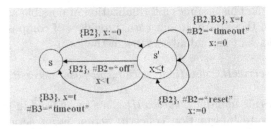

(b) TCA for a t-timer with off and reset options

Fig. 9. Modeling time-aware business processes

formula over the domain $Act =$ enum {'use', 'retain', 'share',...} we can automatically establish whether privacy policies match (state $T1start$ is reachable) or mismatch (state $T1start$ is unreachable). Potentially, more complex matching functions, e.g., ones that take into account action implication (e.g., 'retain' implies 'use', etc.) can be implemented.

In the above model of the investment banking process the system waits until a trader and an auditor perform their activities. Using timer channels we can model a system that notifies the trader about pending requests and the auditor about the need to authorize the performed investment operations if they do not execute their activities in a required time period. Figure 9(a) shows an example of a Reo circuit that uses a *t-timer with off- and reset-option* TIMER(B2,B3) to achieve this goal. A TCA for this channel is shown in Figure 9(b). A *t-timer* channel accepts any input data and returns on its sink end a timeout signal after a delay of t time units. In our case, we use a t-timer to measure how long the investment request waits for authorization. The *off-option* allows the timer to be stopped before the expiration of its delay when a special "off" value is consumed through its source end. This option is used to switch off the timer when the authorization message is received from the auditor. The *reset-option* allows the timer to be reset to 0 after it has been activated, when a special "reset" value is consumed through its source end. We reset the timer after sending a notification message to the auditor.

Additionally, timer channels can be exploited to initiate the rollback of an investment activity that was not authorized in a certain time period after auditor notification. Modeling of long-running business transactions with Reo is discussed in [23].

7   Related Work

The problem of formal business process modeling and high-level property specification has received plenty of attention in the research community. Formal structures such as Petri-nets, transition systems, process algebras and logic-based approaches have been widely employed to formalize the semantics of BPMN [5,24], UML ADs [25] and WS-BPEL [26,27,28]. A comparative analysis of Petri-nets, transactional logics and temporal logics can be found in [29]. At a first glance, Reo is somewhat reminiscent of Petri-nets. However, Petri-nets normally offer synchronization at each transition of a net, whereas in Reo synchronization is defined by the types of channels connected together. This enables more concise representation of complex workflow patterns. Synchronous drain channels in Reo are convenient for modeling processes where token cleaning is required, while Petri-nets are usually extended with inhibitor and reset arcs for this purpose, which significantly reduces the number of software tools able to analyze such models [30]. Due to the compositional nature of Reo, designers can easily model various sub-processes separately, assemble them for verification and testing purposes and later on deploy and execute coordination code on separate machines without any changes in the system behavior. Process algebras have been used for formal modeling and analysis of business processes. Like other traditional models of concurrency, process algebras offer an action based model of concurrency, where more complex actions (i.e., processes) are composed out of simpler ones. In these models, action is the first class concept making the interaction protocols implicit in the static structures of the compound processes that manifest themselves as the sequences of the matching actions of process pairs only as they unravel their behavior in the temporal domain. In contrast, Reo offers a model of concurrency where interaction constitutes the only first class concept. The distinction between Reo and traditional models of concurrency is analogous to the distinction between constraint programming and imperative programming. Every channel in Reo explicitly represents a primitive interaction, as a binary relation that imposes a constraint on the actions at its ends. More complex interaction protocols are constructed by composing such binary constraints into Reo circuits. Having interaction protocols as explicit constraints makes it easier to associate other properties and constraints, such as QoS or compliance, to them. Moreover, Reo/CA-based models are easier than process algebras, which make them a promising technique for practical applications for designers without a strong formal background.

In the area of SOC, the aforementioned formalisms have been applied for web service compatibility checking [31,32] and composition verification [33,34]. Extended CA are suitable for time-, resource- and QoS-aware behavioral compatibility analysis as well. An interesting property of CA as a formal model for web service compositions is their ability to deal with interaction transactions. For example, if a user has to provide his *name, birth date, passport number* and *home address* to a system, it is often not important in what order he/she introduces these data. CA allow us to abstract from such details by modeling the whole interaction as a single transition.

Various types of logic-based languages (First-Order Logic [35,36], LTL [8], CTL [37,38], deontic logic [39,40], temporal deontic assignments [41], concurrent transaction logic [37], etc.) have been applied for high-level process property specification. Existing approaches provide means for formal specification, verification and enforcement of compliance requirements, but their integration appears to be very problematic. Each model is specifically designed to deal with a certain set of requirements representing a single compliance category, e.g., temporal constraints on control flow [42,43], security requirements [44], privacy policies [45,32], task based entailment constraints [46], segregation of duties [47,48], or performance evaluation [49]. The advantage of our approach is that it allows designers to check various types of compliance requirements represented as constraints on transitions in a single CA model. LTL/ASL property specification formats provide powerful means for formalizing and model checking these requirements.

8   Conclusions and Future Work

In this paper, we discussed how Reo/CA can be used for compliance-aware business process modeling and web service composition verification. We aligned various extensions of CA and illustrated their applications using simple but realistic examples. We showed how structural errors in workflow models can be detected, and formalized the problem of process compliance verification to segregation of duties and privacy policies as reachability problems in CA. All steps of business process development, including control/data flow modeling, property specification, process verification and code generation are accomplished with the ECT.

We plan to extend the presented work in several ways. First, additional tools for property specification and verification will be introduced. For example, by integrating appropriate real-time model checking tools with TCA, we can support more powerful time-aware business process analysis. Second, by integrating syntactic/semantic interface matching algorithms with CA bisimulation checking we can enable (semi-)automated service discovery and composition given Reo process models and CA-based specifications of required service operations. Another line of work is related to the generation of graphical Reo circuits from RSL which will provide the basis for efficient process model reconfiguration using RSL-like scripts. Moreover, there is ongoing work on enabling Reo/CA to express priority of certain alternatives and transitions. Such models can be useful for implementing exception and compensation handling in Reo process models.

Acknowledgements

This work is part of the IST COMPAS project, funded by the European Commission, FP7-ICT-2007-1 contract number 215175, http://www.compas-ict.eu/.

References

1. Arbab, F.: Reo: A channel-based coordination model for component composition. Mathematical Structures in Computer Science 14(3), 329–366 (2004)
2. Arbab, F., Chothia, T., Meng, S., Moon, Y.-J.: Component connectors with qoS guarantees. In: Murphy, A.L., Vitek, J. (eds.) COORDINATION 2007. LNCS, vol. 4467, pp. 286–304. Springer, Heidelberg (2007)
3. Arbab, F., Baier, C., Boer, F., Rutten, J.: Models and temporal logical specifications for timed component connectors. Software and Systems Modeling 6(1), 59–82 (2007)
4. Sun, M., Arbab, F.: On resource-sensitive timed component connectors. In: Bonsangue, M.M., Johnsen, E.B. (eds.) FMOODS 2007. LNCS, vol. 4468, pp. 301–316. Springer, Heidelberg (2007)
5. Dijkman, R.M., Dumas, M., Ouyang, C.: Semantics and analysis of business process models in BPMN. In: Information and Software Technology (IST), vol. 50(12), pp. 1281–1294. ACM Press, New York (2008)
6. Awad, A., Decker, G., Weske, M.: Efficient compliance checking using BPMN-Q and temporal logic. In: Dumas, M., Reichert, M., Shan, M.-C. (eds.) BPM 2008. LNCS, vol. 5240, pp. 326–341. Springer, Heidelberg (2008)
7. Wolter, C., Schaad, A.: Modeling of task-based authorization constraints in BPMN. In: Alonso, G., Dadam, P., Rosemann, M. (eds.) BPM 2007. LNCS, vol. 4714, pp. 64–79. Springer, Heidelberg (2007)
8. Liu, Y., Müller, S., Xu, K.: A static compliance-checking framework for business process models. IBM Systems Journal 46(2), 335–361 (2007)
9. Arbab, F., Baier, C., de Boer, F.S., Rutten, J.J.M.M.: Models and temporal logics for timed component connectors. Int. Journal on Software and Systems Modeling 6(1), 59–82 (2007)
10. Baier, C., Sirjani, M., Arbab, F., Rutten, J.: Modeling component connectors in Reo by constraint automata. Science of Computer Programming 61, 75–113 (2006)
11. Arbab, F., Koehler, C., Maraikar, Z., Moon, Y.J., Proenca, J.: Modeling, testing and executing Reo connectors with the Eclipse coordination tools. In: Proc. of the Int. Workshop on Formal Aspects in Component Software. Elsevier, Amsterdam (2008)
12. Arbab, F., Kokash, N., Sun, M.: Towards using Reo for compliance-aware business process modelling. In: Proc. of the Int. Symposium on Leveraging Applications of Formal Methods, Verification and Validation. LNCS, vol. 17. Springer, Heidelberg (2008)
13. Arbab, F., Sun, M.: Synthesis of connectors from scenario-based interaction specifications. In: Chaudron, M.R.V., Szyperski, C., Reussner, R. (eds.) CBSE 2008. LNCS, vol. 5282, pp. 114–129. Springer, Heidelberg (2008)
14. Tasharofi, S., Vakilian, M., Moghaddam, R.Z., Sirjani, M.: Modeling Web Service Interactions Using the Coordination Language Reo. In: Dumas, M., Heckel, R. (eds.) WS-FM 2007. LNCS, vol. 4937, pp. 108–123. Springer, Heidelberg (2008)
15. Chothia, T., Kleijn, J.: Q-automata: Modelling the resource usage of concurrent components. In: Electronic Notes in Theoretical Computer Science: Proc. of the Int. Workshop on the Foundations of Coordination Languages and Software Architectures (FOCLASA 2006), vol. 175(2), pp. 79–94 (2007)
16. Arbab, F., Chothia, T., van der Mei, R., Sun, M., Moon, Y., Verhoef, C.: From coordination to stochastic models of QoS. In: COORDINATION 2009. LNCS, vol. 5521, pp. 268–287. Springer, Heidelberg (2009)

17. Baier, C., Blechmann, T., Klein, J., Klüppelholz, S.: A uniform framework for modeling and verifying components and connectors. In: COORDINATION 2009. LNCS, vol. 5521, pp. 268–287. Springer, Heidelberg (2009)
18. Klüppelholz, S., Baier, C.: Symbolic model checking for channel-based component connectors. Electronic Notes in Theoretical Computer Science 175(2), 19–37 (2007)
19. Concortium, C.: Initial specification of compliance language constructs and operators. COMPAS Deliverable (2008)
20. Blechmann, T., Baier, C.: Checking equivalence for Reo networks. In: Proc. of the Int. Workshop on Formal Aspects of Component Software, FACS (2007)
21. Gligor, V.D., Gavrila, S.I., Ferraiolo, D.: On the formal definition of separation-of-duty policies and their composition. In: Proc. of IEEE Symposium on Research in Security and Privacy (1998)
22. Schaad, A., Lotz, V., Sohr, K.: A model-checking approach to analysing organisational controls in a loan origination process. In: Proc. of the eleventh ACM symposium on Access Control Models and Technologies, SACMAT (2006)
23. Kokash, N., Arbab, F.: Applying Reo to service coordination in long-running business transactions. In: Proceedings of the ACM Symposium on Applied Computing (SAC 2009), pp. 318–319. ACM Press, New York (2009)
24. Wong, P.Y.H., Gibbons, J.: A process semantics for BPMN. In: Liu, S., Maibaum, T., Araki, K. (eds.) ICFEM 2008. LNCS, vol. 5256, pp. 355–374. Springer, Heidelberg (2008)
25. Störrle, H., Hausmann, J.H.: Towards a formal semantics of UML 2.0 activities. Software Engineering, 117–128 (2005)
26. Lucchia, R., Mazzara, M.: A pi-calculus based semantics for WS-BPEL. Journal of Logic and Algebraic Programming 70(1), 96–118 (2007)
27. Lohmann, N.: A feature-complete petri net semantics for WS-BPEL 2.0. In: Dumas, M., Heckel, R. (eds.) WS-FM 2007. LNCS, vol. 4937, pp. 77–91. Springer, Heidelberg (2008)
28. Ouyang, C., Verbeek, E., van der Aalst, W.M.P., Breutel, S., Dumas, M., ter Hofstede, A.H.M.: Formal semantics and analysis of control flow in WS-BPEL. Science of Computer Programming 67(2-3), 162–198 (2007)
29. Oren, E., Haller, A.: Formal frameworks for workflow modelling. Technical Report 2005-04-07, DERI - Digital Enterprise Research Institute (2005)
30. Raedts, I., Petković, M., Usenko, Y.S., van der Werf, J.M., Groote, J.F., Somers, L.: Transformation of BPMN models for behaviour analysis. In: Proceedings of the International Workshop on Modelling, Simulation, Verification and Validation of Enterprise Information Systems (MSVVEIS), pp. 126–137 (2007)
31. Guermouche, N., Perrin, O., Ringeissen, C.: Timed specification for web services compatibility analysis. Electronic Notes in Theoretical Computer Science (ENTCS) 200(3), 155–170 (2008)
32. Mokhtari, K., Benbernou, S., Said, M., Coquery, E., Hacid, M., Leymann, F.: Verification of privacy timed properties in web service protocols. In: Proc. of the Int. Conf. on Services Computing, pp. 593–594. IEEE Computer Society, Los Alamitos (2008)
33. Hamadi, R., Benatallah, B.: A petri net-based model for web service composition. In: Proc. of the Australasian Database Conf. (ADC 2003), ACM Press, New York (2003)
34. Yang, Y., Tan, Q., Xiao, Y.: Verifying web services composition based on hierarchical colored Petri nets. In: Proc. of the Int. Workshop on Interoperability of Heterogeneous Information Systems, pp. 47–54. ACM Press, New York (2005)

35. Dingwall-Smith, A., Finkelstein, A.: Checking complex compositions of web services against policy constraints. In: Proc. of the Int. Workshop on Modelling, Simulation, Verification and Validation of Enterprise Information Systems, MSVVEIS (2007)
36. Halpern, J.Y., Weissman, V.: Using first-order logic to reason about policies. In: Proc. of the Computer Security Foundations Workshop, CSFW (2003)
37. Mukherjee, S., Davulcu, H., Kifer, M., Senkul, P., Yang, G.: Logic based approaches to workflow modeling and verification. In: Logics for Emerging Applications of Databases (2003)
38. Koehler, J., Tirenni, G., Kumaran, S.: From business process model to consistent implementation: A case for formal verification methods. In: Proc. of the Int. Enterprise Distributed Object Computing Conf., pp. 96–107. IEEE Computer Society, Los Alamitos (2002)
39. Sadiq, W., Governatori, G., Namiri, K.: Modeling control objectives for business process compliance. In: Alonso, G., Dadam, P., Rosemann, M. (eds.) BPM 2007. LNCS, vol. 4714, pp. 149–164. Springer, Heidelberg (2007)
40. Cederquist, J., Corin, R., Dekker, M., Etalle, S., den Hartog, J., Lenzini, G.: Audit-based compliance control. Int. Journal of Information Security 6(2), 133–151 (2007)
41. Goedertier, S., Vanthienen, J.: Designing compliant business processes with obligations and permissions. In: Eder, J., Dustdar, S. (eds.) BPM Workshops 2006. LNCS, vol. 4103, pp. 5–14. Springer, Heidelberg (2006)
42. Governatori, G., Milosevic, Z., Sadiq, S.: Compliance checking between business processes and business contracts. In: Proc. of the Int. Enterprize Distributed Object Computing Conf., pp. 221–232. IEEE Computer Society Press, Los Alamitos (2006)
43. Ghose, A.K., Koliadis, G.: Auditing business process compliance. In: Krämer, B.J., Lin, K.-J., Narasimhan, P. (eds.) ICSOC 2007. LNCS, vol. 4749, pp. 169–180. Springer, Heidelberg (2007)
44. Brunel, J., Cuppens, F., Cuppens, N., Sans, T., Bodeveix, J.-P.: Security policy compliance with violation management. In: Proc. of the Workshop on Formal Methods in Security Engineering (FMSE 2007), pp. 31–40. ACM Press, New York (2007)
45. Hamadi, R., Paik, H.-Y., Benatallah, B.: Conceptual modeling of privacy-aware web service protocols. In: Krogstie, J., Opdahl, A.L., Sindre, G. (eds.) CAiSE 2007 and WES 2007. LNCS, vol. 4495, pp. 233–248. Springer, Heidelberg (2007)
46. Wolter, C., Schaad, A., Meinel, C.: Task-based entailment constraints for basic workflow patterns. In: Proc. of the ACM Symposium on Access Control Models and Technologies, pp. 51–60. ACM Press, New York (2008)
47. Li, N., Wang, Q.: Beyond separation of duty: An algebra for specifying high-level security policies. In: Proc. of the ACM Conf. on Computer and Communications Security, pp. 356–369. ACM Press, New York (2006)
48. Knorr, K., Stormer, H.: Modeling and analyzing separation of duties in workflow environments. In: Proc. of the Int. Conf. on Information Security: Trusted Information: the New Decade Challenge, pp. 199–212 (2001)
49. Koizumi, S., Koyama, K.: Workload-aware business process simulation with statistical service analysis and timed Petri net. In: Proc. of the Int. Conf. on Web Services (ICWS), pp. 70–77. IEEE Computer Society, Los Alamitos (2007)

A Real-Time Extension of Creol for Modelling Biomedical Sensors⋆

Marcel Kyas[1] and Einar Broch Johnsen[2]

[1] Department of Computer Science, Freie Universität Berlin, Germany
marcel.kyas@fu-berlin.de
[2] Department of Informatics, University of Oslo, Norway
einarj@ifi.uio.no

Abstract. This paper presents work on object-oriented modelling of wireless biomedical sensors in order to analyse their behaviour. These sensors combine synchronous and asynchronous communication, hard and soft real-time requirements, and have limited resources in terms of memory and energy. Moreover, design decisions tend to influence the validity of other requirements; e.g., higher communication throughput increases energy requirements. A single language is proposed in which design concerns can be expressed and analysed. This language is an extension for real-time systems of Creol, a modelling language specifically designed for distributed, asynchronously communicating, active objects. The extension proposes language primitives to capture requirements on the progress of time and the progress of the system. We integrate the timing requirements and the underlying object-oriented modelling language in a timed denotational semantics. The controller of a biomedical sensor node is used to illustrate the approach, for which there are both hard real-time requirements imposed by taking sensor measurements and soft requirements imposed by the communication network.

1 Introduction

Object-orientation is the leading paradigm for concurrent and distributed systems. It has been recommended by the RM-ODP and standardised by the ISO/IEC [1]. It is also applied in development processes for real-time embedded systems [2]. In particular, model-driven engineering, pushed by the increasing maturity of modelling languages and tools, is increasingly used among software designers and developers [3]. System models, traditionally created using ad-hoc languages and formalisms, are now combined with SysML [4] and other architecture description languages and formalisms. However, the heterogeneity of these approaches form a major obstacle for the formal verification of the models, which is crucial for safety-critical applications [5]. For correctness reasoning, the modelling language needs a well-defined formal semantics and a simple proof theory, which makes it possible to find and check the correctness proofs.

⋆ This work has been supported by the EU-project IST-33826 *CREDO: Modelling and analysis of evolutionary structures for distributed services* (http://credo.cwi.nl).

F.S. de Boer et al. (Eds.): FMCO 2008, LNCS 5751, pp. 42–60, 2009.
© Springer-Verlag Berlin Heidelberg 2009

Creol [6] is a modelling language with these features. The semantics of Creol is formally defined in rewriting logic [7] and is executable in Maude [8]. Creol has a compositional Hoare-style proof system [9]. This proof system is significantly simpler than corresponding proof theories for other object-oriented languages such as, e.g., (subsets of) Java [10]. Creol is therefore a good candidate for modelling distributed safety-critical systems. Creol unites object-orientation and distribution in a natural way [11]: The language is inherently concurrent and separates method invocation from synchronisation. This allows a range of communication and synchronisation forms to be captured in an simple manner. In Creol, all inter-object communication is asynchronous, each object executes on its own virtual processor, and method execution is coordinated using *explicit processor release points*. These release points influence the implicit internal control flow in Creol objects. Since there is only one virtual processor per object, at most one method m may execute at a given time for a given object; any other invocations must wait until m finishes or explicitly releases the processor. This "cooperative" approach to intra-object concurrency has the advantage that while a method is executing between two such release points, no other method activations can access the object's attributes. This leads to a programming and reasoning style reminiscent of monitors [12], but simplified since explicit signalling is not needed. This approach also increases parallelism when objects are waiting for replies and allows objects to combine active and reactive behaviour [13].

This paper proposes an extension of Creol with time, called Creol$_{RT}$, and discusses how this extension can be applied to the modelling of sensor nodes in the biomedical domain. We present the syntax of Creol in Sect. 2 and develop a timed denotational semantics for the language in Sect. 2.2. Based on this timed semantics, language primitives are proposed in Sect. 3 which extend Creol for real-time modelling. The extension to real-time is inspired by timed automatons [14] and is therefore declarative. No specific architecture is assumed, but constraints on time are declared, relating time to the untimed behaviour. The advantage of this approach is that it is platform-independent and allows a simple extension of the underlying semantics and proof theory, as demonstrated in [15]. To illustrate the use of Creol$_{RT}$, we model the timed behaviour of a biomedical sensor controller in Sect. 4. We report on our initial experience in Sect. 6, where we discuss the impact of the timed extension on the object-oriented language and point towards future work.

2   Modelling Distributed Concurrent Objects in Creol

Creol is a concurrent object-oriented modelling language. Communication between concurrent objects is by means of asynchronous method calls only. Await synchronisation is used to coordinate intra-object activities. Consequently, synchronization and communication are a priori decoupled and may be combined in different ways. This makes Creol well-suited for modelling concurrent and distributed systems. In addition, Creol is executable, has a formally defined operational semantics and a concise and compositional proof theory. We can validate

```
interface Radio                              interface Sensor
begin                                        begin
  with Network op send (in data: Data)         with Controller
  with Controller                                op setResolution (in res: Data)
    op write (in data: Data)                     op setEncoding (in encoding: Data)
    op read (out data: Data)                     op switchOn
    op setPower (in power: Int)                  op switchOff
    op setState (in state: State)            end
    op getChannelStatus (out status: Int)
    op getError (out error: Int)             interface PassiveSensor inherits Sensor
end                                          begin
                                               with Controller
interface Controller                             op read(out value: Data)
begin                                          with Radio
  with Sensor op write (in value: Data)          op setRate (in newRate: Duration)
end                                          end
```

Fig. 1. Interfaces of a radio   **Fig. 2.** Interfaces of a sensor

Creol models in various ways, including simulation, script-driven testing, and deductive verification. Creol, its type system, and its operational semantics are described in detail in [6]. For simplicity, we shall assume that all programs are well-typed. This section describes a kernel of the Creol language which we call *Core Creol*. For this language, we define a denotational semantics which we use in Sect. 3 to model timed behaviours.

2.1   Syntax

Creol is an object-oriented modelling language in which *classes* are structured in a multiple-inheritance hierarchy. Classes provide high-level implementations and do not as such declare the behaviour of objects. This means that classes are not types in Creol. Instead, objects are typed by *interfaces*. An interface controls which methods an object exports and which objects may access these methods. An interface may declare a *cointerface*, in which case only objects typed by the cointerface may invoke the methods of the interface. An object may support several interfaces. This allows a fine-grained access control and the static declaration of mutual dependencies. Fig. 1 shows the Radio and Controller interfaces and Fig. 2 shows the interfaces to a simple sensor which only provides methods to objects of the type Controller (the cointerface).

The grammar of class and interface declarations is given in Fig. 3. A Creol class has a list of formal constructor parameters, a list of attributes, and a list of methods. In addition, a class declares a list of the interfaces it implements (specifying its types), a list of interfaces it *contracts*, and a list of super-classes. A class need not inherit the interfaces implemented by its superclasses, so a subclass may reuse the code from superclasses while overriding the superclass' behavior. In contrast, contracted interfaces must be provided by all subclasses. This separation enables flexible code reuse yet supports formal reasoning [16].

A method body is a sequence of variable declarations followed by a statement. We assume a first-order functional language of expressions e, including **this** and **caller**. The latter is bound to the object calling the method and typed

$$If ::= \textbf{interface}\, I\, [\textbf{inherits}\, I\, \{, I\}]\, \textbf{begin}\, \{MDecl\}\, \textbf{end}$$

$$Cl ::= \textbf{class}\, C[(\,Vdecl\, \{, Vdecl\})]\, [\textbf{inherits}\, C[(\vec{e})]\, \{, C[(\vec{e})]\}]$$

$$[\textbf{implements}\, I\, \{, I\}]\, [\textbf{contracts}\, I\, \{, I\}]\, \textbf{begin}\, \{\textbf{var}\, Vdecl\}\, \{Meth\}\, \textbf{end}$$

$$MDecl ::= [\textbf{with}\, \mathit{Type}]\, \textbf{op}\, m[([\textbf{in}\, Vdecl\, \{, Vdecl\}][[;]\, \textbf{out}\, Vdecl\, \{, Vdecl\}])]$$

$$Vdecl ::= v : \mathit{Type}$$

$$Meth ::= MDecl == \{\textbf{var}\, Vdecl;\}\, Stmt$$

$$Stmt ::= \textbf{skip}\mid v := e\mid \ell!o.m(\vec{e})\mid \ell?(\vec{v})\mid \textbf{await}\, c\mid \textbf{release}\mid$$

$$\textbf{if}\, b\, \textbf{then}\, Stmt\, [\textbf{else}\, Stmt]\, \textbf{end}\mid Stmt; Stmt\mid Stmt\,\square\, Stmt$$

Fig. 3. The syntax of the Creol kernel language. The symbol $\{\ldots\}$ represent repetition of the enclosed production. The symbol $[\ldots]$ represents that the enclosed production is optional. The symbol $\square$ is a terminal symbol for the choice operator.

by the declared cointerface. Variables are represented by v. Comma-separated lists of terms and variables are denoted by $\vec{e}$ and $\vec{v}$, respectively. The **await** c statement behaves like **skip** if the guard c holds when the statement is executed, and otherwise suspends the process until c holds (await synchronisation). The **release** statement unconditionally yields control to some other process. The choice statement $S_1 \square S_2$ executes S_1 if S_2 would cause suspension, S_2 if S_1 would cause suspension, and is a non-deterministic choice if neither statement suspends. The choice operator $\square$ is associative and commutative. Finally, $S_1; S_2$ represents the sequential composition of S_1 and S_2.

The communication primitive $\ell!o.m(\vec{e})$ calls a method m with actual parameters $\vec{e}$ on the object o and binds a *handle* to the variable ℓ. This handle uniquely identifies a *future* from which the result of the method invocation can be retrieved. The statement $\ell?(\vec{v})$ is used to retrieve this result and bind it to $\vec{v}$, potentially blocking the execution until the result is available. Control can be suspended until the call has returned by polling the handle in the guard of an await statement; e.g., **await** $\ell?$.

2.2   Denotational Semantics

We develop a timed denotational semantics for Creol models in three steps. First, a denotational semantics of Creol statements is defined. Then, this denotational semantics is extended to objects and, finally, to classes.

Notation. Let N denote the domain of *names* and $\mathbb{D}$ the domain of *values*, and let $\{L, A\}$ partition N into sets of names for local variables and attributes. The domain of *states* $\Sigma = N \to \mathbb{D}$ bind names to values. Exceptional behaviour is reflected by a symbol $\bot \notin \Sigma$. Let $\mathbb{D}_\bot$ denote the domain of values extended with exception and similarly $\Sigma_\bot = \Sigma \cup \{\bot\}$ for the states. The binding of values to local variables and attributes is captured by the maps $\sigma^L : L \to \mathbb{D}_\bot$ and $\sigma^A : A \to \mathbb{D}_\bot$, respectively. A *variant* (or update) of a state σ is defined by

$$\sigma[v \mapsto u](w) \triangleq \begin{cases} u & \text{if } w = v \\ \sigma(v) & \text{if } w \neq v. \end{cases}$$

In a state, the attribute **this** $\in A$ identifies the current object, the local variable **caller** $\in L$ identifies the object which invoked the method, and the local variable **handle** $\in L$ uniquely identifies the method activation and names the *future* to which the result of the call will be returned. These names are read-only and cannot be assigned new values by the modeller. Object states are organised in *heaps* $\mathbb{H} \triangleq O \to \Sigma_\perp$ which map a non-empty set of (observed) objects O to their individual states.

Given a set O of observed objects, let $\mathcal{O}$ denote a set of *observations*:

Silent Action τ represents the internal behaviour of the observed objects or the behaviour of other objects which is hidden to the observed object.

Send Actions are written $o \xrightarrow{n} o'.m(\vec{u})$, where o is the identity of the sender, o' is the identity of the receiver, n is a value, m is the name of the method, and $\vec{u}$ are actual argument values.

Receive Actions are written $o \xleftarrow{n} o'(\vec{u})$, where o is the identity of the sender, o' is the identity of the receiver, n is a value, and $\vec{u}$ are the result values.

Delays are observations of the form $\Delta(t)$ for any $t \in \mathbb{R}_{>t}$ and represent the progress of time. These delays are discussed in detail in Sect. 3.

Statements are defined in the scope of a method. The *meaning* of an atomic statement in a method m is a triple $\langle \sigma, o, \sigma' \rangle \in \mathbb{S}$, where $\mathbb{S} \triangleq \Sigma^m \times \mathcal{O} \times \Sigma_\perp^m \cup \{\perp\} \times \mathcal{O} \times \{\perp\}$. Here, $\sigma \in \Sigma^m$ is a state of the method before executing the statement, $\sigma' \in \Sigma_\perp^m$ is a state of the method after executing the statement, and $o \in \mathcal{O}$ is an observation. Note that even exceptional states must at least admit observations $\langle \perp, \Delta(t), \perp \rangle$, because the failure of an individual object cannot stop the time of the whole system. All other observations $\langle \perp, o, \sigma \rangle$ for any $o \in \mathcal{O}$ and $\sigma \in \Sigma^m$ are disallowed, because objects cannot recover after an exception. We define projections $\mathrm{pre}(\langle \sigma, o, \sigma' \rangle) \triangleq \sigma$, $\mathrm{post}(\langle \sigma, o, \sigma' \rangle) \triangleq \sigma'$, and $\mathrm{obs}(\langle \sigma, o, \sigma' \rangle) \triangleq o$.

The semantics of compound statements is defined in terms of (sets of) *runs*. A run ρ of the system is a possibly infinite sequences of elements from $\mathbb{S}$. Let ϵ represent the empty run, $\rho \cdot \rho'$ the concatenation of runs ρ and ρ', and $|\rho|$ the length of ρ with $|\rho| = \omega$ for infinite sequences. Write $\mathrm{first}(\rho)$ for the first element of a run, $\mathrm{last}(\rho)$ for the last element of a run, $\mathrm{rest}(\rho)$ for the run with its first element removed, and $\rho(i)$ for the ith element of a run ρ. A run ρ is *local* if and only if $\mathrm{pre}(\rho(i))(\textbf{this}) = \mathrm{post}(\rho(i))(\textbf{this})$ for all $0 < i \leq |\rho|$ and $\mathrm{pre}(\rho(i+1))(\textbf{this}) = \mathrm{post}(\rho(i))(\textbf{this})$ for all $0 < i < |\rho|$. We use similar notations for all sequences. A run is called *connected*, when the post state of one statement agrees with the pre-state of a succeeding statement.

For a run ρ, its (communication) *history* $\theta(\rho) \triangleq \langle \mathrm{obs}(\rho(i)) \rangle_{i<|\rho|}$ is the sequence of observations obtained by projection from ρ. Given a set $\mathcal{O}$ of observations, let $\mathcal{O}^*$ denote the set of all finite histories, $\mathcal{O}^\omega$ the set of all infinite histories, and $\bar{\mathcal{O}}$ the set of finite and infinite histories (i.e., $\bar{\mathcal{O}} = \mathcal{O}^* \cup \mathcal{O}^\omega$). Histories form a partially ordered set $\langle \mathcal{O}^*; \preceq \rangle$ with least element ϵ, where $\preceq$ is the prefix order on

$\mathcal{O}^*$. Observe that $\theta \preceq \theta'$ implies that there exists $\theta'' \in \mathcal{O}^*$ such that $\theta\theta'' = \theta'$. This motivates the extension of the prefix order $\preceq$ to $\bar{\mathcal{O}}$ as follows:

1. If $\theta \in \mathcal{O}^*$ and $\theta' \in \bar{\mathcal{O}}$, then $\theta \preceq \theta'$ if and only if there exists $\theta'' \in \bar{\mathcal{O}}$ such that $\theta\theta'' = \theta'$.
2. If $\theta \in \mathcal{O}^\omega$ and $\theta' \in \bar{\mathcal{O}}$, then $\theta \preceq \theta'$ if and only if $\theta = \theta'$.

An observation d is *local* to an object o, if and only if $d = \tau$, $d = \Delta(t)$ for some $t \in \mathbb{R}_{>0}$, $d = o \xrightarrow{n} o'.m(\vec{u})$, or $d = o \xleftarrow{n} o'(\vec{u})$ for some values o', n, m, and $\vec{u}$. Let $\mathcal{O}_o$ denote the set of observations local to o. A history θ is called *local* to an object o if and only if $\forall i < |\theta| : \theta(i) \in \mathcal{O}_o$. Let θ/o denote the *projection* of a history $\theta \in \bar{\mathcal{O}}$ to the local observables $\mathcal{O}_o$ of an object o, so $\theta/o \in \bar{\mathcal{O}}_o$. For a history θ, the sets of *call handles* $C(\theta)$ and *reply handles* $R(\theta)$ are given by

$$C(\theta) \triangleq \{n \mid \exists i, o, o', m, \vec{u} : i < |\theta| \wedge \theta(i) = o \xrightarrow{n} o'.m(\vec{u})\}$$
$$R(\theta) \triangleq \{n \mid \exists i, o, o', m'\vec{u} : i < |\theta| \wedge \theta(i) = o \xleftarrow{n} o'(\vec{u})\} \quad .$$

Objects only have *well-formed* histories, which are formally defined as follows:

Definition 1 (Well-formedness). *A history $\theta \in \mathcal{O}_o^*$ is well-formed, written* $\mathrm{wf}(\theta)$, *if and only if:*

$$\mathrm{wf}(\epsilon) = \mathit{true}$$
$$\mathrm{wf}(\theta \cdot \tau) = \mathrm{wf}(\theta)$$
$$\mathrm{wf}(\theta \cdot \Delta(t)) = \mathrm{wf}(\theta)$$
$$\mathrm{wf}(\theta \cdot o \xrightarrow{n} o'.m(\vec{u})) = \mathrm{wf}(\theta) \wedge n \notin C(\theta)$$
$$\mathrm{wf}(\theta \cdot o \xleftarrow{n} o'(\vec{u})) = \mathrm{wf}(\theta) \wedge n \in C(\theta) \wedge n \notin R(\theta)$$

For a set O of observed objects, a history $\theta \in \mathcal{O}^*$ is well-formed if it is well-formed for all the objects in the set; i.e., $\mathrm{wf}(\theta) \triangleq \forall o \in O : \mathrm{wf}(\theta/o)$.

We define the following extensions to well-formed histories (recall that the local state is denoted σ^L):

Definition 2. *Let O be a set of observed objects, $\theta' \in \bar{\mathcal{O}}$, and $\theta \in \mathcal{O}^*$ such that* $\mathrm{wf}(\theta)$. *Then*

- θ' *is an extension of θ, written $\theta \leqslant \theta'$, if and only if $\theta \preceq \theta'$, $\mathrm{wf}(\theta)$, $\mathrm{wf}(\theta')$ and for all $|\theta| \leq i < |\theta'|$ we have $\mathrm{post}(\mathrm{last}(\theta))^L = \mathrm{pre}(\theta'(i))^L$ and $\mathrm{pre}(\theta'(i))^L = \mathrm{post}(\theta(i))^L$.*
- θ' *is an input extension of θ, written $\theta \unlhd \theta'$, if and only if $\theta \leqslant \theta'$, $\exists \theta'' \in \bar{\mathcal{O}}$ such that $\theta' = \theta \cdot \theta''$, and for any $o \in O$ we have $\forall o', n, m, \vec{u} : \theta''(i) \neq o \xrightarrow{n} o'.m(\vec{u})$ (o does not call a method) or $\forall o', n, m, \vec{u} : \theta''(i) \neq o' \xleftarrow{n} o.m(\vec{u})$ (o does not emit a reply to a call) for all $i < |\theta''|$.*

Prefix relations admit time progression, since $\langle \sigma, \Delta(t), \sigma' \rangle$ is always allowed as an extension. Input extensions will extend histories with messages (calls and replies) from objects outside of the observed objects O to objects in of O, but *not* in the other direction.

A Denotational Representation of Creol Statements is given in Fig. 4 and explained below. The denotation of a Creol statement is an *extended reactive sequence*; i.e., a sequence of triples $\langle \sigma, o, \sigma' \rangle$, where o is an observation and σ and σ' are the states before and after the statement is executed. The state after executing some statement need not be the same as the state before executing the following statement. This models possible interleaving between objects or between different method activations within the same object. Once all statements are considered, the semantics of the *system* is given by *connected* sequences; i.e., sequences in which the post-state of one statement agrees with the pre-state of a succeeding statement, but the succeeding statement may belong to another method or object.

Lets motivate our choice for using these reactive sequences. Reactive sequences have been introduced to obtain a compositional semantics for shared-variable programs [17]. Each Creol object is, to some extend, a shared variable program, because many method activations may exist in each object and execution may change between these activations, e.g. by executing a **release** statement. Whenever control yields to another activation, we cannot assume that the object's state remains unchanged once control returns. The behaviour between objects, however, should be defined by the exchanged messages. Consequently, the internal observation is a sequence of object-states and the external observation is a sequence of observations.

Let the auxiliary predicate fresh(n, θ) assert that a handle value or object identifier n does not occur in the history θ and the function eval(e, σ, θ) evaluate expressions e in the context of a state σ and a history θ. Histories record the communication history of objects and are used to evaluate the polling of handle variables, for example in a statement in **await** v?.

Equation (1) states that **skip** has no effect and Eq. (2) that an assignment evaluates the expressions on its right hand side and updates the object's state with the new values. Equation (3) describes object creation; the freshness of the new object's name o is ensured by requiring that the name o has not been seen in the current run. We assume the presence of a constructor method *init*, which describes initialisation and activates the on-going behaviour of the object. This method is called upon object creation. Equation (4) describes the call statement, which evaluates all actual parameter expressions, binds a fresh handle value n to the handle ℓ, and appends the send action $\sigma(\textbf{this}) \xrightarrow{n} \text{eval}(o, \sigma, \rho).m(\text{eval}(\vec{e}, \sigma, \rho))$ to the history. Equation (5) describes the *reply statement*; if the reply to the call with handle ℓ occurs in the history θ, the received reply values are assigned to the variables $\vec{v}$. Equation (6) explains **release**; after the release statement, the values of the attributes may have changed and the history extended as an effect of other activities in the object. Similarly for the **await** statement in Eq. (7); either b holds when the statement is executed (then it behaves like **skip**) or the thread suspends, in which case the values of the attributes may change and the history extended by some input-extension. The last observation of ρ' is the time when the method is reactivated after suspension. However, the **release** and **await** statements need not return. Equation (8) explains the (standard) meaning

$$\mathcal{D}_m^C[\![\mathbf{skip}]\!]\rho \triangleq \{\rho \cdot \langle \sigma, \tau, \sigma \rangle \mid \sigma \in \Sigma\} \tag{1}$$

$$\mathcal{D}_m^C[\![v := e]\!]\rho \triangleq \{\rho \cdot \langle \sigma, \tau, \sigma[v \mapsto \mathrm{eval}(e, \sigma, \rho)] \rangle \mid \sigma \in \Sigma\} \tag{2}$$

$$\mathcal{D}_m^C[\![v := \mathbf{new}\ C(e)]\!]\rho \triangleq \{\rho \cdot \langle \sigma, \sigma(\mathbf{this}) \xrightarrow{n} o.\mathit{init}(), \sigma[v \mapsto o] \rangle \tag{3}$$
$$\mid \sigma \in \Sigma \wedge \mathrm{fresh}(n, \rho) \wedge \mathrm{fresh}(o, \rho)\}$$

$$\mathcal{D}_m^C[\![\ell!o.m(\vec{e})]\!]\rho \triangleq \{\rho \cdot \langle \sigma, \sigma(\mathbf{this}) \xrightarrow{n} \mathrm{eval}(o, \sigma, \rho).m(\mathrm{eval}(\vec{e}, \sigma, \rho)), \sigma[\ell \mapsto n] \rangle \tag{4}$$
$$\mid \sigma \in \Sigma \wedge \mathrm{fresh}(n, \rho)\}$$

$$\mathcal{D}_m^C[\![\ell?(\vec{v})]\!]\rho \triangleq \{\rho \cdot \langle \sigma, \sigma(\mathbf{this}) \xrightarrow{\mathrm{eval}(\ell, \sigma, \rho)} o.m(\vec{u}), \sigma[\vec{v} \mapsto \vec{u}] \rangle \tag{5}$$
$$\mid \sigma \in \Sigma \wedge \exists m', o : m' = m \wedge o' = o\}$$

$$\mathcal{D}_m^C[\![\mathbf{release}]\!]\rho \triangleq \{\rho \cdot \rho' \mid \rho \leqslant \rho \cdot \rho' \wedge \mathrm{obs}(\mathrm{first}(\rho')) = \tau\} \tag{6}$$

$$\mathcal{D}_m^C[\![\mathbf{await}\ b]\!]\rho \triangleq \{\rho \cdot \langle \sigma, \tau, \sigma \rangle \mid \mathrm{eval}(b, \sigma, \rho)\} \tag{7}$$
$$\cup \{\rho \cdot \rho' \mid \rho \leqslant \rho \cdot \rho' \wedge \mathrm{obs}(\mathrm{first}(\rho')) = \tau$$
$$\wedge \neg\, \mathrm{eval}(b, \mathrm{post}(\mathrm{last}(\rho)), \rho) \wedge \mathrm{eval}(b, \mathrm{pre}(\mathrm{last}(\rho')), \rho \cdot \rho')\}$$

$$\mathcal{D}_m^C[\![\mathbf{if}\ b\ \mathbf{then}\ S\ \mathbf{else}\ S'\ \mathbf{end}]\!]\rho \triangleq$$
$$\{\rho \cdot \rho' \in \mathcal{D}_m^C[\![S]\!]\rho \mid \mathrm{eval}(b, \mathrm{pre}(\mathrm{first}(\rho')), \rho \cdot \mathrm{first}(\rho'))\} \tag{8}$$
$$\cup \{\rho \cdot \rho' \in \mathcal{D}_m^C[\![S']\!]\rho \mid \neg\, \mathrm{eval}(b, \mathrm{pre}(\mathrm{first}(\rho')), \rho \cdot \mathrm{first}(\rho'))\}$$

$$\mathcal{D}_m^C[\![S \,\square\, S']\!]\rho \triangleq \mathcal{D}_m^C[\![S]\!]\rho \cup \mathcal{D}_m^C[\![S']\!]\rho \tag{9}$$

$$\mathcal{D}_m^C[\![S; S']\!]\rho \triangleq \{\rho''' \mid \exists \rho' \in \mathcal{D}_m^C[\![S]\!]\rho \wedge (\exists \rho'' : \rho' \trianglelefteq \rho'' \wedge \rho''' \in \mathcal{D}_m^C[\![S']\!]\rho'')\} \tag{10}$$

Fig. 4. The denotational semantics of Creol statements

of a conditional statement and the *choice* statement in Equation (9) is simply the union of the denotations of its branches.

Equation (10) captures the sequential composition of statements. The run ρ which leads to the composed statement $S; S'$ is extended with the effect of the first statement S. The resulting run ρ' is extended with an *arbitrary input extension* to a run ρ'', which captures incoming messages and the passage of time. Finally, ρ'' is extended with the effect of the second statement S'. If the first statement fails, the second statement will not be executed. The meaning of a sequential statement is, consequently, the history that leads to the first statement, an extension, followed by the effect of the last statement. All messages received between both statements are remembered in the resulting history.

The denotational semantics for methods and classes is given in Fig. 5. Equation 11 describes a method m with input parameters $\vec{p}$, output parameters $\vec{q}$ and method body S: The run ρ is extended with the effect of the method body (which may be interleaved with the effect of other suspended method bodies), if a call to that method has not been answered and the initial state of that method body is updated to assign the actual arguments to the formal parameters.

Finally, consider the denotational semantics of a *flattened* class in Eq. (12). We first focus on a single instance of the class, since the behavior of other instances can be obtained by substituting the value of **this**. A single object may execute many methods in an arbitrary order, but it always starts with executing its

$$\mathcal{D}^C[\![m(\vec{p};\vec{q}) == S]\!]\rho \triangleq \{\rho' \cdot \langle \sigma', \sigma'(\textbf{caller}) \xleftarrow{n} \sigma'(\textbf{this})(\sigma'(\vec{q})), \sigma' \rangle \mid$$
$$\sigma = \mathrm{post}(\mathrm{last}(\rho)) \wedge \sigma' = \mathrm{post}(\mathrm{last}(\rho')) \wedge \exists c, n, \vec{u}, i : n \notin R(\theta(\rho)) \wedge \qquad (11)$$
$$\mathrm{obs}(\rho(i)) = c \xrightarrow{n} \sigma'(\textbf{this}).m(\vec{u}) \wedge$$
$$\rho' \in \mathcal{D}^C_m[\![S]\!](\rho \cdot \langle \sigma, \tau, \sigma[handle \mapsto n, \textbf{caller} \mapsto c, \vec{p} \mapsto \vec{u}]\rangle)\}$$

$$\mathcal{D}[\![C]\!] \triangleq \{\rho \mid \exists o', o, \sigma, \rho', \rho'', n, n' :$$
$$\rho' \in \mathcal{D}^C[\![init == S]\!]\langle \sigma, o' \xrightarrow{n} o.init(), \sigma[\textbf{this} \mapsto o]\rangle \wedge$$
$$\rho'' \in \mathcal{D}^C[\![run == S']\!]\rho' \cdot \langle \sigma', \sigma(\textbf{this}) \xrightarrow{n'} \sigma(\textbf{this}).run(), \sigma' \rangle \wedge \qquad (12)$$
$$\sigma' = \mathrm{post}(\mathrm{last}(\rho')) \wedge \rho'' \trianglelefteq \rho \wedge \mathrm{wf}(\rho) \wedge \mathrm{conn}(\rho)\}$$

Fig. 5. The denotational semantics of Creol methods and classes

constructor *init* and continues by executing the method *run* which models the active behaviour. Self calls are needed to maintain that behaviour. The meaning of these calls is usually provided by the extensions of Eqs. (6) and (7), together with the input extensions of Eq. (10) and finally, by Eq. (11) providing the meaning of the executed code. The meaning of an object that executes a number of methods can be obtained by composing the semantics of those methods. A run of a class is *connected* if the post-state of one observation corresponds to the pre-state of its successor component; i.e.,

$$\mathrm{conn}(\rho) \triangleq \forall i < |\rho| : \mathrm{post}(\rho(i)) = \mathrm{pre}(\rho(i+1)) \quad .$$

Connected sequences have been used as a compositional semantic model for shared variable concurrency [17].

The semantics of a model is obtained from the semantics of objects by reformulating runs in terms of heaps. We assume one instance of a root class in the heap and consider all runs from that root class. Observe that well-formedness will guarantee causality between all communication events, whereas progress of time is observed equally by all objects. Furthermore, when executing **new** statements, the heap must be extended to include the state of the newly created object in addition to the effect described in Eq. (3).

3   Creol$_{RT}$: Extending Creol with Real-Time Constraints

Based on the timed denotational semantics introduced in Sect. 2.2, we now propose an extension Creol$_{RT}$ of Creol to model real-time behaviours. The model is intended to capture the timing requirements of the original specification and to help find inconsistencies and identify conditions under which these requirements can be met. The proposed extension follows Hooman [15].

The time-dependent properties of a system can be captured using two data types and two statements. The first data type is *Time*, with domain $\mathbb{R}_{\geq 0}$, and which is the type of the value of clocks. We assume one global clock, which all objects can read through the expression **now**. This expression behaves like a read-only global system variable. Values read from **now** can be stored in variables

$$
\begin{aligned}
&\mathbf{now} : \mathit{Time} && 0, 1, 1.5, \ldots : \mathit{Duration} \\
&= : \mathit{Time} \times \mathit{Time} \to \mathit{Bool} && = : \mathit{Duration} \times \mathit{Duration} \to \mathit{Bool} \\
&< : \mathit{Time} \times \mathit{Time} \to \mathit{Bool} && < : \mathit{Duration} \times \mathit{Duration} \to \mathit{Bool} \\
&- : \mathit{Time} \times \mathit{Time} \to \mathit{Duration} && - : \mathit{Duration} \times \mathit{Duration} \to \mathit{Duration} \\
&+ : \mathit{Time} \times \mathit{Duration} \to \mathit{Time} && + : \mathit{Duration} \times \mathit{Duration} \to \mathit{Duration} \\
& && \cdot : \mathit{Real} \times \mathit{Duration} \to \mathit{Duration}
\end{aligned}
$$

Fig. 6. Real-time expressions and constraints

of type *Time* and compared to other values of type *Time*. There is no absolute notion of time available to the modeller, instead timing must be expressed relative to observations in the model. A practical advantage of this design choice is that the specifications are *shift invariant*; i.e., properties that hold for histories starting with time t_0 also hold for histories starting at another time. In addition, a second data type *Duration* is used to express the difference between two clock values. All floating-point literals can be used as values of type *Duration*. The operations on *Time* and *Duration* are summarised in Fig. 6.

The denotational semantics of Sect. 2.2 already supports observations of the passage of time. For all $t \in \mathbb{R}_{>0}$, delay events $\Delta(t)$ represent that the clock advances by t time units. Consequently, delays may be seen as a form of *inputs* to the object, which increase the clock value of the object. Thus, the timed semantics is very similar to the semantics formulated for timed automatons [14]; time progresses in states, while executing statements is instantaneous.

With these operations, a modeller can observe time, express durations, and formulate predicates on time. In the sequel, a *timed* constraint is any Boolean predicate in which all non-Boolean expressions have the type *Time* or *Duration*. The latter clause allows scalar multiplication of durations in timed constraints (the scalar has type *Real*) without admitting comparisons of real numbers as part of timed constraints.

The value of **now** in an object can be obtained from the history leading to that statement by summing up all delay values in the run

$$
\mathrm{eval}(\mathbf{now}, \sigma, \rho) = \sum_i^{|\rho|} \delta(\rho(i)), \text{ where } \delta(\langle \sigma, o, \sigma' \rangle) \triangleq \begin{cases} t & \text{if } o = \Delta(t) \\ 0 & \text{otherwise} \end{cases}.
$$

We now consider how time constraints may be combined with untimed behavior.

Waiting. As in timed automatons, the execution of statements is instantaneous, that is, time does not progress while a statement is executed. Time can only progress while an object is not executing any statements; e.g., when it is waiting for a reply or a condition. Using the **await** statement with a time constraint forces the advance of time before the process can proceed. The fragment

var t: Time :=**now**; S; **await now** $\geq$t +1

expresses that the execution of S takes at least 1 time unit: it stores the value of the current time in t, executes S, and then waits until **now** has advanced for at least 1 time unit since storing t. In this example, time may advance before executing S, after executing S or, if S is compound, anywhere between executing statements in S. Rather, we express that at least 1 time unit has passed from the assignment to t until the termination of the **await** statement.

This kind of **await** statement is easily implementable; e.g., by a busy waiting loop. Creol does not guarantee that the method activation resumes execution as soon as the condition is true, but that the condition is true in the moment the busy waiting loop terminates.

The elapse of time can be modelled by **await** statements with timed constraints. Combined with the non-deterministic choice operator these statements can be used to model time-dependent execution of statements, as shown in

> **var** t: Time :=**now**; S;
> **begin**
>   **await now** $\geq$t +1; S1 $\square$ **await now** <t +1; S2
> **end**

This example suggests a way to model a time-out. Here, S_1 should be chosen if S terminates after 1 time unit and S_2 should be chosen otherwise.

Timed constraints may also be used in **while** and **if** conditions. Time does not advance while the condition is evaluated, but it may advance before, while, and after executing the substatements.

Combining **await** statements with timed constraints imposes constraints on how time is supposed to advance. Furthermore, we require that all infinite runs are *non-Zeno*; i.e., for all $t \in \mathbb{R}_{>0}$ there is an $i < \omega$ such that $\sum_{j<i}^{|\rho|} \delta(\rho(i)) > t$. However, this requirement allows undesired or uninteresting behaviour, where runs only consist of delay observations.

Progress could in principle be captured similarly. However, the fragment

> **var** t: Time :=**now**; S; **await now** <t +1

does not express that executing S takes at most 1 time unit. If the execution of S takes more than 1 time unit, the method would be suspended and never reactivated. Similarly, the fragment

> **await now** $\geq$t +1; S1 $\square$ **await now** <t +1; S2

allows to wait forever instead of selecting a branch. Consequently, the **await** statement is not expressive enough to ensure *progress* of the system.

We introduce the declarative "statement" **posit** φ to express *progress*, where φ is a time constraint. A **posit** statement is not executable, but it declares a property on time which should hold for all computations of the system. Thus, the **posit** statement acts like a filter on acceptable runs of the model. The semantics of **posit** statements ressemble *invariants* in timed automatons [14]: Each timed history must satisfy all **posit** constraints in order to be considered a timed history of the Creol$_{RT}$ model.

If ρ is a run of a system and the prefix of length j leads to a statement **posit** φ, the run is *valid*, if and only if $\rho_j \models \varphi$. As a consequence, the **posit** statement conceptually blocks execution unless the condition φ holds. Remark that time-constraints do not necessarily describe convex sets, but may contain "holes". Our semantics allows time to "jump" over these holes without violating the **posit** constraint. For example, in the fragment

posit $(t0 <$**now** $\wedge$**now** $< t0 + 10) \vee t1 <$**now**

the constraint $t0+10<t1$ contains such a hole. The **posit** constraint states that local observations do not occur between time $t0+10$ and $t1$.

Observe that the timing requirements of different **posit** statement may result in systems with objects that do not have any computations at all; e.g., **posit false** or **await now** $>c$; **posit now** $<c$. If one object allows no run to satisfy all its **posit** constraints, then the whole system has no run, too. This is because a **posit** constraint is a constraint on time, and time is a global entity. If a time fails for one object, it fails for every other object in the same instant. Furthermore, **posit** statement may make the behaviour of objects incompatible; i.e., their composition does not contain any behaviour. Proving that there exists a connected sequence that satisfies all relevant posit constraints implies that the objects' behaviours are compatible.

The addition of the declarative **posit** statements to Creol$_{RT}$ has as a consequence that models need not be realisable. The **posit** declarations are assumed as axioms of the model and therefore become proof obligations at the implementation level. In order to discharge these proof obligations, suitable schedulers may be needed for each object. In addition,the inter-object communication must be *realisable* as postulated by the modeller.

To implement a Creol$_{RT}$ model we would usually use the facilities of some real-time operating system, which would select the next method activation by following some priority scheme. There, it is usually assumed that the operating system will avoid undue waiting by trying to schedule and execute tasks eagerly, i.e. as soon as a task is eligible for execution. This assumption makes one motivation for our **posit** statement redundant, whereas a second aspect still remains: Priorities ought to be assigned in a way that all **posit** conditions are never violated. After priorities have been assigned, as described in, e.g., [18], the **posit** statements may take the rôle of *assertions* when validating the objects behaviour.

The semantics of a Creol$_{RT}$ model is a set of timed histories. We explain why we did not cover inheritance in Sect. 6. We continue with representing how Creol$_{RT}$ is used to model a simple case study.

4   Modelling Biomedical Sensor Nodes in Creol$_{RT}$

Biomedical sensor nodes are used to monitor biological parameters in tissues and organs and to detect any biological changes in patients. A range of different sensor nodes may be used on patients in diagnostic, surgical, and post-operative phases. To facilitate patient mobility and avoid blind phases when moving patients, we are interested in sensor nodes which use wireless communication.

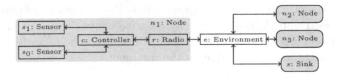

Fig. 7. The architecture of a sensor node and its relation to other nodes

A wireless biomedical sensor *node* controls one or more sensors, collects data with fixed sampling rates, and sends the data to a base station for further processing; e.g., visualisation. Different requirements have to be balanced for this application: The sensor node runs on battery and is expected to last for some time (e.g., 7 days) and as a consequence, the sensor node needs to manage power carefully. To this end, biomedical controllers support two different modes: the *monitoring mode* is used in situations where approximate data about the patient's condition suffice, and the *diagnostic mode*, in which precise high-resolution data are required. For example, to monitor ECG data a sampling-frequency of 150 Hz is used in monitoring mode and up to 600 Hz in diagnostic mode. The *quality* of a network of such sensor nodes is determined by the time and the duration with which the sensor nodes listen to neighbouring sensor nodes: The longer a sensor node listens, the more data will be delivered successfully to the base station, but the shorter the battery will last. A certain loss of data packets is acceptable to conserve energy. Combined with the soft real-time tasks of transporting and routing data, the sensor node has to execute the hard real-time task of sampling biological values. The sampling frequency must be observed strictly: if the sensor samples too often, the sampled signal needs to be time-stamped to obtain the correct data, more packets have to be sent, and the battery charge is depleted too fast. If the sampling frequency is too low, the sampled signal will contain erroneous information [19] and cannot be used at all.

The overall architecture of the sensor nodes is shown in Fig. 7. A sensor node n_1 consists of a controller c and a radio r, whose interface is specified in Fig. 1, as well as two sensors s_0 and s_1, whose interface is specified in Fig. 2. The controller decides whether it operates in monitoring or diagnostic mode, and in each mode it reads data from the sensor with a fixed frequency. After a certain number of values have been sampled from a sensor, the node sends these values via the radio to a neighbour node or the sink node. In addition, the controller listens for packets on the network and forwards them towards the sink node if necessary. In the considered architecture, the object e represents the environment and decides whether a node is within reach of another node. Here, we assume that the network contains a single sink node s. Finally, neighbouring nodes can be dynamically introduced and removed from the environment.

To ensure that the sensor node will work as expected, the sensor node was modelled in Creol$_{RT}$ as part of a case study on biomedical sensor networks. The satisfaction of all timing constraints has been checked on that model. The timing assumptions of our model are coarse and need to be validated by testing or simulation of the real implementation. Nonetheless, modelling the sensor node helped in finding ambiguities, omissions, and errors in the specification. We focus on the timing aspects of the sensor node, and abstract from the behaviour of the sensor. The sensors will therefore provide the data of a "healthy patient." Furthermore, the behaviour of the sensors does not impose any constraints on time. They can be read at any time providing an appropriate value.

A Creol$_{RT}$ model of a sensor node with two simple sensors is given in the class *TwoSimpleSensorNode* in Fig. 8. The *run* method describes the active behaviour of the object. It cycles the radio through three different modes: in *off* mode the radio is turned off and the node cannot receive any messages from the environment, in *rx* mode the radio is listening for messages. In *tx* mode the radio can send messages. The hardware of the radio is not able to send and receive at the same time. The controller maintains a buffer with a number of free slots. Once that buffer is full, its content should be sent to the network.

The listening task reads data from the radio while the radio is in *rx* mode. We have elided the code that reads data sent by neighbouring nodes. In that case the message are queued for resending when the radio enters *tx* mode. If energy is low, the controller may decide to drop data. In addition, protocol information has to be processed. We only consider control messages pertaining to the switch between monitoring and diagnostic mode.

The sensor node has to support switching between the monitor mode and the diagnostic mode at run-time. While listening to the network, it may receive a message which triggers such a change. Switching between the modes of operation entails changing the sampling frequency of the sensor, and therefore the overall timed behaviour. Switching from the diagnostic mode to the monitor mode is simple, because it increases the duration of the period of activity. Switching from monitor mode to diagnostic mode is more difficult, because the duration between taking samples is decreased. Naively setting the new rate may invalidate the model by violating **posit now** $\leq$clock0 +rate0 in the *run0* method. A common idiom is **await now** $\geq$t0 +rate0; **posit now** $\leq$t0 +rate0; S, which expresses that S is executed precisely at time t0+rate0 (this is convenient for modelling, but hardly implementable).

Figure 9 illustrates the possible scenarios. Assume that the sensor node started sampling the latest value from the sensor at t_0 (the black area suggests the time needed for sampling). Then reading the next sample is scheduled at time $t_0 + p$, where p is the sampling period in monitoring mode. If a request to change to diagnostic mode is received at t_1, and the new sampling period is set to p', such that $t_1 \leq t_0 + p'$, then we can safely change the mode and start reading the next sample at $t_0 + p'$. However, if a request to change to diagnostic mode is received at t_2 with $t_2 > t_0 + p'$ then the change cannot happen easily, since we must not violate the **posit** constraint.

Completing the cycle with the old rate may cause an unnecessary delay and render some data unusable. In the ECG scenario, changing from 150 Hz to 600 Hz could mean to lose up to 5 samples and the packed data could become hard to interpret. This may be unacceptable. Instead, we decided in our model to send

```
class TwoSimpleSensorNode(sensor0: PassiveSensor, sensor1: PassiveSensor,
                          radio: Radio, size: Int,
                          initialRate0: Duration, initialRate1: Duration)
  contracts Controller
begin
  var buffer: List[Data] :=nil
  var slots: Int :=size
  var rate0: Duration :=initialRate0
  var rate1: Duration :=initialRate1
  var t0: Time
  var t1: Time

  op init == t0, t1 :=now, now

  op run == !run0() ; !run1()

  op run0 == read0(;); await now ≥t0 +rate0; posit now ≤t0 +rate0;
    t0 :=now; !run0()

  op read0 == var temp: Data; sensor0.read(; temp); posit now ≤t0;
    await slots >0; buffer :=buffer ⊢temp; slots :=slots − 1;
    if slots = 0 then packAndSend(;) end

  op run1 == read1(;); await now ≥t1 +rate1; posit now ≤t1 +rate1;
    t1 :=now; !run1()

  op read1 == var temp: Data; sensor1.read(; temp); posit now ≤t1;
    await slots >0; buffer :=buffer ⊢temp; slots :=slots − 1;
    if slots = 0 then packAndSend(;) end

  op packAndSend == var x: Time; var l: Label □ ; radio.setMode(1;);
    l!radio.write(this ⊣now ⊣buffer); await l?;
    buffer, slots :=nil, size; await now ≥x +5; radio.setMode(0;);

  with Radio
    op setRate0(in newRate: Duration) ==
      if newRate <rate0 ∧now >t0 +newRate then t0 :=now; read0(;) end;
      rate0 :=newRate; posit now <t0 +rate0

    op setRate1(in newRate: Duration) ==
      if newRate <rate1 ∧now >t1 +newRate then t1 :=now; read1(;) end;
      rate1 :=newRate; posit now <t1 +rate1

  with Sensor
    op write(in data: Data) == skip
end
```

Fig. 8. A sensor node class which reads two sensors with different rates. Here, the expression buffer ⊢temp states, that the element temp is appended to the list buffer.

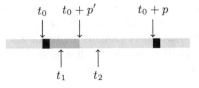

Fig. 9. Sampling time line

a short packet, read a new sample immediately, and set the new sampling rate. This may cost slightly more energy, but ensures a timely reaction and quality.

It is also possible to delay the switch to diagnostic mode. While the timely reading of samples is necessary to ensure the quality of the data, delays in delivery can be hidden by the tolerated packet loss. It depends on the overall network, if such a calculated loss is acceptable, since packet loss due to sleeping neighbours and environmental noise could prove sufficient for reducing the number of packages to barely acceptable levels.

5 Analysis

We use the denotational semantics described in Sect. 2 to assign a meaning to the model of Sect. 4. Asserting that the set of runs is non-empty implies that all timing constraints can be satisfied. Conversely, showing that there is no denotation shows that some constraints cannot be satisfied.

For the *TwoSimpleSensorNode* class, we manually proved the existence of an infinite run. To satisfy all timing constraints, all long-running methods must be preemptable by means of **await** statements to allow the timely reading of sensor values. For example when a buffer for sending on the radio has been prepared, the buffer used by the sensor node is freed in the *packAndSend* method: the radio is instructed to send that package and control is then preempted to other tasks by the **await** l? statement. The condition becomes true when the radio finishes sending the message, after which the buffer is freed for further processing.

Verifying scheduling properties of the models often shows at which program locations a task should be preempted by an **await** statement and a timing constraint. Thus, the described method can be applied to designing real-time systems in Creol. On the other hand, the described method is deductive and therefore expensive to apply. Automatic methods that reduce the verification effort might not exist, because the problem is undecidable in the presence of preemption. Creol's cooperative nature restricts preemption to explicit locations and may help in making automatic methods applicable.

In time-critical systems, everything depends on timing and the timing requirements must be strictly enforced. The time needed to execute a method is often part of the implicit assumptions of the callers. Overriding or replacing a method body with one with different timing characteristics can therefore be fatal to the system's behaviour. The timing *guarantees* of a method must therefore be stated explicitly in the interface of that method. Moreover, the *assumptions* made on all methods called from this method need also be explicit.

The complete design of this example contains many other challenges for the modeller. Most of the results about the model, which we described in this section, have been obtained by deductive reasoning techniques. Many omissions and ambiguities have been identified in that process, which increases our confidence in the soundness of the design.

6 Discussion

This paper describes Creol$_{RT}$, an extension of the concurrent object-oriented modelling language Creol with constructs for modelling real-time systems. This extension is illustrated on a small case study, modelling the behaviour of a biomedical sensor node. Modelling the sensor node in Creol$_{RT}$ was instrumental in deriving an improved specification of its timed behaviour.

The Creol$_{RT}$ extension combines a timed-automatons based timing model with Creol's concurrent object model, and necessitated a close examination of the particular semantics of the Creol language in the timed setting: asynchronous communication and cooperative multiprogramming within objects. A fine-grained model of the real-time behaviour of a system is very difficult to obtain, because it often involves an analysis of the system at the level of its *machine code*, which must take the actual target platform into account [20]. Such models are unnecessarily detailed for our purposes, and focusing on time is often harmful for modelling [21]. The declarative approach taken here allows to abstract from the concrete details of the hardware and makes the necessary requirements explicit. Furthermore, the cooperative multiprogramming model of Creol significantly helps in controlling possible interference between processes in the same object.

We have not considered the challenges of combining inheritance and late binding with the timed semantics in this paper. Inheritance interacts with the time extension by breaking encapsulation. The problems are similar to such anomalies as the *fragile base class problem* [22] for the sequential setting and the *inheritance anomaly* [23] in the concurrent setting. Specifically, the timing requirements and guarantees of a method that arise from the implementation become part of the method's interface and should be documented. Overriding a method should *not* change the timing-characteristics of the overridden method: the execution of that method should not take more or less time than specified. This has already been observed in [24].

For the case study, all proofs needed to verify the consistency of the specification have been obtained by hand. Formalising the theory described in this paper has been definitely helpful in increasing our confidence in our extension and the models. We are looking into formalising the described theory within a proof assistant in order to help automate many proof steps. In this work, the focus has not been so much on execution times but on *timeliness* properties. Methods can specify when they are expected to be executed: The execution times of the sensor controllers in the example are less important than the execution *frequency*. The requirements state that a method must be called once every t time units. As a next step, we intend to refine the *tx* and *rx* modes of the radio. We are currently able to reason about the time spent in each mode and we are able to derive how long each node needs to send a message.

To analyse sensor networks, we need to specify the properties of the (asynchronous and reordering) communication media. In addition, timed specifications impose global constraints on communication and couple objects in unexpected ways, because the caller decides whether to block on a method call and imposes constraints on the round-trip time of calls. The conjunction of all such local constraints need not be satisfiable, leading to inconsistent models. Time requires an *explicit* model of the communication medium with which objects are synchronising, e.g., in the form of timed automatons. This helps identify inconsistencies.

To facilitate simulation and verification, we consider translating a subset of the Creol$_{RT}$ modelling language to timed automatons, preferably the language used by the UPPAAL model checker [25]. Obtaining finite-state timed models from Creol$_{RT}$ models is a major challenge: Asynchronous channels need bounds to have a finite queue, reductions need to deal with message overtaking, and data abstractions have to be applied. A translation to UPPAAL will enable us to combine our model of the controller with the radio model presented by Tschirner and Wang in [26]. Then we can analyse the global behaviour of the system. However, the generated automaton will generally be an under-approximations of the Creol$_{RT}$ model, because we need to limit the number of active tasks to keep the state space finite. This will only preserve *existential* properties: If an error can be reproduced in the finite system, then it is also present in the unbounded one. It is a challenge to infer reasonable bounds which guarantee that the universal properties required by the system are indeed satisfied.

Acknowledgements. Bjarte Østvold and Wolfgang Leister commented on drafts of this paper. Xuedong Liang provided the initial model of the case study.

References

1. International Organization for Standardization Geneva: Information technology – Open Distributed Processing – Reference model: Overview. Iso/iec 10746-1:1998 edn (1998)
2. Graf, S., Hooman, J.: Correct development of embedded systems. In: Oquendo, F., Warboys, B.C., Morrison, R. (eds.) EWSA 2004. LNCS, vol. 3047, pp. 241–249. Springer, Heidelberg (2004)
3. Oliver, I.: Model driven embedded systems. In: ACSD, vol. 5. IEEE Computer Society Press, Los Alamitos (2003)
4. SysML Partners: OMG SysML Specification. (March 2007), http://www.sysml.org/specs.htm
5. Bowen, J.: The ethics of safety-critical systems. Communications of the ACM 43(4), 91–97 (2000)
6. Johnsen, E.B., Owe, O., Yu, I.C.: Creol: A type-safe object-oriented model for distributed concurrent systems. Theoretical Computer Science 365(1-2), 23–66 (2006)
7. Meseguer, J.: Conditional rewriting logic as a unified model of concurrency. Theoretical Computer Science 96, 73–155 (1992)
8. Clavel, M., Durán, F., Eker, S., Lincoln, P., Martí-Oliet, N., Meseguer, J., Quesada, J.F.: Maude: Specification and programming in rewriting logic. Theoretical Computer Science 285(2), 187–243 (2002)
9. Dovland, J., Johnsen, E.B., Owe, O.: Verification of concurrent objects with asynchronous method calls. In: SwSTE, pp. 141–150. IEEE Computer Society Press, Los Alamitos (2005)
10. Ábrahám-Mumm, E., de Boer, F.S., de Roever, W.-P., Steffen, M.: Verification for java's reentrant multithreading concept. In: Nielsen, M., Engberg, U. (eds.) FOSSACS 2002. LNCS, vol. 2303, p. 5. Springer, Heidelberg (2002)
11. Johnsen, E.B., Owe, O.: An asynchronous communication model for distributed concurrent objects. Software and Systems Modeling 6(1), 35–58 (2007)

12. Hoare, C.A.R.: Monitors: An operating system structuring concept. Communications of the ACM 17(10), 549–557 (1974)
13. Johnsen, E.B., Owe, O., Arnestad, M.: Combining active and reactive behavior in concurrent objects. In: Langmyhr, D. (ed.) NIK, November 2003, pp. 193–204. Tapir Academic Publisher (2003)
14. Alur, R., Dill, D.L.: A theory of timed automata. Theoretical Computer Science 126(2), 183–235 (1994)
15. Hooman, J.: Extending Hoare logic to real-time. Formal Aspects of Computing 6(6A), 801–825 (1994)
16. Dovland, J., Johnsen, E.B., Owe, O., Steffen, M.: Lazy behavioral subtyping. In: Cuellar, J., Maibaum, T., Sere, K. (eds.) FM 2008. LNCS, vol. 5014, pp. 52–67. Springer, Heidelberg (2008)
17. de Boer, F.S., Kok, J.N., Palamidessi, C., Rutten, J.J.M.M.: The failure of failures in a paradigm for asynchronous communication. In: Groote, J.F., Baeten, J.C.M. (eds.) CONCUR 1991. LNCS, vol. 527, pp. 111–126. Springer, Heidelberg (1991)
18. Liu, J.W.: Real-Time Systems. Prentice Hall, Upper Saddle River (2000)
19. Shannon, C.E.: Communication in the presence of noise. Proceedings of the Institute of Radio Engineers 37(1), 10–21 (1949)
20. Ferdinand, C., Heckmann, R., Langenbach, M., Martin, F., Schmidt, M., Theiling, H., Thesing, S., Wilhelm, R.: Reliable and precise WCET determination for a real-life processor. In: Henzinger, T.A., Kirsch, C.M. (eds.) EMSOFT 2001. LNCS, vol. 2211, pp. 469–485. Springer, Heidelberg (2001)
21. Turski, W.M.: Time considered irrelevant for real-time systems. BIT 28(3), 473–486 (1988)
22. Mikhajlov, L., Sekerinski, E.: A study of the fragile base class problem. In: Jul, E. (ed.) ECOOP 1998. LNCS, vol. 1445, pp. 355–382. Springer, Heidelberg (1998)
23. Matsuoka, S., Yonezawa, A.: Analysis of inheritance anomaly in object-oriented concurrent programming languages. In: Agha, G., Wegner, P., Yonezawa, A. (eds.) Research Directions in Concurrent Object-Oriented Programming, pp. 107–150. MIT Press, Cambridge (1993)
24. Aksit, M., Bosch, J., van der Sterren, W., Bergmans, L.: Real-time specification inheritance anomalies and real-time filters. In: Tokoro, M., Pareschi, R. (eds.) ECOOP 1994. LNCS, vol. 821, pp. 386–407. Springer, Heidelberg (1994)
25. Bengtsson, J., Larsen, K.G., Larsson, F., Pettersson, P., Yi, W.: Uppaal — a tool suite for automatic verification of real–time systems. In: Alur, R., Sontag, E.D., Henzinger, T.A. (eds.) HS 1995. LNCS, vol. 1066, pp. 232–243. Springer, Heidelberg (1996)
26. Tschirner, S., Xuedong, L., Yi, W.: Model-based validation of QoS properties of biomedical sensor networks. In: de Alfaro, L., Palsberg, J. (eds.) EMSOFT, pp. 69–78. ACM Press, New York (2008)

Conformance Testing of Distributed Concurrent Systems with Executable Designs[*]

Bernhard K. Aichernig [1,2], Andreas Griesmayer [1],
Einar Broch Johnsen [3], Rudolf Schlatte [1,2], and Andries Stam [4]

[1] International Institute for Software Technology, United Nations University
(UNU-IIST), Macao S.A.R., China
{agriesma,bka,rschlatte}@iist.unu.edu
[2] Institute for Software Technology, Graz University of Technology, Austria
{aichernig,rschlatte}@ist.tugraz.at
[3] Department of Informatics, University of Oslo, Norway
einarj@ifi.uio.no
[4] Almende BV, The Netherlands
andries@almende.org

Abstract. This paper presents a unified approach to test case generation and conformance test execution in a distributed setting. A model in the object-oriented, concurrent modeling language Creol is used both for generating test inputs and as a test oracle. For test case generation, we extend Dynamic Symbolic Execution (also called Concolic Execution) to work with multi-threaded models and use this to generate test inputs that maximize model coverage. For test case execution, we establish a conformance relation based on trace inclusion by recording traces of events in the system under test and replaying them in the model. User input is handled by generating a test driver that supplies the needed stimuli to the model. An industrial case study of the Credo project serves to demonstrate the approach.

Keywords: Model-based testing, conformance testing, concolic execution, Creol, Maude.

1   Introduction

Model-based testing has become an increasingly important part of robust software development practices. Specifying a system's behavior in a formal model helps to uncover specification ambiguities that would otherwise be resolved in an ad-hoc fashion during implementation. Using the model as a test oracle as well as a specification aid reinforces its critical role in the development process.

The techniques presented in this paper are based on the object-oriented modeling language Creol, a language designed to model concurrent and distributed

---

[*] This research was carried out as part of the EU FP6 project *Credo*: Modeling and analysis of evolutionary structures for distributed services (IST-33826).

F.S. de Boer et al. (Eds.): FMCO 2008, LNCS 5751, pp. 61–81, 2009.
© Springer-Verlag Berlin Heidelberg 2009

systems. Creol models are high-level as they abstract from, e.g., particular network properties as well as specific local schedulers. However, Creol is an executable language with a formal semantics defined in rewriting logic [19]. Thus, Creol models may be seen as executable designs. Test cases are written in Creol as well, and *dynamic symbolic execution* (DSE) is applied to calculate a test suite that reaches the desired model coverage. DSE is a combination of concrete and symbolic execution, and therefore, it is also known as *concolic execution.*

To show conformance between model and implementation, sequences of events are recorded from the instrumented implementation and replayed on the model. This approach allows reasoning about control flow and code coverage and goes beyond observations on program input/output. The conformance relation is based on trace inclusion, that is, every behavior shown by the implementation must be observable on the model as well. In case of non-deterministic models, we apply model-checking techniques in order to reach conclusive fail verdicts. To deal with user input events, the generated test driver stimulates the model in the same way as was observed in the implementation.

This testing methodology is applied in the context of the ASK system, one of the industrial demonstrators of the Credo project. However, Creol and the presented model-based testing technique is general and covers a wide range of distributed architectures.

The major contributions of this paper are:

- A tool-supported method for calculating optimal-coverage test cases from a model that serves as a test oracle.
- An extension of DSE to deal with concurrency.
- A conformance relation that can handle both input/output events and internal actions in a uniform way and allows reasoning about program flow and code coverage.
- A tool to generate a test driver from recorded implementation behavior that copes with arbitrary input events.

The rest of the paper is organized as follows: Section 2 gives an in-depth overview of the approach, including the techniques and the conformance relation developed, and Section 3 presents the unique features of the Creol modeling language that enable parallel DSE. Section 4 explains how to calculate test inputs from a Creol model, and Section 5 shows how to generate full test cases by recording an implementation's behavior responding to these test inputs, and checking whether its Creol model can exhibit the same behavior. Finally, Sections 6 and 7 contain related work and a conclusion to the paper.

2   Overview: The Testing Approach

The method described in this paper consists of two parts: generating test cases from a Creol model, and validating the implementation against the model. *Generating test cases* is done by computing test input values to achieve maximal model coverage. To handle the parallelism in the models, dynamic symbolic execution is used to avoid the combinatorial state space explosion that is inherent in static analysis of such systems. *Validating the implementation* is achieved via light-weight instrumentation of both model and implementation, and replaying traces that were recorded on the implementation on the model in order to verify the conformance of the implementation's behavior.

2.1   Finding Test Cases with Dynamic Symbolic Execution

This section gives a brief introduction to dynamic symbolic execution (DSE) and its application to test case generation of sequential programs. Our extensions for distributed and concurrent systems are presented in Section 4.1. Conventional symbolic execution uses symbols to represent arbitrary values during execution. When encountering a conditional branch statement, the run is forked. This results in a tree covering all paths in the program. In contrast, dynamic symbolic execution calculates the symbolic execution *in parallel* with a concrete run that is actually taken, avoiding the usual problem of eliminating infeasible paths. Decisions on branch statements are recorded, resulting in a set of conditions over the symbolic values that have to evaluate to *true* for the path to be taken. We call the conjunction of these conditions the *path condition*; it represents an equivalence class of concrete input values that *could* have taken the same path. Note, in the case of non-determinism, there is no guarantee that all inputs of this equivalence class will take this path. For the application of DSE to systematic test case generation, the symbolic values represent the inputs of a program; concrete input values from outside this equivalence class are selected to force new execution paths, and thereby new test cases. Hence, the selection of new input values for finding new paths is a typical constraint solving problem.

Example 1. Consider the following piece of code from an agent system calculating the number of threads needed to handle job requests.

```
1    amountToCreate:= tasks − idlethreads + ... ;
2    if (amountToCreate > (maxthreads − threads)) then
3      amountToCreate:= maxthreads − threads;
4    end;
5    if (amountToCreate > 0) then ... end;
```

Testers usually analyze the control flow in order to achieve a certain coverage. For example, a run evaluating both conditions above to **true** is sufficient to ensure *statement coverage*. *Branch coverage* needs two cases at least and *path coverage* all four combinations. The symbolic computation calculates all possible conditions, expressed in terms of symbolic input values. We denote the symbolic value of an input parameter by appending s to the parameter's variable name. Let threads, idlethreads, and tasks denote the input parameters for testing, and maxthreads being a constant. Then statement coverage (both conditions evaluate to **true**) is obtained for all input values fulfilling the condition

$$(tasks_s - idlethreads_s) > (maxthreads - threads_s)$$
$$\wedge (maxthreads_s - threads_s) > 0$$

Dynamic symbolic execution calculates these input conditions for a concrete execution path. The next test case is generated in such a way that the same path is avoided by negating the input conditions of the previous paths and choosing new input values satisfying this new condition. For example, inputs satisfying

$(tasks_S - idlethreads_S) \leq (\texttt{maxthreads} - threads_S)$
$\wedge (\texttt{maxthreads} - threads_S) > 0$

will avoid the first **then**-branch, resulting in a different execution path.

One immediately realizes that the choice of which sub-condition to negate determines the kind of coverage obtained, but the coverage that can actually be achieved also depends on the actual program and the symbolic values used. For example, the presence of unreachable code obviously makes full statement coverage impossible. The concrete test values from symbolic input vectors can be found by modern constraint solvers (e.g., ILOG Solver) or SMT-solvers (e.g., Yices, Z3).

2.2   Conformance Testing Using Recorded Event Traces

In the setting of asynchronous, concurrent systems, and when facing non-determinism, testing for expected behavior by examining the outputs of the *system under test* (SuT) is not always sufficient. Our approach utilizes the observed structural similarity of a model written in Creol and its implementation to test that the implementation has a similar control flow as the executable model. To this end, both model and implementation are *instrumented* at points in the code where meaningful *events* occur. At a high level, an implementation can be seen as a mapping I from an initial configuration $conf_I$ to an event trace $events_I$ – or more generally, in the face of nondeterminism, to a set of event traces $\{events_I\}$. Similarly, the instrumented model M maps an initial configuration $conf_M$ to a set of traces $\{events_M\}$.

Given a function ρ that converts (refines) configurations from the model to the implementation view, and a function α to abstract event traces from implementation to the model, the relationship between model and implementation can be seen in Diagram 1:

$$
\begin{array}{ccc}
conf_M & \xrightarrow{\ M\ } & \{events_M\} \\
\downarrow \rho & & \uparrow \alpha \\
conf_I & \xrightarrow{\ I\ } & \{events_I\}
\end{array}
\tag{1}
$$

In the literature this is also called U-simulation [12]. The conformance relation of the approach can then be described as follows: given a test input (written by a test engineer or calculated via DSE), all possible event traces resulting from stimulating the implementation by that input must also be observable on the model. Equation 2 shows the formulation of this trace inclusion relation:

$$
\alpha(I(\rho(conf_M))) \subseteq M(conf_M)
\tag{2}
$$

Section 5.2 shows an implementation of the α function as a generated Creol test driver class that is run in parallel with the instrumented model to reach a test verdict. Some of the recorded events correspond to user input to the implementation; the generated test driver supplies the equivalent stimuli to the model.

In contrast to the automated α mapping, currently the ρ mapping between initial configurations is manual.

3   Creol

Creol is a modeling language for executable designs, targeting distributed systems in which concurrent objects communicate asynchronously [18]. The language decouples communication from synchronization. Furthermore, it allows local scheduling to be left underspecified but controlled through explicitly declared process release points. The language has a formal semantics defined in rewriting logic [19] and executes on the Maude platform [9]. In the remainder of this section, we present Creol and emphasize its essential features for DSE.

A concurrent object in Creol executes a number of processes that have access to its local state. Each process corresponds to the activation of one of the object's methods; a special method run is automatically activated at object creation time, if present, and represents the object's active behavior. Objects execute concurrently: each object has a processor dedicated to executing the processes of that object, so processes in different objects execute in parallel. In contrast to, e.g., Java, each Creol object strictly encapsulates its state; i.e., external manipulation of the object state happens via calls to the object's methods only.

Only one process can be active in an object at a time; the other processes in the object are *suspended*. We distinguish between *blocking* a process and *releasing* a process. Blocking causes the execution of the process to stop, but does not let a suspended process resume. Releasing a process suspends the execution of that process and lets another (suspended) process resume. Thus, if a process is blocked there is no execution in the object, whereas if a process is released another process in the object may execute. The execution of several processes within an object can be combined using *release points* within method bodies. At a release point, the active process may be released and *some* suspended process resumes. Note, due to the non-deterministic scheduling semantics of Creol it is possible that the active process may be immediately rescheduled for execution. Hence, (non-terminating) active and reactive behavior are easily combined within a concurrent object in Creol.

Communication in Creol is based on method calls. These are a priori asynchronous; method replies are assigned to labels (also called *future variables*, see [10]). There is no synchronization associated with *calling* a method. However, *reading a reply* from a label is a blocking operation and allows the calling object to synchronize with the callee. A method call that is directly followed by a read operation models a synchronous call. Thus, the calling process may decide at runtime whether to call a method synchronously or asynchronously. The local scheduling of processes inside an object is given by conditions associated with release points. These conditions may depend on the value of the local

$T::= C \mid \textbf{Bool} \mid \textbf{Void}$ $L ::= \textbf{class } C(\overline{v}) \textbf{ begin } \overline{\textbf{var } f : T}; \overline{M} \textbf{ end}$
  $\mid \textbf{Int} \mid \textbf{String} \mid ...$ $M::= \textbf{op } m(\textbf{in } \overline{x : T} \textbf{ out } \overline{x : T}) == \overline{\textbf{var } x : T}; \overline{s} \textbf{ end}$
$v::= f \mid x$ $e ::= v \mid \textbf{new } C(\overline{v}) \mid \textbf{null} \mid \textbf{this} \mid v + v \mid ...$
$b::= \textbf{true} \mid \textbf{false} \mid v$ $s ::= l!e.m(\overline{e}) \mid !e.m(\overline{e}) \mid l?(v) \mid e.m(\overline{e};\overline{v}) \mid \textbf{await } g$
$g::= b \mid v? \mid g \wedge g$ $\mid v := e \mid \textbf{skip} \mid \textbf{release} \mid \textbf{await } e.m(\overline{e};\overline{v})$
          $\mid \textbf{while } g \textbf{ do } \overline{s} \textbf{ end} \mid \textbf{if } g \textbf{ then } \overline{s} \textbf{ end}$

Fig. 1. Language syntax of a subset of Creol

state, allowing cooperative scheduling between the processes within an object, but may also depend on the object's communication with other objects in the environment. Guards on release points include synchronization operations on labels, so the local scheduling can depend on both the object's state and the arrival of replies to asynchronous method calls.

In summary, only one process is executing on each object's local state at a time, and the interleaving of processes is flexibly controlled via (guarded) release points. Together with the fact that objects communicate exclusively via messages (strict encapsulation), this gives us the concurrency control necessary for extending DSE to the distributed paradigm.

Syntax. The language syntax of the subset of Creol used in this paper is presented in Figure 1. In this overview, we omit some features of Creol, including inheritance, non-deterministic choice, and many built-in data types and their operations. For a full overview of Creol, see for example [18]. In the language subset used in the examples of this paper, classes L are of type C with a set of methods $\overline{M}$. Classes can implement zero or more interfaces, which define methods that the class must then implement. *Expressions* e over variables v (either fields f or local variables x) are standard. *Statements* s are standard apart from the asynchronous method call $l!e.m(\overline{e})$ where the label l points to a reference to the reply, the (blocking) read operation $l?(\overline{v})$, and release points **await** g and **release**. *Guards* g are conjunctions of Boolean expressions b and synchronization operations $l?$ on labels l. When the guard in an **await** statement evaluates to *false*, the statement is *disabled* and becomes a **release**, otherwise it is *enabled* and becomes a **skip**. A **release** statement suspends the active process and another suspended process may be rescheduled. Hence, the suspended process releases lock on the object's attributes. The *guarded call* **await** $e.m(\overline{e};\overline{v})$ is a typical pattern which suspends the active process until the reply to the call has arrived and abbreviates $l!e.m(\overline{e})$; **await** $l?; l?(\overline{v})$.

3.1 Representation of a Run

A run of a Creol system captures the parallel execution of processes in different concurrent objects. Such a run may be perceived as a sequence of atomic execution steps where each step contains a set of local state-transitions on a subset of the system's objects. However, only one process may be active at a time in each object and different objects operate on disjoint data. Therefore, the transitions in each execution step may be performed in a truly concurrent manner or in any sequential order, so long as all transitions in one step are completed before the next execution step commences. For the purposes of dynamic symbolic execution the run is represented as a sequence of statements which manipulate the state variables, together with the conditions which determine the control flow, as follows.

The representation of an assignment $\overline{v} := \overline{e}$ is straightforward: Because fields and local variables in different processes can have the same name and statements from different objects are interleaved, the variable names are expanded to unique identifiers by adding the object id for fields and the call label for local variables. This expansion is done transparently for all variables and we will omit the variable scope in the sequel.

An asynchronous method call in the run is reflected in four execution steps (remark that the label value l uniquely identifies the steps that belong to the same method call): $o_1 \xrightarrow{l} o_2.m(\overline{e})$ represents the *call* of method m in object o_2 from object o_1 with arguments $\overline{e}$; $o_1 \xrightarrow{l} o_2.m(\overline{v})$ represents the moment when a called object starts execution, where $\overline{v}$ are the local names of the parameters for m; $o_1 \xleftarrow{l} o_2.m(\overline{e})$ represents the emission of the return values from the method execution; and $o_1 \xleftarrow{l} o_2.m(\overline{v})$ represents the corresponding reception of the values. These four events fully describe method calling in Creol. In this execution model the events reflecting a specific method call always appear in the same order, but they can be interleaved with other statements.

Object creation, **new** $C(\overline{v})$, is similar to a method call. The actual object creation is reduced to generating a new identifier for the object and a call to the object's **init** and **run** methods, which create the sequences as described above.

Conditional statements in Creol are side effect free, i.e. they do not change an object's state. In order to record the choice made during a run, the condition or its negated version are included into the run as Boolean guard $\langle g \rangle$. Hence, a run represents both, the variable changes together with the taken branch. As will be shown later, the conditions in a run are used to calculate the equivalence class of all input values that may take this path.

Await statements **await** g require careful treatment: if they evaluate to *false*, no code is executed. To reflect the information that the interpreter failed to execute a process because the condition g of the **await** statement evaluated to *false*, the negated condition $\langle \neg g \rangle$ is recorded.

3.2   The ASK Case Study

We demonstrate the approach using the ASK system as a running example throughout the paper. ASK is an industrial software system for connecting people based on context-aware response, developed by the research company Almende [3] and marketed by ASK Community Systems [4]. The ASK system provides mechanisms for matching users requiring information or services with potential suppliers and is used by various organizations for applications such as

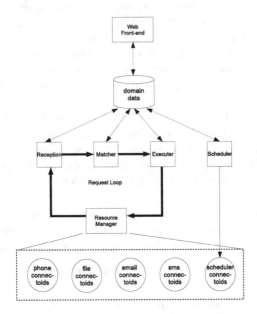

Fig. 2. Overview of the ASK system architecture

workforce planning and emergency response. The number of people connected varies from several hundred to several thousand, making it imperative to have good testing support.

Figure 2 shows the basic architectural view of the existing ASK systems. The "heartbeat" of the system is the *Request loop*, indicated with thick arrows. A request contains the information of two *participants* (a requester and a responder). Based on the request, the ASK system attempts to provide a connection between the two participants if possible, and otherwise attempts to suggest an alternative responder. A number of more or less independent components work together to search for appropriate participants for a request, determine how to connect them, or in general figure out the best way in which a request can be fulfilled.

Each of these components is itself multi-threaded. The threads act as workers in a thread pool, executing tasks put into a component-wide shared task queue. Tasks are used to implement the requests described above. Within a single component, threads do not communicate directly with each other. However, they can dispatch new tasks to the task queue that are eventually executed by another or the same thread. Threads are also able to send messages to other components. In most of the components, the number of threads can change over time, depending on the number of pending tasks in the task queue and on the number of idle threads.

A reference model for ASK systems has been developed in Creol, in collaboration with Almende [2]. An example of a class in Creol is given in Figure 3, which shows the implementation of the ThreadPool and also contains the system-wide

```
1  class ThreadPool(size : Int, maxNofThreads : Int)
2    contracts ThreadPool
3  begin
4    vars taskCtr, threadCtr, busyCtr :Counter;
5    var taskQueue : TaskQueue;
6    var threads : List[Thread];
7    var balancer : Task;
8
9    op init ==
10   // removed variable initialization
11     balancer:= new BalancerTask(1, taskCtr, threadCtr, busyCtr,
12       maxNofThreads, mrate, taskQueue, this);
13     this.dispatchTask(balancer;)
14
15   with Any op dispatchTask(in task : Task) ==
16     taskQueue.enqueueTask(task;)
17
18   with Any op createThreads(amount : Int) ==
19     var i : Int;
20     var thread : Thread;
21     i:= 0;
22     while (i < amount) do
23       thread:= new Worker(taskQueue, busyCtr, threadCtr);
24       threads:= threads ⊢ thread; // append thread
25       threadCtr.inc(;);
26       i:= i +1
27     end
28
29   with Any op start ==
30     this.createThreads(size;)
31 end
```

Fig. 3. ThreadPool of the ASK system (instantiation of Counter and TaskQueue omitted)

task queue. The thread pool is initialized with the parameters size and maxNofThreads which determine the initial number of threads in the pool and the maximum allowed number respectively. It also contains a number of counters to keep record of tasks and threads (number of pending tasks taskCtr, total number of worker threads threadCtr, and number of worker threads that currently execute a task busyCtr). The initialization of these variables is straightforward and omitted in the shown code for matters of presentation. When the class is initialized, the init method is automatically executed and creates the *balancer* task which is responsible for creating and deleting working threads when needed. We will discuss this thread in more detail in Section 4.2. The dispatch method inserts tasks into the task queue to be executed by an idle worker thread. Method createThreads creates a given number of worker threads, which themselves look into the task queue for open tasks. Note that in Creol input and output parameters are separated by semicolon. Hence, the absence of output is indicated by a semicolon at the end of the actual parameter list, as e.g. in the call to `createThreads` at the end. When the system is set up, the thread pool is activated by the `start` method (being called from a client object), which calls `createThreads` with the initial number of worker threads (as set by the class parameter `size`).

This reference model forms the basis for our work on testing ASK systems. Note that in this paper we only show excerpts of the model and omit some of the details for better demonstration of the approach. This simplified model consist of six different kinds of objects with various instances and does not induce any performance problems.

4   Test Case Generation

To generate test cases from the Creol model, we extend dynamic symbolic execution from Section 2.1 to distributed concurrent objects. Coverage criteria define a measurement of the amount of the program that is covered by the test suite. Two runs that cover the same parts of a system can be considered equivalent. A good test suite maximizes the coverage while minimizing the number of equivalent runs in order to avoid superfluous effort in executing the tests.

To set up a test case, the testing engineer first selects a test scenario, a description of the intention of the test, either from use cases or a high level specification of the system. Using this scenario, a first test run is set up that triggers a corresponding execution of the system. Starting with this run, the coverage is enhanced by introducing symbolic values t_S in the test object and computing new values such that new, non-equivalent runs are performed.

Dynamic symbolic execution on a run gives the set of conditions that are combined to the path condition $\mathcal{C} = \bigwedge_{1 \leq i \leq n} c_i$ (for n conditions), characterizing exactly the equivalence class of t_S that can repeat the same execution path. Only one test case that fulfills $\mathcal{C}$ is required. A new test case is then chosen by violating some c_i so that another branch is executed. Note that by executing new branches, also new conditions may be discovered. To reach decision coverage (DC) in a test suite, for instance, test cases are created until for each condition c_i there is at least one test case that reach and fulfill as well as violate this condition. The process of generating new test cases ends after all combinations required for the required coverage criterion are explored.

In the case of distributed concurrent systems, however, we frequently deal with scenarios in which the naive approach does not terminate. Most importantly, such concurrent systems often contain active objects that do not terminate and thus create an infinite run. In this case, execution on the model has to be stopped after exceeding some threshold. The computation of the path condition can be performed as before and will prohibit the same partial run in future computations. Creol also supports infinite datatypes. For a code sample such as **while** (i > 0) **do** i := i - 1 **end**, there is a finite run for each i, but there are infinitely many of them. To make sure that the approach terminates, a limiting condition has to be introduced manually, for example by creating an equivalence class for all i greater than a user defined constant.

4.1 Dynamic Symbolic Execution in the Parallel Setting

We now present the rules to compute the symbolic values for a given run. The formulas given in this section very closely resemble the rewrite rules of the Creol simulation environment [18], defined in rewriting logic [19] and implemented in Maude [9]. A rewrite rule $t \implies t'$ may be interpreted as a *local transition rule* allowing an instance of the pattern t in the configuration of the rewrite system to evolve into the corresponding instance of the pattern t'. When auxiliary functions are needed in the semantics, these are defined in equational logic, and are evaluated in between the state transitions [19]. The rules are presented here in a slightly simplified manner to improve readability.

Denote by $\bar{s}$ the representation of a sequence of program statements. Let $\sigma = \langle v_1 \triangleright e_1, v_2 \triangleright e_2, \ldots, v_n \triangleright e_n \rangle = \langle \bar{v} \triangleright \bar{e} \rangle$ be a map which records *key–value* entries $v \triangleright e$, where a variable v is bound to a symbolic value e. The value assigned to the key v is accessed by $v\sigma$. For an expression e and a map σ, define a parallel substitution operator $e\sigma$ which replaces all occurrences of every variable v in e with the expression $v\sigma$ (if v is in the domain of σ). For simplicity, let $\bar{e}\sigma$ denote the application of the parallel substitution to every expression in the list $\bar{e}$. Furthermore, let the expression $\sigma_1 \uplus \sigma_2$ combine two maps σ_1 and σ_2 so that, when entries with the same key exist in both maps, the entry in σ_2 is taken. In the symbolic state σ, all expanded variable names are bound to symbolic expressions. However, operations for method calls do not change the value of the symbolic state, but generate or receive *messages* that are used to communicate actual parameter values between the calling and receiving objects. Similar to the expressions bound to variables in the symbolic state σ, the symbolic representations of these actual parameters are bound in a map Θ to the actual and unique label value l provided for each method call by Creol's operational semantics. Finally, the conditions of control statements along an execution path are collected in a list $\mathcal{C}$; the concatenation of a condition c to $\mathcal{C}$ is denoted by $\mathcal{C}\hat{\ }c$.

The *configurations* of the rewrite system for dynamic symbolic execution are given by $\bar{s}[\Theta, \sigma, \mathcal{C}]$, where $\bar{s}$ is a sequence of statements, Θ and σ are the maps for messages and symbolic variable assignments as described above, and $\mathcal{C}$ is the list of conditions. Recall that the sequence $\bar{s}$ (as described in Section 3.1) is in fact generated on the fly by the concrete rewrite system for Creol executed in parallel with the dynamic symbolic execution. Thus, the *rules* of the rewrite system have the form

$$\bar{s}[\Theta, \sigma, \mathcal{C}] \implies \bar{s}'[\Theta', \sigma', \mathcal{C}'].$$

The primed terms on the right-hand side are updated results from the execution of the rule. The rules are given in Figure 4 and explained below.

Rule ASSIGN defines the variable updates that are performed for an assignment. All variables in the right hand side are replaced by their current values in

$$\bar{v} := \bar{e}; \bar{s}[\varTheta, \sigma, \mathcal{C}] \Longrightarrow \bar{s}[\varTheta, \sigma \uplus \langle \bar{v} \rhd (\bar{e}\sigma) \rangle, \mathcal{C}]. \qquad \text{(ASSIGN)}$$

$$o_1 \xrightarrow{l} o_2.m(\bar{e}); \bar{s}[\varTheta, \sigma, \mathcal{C}] \Longrightarrow \bar{s}[\varTheta \uplus \langle l \rhd \bar{e}\sigma \rangle, \sigma, \mathcal{C}]. \qquad \text{(CALL)}$$

$$o_1 \xrightarrow{l} o_2.m(\bar{v}); \bar{s}[\varTheta, \sigma, \mathcal{C}] \Longrightarrow \bar{s}[\varTheta, \sigma \uplus \langle \bar{v} \rhd l\varTheta \rangle, \mathcal{C}]. \qquad \text{(BIND)}$$

$$\langle g \rangle; \bar{s}[\varTheta, \sigma, \mathcal{C}] \Longrightarrow \bar{s}[\varTheta, \sigma, \mathcal{C}^\frown \langle g\sigma \rangle]. \qquad \text{(COND)}$$

Fig. 4. Rewrite rules for symbolic execution of Creol statements

σ, which is then updated by the new expressions. Note that we do not handle variable declarations, but work in the runtime-environment. We expect that a type check already happened during compile time and insert variables into σ the first time they appear. A method call as defined by Rule CALL emits a message that records the expressions that are passed to the method. Because of the asynchronous behavior of Creol, the call might be received at a later point in the run (or not at all if the execution terminates before the method was selected for execution) by Rule BIND, which handles the binding of a call to a new process and assigns the symbolic representation of the actual parameter values to the local variables in the new process. The emission and reception of return values are handled similarly to call statements and call reception.

Object creation is represented as a call to the constructor method init of the newly created object. In this case there is no explicit label for the call statement, so the object identifier is used to identify the messages to call the init and run methods, which are associated to the **new** statement. For conditionals, the local variables in the condition are replaced by their symbolic values (Rule COND). This process is identical for the different kinds of conditional statements (**if**, **while**, **await**). The statement itself acts as a **skip** statement; it changes no variables and does not produce or consume messages. The expression $g\sigma$ characterizes the equivalence class of input values that fulfill the condition if it is reached. The conjunction of all conditions found during symbolic evaluation represents the set of input values that can trigger that run. The tool records the condition that evaluated to *true* during runtime. Therefore, if the **else** branch of an **if** statement is entered or a disabled **await** statement with g is approached, the recorded condition will be $\neg g$.

4.2 The ASK Case Study Revisited

We revisit our running example to demonstrate the parallel version of DSE and the way test cases are generated. The *balancer* Task is instantiated by the ThreadPool in Figure 3 to compute the number of worker threads to create or destroy depending on a given maximal number of threads, the currently existing number of threads and the number of remaining tasks. Figure 5 shows one central part of this balancing task: the tail-recursive method createThreads. This method and its opponent in the model, killThreads, are responsible for creating and killing threads as needed. The balancer is initialized with *maxthreads_s*,

```
1   op init ==
2     maxthreads:=maxthreads +1;
3
4   op createThreads ==
5     var amountToCreate : Int;
6     var idlethreads : Int:=threads -busythreads;
7     await ((threads<maxthreads)
8          ∧((idlethreads - tasks)<(threads/2)));
9     amountToCreate:=tasks - idlethreads +(threads/2);
10    if (amountToCreate > (maxthreads - threads)) then
11      amountToCreate:=maxthreads - threads;
12    end;
13    if (amountToCreate >0) then
14      await threadpool.createThreads(amountToCreate);
15    end;
16    createThreads();// infinite loop by tail- recursion
```

Fig. 5. Parts of the balancing thread to initialize and create new threads. The fields threads, idlethreads and tasks are updated by outside method calls, so the conditions in the **await** statements can become true.

the maximum number of threads that are allowed in the thread pool. In the balancer's init method (not shown here), the local variable maxthreads is incremented by one to account for the balancer task itself, which also runs inside the thread pool. The balancer has access to the number of threads that are active (threads), the number of threads that are processing some task (busythreads), and the number of tasks that are waiting to be assigned to a worker thread (tasks).

The **await** statement in the line 7 suspends the process while it is not necessary to create further worker threads; i.e., if the maximal number of threads is already reached or half of the threads are without a task (they are neither processing a task nor is there a task open for processing). The **if** statement in line 10 checks that there are not more tasks created than allowed by maxthreads. Finally, the thread pool is instructed to create the required numbers of threads in the line 14.

Figure 6 shows the code to instantiate the model and create a fixed number of tasks (10 in our example). The dynamic symbolic interpreter allows to treat special *variables* as *values*. Such variables are treated as a symbolic value for the dynamic symbolic execution and are selected by a special naming scheme, here denoted by the subscript s. This enables a flexible monitoring of symbolic values of variables at any arbitrary level in the code.

The test case setup of Figure 6 uses two symbolic variables as parameters: the maximum number of working threads $maxWorkThreads_s$ and the initial number of threads $nthreads_s$. DSE is used to find different concrete values for those symbolic values to optimize the coverage of the model.

```
1  class Main(nthreadss : Int, maxWorkThreadss : Int)
2  begin
3    var threadpool : ThreadPool;
4    var executionCounter : Counter;
5
6    op init ==
7      threadpool:= new ThreadPool(nthreadss, maxWorkThreadss);
8      executionCounter:= new Counter;
9
10   op run ==
11     var task : Task;
12     var i : Int;
13     i:= 0;
14     while (i < 10) do
15       task:= new CounterTask(i, executionCounter);
16       threadpool.dispatchTask(task; );
17       i:= i +1;
18     end
19     threadpool.start(; )
20   // After running, the executionCounter should be 10
21 end
```

Fig. 6. Setting up a model for DSE. Here, $nthreadss$ is the number of initial threads to be created and $maxthreadss$ is the maximal size of the thread pool.

For a first run we randomly choose the initial values $maxWorkThreadss==0$ and $nthreadss==1$. Dynamic symbolic execution with these starting values results in the path condition:

```
{"ifthenelse" : (0 < nthreadss)}
{"ifthenelse" : not(1 < nthreadss)}
{"disabled_await" : not( 1 < (maxWorkThreadss +1) ∧ true)}
```

The first two conditions are from the loop in the line 22 of Figure 3 and correspond to one loop traversal in which a thread is created. The third condition corresponds to the line 7 in Figure 5 and shows that the path was taken because $0 >= maxWorkThreadss$ and the balancer is not allowed to create any worker threads. Any other start values will lead to a different run.

Each of the conjuncts in the path condition depends only on the input $maxWorkThreadss$. For easier presentation, we will exploit this fact in the following and compute new values only for this input and leave $nthreadss$ constant. Note that this is generally not the case, conditions that rely on several symbolic values require that the input space is partitioned considering all variables.

For the second run we choose a value that it outside the previously computed path condition and continue with $maxWorkThreadss==15$, which records the conditions:

```
{"enabled_await" : (1< (maxWorkThreads_S +1) ∧ true) }
{"ifthenelse" : not(10 > maxWorkThreads_S ) }
```

for the **await** in line 7 and the **if** in line 10 of Figure 5. The number 10 in the second condition reflects that we create ten tasks at initialization in in Figure 6. The path condition reflects that all inputs with $maxWorkThreads_S$ >= 10 lead to the same path because there will not be more threads created than the number of outstanding tasks. There is no condition for the **if** in the line 13 because the amount to create does not exceed $maxWorkThreads_S$ and therefore is not dependent on it.

A third run, created with $maxWorkThreads_S$ == 5, results in

```
{"disabled_await" : (1< (maxWorkThreads_S +1) ∧ true) }
{"ifthenelse" : 10 > maxWorkThreads_S }
{"ifthenelse" : maxWorkThreads_S > 0 }
```

In this test case the amount of threads to create exceeded the maximal allowed number of threads and therefore was recomputed in line 11. The new value depends on $maxWorkThreads_S$, which causes the **if** statement in the line 13 to contribute to the path condition. The new path condition does not further divide the input space, so the maximal possible coverage according to the chosen coverage criterion is reached.

The $nthreads_S$ variable controls the initial number of threads in the threadpool, and is the only variable that determines the number of traversals through the loop in the line 22 of Figure 3. This is also reflected in the path condition that we got from $nthreads_S$==1 — it states that the same path through the loop will be taken if $(0 < nthreads_S)$ and $(1 \geq nthreads_S)$, i.e., $nthreads_S == 1$. Thus, using this condition for test case selection, we need a test case for each value of $nthreads_S$, it is not possible to create bigger equivalence classes. A closer look at the path condition shows us how to create a new run that never traverses the loop: negating the first condition, $(0 < nthreads_S)$. Thus, we get a new test case with $nthreads_S$==0 (we keep the value $maxWorkThreads_S$==5 from the initial test case). The path condition only consists of:

```
{"ifthenelse" not(0< nthreads_S) }
```

None of the conditions of Figure 5 is reached. This is due to the fact that in this case no worker thread is created on initialization of the threadpool, thus, the balancer cannot be executed.

Test cases with $nthreads_S$>1 lead to similar test cases as the initial one, with the variation that a different number of threads are calculated to be created. If too many threads are created in the beginning, the tasks are all completed before the balancer is called. This is because the tasks in the model are strongly abstracted versions of the real implementation and complete instantly. A delay in the tasks or more tasks in the test setup can be used to solve that problem.

The computation of the values for $maxWorkThreads_S$ can be automatized by constraint- or SMT solvers. For the example above we used Yices [11], which takes the negated path condition as input and computes an valuation for the variables if it is satisfiable.

```
<trace>
  <createThreads thread="3079972528" time="501911878"
                    number="10"/>
  <starting thread="3075214224" time="501911929" info=""/>
  <waiting thread="3075214224" time="501911951" info=""/>
  <starting thread="3066821520" time="501911980" info=""/>
  <waiting thread="3066821520" time="501911999" info=""/>
  ...
  <enqueue thread="3079972528" time="501912403"
            info="Sabbey - balancer (Sabbey.c 353)"/>
  ...
</trace>
```

Fig. 7. Parts of a recorded event trace from the ASK system. At the beginning, 10 threads are created; each thread emits a starting and a waiting event when created. Later, a task is added to the system.

5   Test Case Execution

Section 4 explained how to calculate test inputs for the implementation. This section describes how to reach test verdicts by generating test drivers to run the test cases and validate the implementation's behavior against the model. As mentioned in Section 2, our test assumption is that a sequence of events that is observed on the implementation can be reproduced (replayed) by the model.

5.1   Obtaining Traces from the Implementation

In order to obtain traces of events, the implementation is instrumented via code injection. The case study, where the system under test is implemented in C, uses AspectC [5] for this purpose; similar code injection or aspect-oriented programming solutions can be used for systems implemented in other languages.

Traces are recorded in a simple XML-based format, for ease of automatic processing. Figure 7 shows parts of a trace from the ASK system. At the start, a createThreads event occurs, followed by the events associated with threads being started and waiting for a task to work on (starting and waiting, respectively). Other events used in the case study are killThreads (recorded when the balancing thread decides to remove some threads), enqueue (recorded when a new Task is created) and dequeue (recorded when a thread starts working on a task).

5.2   Generating the Test Driver

As mentioned in Section 2.2, some of the events recorded in the implementation originate from the environment (user input, incoming network data, etc.). We call these "external" events *actions*, and generate a test driver that stimulates the model in the same way. In the example, enqueue is an event that comes from outside – in the implementation, it is typically triggered by an incoming phone call or by a database-stored work queue; the test driver has to trigger the same action when replaying the trace on the model.

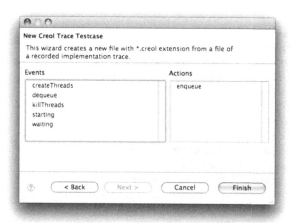

Fig. 8. Generating the tester from a recorded trace: separating Actions and Events. "enqueue" is to be triggered by the tester, so is designated to be an Action using this dialog.

```
1  interface TestActions
2  begin
3    with Any op enqueue(in thread :Int, time :Int, info :String)
4  end
5
6  class TestAdapter implements TestActions
7  begin
8    op init ==
9      skip// TODO : implement test driver setup here
10   with Any op enqueue(in thread :Int, time :Int, info :String) ==
11     skip// TODO : implement enqueue action
12 end
```

Fig. 9. Test actions interface and test adapter class template, created from the implementation trace

Figure 8 shows the dialog that is used to differentiate actions and events from the recorded trace for the purpose of generating the tester. Each action is a stimulus that the tester gives to the model. The tool generates a Creol interface TestActions and a class TestAdapter which is ready to contain code for initializing the model and for stimulating the model from the test case implementation. Methods with empty bodies are generated for these purposes.

Figure 9 shows the interface TestActions and class TestAdapter that are generated using the choices made in Figure 8. The one designated action ("enqueue") results in a method called enqueue, which will be called by the generated tester code. In the TestAdapter class, the test engineer then supplies implementations for model initialization (Figure 9, line 9) and any actions (line11).

```
1   op run ==
2     ok:= false;
3     this.allow("createThreads";);
4     await get(sem, "createThreads") = 0;
5     this.allow("starting";);
6     await get(sem, "starting") = 0;
7     this.allow("waiting";);
8     await get(sem, "waiting") = 0;
9     this.allow("starting";);
10    await get(sem, "starting") = 0;
11    this.allow("waiting";);
12    await get(sem, "waiting") = 0;
13  ...
14    this.enqueue(3079972528, 501912403,
15                    "Sabbey_-_balancer_(Sabbey.c_353)";);
16  ...
17    ok:= true
```

Fig. 10. Replaying the trace of Figure 7: tester event and action behavior in the model

In addition to implementing the methods in TestAdapter, the test engineer
has to add events to the model at the place equivalent to where they were added
in the implementation to record the trace. At each point where an event occurs,
the model communicates with the tester, indicating which event is about to happen. The thread of execution which generates an event is *blocked* until the tester
accepts the event; other threads can continue executing. The tester, in turn, waits
for each event in sequence and then unblocks the model so that it can continue.
The model thus synchronizes with the sequence of events recorded from the implementation, as implemented by the tester. The following code snippet shows the
createThreads event added to the createThreads method from Figure 5:

```
if (amountToCreate > 0) then
  tester.request("createThreads"); // EVENT
  await threadpool.createThreads(amountToCreate);
end;
```

Figure 10 shows parts of the tester's run method; the sequence of Creol statements corresponds one-to-one to the sequence of events and actions in the trace
of Figure 7. The ok variable is set to false at the beginning and to true at the
end of the run method; this allows us to use model checking to find a successful
run. Each action in the trace is converted to a call to the corresponding method
in the TestAdapter class, as implemented by the user. In line 14 is a call
to action. Each event is converted to a pair of statements, the first statement
(this.allow(...)) unblocks the model and allows the event to occur, the
second statement (await get(...)) blocks the tester until the event actually
occurs in the model.

5.3 Obtaining Test Verdicts

To actually run the test case, an instance of the generated TestCase class is generated. Its init method, inherited from TestAdapter and implemented by the user, sets up and starts the model, and its run method (Figure 10), generated from the recorded implementation trace, steers the model to generate the expected events in sequence.

A test results in a verdict of "pass" if the model can reproduce the trace recorded from the implementation and if all assertions and invariants in the model hold. If an assertion in the model is violated, the model itself has an inconsistency and is in error (assuming the model is supposed to be valid for all inputs); no verdict about the implementation can be reached. If the run method of TestCase runs to completion, the test passes. If the tester deadlocks when running in parallel with the model, the implementation potentially violates the test assumption. But this result is inconclusive, it is still a possibility that a different scheduling in the model allows the test to pass; model checking the combination of model and tester can give a definitive answer and let us reach a verdict of "pass" or "fail".

6 Related Work

To our knowledge, the first to use symbolic execution on single runs were Boyer et al. in 1975 [8] who developed the interactive tool SELECT that computes input values for a run selected by the user. Some of the first automated tools for testing were DART (Directed Automated Random Testing) from Godefroid et al. [15], and the CUTE and jCUTE tools from Sen at al. [20]. Perhaps the most prominent and most widely used tool in that area is PEX by Tillmann et al. [21], which creates parameterized unit tests for single-threaded .NET programs. A closer look at DSE for generating test input in a parallel setting can be found in [17,16], recent work on examining all relevant interleavings in [1].

The use of formal models for testing has a long history, some of the more influential work are [14] and [22]. Various conformance relations have been proposed. They place varying demands w.r.t. controllability and observability placed on the SuT; for example *ioco* [23] by Tretmans et al. demands that implementations be input-enabled, while Petrenko and Yevtushenko's *queued-quiescence testing* does away with that assumption. Our proposed conformance relation is even more permissive, in that arbitrary input can become part of the test case and conforming behavior is checked after the fact instead of in parallel with the implementation.

Most tools for automated or semi-automated model-based software testing, including TorX [6] and TGV [13], work by simulating a user of the system, controlling input and checking output. A testing method similar to the one described in this paper, also relying on event traces, was developed by Bertolino et al. [7], whereby at run-time traces are extracted and model-checked to verify conformance to a stereotyped UML2 model. They emphasize black-box testing of components and reconstruct cause-effect relationships between observed events to construct message sequence charts. Consequently, they have to employ more intrusive monitoring than our approach.

7   Conclusions

We have presented an approach to test case generation and conformance testing which is integrated into the development cycle of distributed systems. We specify models in Creol, a concurrent object-oriented modeling language for executable designs of distributed systems. A single model serves to both optimize test cases in terms of coverage, and as test oracle for test runs on the actual implementation. Test input generation and model coverage are controlled via dynamic symbolic execution extended to a parallel setting, which has been implemented on top of the Maude execution platform for Creol. The conformance relation is based on U-simulation. Only a lightweight level of instrumentation of the implementation is needed, which is here achieved by means of aspect-oriented programming. The problem of reaching conclusive verdicts in case of non-determinism is handled by replaying the traces using Maude's search facilities. The techniques have been successfully applied in the context of the ASK systems, one model serving as a reference for several versions of the system.

Acknowledgments. The authors wish to thank the anonymous reviewers for their helpful comments and clarifications.

References

1. Aichernig, B., Griesmayer, A., Kyas, M., Schlatte, R.: Exploiting distribution and atomic transactions for partial order reduction. Technical Report No. 418, UNU-IIST (June 2009)
2. Aichernig, B., Griesmayer, A., Schlatte, R., Stam, A.: Modeling and testing multi-threaded asynchronous systems with Creol. In: Proceedings of the 2nd International Workshop on Harnessing Theories for Tool Support in Software (TTSS 2008). ENTCS. Elsevier, Amsterdam (2009)
3. Almende website, http://www.almende.com
4. ASK community systems website, http://www.ask-cs.com
5. ACC: The AspeCt-oriented C compiler, http://www.aspectc.net
6. Belinfante, A., Feenstra, J., de Vries, R.G., Tretmans, J., Goga, N., Feijs, L.M.G., Mauw, S., Heerink, L.: Formal test automation: A simple experiment. In: Csopaki, G., Dibuz, S., Tarnay, K. (eds.) 12th International Workshop on Testing of Communicating Systems. IFIP Conference Proceedings, vol. 147, pp. 179–196. Kluwer, Dordrecht (1999)
7. Bertolino, A., Muccini, H., Polini, A.: Architectural verification of black-box component-based systems. In: Guelfi, N., Buchs, D. (eds.) RISE 2006. LNCS, vol. 4401, pp. 98–113. Springer, Heidelberg (2007)
8. Boyer, R.S., Elspas, B., Levitt, K.N.: Select-A formal system for testing and debugging programs by symbolic execution. SIGPLAN Not. 10(6), 234–245 (1975)
9. Clavel, M., Durán, F., Eker, S., Lincoln, P., Martí-Oliet, N., Meseguer, J., Quesada, J.F.: Maude: Specification and programming in rewriting logic. Theoretical Computer Science 285, 187–243 (2002)
10. de Boer, F.S., Clarke, D., Johnsen, E.B.: A complete guide to the future. In: De Nicola, R. (ed.) ESOP 2007. LNCS, vol. 4421, pp. 316–330. Springer, Heidelberg (2007)

11. de Moura, L., Dutertre, B.: A fast linear-arithmetic solver for DPLL(T). In: Ball, T., Jones, R.B. (eds.) CAV 2006. LNCS, vol. 4144, pp. 81–94. Springer, Heidelberg (2006)
12. de Roever, W.-P., Engelhardt, K.: Data Refinement: Model-Oriented Proof Methods and their Comparison. Cambridge University Press, Cambridge (1998)
13. Fernandez, J.-C., Jard, C., Jéron, T., Viho, C.: Using on-the-fly verification techniques for the generation of test suites. In: Alur, R., Henzinger, T.A. (eds.) CAV 1996. LNCS, vol. 1102, pp. 348–359. Springer, Heidelberg (1996)
14. Gaudel, M.-C.: Testing can be formal, too. In: Mosses, P.D., Schwartzbach, M.I., Nielsen, M. (eds.) CAAP 1995, FASE 1995, and TAPSOFT 1995. LNCS, vol. 915, pp. 82–96. Springer, Heidelberg (1995)
15. Godefroid, P., Klarlund, N., Sen, K.: DART: directed automated random testing. In: PLDI 2005: Proceedings of the 2005 ACM SIGPLAN conference on Programming language design and implementation, pp. 213–223. ACM Press, New York (2005)
16. Griesmayer, A., Aichernig, B., Johnsen, E., Schlatte, R.: Dynamic symbolic execution for testing distributed objects. In: TAP 2009. LNCS, vol. 5668, pp. 105–120. Springer, Heidelberg (2009)
17. Griesmayer, A., Aichernig, B., Johnsen, E., Schlatte, R.: Dynamic symbolic execution of distributed concurrent objects (short paper). In: Lee, D., Lopez, A., Poetzsch-Heffter, A. (eds.) FMOODS/FORTE 2009. LNCS, vol. 5522, pp. 225–230. Springer, Heidelberg (2009)
18. Johnsen, E.B., Owe, O.: An asynchronous communication model for distributed concurrent objects. Software and Systems Modeling 6(1), 35–58 (2007)
19. Meseguer, J.: Conditional rewriting logic as a unified model of concurrency. Theoretical Computer Science 96, 73–155 (1992)
20. Sen, K., Agha, G.A.: CUTE and jCUTE: Concolic unit testing and explicit path model-checking tools. In: Ball, T., Jones, R.B. (eds.) CAV 2006. LNCS, vol. 4144, pp. 419–423. Springer, Heidelberg (2006)
21. Tillmann, N., de Halleux, J.: Pex–white box test generation for.NET. In: Beckert, B., Hähnle, R. (eds.) TAP 2008. LNCS, vol. 4966, pp. 134–153. Springer, Heidelberg (2008)
22. Tretmans, J.: Test generation with inputs, outputs, and quiescence. In: Margaria, T., Steffen, B. (eds.) TACAS 1996. LNCS, vol. 1055, pp. 127–146. Springer, Heidelberg (1996)
23. van der Bijl, M., Rensink, A., Tretmans, J.: Compositional testing with ioco. In: Petrenko, A., Ulrich, A. (eds.) FATES 2003. LNCS, vol. 2931, pp. 86–100. Springer, Heidelberg (2004)

Formal Verification for Components and Connectors

Christel Baier, Tobias Blechmann, Joachim Klein, and Sascha Klüppelholz[*]

Faculty of Computer Science,
Technische Universität Dresden, Germany

Abstract. In previous work, constraint automata have been introduced
as a uniform model for behavioral interfaces of components, (possibly
dynamic) component connectors and systems consisting of several components and their glue code. The purpose of the paper is to provide
an overview of the techniques for specifying and verifying temporal requirements, conditions on the data flow at the I/O-ports of components
and alternating-time properties that have been designed for constraint
automata. The paper presents the syntax and semantics of the logics,
sketches the model checking algorithms, summarizes the main features of
the implementation within the tool Vereofy and reports on experimental
studies.

1 Introduction

The main idea of component-based software engineering is to divide a complex
system into smaller logical components with well-defined interfaces. For this
purpose, a variety of coordination models and languages have been introduced
which support the separation between computations inside the components and
the interactions between the components. All these models and languages aim
to improve productivity, enhance maintainability, advocate modularity, promote
reusability, and lead to software organizations and architectures that are more
tractable and more amenable to verification and analysis. For providing tool
support for the verification of such systems one needs operational models that
are powerful enough to describe both the coordination imposed by the connectors
and the behavioral interfaces of the connected components and that can serve
as structures for temporal logics and as basis for model checking algorithms.
For this purpose, constraint automata have been introduced in [6]. They have
been used as a compositional semantics for the exogenous coordination language
Reo [3]. In the exogenous setting the components are not aware of the context in
which say are used. The component interactions and communication is handled
by a network from outside the components.

Constraint automata are a special variant of labeled transition systems where
the transitions are labeled with sets of I/O-ports and constraints on the data

---

[*] The authors are supported by the EU-project Credo and the DFG-project Syanco.

F.S. de Boer et al. (Eds.): FMCO 2008, LNCS 5751, pp. 82–101, 2009.

transferred at those ports. This special type of automata is adequate to represent any kind of synchronous and asynchronous peer-to-peer communication, to model exogenous and endogenous coordination mechanisms and to deal with component connectors with dynamically changing network topologies [4]. In this paper, we provide an overview of the approaches that have been designed for the analysis of systems modeled by constraint automata and implemented to a large extent within our toolkit Vereofy, see www.vereofy.de. These approaches cover model checking techniques against temporal properties as well as equivalence checking techniques. The formalisms to specify temporal properties rely on the modalities of classical temporal logics (dynamic linear temporal logic [17,12], computation tree logic [9] and alternating-time temporal logic [2]) and operators to specify regular temporal conditions on the data streams at the I/O-ports of components or observable "inner nodes" of the network. Since constraint automata are a generic model for connectors, behavioral interfaces of components and the composite system (consisting of several components and a connector), our techniques are adequate to verify (i) coordination mechanisms with black-box components, (ii) the observable behavior of components, and (iii) special scenarios of coordination algorithms where assumptions are made on the component interfaces. While the model checking algorithms for linear and branching-time logics rely on standard concepts, the alternating-time approach is based on a concurrent game structure where the components serve as players and a nonstandard notion of strategies is required due to the special mixture of synchrony and asynchrony and the mutual dependencies of I/O-operations.

The main concepts of the verification approaches introduced in this paper are supported by our toolkit Vereofy, see Figure 1. For modeling, Vereofy relies on a hybrid approach with two input languages [4], the guarded command language CARML, which is most appropriate to specify the behavioral interfaces of the components, and the scripting language RSL (Reo scripting language), which mainly serves to specify the coordination mechanism. CARML provides a convenient way to specify the component interfaces and to provide a high-level description of the operational behavior of components. It supports channel-based message passing and is even expressive enough to specify complex component connectors. In CARML, the transitions of constraint automata are described in a symbolic way, i.e., by means of Boolean conditions on the current state and on the enabled concurrent I/O-operations (guards) and assignments that specify the effect of the taken transitions.

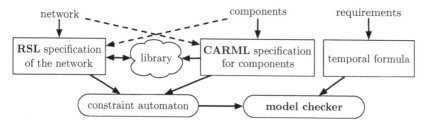

Fig. 1. Vereofy overview

RSL combines the major features of the exogenous coordination language Reo [3] with concepts to specify connectors with dynamically changing network topologies and some features of other languages. Reo's coordination primitives (creation of channels of an arbitrary type, joining channel ends or nodes, hiding) allow to reason about all kinds of coordination patterns with an arbitrary mixture of synchronous or asynchronous peer-to-peer communication. In particular, standard CCS-like handshaking or message passing over FIFO can be modeled in Reo (and RSL). Besides Reo's coordination primitives, RSL contains operators for the instantiation of component connectors or components. The code for the templates of components or connectors can be provided in RSL or CARML as part of the RSL main script or taken from a library. In this way, our approach with RSL and CARML naturally supports the reuse of components and connectors by instantiation and offers an elegant way for the compositional, hierarchical construction of component connectors and components. To ease the automatic translation of CARML specifications into a compact internal representation based on Binary Decision Diagrams (BDD), we adapted some concepts of reactive modules [1] for the syntax of CARML modules. Our symbolic implementation constructs BDDs for the constraint automata semantics of CARML modules directly and BDDs for RSL scripts compositionally using a product construction of constraint automata [6,7]. A more detailed description of both languages can be found in [4] or in the Vereofy manual available at www.vereofy.de. Our tool Vereofy can be used as as stand-alone version working on models stated in RSL and CARML or via the graphical user interface offered by the Eclipse Coordination Tools [18].

Organization. Section 2 presents the definition of constraint automata and related notations. The syntax, semantics and model checking algorithms for the temporal logics LTL_{IO} and ASL that have been designed for constraint automata are presented in Section 3. Furthermore this section explains the connection between these logics and bisimulation equivalence for constraint automata. Section 4 reports on the main features of our implementation, presents some experimental results and summarizes future directions.

2   Constraint Automata

Constraint automata (CA) provide a generic operational model to formalize the behavioral interfaces of the components, the network that coordinates the components (i.e., the glue code or connector), and the composite system consisting of the components and the glue code. Constraint automata are variants of labeled transition systems (LTS) where the labels of the transitions represent the (possibly data-dependent) I/O-operations of the components and the network. Thus, they support any kind of synchronous and asynchronous peer-to-peer communication.

The nodes of a CA play the role of the I/O-ports of the components or the network. The states of a CA represent the local states of components and/or configurations of a connector. The transitions in a CA describe the potential one-step behavior. In the approach of [6] transitions in a CA are labeled with a set of active nodes and Boolean conditions on the data values observable at active nodes. In the sequel, let Data be a finite nonempty data domain and $\mathcal{N}$ a finite, nonempty set of nodes. We slightly depart from the syntax of CA as introduced in [6] and deal with transitions $q \xrightarrow{c} p$, where c is a *concurrent I/O-operation*, i.e., c consists of a (possibly empty) node-set $N \subseteq \mathcal{N}$ together with data items for each $A \in N$ that are written or received at node A. In the moment where c is executed there is no data flow (i.e., no read or write operation) at the nodes $A \in \mathcal{N} \setminus N$.

Concurrent I/O-operations (CIO). A concurrent I/O-operation is a partial function assigning data values to the nodes, i.e., a function $c : \mathcal{N} \to \text{Data} \cup \{\bot\}$, where the symbol $\bot$ means "undefined". We write Nodes(c) for the set of nodes $A \in \mathcal{N}$ such that $c(A) \in$ Data. The *empty* concurrent I/O-operation, denoted $c_\emptyset$, is the unique concurrent I/O-operation where Nodes$(c_\emptyset) = \emptyset$. CIO$_\mathcal{N}$, or briefly CIO, denotes the set of all concurrent I/O-operations (including $c_\emptyset$). The empty concurrent I/O-operation $c_\emptyset$ represents any step where no data flow at some node $A \in \mathcal{N}$ is observable. Thus, it models any internal step of some component or any non-observable step of the network where data flow appears at most at some "hidden nodes" of the network. As $\mathcal{N}$ and Data are supposed to be finite, the set CIO = CIO$_\mathcal{N}$ of concurrent I/O-operations is finite as well.

Our logical framework refers to two kinds of labels. One refers to the I/O-operations in the network and the other to the states of constraint automata. The labels for the states can be regarded as unary state predicates. They are called atomic propositions. For example, if the network (i.e., connector) contains a FIFO channel then there might be atomic propositions stating, e.g., that all buffer cells are empty or that the first buffer cell contains a value d in some set $D \subseteq$ Data.

Constraint automata [6]. A constraint automaton (CA) is a tuple $\mathcal{A} = \langle Q, \mathcal{N}, \longrightarrow, Q_0, \text{AP}, L \rangle$ where Q is a finite and non-empty set of states, $\mathcal{N}$ a finite set of nodes, $\longrightarrow$ is a subset of $Q \times \text{CIO} \times Q$, called the transition relation of $\mathcal{A}$, $Q_0 \subseteq Q$ a non-empty set of initial states, AP a finite set of atomic propositions, and $L : Q \to 2^{\text{AP}}$ a labeling function. We write $q \xrightarrow{c} p$ instead of $(q, c, p) \in \longrightarrow$. The set of all I/O-operations enabled in state $q \in Q$ is defined by

$$\text{CIO}(q) \stackrel{\text{def}}{=} \{ c \in \text{CIO} : q \xrightarrow{c} p \text{ for some } p \in Q \}.$$

The meaning of a transition $q \xrightarrow{c} p$ is that in configuration q, the concurrent I/O-operation c is enabled and state p is a possible successor state of q executing the concurrent I/O-operation c.

Example 1 (Railway track). To illustrate the main features of CA we model a simple railway track. The node set $\mathcal{N} = \{A, B\}$ consists of two nodes. The track can be entered if a signal has been received from A and left via synchronizing with B. A train may pass the track if both ports A and B are ready for synchronization and it has to stop on the track if A is ready only. In the latter case the

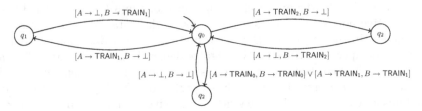

Fig. 2. Example constraint automaton for a railway track

train has to wait until B is ready for synchronization. Figure 2 shows the constraint automaton for two trains, i.e., $\mathsf{Data} = \{\mathsf{TRAIN_1}, \mathsf{TRAIN_2}\}$. We use $\mathsf{AP} = \{\mathsf{FREE}, \mathsf{OCCUPIED}, \mathsf{TRANSIT}, \mathsf{WAITING}\}$ as the set of atomic propositions and labeling function L with $L(q_0) = \{\mathsf{FREE}\}$, $L(q_1) = L(q_2) = \{\mathsf{OCCUPIED}, \mathsf{WAITING}\}$, and $L(q_2) = \{\mathsf{OCCUPIED}, \mathsf{TRANSIT}\}$. State q_0 is the initial state, i.e., initially there is no train on the track.   □

To simplify the presentation of the paper, we describe here our logical approach under the assumption that there are no terminating behaviors. That is, we depart here from [6] and require that for every state of a CA there is at least one outgoing transition. This assumption is somehow unrealistic since deadlock situations can appear, e.g., when the requested interactions of the components are contradicting. The treatment of infinite and terminating behaviors causes some technical difficulties which are avoided here to provide a clear and simple presentation of the major concepts.

Executions, paths, I/O-streams. As in standard LTS an *execution* in $\mathcal{A}$ is a finite or infinite sequence built by consecutive transitions:

$$\eta \;=\; q_0 \xrightarrow{c_1} q_1 \xrightarrow{c_2} \ldots$$

where $q_i \in Q$, $c_i \in \mathsf{CIO}$, and $q_i \xrightarrow{c_{i+1}} q_{i+1}$ for all $i \geq 0$. As stated above, in this paper we focus on explanations of our approaches to reason about infinite behaviors. We therefore define a *path* of $\mathcal{A}$ to be an infinite execution. We write $\mathsf{Paths}(q)$ to denote the set of all paths starting in q. Let $\pi = q_0 \xrightarrow{c_1} q_1 \xrightarrow{c_2} \ldots$ be a path and $0 \leq n$. Then, $\pi \downarrow n$ denotes the prefix of path π with length n and $\pi \uparrow n$ the suffix starting at the n-th state. Thus,

$$\pi \downarrow n \;\stackrel{\text{def}}{=}\; q_0 \xrightarrow{c_1} \ldots \xrightarrow{c_n} q_n$$
$$\pi \uparrow n \;\stackrel{\text{def}}{=}\; q_n \xrightarrow{c_{n+1}} q_{n+1} \xrightarrow{c_{n+2}} q_{n+2} \xrightarrow{c_{n+3}} \ldots.$$

The notion of an *I/O-stream* for CA corresponds to action sequences in LTS. The I/O-stream $\mathsf{ios}(\eta)$ of a finite execution η is the finite word over CIO that is obtained by taking the projection to the labels of the transitions. Formally, if $\eta = q_0 \xrightarrow{c_1} \ldots \xrightarrow{c_n} q_n$ is a finite execution then $\mathsf{ios}(\eta) \stackrel{\text{def}}{=} c_1 \ldots c_n \in \mathsf{CIO}^*$. The set of all I/O-streams is denoted by $\mathsf{IOS} \stackrel{\text{def}}{=} \mathsf{CIO}^*$.

I/O constraints (IOC). Sometimes it is useful to switch to a symbolic representation of the transition relation by combining transitions with the same starting and target state. (For example, our implementation of the model checker relies on a symbolic representation of CA.) For this purpose, we deal with I/O-constraints, i.e., propositional formulas in positive normal form that stand for *sets* of concurrent I/O-operations. The I/O-constraints may impose conditions on the nodes that may or may not be involved and on the data items written on or read from them. The abstract syntax of *I/O-constraints* over the node-set $\mathcal{N}$ is given by the grammar:

$$\text{ioc} ::= \quad tt \mid ff \mid A \mid \neg A \mid (d_{A_1}, \ldots, d_{A_k}) \in D \mid \text{ioc}_1 \wedge \text{ioc}_2 \mid \text{ioc}_1 \vee \text{ioc}_2$$

where $A \in \mathcal{N}$, $A_1, \ldots, A_k$ are pairwise distinct nodes in $\mathcal{N}$, d_{A_i} the data value written or read at port A_i, and $D \subseteq \mathsf{Data}^k$. The meaning of an I/O-constraint ioc is a subset $\lceil \text{ioc} \rceil$ of CIO defined in the expected way. We define $\lceil tt \rceil \overset{\text{def}}{=} \mathsf{CIO}$, $\lceil ff \rceil \overset{\text{def}}{=} \emptyset$, and for the literals $A \in \mathcal{N}$ and their negations $\neg A$:

$$\lceil A \rceil \overset{\text{def}}{=} \{ c \in \mathsf{CIO} : A \in \mathsf{Nodes}(c) \}$$
$$\lceil \neg A \rceil \overset{\text{def}}{=} \{ c \in \mathsf{CIO} : A \notin \mathsf{Nodes}(c) \}$$

The I/O-constraints $(d_{A_1}, \ldots, d_{A_k}) \in D$ impose conditions for the written and read data items. That is, $\lceil (d_{A_1}, \ldots, d_{A_k}) \in D \rceil$ agrees with the set

$$\{ c \in \mathsf{CIO} : \{A_1, \ldots, A_k\} \subseteq \mathsf{Nodes}(c), (c(A_1), \ldots, c(A_k)) \in D \}.$$

Conjunction and disjunction have their standard meaning, i.e.,

$$\lceil \text{ioc}_1 \wedge \text{ioc}_2 \rceil \overset{\text{def}}{=} \lceil \text{ioc}_1 \rceil \cap \lceil \text{ioc}_2 \rceil$$
$$\lceil \text{ioc}_1 \vee \text{ioc}_2 \rceil \overset{\text{def}}{=} \lceil \text{ioc}_1 \rceil \cup \lceil \text{ioc}_2 \rceil$$

We often use simplified notations for the IOC of the form $(d_{A_1}, \ldots, d_{A_k}) \in D$. E.g., the notation $d_A = d_B$ is a shorthand for $(d_A, d_B) \in \{(d_1, d_2) \in \mathsf{Data}^2 : d_1 = d_2\}$. The notation $\{A, B\}$ is used as a shorthand for $A \wedge B \bigwedge_{C \in \mathcal{N}} \neg C$ with meaning $\lceil \{A, B\} \rceil \overset{\text{def}}{=} \{c \in \mathsf{CIO} : \mathsf{Nodes}(c) = \{A, B\}\}$.

Example 2 (Railway track). An ioc for the railway track example may state that either a train has to stop or pass through.

$$(\{A\} \wedge d_A \in \{\mathsf{TRAIN}_1, \mathsf{TRAIN}_2\}) \vee (\{A, B\} \wedge d_A = d_B) \qquad \square$$

Stream expressions. To impose conditions on the data flow at the I/O-ports of components or nodes in the network, our logics will use a symbolic representation for sets of I/O-streams by means of regular I/O-stream expressions, briefly called stream expressions. The abstract syntax of stream expressions over $\mathcal{N}$ is given by the following grammar:

$$\alpha \quad ::= \quad \text{ioc} \mid \alpha^* \mid \alpha_1; \alpha_2 \mid \alpha_1 \cup \alpha_2$$

where ioc ranges over all I/O-constraints over $\mathcal{N}$. The formal definition of the regular languages $\mathsf{IOS}(\alpha) \subseteq \mathsf{IOS}$ is defined by structural induction. $\mathsf{IOS}(\mathsf{ioc})$ is the set consisting of the I/O-streams of length 1 given by ioc, i.e., $\mathsf{IOS}(\mathsf{ioc}) = \lceil \mathsf{ioc} \rceil$. Union ($\cup$), Kleene star ($*$) and concatenation (;) have their standard meaning.

3   Specifying and Verifying Components and Connectors

Constraint automaton yield a general framework for the behavior of a component, a connector or a composite system and serve as starting point for model checking. The model checking problem asks whether a given property holds for the automaton. In our framework and the tool Vereofy, the properties can be specified by temporal formulas with classical modalities to formalize safety or liveness conditions, but also constraints on the observable data flow (I/O-streams). Vereofy supports model checking against linear-time, branching-time or alternating-time properties formalized in the logics $\mathsf{LTL_{IO}}$ or ASL. The logic $\mathsf{LTL_{IO}}$ (see Section 3.1) is a variant of linear temporal logic LTL which is closely related to dynamic LTL [12] and combines the standard temporal modalities of LTL with stream expressions. It is appropriate to specify complex temporal conditions on paths (such as Boolean combinations of reachability, repeated reachability or persistence conditions), possibly in combination with regular conditions on I/O-streams of their prefixes. Alternating-time stream logic ASL (see Section 3.2) allows reasoning about the branching structure of the states by means of branching-time temporal formulas stating, e.g., the existence of a path where a certain path property holds (as in CTL [9]), or alternating-time conditions stating, e.g., the possibility of selected components to enforce a certain path property (as in ATL [2]). The path properties expressible in ASL rely on the ATL-syntax extended by stream expressions that can be attached to the until operator (as in $\mathsf{LTL_{IO}}$). Furthermore, Vereofy supports equivalence checking by means of a notion of bisimulation equivalence for constraint automata that preserves all properties expressible in $\mathsf{LTL_{IO}}$ and ASL (see Section 3.3). Throughout this section, we fix a finite set AP of atomic propositions for the states and a finite node-set $\mathcal{N}$.

3.1   Linear-Time Properties

In this section we describe the logic $\mathsf{LTL_{IO}}$, which is adapted from Dynamic Linear Time Temporal Logic (DLTL) [12] to the context of constraint automata and I/O-stream expressions. DLTL itself extends LTL with regular expressions to achieve the full expressiveness of omega-regular languages. For $\mathsf{LTL_{IO}}$ the concurrent I/O-operations over the given node-set $\mathcal{N}$ (i.e., the elements in the set $\mathsf{CIO}_{\mathcal{N}} = \mathsf{CIO}$) serve as names for actions and the I/O-stream expressions take the role of the propositional dynamic logic programs (regular expressions) of DLTL.

Syntax of $\mathsf{LTL_{IO}}$. The abstract syntax of $\mathsf{LTL_{IO}}$ formulas over AP and $\mathcal{N}$ is defined by the following grammar.

$$\varphi \ ::= \ \text{true} \ \Big| \ a \ \Big| \ \neg\varphi \ \Big| \ \varphi_1 \wedge \varphi_2 \ \Big| \ \varphi_1 \, \mathsf{U}^\alpha \, \varphi_2$$

where $a \in \mathsf{AP}$ and α is a stream expression over $\mathcal{N}$. Recall that the syntax and semantics of stream expressions has been provided in the end of Section 2.

Semantics of LTL$_{\mathsf{IO}}$. Let $\pi = q_0 \xrightarrow{c_1} q_1 \xrightarrow{c_2} \dots$ be a path in a constraint automaton, with $q_i \in Q$ and $c_i \in \mathsf{CIO}$. Let φ be LTL$_{\mathsf{IO}}$ formula over AP and $\mathcal{N}$. The satisfaction relation $\pi \models \varphi$ is defined as follows:

$$
\begin{aligned}
&\pi \models \text{true} \\
&\pi \models a && \text{iff } a \in L(q_0) \\
&\pi \models \neg\varphi && \text{iff } \pi \not\models \varphi \\
&\pi \models \varphi_1 \wedge \varphi_2 && \text{iff } \pi \models \varphi_1 \text{ and } \pi \models \varphi_2 \\
&\pi \models \varphi_1 \, \mathsf{U}^\alpha \, \varphi_2 && \text{iff there exists } n \geq 0 \text{ such that } \pi{\uparrow}n \models \varphi_2 \text{ and} \\
& && \text{ios}(\pi{\downarrow}n) \in \mathsf{IOS}(\alpha) \text{ and } \pi{\uparrow}i \models \varphi_1 \text{ for all } 0 \leq i < n
\end{aligned}
$$

Recall that $\pi{\downarrow}n$ is the prefix of π of length n, $\pi{\uparrow}n$ is the suffix of π starting at the n-th state, $\text{ios}(\eta)$ is the projection on the corresponding I/O-operation and $\mathsf{IOS}(\alpha)$ is the set of finite executions satisfying the stream expression α.

The until operator is indexed by a stream expression α over I/O-constraints. Intuitively, it is satisfied on a given path if there exists a finite prefix such that its I/O-stream satisfies α and φ_1 holds for all the suffixes starting at a state in this prefix and φ_2 holds for the suffix starting in the state after the prefix matching α. In addition to the usual propositional operators ($\vee$, $\rightarrow$, $\leftrightarrow$, etc.) we can derive the path modalities $\langle\alpha\rangle\varphi$ and $[\![\alpha]\!]\varphi$ by

$$
\langle\alpha\rangle\varphi \stackrel{\text{def}}{=} \text{true}\,\mathsf{U}^\alpha\,\varphi \quad \text{and} \quad [\![\alpha]\!]\varphi \stackrel{\text{def}}{=} \neg\langle\alpha\rangle\neg\varphi.
$$

Intuitively, $\langle\alpha\rangle\varphi$ holds if there **exists a prefix** whose I/O-stream matches α and afterwards φ holds for the suffix. The dual operator, $[\![\alpha]\!]\varphi$, holds if **for all prefixes** with I/O-streams matching α afterwards φ holds for the suffix. For convenience, we also derive $\langle\alpha\rangle^t \stackrel{\text{def}}{=} \langle\alpha\rangle\,\text{true}$, which holds if there is a prefix with I/O-stream matching α. The standard LTL until operator without stream expressions can be derived by $\varphi_1 \, \mathsf{U} \, \varphi_2 \stackrel{\text{def}}{=} \varphi_1 \, \mathsf{U}^{tt^*} \, \varphi_2$, where tt^* is the stream expression signifying an I/O-stream of any length. We can derive as well the standard LTL operators "eventually $\Diamond$" "always $\square$" and "neXt X":

$$
\Diamond\varphi \stackrel{\text{def}}{=} \text{true}\,\mathsf{U}\,\varphi, \quad \square\varphi \stackrel{\text{def}}{=} \neg\Diamond\neg\varphi, \quad \mathsf{X}\varphi \stackrel{\text{def}}{=} \langle tt\rangle\varphi.
$$

Given a constraint automaton $\mathcal{A}$, the model checking problem asks whether all paths in $\mathcal{A}$ starting in an initial state satisfy the formula φ:

$$
\mathcal{A} \models \varphi \stackrel{\text{def}}{\iff} \pi \models \varphi \text{ for all } \pi \in \mathsf{Paths}(q_0) \text{ and all } q_0 \in Q_0
$$

Example 3 (Railway track). For the CA modeling a railway track depicted in Figure 2 the LTL$_{\mathsf{IO}}$ formula $\square\,(\langle A \wedge B\rangle^t \rightarrow \langle d_A = d_B\rangle^t)$ can be used to verify that if both A and B send/ receive a signal concurrently then the data values at A and B agree, i.e. that the train entering through A is the same as the one leaving through B. The property specified by the LTL$_{\mathsf{IO}}$ formula

$$
\square\,(\texttt{WAITING} \rightarrow \langle(\neg A)^*; B\rangle\texttt{FREE})
$$

can be used to check that whenever the track is occupied by a waiting train there will be no new train entering at A until the train has left through B and the track has thus become unoccupied again.   □

Model checking LTL$_{IO}$ formulas. Checking whether $A \models \varphi$ can be performed using the standard automata theoretic approach to LTL model checking [20,19], as illustrated in Figure 3. For an LTL$_{IO}$ formula ϕ, we can construct a non-deterministic Büchi automaton recognizing exactly the paths $\pi \models \phi$ (e.g., using the construction in [11]). Non-deterministic Büchi automata are similar to non-deterministic finite automata over finite words, but range over infinite words/paths. The Büchi acceptance condition specifies a subset of automata states that has to be visited infinitely often for a path to be accepted. To check whether $A \models \varphi$, we construct a non-deterministic Büchi automaton $\mathcal{Z}_{\neg\varphi}$ for the negation of φ. $\mathcal{Z}_{\neg\varphi}$ recognizes all the paths that violate φ. Then the product automaton $A \bowtie \mathcal{Z}_{\neg\varphi}$ is built, resulting in a constraint automaton augmented with a Büchi acceptance condition. The paths of the product can be viewed as pairs $\langle \pi, s \rangle$ of a path in A and a run s for π in $\mathcal{Z}_{\neg\varphi}$. The model checking algorithm seeks for a path in the product such that s meets the acceptance condition of $\mathcal{Z}_{\neg\varphi}$. If such a path $\langle \pi, s \rangle$ exists then π is a path in A that violates φ. Otherwise no such path in A violates φ and consequently $A \models \varphi$. In the case that $A \not\models \varphi$, the path in A violating φ can be output to the user as a counterexample to φ. This allows the user to inspect the model and find the cause of the property violation.

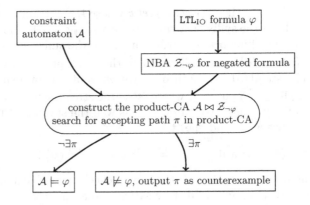

Fig. 3. Schema for model checking an LTL$_{IO}$ formula

Fairness. It is often useful to restrict the behavior of an interleaving model to those paths that satisfy some fairness constraints, e.g., to rule out infinite behavior that is considered unrealistic as the activities of some components are ignored forever. Unconditional, weak and strong fairness constraints can be directly expressed using LTL$_{IO}$ and model checking a formula φ under fairness constraints ψ_i can be performed by checking the formula $\varphi' = (\bigwedge_i \psi_i) \rightarrow \varphi$.

To specify fairness conditions, atomic propositions of the form enabled(ioc) (where ioc is an I/O-constraint) will be used that assert the enabledness of some concurrent I/O-operation that satisfies ioc. That is, we suppose that enabled(ioc) is an atomic proposition such that the labeling function L of the given CA enjoys the following property:

$$\texttt{enabled(ioc)} \in L(q) \quad \Leftrightarrow \quad \exists\, q \xrightarrow{c} q' : c \in \lceil \texttt{ioc} \rceil$$

For example, the following formula ψ specifies a weak fairness constraint for the railway track example. We require that, whenever infinitely often there is a train occupying the track and the train is allowed to leave the track via B infinitely many times, then infinitely often a train does leaves the track via B. This averts infinite paths where the train always has the chance to leave but does not, e.g. because another train is always scheduled to move instead.

$$\psi = \Diamond \Box \, (\texttt{enabled}(B) \wedge \neg \texttt{FREE}) \; \rightarrow \; \Box \Diamond \, \langle B \rangle^t$$

Example 4 (A railway network). As a more complex example consider the system in Figure 4, which shows a high-level view of a railway network composed out of the railway tracks from Example 1, as well as tracks with a train initially occupying the track, a train station (where trains have to stop, i.e. no instantaneous pass-through) and non-deterministic switches connecting the tracks. Each of the building blocks is modeled by means of a constraint automaton and the constraint automaton for the composite system results from a product construction [6]. The constraint automaton corresponding to the composed system has three nodes $\mathcal{N} = \{A_1, A_2, A_3\}$ where data flow – in this case modeling train travel – can be observed. The data domain is again $\mathsf{Data} = \{\mathsf{TRAIN}_1, \mathsf{TRAIN}_2\}$.

The following fairness constraint ψ ensures that the switch *switch₁* will behave fairly in the sense that the non-deterministic choice will not be resolved in such a way that one of its two entries A_1, A_2 will be blocked forever:

$$\psi = \big(\Box \Diamond \texttt{enabled}(A_1) \rightarrow \Box \Diamond \, \langle A_1 \rangle^t \big) \wedge \big(\Box \Diamond \texttt{enabled}(A_2) \rightarrow \Box \Diamond \, \langle A_2 \rangle^t \big)$$

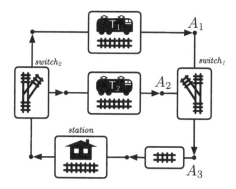

Fig. 4. High-level view of a small railway network composed out of basic elements

Using ψ as fairness constraint, the following formula is satisfied, specifying that both trains can be observed at node A_3 infinitely often:

$$\varphi = \Box\Diamond \langle A_3 \wedge d_{A_3} = \mathsf{TRAIN_1}\rangle^t \quad \wedge \quad \Box\Diamond \langle A_3 \wedge d_{A_3} = \mathsf{TRAIN_2}\rangle^t$$

Without the fairness constraint ψ, it would be possible – due to the non-deterministic choice between the entries of *switch$_1$* – that one train cycles through the railway network and the other train never gets the chance to pass through switch *switch$_1$*. Thus formula φ would be violated, as the blocked train would never be observed at A_3. □

3.2 Branching and Alternating-Time Properties

Alternating-time stream logic, ASL for short, is a branching-time logic with ATL-like [2] modalities to reason about the possibility for components to cooperate in such way that a certain temporal property or property on the observable data flow holds.

Constraint automata as multi-player games. The logic ASL relies on a game-based view of constraint automata. In this context, it is assumed that the CA under consideration models a system where several components are glued together using (a)synchronous peer-to-peer communication. The players of the game are the individual components. Each of the players has control over his write and read operations at its interface ports. A player might refuse some or even any synchronization operation with other players. Players might build arbitrary coalitions to achieve a certain common goal, e.g., to enforce that a certain temporal property holds. In our approach, a coalition of players is given by a set of controllable nodes $N \subseteq \mathcal{N}$, the union of all controllable coalition nodes, for which the players might try to develop a common strategy to achieve their objectives.

Intuitively, a strategy for the set N of controllable nodes, briefly called an N-strategy, takes the history of the system formalized by a finite execution as input, and declares the conditions under which the N-agents (members of the coalition) are willing to cooperate with each other and their opponents. For instance, an N-strategy might offer to write data value 0 at a source node $A \in N$, but refuse to write data value 1. Furthermore, an N-strategy might suggest the N-agents to completely refuse any participation in concurrent I/O-operations. To meet the simplifying assumption that all potential "behaviors" under $\mathfrak{S}$ are infinite, one might suppose that $c_\emptyset$ is enabled in all states.

Definition 1 (Strategy). *Let $\mathcal{A} = \langle Q, \mathcal{N}, \longrightarrow, Q_0, \mathsf{AP}, L\rangle$ be a constraint automaton, and let $N \subseteq \mathcal{N}$ be a node-set. An N-strategy is a function*

$$\mathfrak{S} : \mathsf{Exec}_{fin}(\mathcal{A}) \to 2^{\mathsf{CIO}},$$

assigning to any finite execution η a set $\mathfrak{S}(\eta)$ consisting of I/O-operations $c \in \mathsf{CIO}$ such that if $c \in \mathsf{CIO}$ and $\mathsf{Nodes}(c) \cap N = \emptyset$ then $c \in \mathfrak{S}(\eta)$. □

Unlike strategies in standard multi-player games, an N-strategy does not necessarily determine unique activities for the controlled components. Instead it yields a set of potential interactions. This is reasonable for the game semantics of CA since the enabledness of a concurrent I/O-operations c with node-set $\mathsf{Nodes}(c) = M$ depends on the agreement of all components that have an I/O-port in M to perform synchronized write and read operations according to c. Hence, only if M is a nonempty subset of N then c is controllable by N in the sense that the N-nodes can offer c, although they cannot enforce that c will indeed we taken. The ratio behind the condition requiring that $c \in \mathfrak{S}(\eta)$ whenever c is a concurrent I/O-operation with $\mathsf{Nodes}(c) \cap N = \emptyset$ is that the N-nodes are not in the position to refuse an I/O-operation c where none of the N-nodes is involved. In particular, invisible actions (i.e., the concurrent I/O-operation $c_\emptyset$ with the empty node-set) cannot be ruled out by an N-strategy. Thus, $c_\emptyset \in \mathfrak{S}(\eta)$ for each execution η and N-strategy $\mathfrak{S}$.

Given an N-strategy $\mathfrak{S}$, the $\mathfrak{S}$-paths are those paths in $\mathcal{A}$ that can be obtained when the I/O-operations performed at the nodes in N are consistent with $\mathfrak{S}$. Formally, a $\mathfrak{S}$-*path* is a path $\pi = q_0 \xrightarrow{c_1} q_1 \xrightarrow{c_2} \ldots$ such that $c_{i+1} \in \mathfrak{S}(\eta \downarrow i)$ for all positions $i \in \mathbb{N}$. We write $\mathsf{Paths}(q, \mathfrak{S})$ to denote all $\mathfrak{S}$-paths starting in q.

The general definition of strategies does not impose any restrictions on their realizability. E.g., strategies may even be not computable. As we will see later, for our purposes it suffices to consider strategies that make their decisions on the basis of a finite automaton rather than the full history. Formally, a *finite-memory N-strategy* is a tuple $\mathfrak{M} = (\mathsf{Modes}, \Delta, \mu, m_0)$, where

- Modes is a finite set (of so-called modes),
- $m_0 \in$ Modes the starting mode,
- $\mu : Q \times$ Modes $\to 2^{\mathsf{CIO}}$ the decision function, and
- $\Delta :$ Modes $\times (Q \times \mathsf{CIO} \times Q) \to$ Modes the next-mode function.

For the decision function μ we require that $\mu(q, m) \subseteq \{c \in \mathsf{CIO} : \mathsf{Nodes}(c) \cap N = \emptyset\}$ for all states $q \in Q$ and modes $m \in$ Modes. If Modes is a singleton then we refer to $\mathfrak{M}$ as a *memoryless* strategy. Memoryless strategies are typically specified as functions $\mathfrak{S} : Q \to 2^{\mathsf{CIO}}$. Given a finite-memory N-strategy $\mathfrak{M}$ then the associated N-strategy $\mathfrak{S}_{\mathfrak{M}}$ (in the sense of Definition 1) is given by:

$$\mathfrak{S}_{\mathfrak{M}}\left(q_0 \xrightarrow{c_1} \ldots \xrightarrow{c_i} q_i\right) = \mu\left(q_i, \Delta^*(m_0, q_0 \xrightarrow{c_1} \ldots \xrightarrow{c_i} q_i)\right)$$

where $\Delta^*(m, \eta)$ denotes the mode that $\mathfrak{M}$ reaches when starting in mode m and scanning the execution η. That is, $\Delta^*(m, q_0) = m$, $\Delta^*(m, q_0 \xrightarrow{c_1} q_1) = \Delta(m, q_0 \xrightarrow{c_1} q_1)$, and $\Delta^*\left(m, q_0 \xrightarrow{c_1} q_1 \xrightarrow{c_2} \ldots \xrightarrow{c_i} q_i\right) = \Delta^*\left(\Delta(m, q_0 \xrightarrow{c_1} q_1), q_1 \xrightarrow{c_2} \ldots \xrightarrow{c_i} q_i\right)$.

Syntax of ASL. To reason about the components from a game-based point of view, *alternating-time stream logic* (ASL) has been introduced in [16] as an ATL-like logic [2] for the game-structures associated with constraint automata. We present here a slightly different syntax for ASL than in [16] and deal here with the modality U^α (as in LTL_{IO}). Furthermore, in [16] and [15] we discussed the treatment of finite and infinite paths, while in this paper we restrict our observations on infinite paths only to simplify the notations. Infinite behavior could e.g. be achieved my assuming that in each state of the automaton the empty concurrent I/O-operation $c_\emptyset$ is enabled.

As in other CTL-like branching time logics, ASL distinguishes between state and path formulas. The state formula fragment is as in ATL, but adapted to the CA framework where the alternating-time quantifiers range over the strategies of certain node-sets. Intuitively, these node-sets stand for the interface nodes of one or more components. The existential quantifier $\mathbb{E}_N$ is used to indicate that the components with sink and source nodes in N have a strategy ensuring to reach a certain goal, no matter how the other components connected to the nodes in $\mathcal{N} \setminus N$ behave. The universal quantifier $\mathbb{A}_N$ is dual and serves to state that the components providing the write and read actions at the N-nodes cannot avoid that a certain condition holds.

In the sequel, we assume a fixed, non-empty and finite node-set $\mathcal{N}$ and a non-empty and finite set AP of atomic propositions. $\mathcal{N}$ and AP will serve as signature for ASL-formulas. State-formulas (denoted by capital Greek letters Φ, Ψ) and path-formulas (denoted by small Greek letters φ, ψ) of ASL are built by the following grammar:

$$\Phi ::= \text{true} \mid a \mid \Phi_1 \wedge \Phi_2 \mid \neg\Phi \mid \mathbb{E}_N\varphi \mid \mathbb{A}_N\varphi$$

$$\varphi ::= \Phi_1 U^\alpha \Phi_2$$

where $N \subseteq \mathcal{N}$, $a \in$ AP and α is a stream expression. The operator $\mathbb{E}_N$ corresponds to an existential quantification while the $\mathbb{A}_N$ corresponds to an universal quantification over all N-strategies. In the following, we shortly write $\mathbb{E}_A\varphi$ for $\mathbb{E}_{\{A\}}\varphi$ and $\mathbb{A}_A\varphi$ for $\mathbb{A}_{\{A\}}\varphi$. The standard CTL path quantifiers that range over all paths can be derived using the $\mathbb{E}_N$ and $\mathbb{A}_N$-quantifiers with the empty node-set $N = \emptyset$, by $\forall\varphi \stackrel{\text{def}}{=} \mathbb{E}_\emptyset\varphi$ and $\exists\varphi \stackrel{\text{def}}{=} \mathbb{A}_\emptyset\varphi$.

Derived path modalities. The path modalities $\langle\alpha\rangle\Phi$ and $[\alpha]\Phi$ from BTSL [15] can be derived by $\langle\alpha\rangle\Phi \stackrel{\text{def}}{=} (\text{true} U^\alpha\Phi)$ and

$$\mathbb{E}_N[\alpha]\Phi \stackrel{\text{def}}{=} \neg\mathbb{A}_N\langle\alpha\rangle\neg\Phi \quad \text{and} \quad \mathbb{A}_N[\alpha]\Phi \stackrel{\text{def}}{=} \neg\mathbb{E}_N\langle\alpha\rangle\neg\Phi.$$

The standard CTL operators for "next step", "until" and "eventually" are obtained by $X\Phi \stackrel{\text{def}}{=} (\text{true} U^{tt}\Phi) = \langle tt\rangle\Phi$, $\Phi_1 U\Phi_2 \stackrel{\text{def}}{=} (\Phi_1 U^{tt^*}\Phi_2)$ and $\Diamond\Phi \stackrel{\text{def}}{=} (\text{true} U\Phi)$. The definition of the always operator $\Box$ in ASL is as follows:

$$\mathbb{E}_N\Box\Phi \stackrel{\text{def}}{=} \neg\mathbb{A}_N(\text{true} U \neg\Phi) \quad \text{and} \quad \mathbb{A}_N\Box\Phi \stackrel{\text{def}}{=} \neg\mathbb{E}_N(\text{true} U \neg\Phi).$$

Other Boolean connectives, like disjunction or implication, are obtained in the obvious way.

Semantics of ASL. Let $\mathcal{A}$ be a CA and π a path in $\mathcal{A}$. The satisfaction relation $\models$ for ASL state formulas is defined by structural induction as shown below:

$$q \models \text{true}$$
$$q \models a \quad\quad\quad \text{iff} \quad a \in L(q)$$
$$q \models \Phi_1 \wedge \Phi_2 \quad \text{iff} \quad q \models \Phi_1 \text{ and } q \models \Phi_2$$
$$q \models \neg\Phi \quad\quad \text{iff} \quad q \not\models \Phi$$
$$q \models \mathbb{E}_N\varphi \quad\quad \text{iff} \quad \text{there is an } N\text{-strategy } \mathfrak{S} \text{ such that}$$
$$\text{for all } \pi \in \text{Paths}(q, \mathfrak{S}) \text{ we have: } \pi \models \varphi$$
$$q \models \mathbb{A}_N\varphi \quad\quad \text{iff} \quad \text{for all } N\text{-strategies } \mathfrak{S} \text{ there exists } \pi \in \text{Paths}(q, \mathfrak{S})$$
$$\text{such that } \pi \models \varphi$$

The satisfaction relation $\models$ for ASL path-formulas and the path π in $\mathcal{A}$ is defined as follows:

$$\pi \models \Phi_1 \, \mathsf{U}^\alpha \Phi_2 \quad \text{iff} \quad \text{there exists } n \in \mathbb{N} \text{ such that } \text{ios}(\pi \!\downarrow\! n) \in \text{IOS}(\alpha)$$
$$\text{and } q_i \models \Phi_1 \text{ for all } 0 \le i < n \text{ and } q_n \models \Phi_2$$

Given a state q and an ASL path formula φ, an N-strategy $\mathfrak{S}$ is called *winning* for the tuple $\langle q, \varphi \rangle$ if φ holds for all $\mathfrak{S}$-paths starting in q. Thus, $q \models \mathbb{E}_N\varphi$ iff there exists a winning N-strategy for $\langle q, \varphi \rangle$. We say that $\mathfrak{S}$ is winning for φ if $\mathfrak{S}$ is winning for all pairs $\langle q, \varphi \rangle$ where $q \models \mathbb{E}_N\varphi$. An ASL state formula Φ is said to hold for a constraint automaton $\mathcal{A}$, written $\mathcal{A} \models \Phi$, if $q_0 \models \phi$ for all initial states q_0 of $\mathcal{A}$.

Example 5 (Railway track). To illustrate some ASL example formulas we reconsider the railway track from Example 1. The following formula asks for a $\{B\}$-strategy $\mathfrak{S}$ ensuring that for all $\mathfrak{S}$-paths we have that the first train passes through until the second train has to stop.

$$\mathbb{E}_B((\text{FREE} \vee \text{TRANSIT}) \, \mathsf{U}^\alpha \, \text{OCCUPIED}),$$

where $\alpha = (((A \wedge B \wedge d_A = \text{TRAIN}_1); (\neg A \wedge \neg B))^*; \{A\} \wedge d_A = \text{TRAIN}_2)$. Obviously, the formula does not hold, since no $\{B\}$-strategy can detain the first train to stop as well. But even if we use $\alpha' = ((d_A \neq \text{TRAIN}_2)^*; \{A\} \wedge d_A = \text{TRAIN}_2)$ instead of α the path where the second train never arrives is a $\mathfrak{S}$-path for all $\{B\}$-strategies $\mathfrak{S}$. This can be illustrated by the following ASL formula

$$\mathbb{A}_B [\![(d_A \neq \text{TRAIN}_2)^*; d_A = \text{TRAIN}_2]\!] \text{false}.$$

Standard turn-based games are determined which means that given a state q, a coalition $\mathcal{C}$ and a winning objective φ then either $\mathcal{C}$ has a strategy to ensure that φ holds or the opponents, i.e., all agents not in $\mathcal{C}$, have a strategy to ensure that $\neg\varphi$ holds. As shown in [16], this does not hold for the ASL games. For the example above, neither A has a winning strategy for the ASL path formula $\langle (tt)^*; \{A\} \wedge d_A = \text{TRAIN}_2 \rangle$true nor can the opponent B enforce the dual path property. □

ASL model checking. The model checking problem for ASL asks whether, for a given CA $\mathcal{A}$ and ASL state formula Φ_0, all initial states q_0 of $\mathcal{A}$ satisfy Φ_0. The main procedure for ASL model checking follows the standard approach for CTL-like branching time logics [10] and recursively calculates the satisfaction sets

$$\mathsf{Sat}(\Psi) \stackrel{\text{def}}{=} \{q \in Q : q \models \Psi\}$$

for all subformulas Ψ of Φ_0. To compute the satisfaction sets of $\mathbb{E}_N(\Phi_1 \,\mathsf{U}^\alpha \Phi_2)$ and $\mathbb{A}_N(\Phi_1 \,\mathsf{U}^\alpha \Phi_2)$, we follow an automata-theoretic approach which resembles the standard automata-based LTL model checking procedure and relies on a representation of α by means of a finite automaton $\mathcal{Z}$ and model checking ASL state formulas of the form $\mathbb{E}_N(\Psi_1 \,\mathsf{U} \Psi_2)$ and $\mathbb{A}_N(\Psi_1 \,\mathsf{U} \Psi_2)$, respectively, in the product of $\mathcal{A}$ and $\mathcal{Z}$. Using standard methods for regular languages, we first generate a deterministic finite automata (DFA) $\mathcal{Z}$ over the alphabet CIO such that the accepted language of $\mathcal{Z}$ agrees with $\mathsf{IOS}(\alpha)$. In the sequel, let

$$\mathcal{Z} \;=\; (Z, \mathsf{CIO}, \delta, z_0, Z_F),$$

where Z stands for the state space, z_0 denotes the initial state, Z_F is the set of final (accept) states and $\delta : Z \times \mathsf{CIO} \to Z$ the transition function. In fact, $\mathcal{Z}$ can be viewed as a CA where the set Z_F plays the role of the labeling function which separates the final states from the non-final states. Given $\mathcal{A}$ and $\mathcal{Z}$, we built the product $\mathcal{A} \bowtie \mathcal{Z}$, similar to the product of finite automata and the join operator for CAs [6].

Let $\mathcal{A}$ be a CA as in Definition 1 and $\mathcal{Z}$ a DFA as above. Furthermore, let $\emptyset \neq N \subseteq \mathcal{N}$ and Φ an ASL state formula. We define the CA $\mathcal{A} \bowtie_{N,\Phi} \mathcal{Z}$, or briefly $\mathcal{A} \bowtie \mathcal{Z}$ if N and Φ are clear from the context, as follows:

$$\mathcal{A} \bowtie \mathcal{Z} \stackrel{\text{def}}{=} (S, \mathcal{N}, \longrightarrow, S_0, \mathsf{AP}', L').$$

The state space S is $Q \times Z$, the set of initial states is given by $S_0 \stackrel{\text{def}}{=} \big\{ \langle q, z_0 \rangle : q \in Q_0 \big\}$. The transitions in $\mathcal{A} \bowtie \mathcal{Z}$ are obtained by the following synchronization rule for concurrent I/O-operations $c \in \mathsf{CIO}$ state q in $\mathcal{A}$, and state $z \in Z$:

$$\frac{q \xrightarrow{c} q' \;\wedge\; z' = \delta(z, c)}{\langle q, z \rangle \xrightarrow{c} \langle q', z' \rangle}$$

The set of atomic propositions in $\mathcal{A} \bowtie \mathcal{Z}$ is $\mathsf{AP}' = \{a_\Phi, \mathsf{accept}\}$, while the labeling function L' is given by the requirements (i) $a_\Phi \in L'(\langle q, z \rangle)$ iff $q \models \Phi$ and (ii) $\mathsf{accept} \in L'(\langle q, z \rangle)$ iff $z \in Z_F$.

The following lemmas formalize the reduction of the model checking problem for ASL state formulas of the form $\mathbb{E}_N(\Phi_1 \,\mathsf{U}^\alpha \Phi_2)$ and $\mathbb{A}_N(\Phi_1 \,\mathsf{U}^\alpha \Phi_2)$ to the problem of computing satisfaction sets for formulas of the type $\mathbb{E}_N(\Psi_1 \,\mathsf{U} \Psi_2)$ and $\mathbb{A}_N(\Psi_1 \,\mathsf{U} \Psi_2)$ in the product, respectively. See Figure 5.

Lemma 1 (Treatment of $\mathbb{E}_N(\Phi_1 \,\mathsf{U}^\alpha \Phi_2)$). *Let $\mathcal{A}$ be a CA, and $\mathcal{Z} = (Z, \mathsf{CIO}, \delta, z_0, Z_F)$ a DFA for a stream expression α. Furthermore, let q be a state in $\mathcal{A}$, $N \subseteq \mathcal{N}$ and Φ_1 and Φ_2 ASL state formulas. Then, the following statements are equivalent:*

(a) $q \models \mathbb{E}_N(\Phi_1 \mathsf{U}^{\alpha} \Phi_2)$ in $\mathcal{A}$

(b) $\langle q, z_0 \rangle \models \mathbb{E}_N(a_{\Phi_1} \mathsf{U}(a_{\Phi_2} \wedge \mathsf{accept}))$ in $\mathcal{A} \bowtie \mathcal{Z}$

(c) There exists a finite-memory N-strategy $\mathfrak{S}$ for $\mathcal{A}$ that is winning for $\langle q, \Phi_1 \mathsf{U}^{\alpha} \Phi_2 \rangle$.

Lemma 2 (Treatment of $\mathbb{A}_N(\Phi_1 \mathsf{U}^{\alpha} \Phi_2)$). Let $\mathcal{A}, \mathcal{Z}, \alpha, \Phi_1, \Phi_2$ be as in Lemma 1. Then, for all states $q \in Q$ the following statements are equivalent:

(a) $q \models \mathbb{A}_N(\Phi_1 \mathsf{U}^{\alpha} \Phi_2)$ in $\mathcal{A}$

(b) $\langle q, z_0 \rangle \models \mathbb{A}_N(a_{\Phi_1} \mathsf{U}(a_{\Phi_2} \wedge \mathsf{accept}))$ in $\mathcal{A} \bowtie \mathcal{Z}$

(c) For all finite memory N-strategies $\mathfrak{S}$ there is a path $\pi \in \mathsf{Paths}(q, \mathfrak{S})$ in $\mathcal{A}$ such that $\pi \models (\Phi_1 \mathsf{U}^{\alpha} \Phi_2)$.

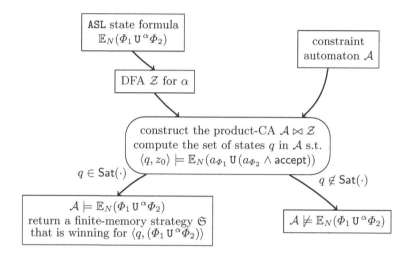

Fig. 5. Schema for the treatment of $\mathbb{E}_N(\Phi_1 \mathsf{U}^{\alpha} \Phi_2)$

It remains to explain how to calculate $\mathsf{Sat}(\mathbb{E}_N(\Phi_1 \mathsf{U} \Phi_2))$ and $\mathsf{Sat}(\mathbb{A}_N(\Phi_1 \mathsf{U} \Phi_2))$ for a node-set $N \subseteq \mathcal{N}$. The essential ingredient for this are the predecessor operators $\mathsf{Pre}(P, N)$ and $\widetilde{\mathsf{Pre}}(P, N)$ where P is a set of states and N a set of nodes. The former denotes the set of all states q such that the N-nodes have a strategy which guarantees to move within one step to a state in P, while $\widetilde{\mathsf{Pre}}(P, N)$ denotes the set of all states q such that no N-strategy can avoid that a transition emanating from q and leading to a state in P will be taken.

Post, Pre-operators. Let $\mathcal{A} = \langle Q, \mathcal{N}, \longrightarrow, Q_0, \mathsf{AP}, L \rangle$ be a constraint automaton, $q \in Q$, $N \subseteq \mathcal{N}$ and $P \subseteq Q$. If c is a concurrent I/O-operation then

$$\mathsf{Post}[c](q) \overset{\text{def}}{=} \{p \in Q : q \overset{c}{\rightarrow} p\}.$$

Let $P \subseteq Q$ and $N \subseteq \mathcal{N}$ a node-set. Then, $\mathsf{Pre}(P, N)$ denotes the set of all states $q \in Q$ such that the following two conditions hold:

(1) for all $c \in \mathsf{CIO}(q)$ such that $\mathsf{Nodes}(c) \cap N = \emptyset$ we have $\mathsf{Post}[c](q) \subseteq P$
(2) there exists $c \in \mathsf{CIO}(q)$ such that $\mathsf{Nodes}(c) \subseteq N$ and $\mathsf{Post}[c](q) \subseteq P$

Recall that $\mathsf{CIO}(q)$ denotes the set of all concurrent I/O-operations that are enabled in state q. Condition (1) is needed to ensure that no uncontrollable transition (from the view of the N-agents) leads to a state outside of P, while condition (2) asserts the existence of at least one concurrent I/O-operation that is controllable by the N-agents and certainly leads to a state in P. The set

$$\widetilde{\mathsf{Pre}}(P, N) \stackrel{\text{def}}{=} Q \setminus \mathsf{Pre}(Q \setminus P, N)$$

denotes the set of all states $q \in Q$ such that there is a concurrent I/O-operation $c \in \mathsf{CIO}(q)$ with $\mathsf{Nodes}(c) \cap N = \emptyset$ and $\mathsf{Post}[c](q) \cap P \neq \emptyset$. (Recall that we suppose that each state q has an outgoing c_0-transition. Thus, the N-agents can never avoid that some transition will be taken.) We then have:

$$\mathsf{Pre}(P, N) = \left\{ q \in Q : q \models \mathbb{E}_N \mathsf{X} P \right\}$$
$$\widetilde{\mathsf{Pre}}(P, N) = \left\{ q \in Q : q \models \mathbb{A}_N \mathsf{X} P \right\}$$

As for standard CTL (and ATL), the semantics of until has a least fixed point characterization. Formally, the sets $P = \mathsf{Sat}(\mathbb{E}_N(\Phi_1 \cup \Phi_2))$ and $\mathsf{Sat}(\mathbb{A}_N(\Phi_1 \cup \Phi_2))$ are the least fixpoints of the following functions $2^Q \to 2^Q$:

$$P \mapsto \mathsf{Sat}(\Phi_2) \cup (\mathsf{Pre}(P, N) \cap \mathsf{Sat}(\Phi_1)) \quad (\mathbb{E}_N)$$
$$P \mapsto \mathsf{Sat}(\Phi_2) \cup (\widetilde{\mathsf{Pre}}(P, N) \cap \mathsf{Sat}(\Phi_1)) \quad (\mathbb{A}_N)$$

Hence, we have the following *expansion laws*:

$$\mathbb{E}_N(\Phi_1 \cup \Phi_2) \equiv \Phi_2 \vee (\Phi_1 \wedge \mathbb{E}_N \mathsf{X} \mathbb{E}_N(\Phi_1 \cup \Phi_2))$$
$$\mathbb{A}_N(\Phi_1 \cup \Phi_2) \equiv \Phi_2 \vee (\Phi_1 \wedge \mathbb{A}_N \mathsf{X} \mathbb{A}_N(\Phi_1 \cup \Phi_2))$$

where $\equiv$ denotes equivalence of ASL state formulas. On the basis of the expansion laws, we obtain that for winning objectives formalized by ASL state formulas of the form $\mathbb{E}_N(\Phi_1 \cup \Phi_2)$ and $\mathbb{A}_N(\Phi_1 \cup \Phi_2)$, memoryless strategies are sufficient. Furthermore, the satisfaction sets $\mathsf{Sat}(\mathbb{E}_N(\Phi_1 \cup \Phi_2))$ and $\mathsf{Sat}(\mathbb{A}_N(\Phi_1 \cup \Phi_2))$ can be computed by means of the standard procedures to compute least fixed points of monotonic operators.

3.3   Bisimulation Equivalence for Constraint Automata

Besides verifying constraint automaton against temporal logic formulas, Vereofy provides an equivalence checker that relies on the notion of bisimulation equivalence for CA. The problem of checking bisimulation equivalence appears naturally in the design and optimization of complex systems. For example, given a complex component connector $\mathcal{C}$ that uses many internal channels, one might ask whether $\mathcal{C}$ can be replaced by a simpler connector $\mathcal{C}'$ that is cheaper according to some cost function. One possibility to verify that $\mathcal{C}$ and $\mathcal{C}'$ realize the same coordination mechanism is to prove the bisimulation equivalence of the CA associated with $\mathcal{C}$ and $\mathcal{C}'$. Furthermore, bisimulation equivalence can also serve as a specification formalism. For example, the specification of a connector might be provided by means of a CA $\mathcal{A}_{\mathrm{spec}}$ and the task is to provide the code for a connector $\mathcal{C}$ in some coordination language (e.g., Reo [3]) such that the CA for $\mathcal{C}$ and $\mathcal{A}_{\mathrm{spec}}$ are bisimulation equivalent.

Let $\mathcal{A}$ be a CA as before, $q \in Q$, and $P \subseteq Q$. Then $\mathsf{CIO}(q, P)$ denotes the set of all I/O-operations that are enabled in state q and can lead to a state in P. That is, $\mathsf{CIO}(q, P) = \{\, c \in \mathsf{CIO} : q \xrightarrow{c} p \text{ for some } p \in P \,\}$.

Definition 2 (Bisimulation). Let $\mathcal{A}$ be as above. An equivalence relation $\mathcal{R}$ on Q is called bisimulation for $\mathcal{A}$ if for all pairs $(q_1, q_2) \in \mathcal{R}$ the following two conditions (i) and (ii) are satisfied:

(i) $L(q_1) = L(q_2)$
(ii) $\mathsf{CIO}(q_1, P) = \mathsf{CIO}(q_2, P)$ for all $\mathcal{R}$-equivalence classes $P \in Q/\mathcal{R}$.

Two states $q_1, q_2 \in Q$ are called bisimilar (or bisimulation equivalent) iff there exists a bisimulation $\mathcal{R}$ with $(q_1, q_2) \in \mathcal{R}$.   □

As usual, the above definition of bisimulation equivalence for the states of a single CA can be adapted to define bisimulation equivalence of two CA. Suppose that $\mathcal{A}_1$ and $\mathcal{A}_2$ are CA with the same node-set $\mathcal{N}$ and the same set AP of atomic propositions. Let $\mathcal{A}_1 \uplus \mathcal{A}_2$ be the "large" automaton obtained through the disjoint union of the state spaces of $\mathcal{A}_1$ and $\mathcal{A}_2$. Automata $\mathcal{A}_1$ and $\mathcal{A}_2$ are called bisimilar, denoted $\mathcal{A}_1 \sim \mathcal{A}_2$, if for each bisimulation equivalence class P in $\mathcal{A}_1 \uplus \mathcal{A}_2$ either P does not contain any initial state of $\mathcal{A}_1$ or $\mathcal{A}_2$ or P contains at least one initial state of both automata $\mathcal{A}_1$ and $\mathcal{A}_2$.

The classical partitioning refinement approach [14] for computing the bisimulation equivalence classes of a finite labeled transition system can be adapted for CA [6,7]. This algorithm serves at the same time for checking bisimulation equivalence of two constraint automata and can also be used as a reduction technique by replacing a "large" CA with its the bisimulation quotient. Indeed the switch from a constraint automaton $\mathcal{A}$ to a bisimilar automaton $\mathcal{A}'$ preserves all properties that are expressible in the logics $\mathrm{LTL_{IO}}$ and ASL.

Lemma 3. *If $\mathcal{A}_1 \sim \mathcal{A}_2$ then $\mathcal{A}_1$, $\mathcal{A}_2$ satisfy the same ASL and LTL_{IO} formulas.*

The proof for these statements are standard (see e.g. [5]) and can be provided by structural induction. As for other CTL-like branching-time logics (see [8]), even a small fragment of ASL is sufficient to provide a complete logical characterization of bisimulation equivalence. Constraint automata $\mathcal{A}_1$ and $\mathcal{A}_2$ are called equivalent with respect to a logic L, denoted $\mathcal{A}_1 \equiv_{\mathrm{L}} \mathcal{A}_2$, if $\mathcal{A}_1$ and $\mathcal{A}_2$ yield the same truth value for all formulas in L, i.e.,

$$\mathcal{A}_1 \equiv_L \mathcal{A}_2 \quad \text{iff} \quad \text{for all } \phi \in \mathrm{L}\colon \mathcal{A}_1 \models \phi \iff \mathcal{A}_2 \models \phi$$

Let us now consider the sublogic L of ASL consisting of all ASL state formulas which can be build using the propositional fragment of ASL (i.e., atomic propositions and the Boolean connectors $\wedge$ and $\neg$) and formulas of the form $\exists\langle\text{ioc}\rangle\Phi$ where Φ is a formula of L and ioc a basic stream expression given by an I/O-constraint (and representing a set consisting of I/O-streams of length 1). Then, $\mathcal{A}_1 \equiv_L \mathcal{A}_2$ implies that $\mathcal{A}_1$ and $\mathcal{A}_2$ are bisimilar. Thus:

$$\mathcal{A}_1 \equiv_L \mathcal{A}_2 \text{ iff } \mathcal{A}_1 \equiv_{\text{ASL}} \mathcal{A}_2 \text{ iff } \mathcal{A}_1 \sim \mathcal{A}_2$$

Hence, in order to show that two constraint automata are not bisimilar then a formula Φ in L can be provided that holds for $\mathcal{A}_1$, but not for $\mathcal{A}_2$. Such a formula Φ can be understood as a counterexample.

4   Results, Conclusion and Future Work

Our verification toolkit Vereofy currently supports model checking the LTL_{IO} fragment consisting of propositional logic, the standard LTL until operator (and the derived temporal operators) as well as the indexed next step operator $\langle\text{ioc}\rangle\varphi$ where ioc is an I/O-constraint. It also supports the use of enabled(ioc) to talk about the enabled CIO at a state, which can be used to specify fairness constraints. The ASL-fragment of our implementation cannot yet treat the U^α-operator, but directly supports the derived operators on path formulas $\langle\alpha\rangle\Phi$ and $[\![\alpha]\!]\Phi$. The currently implemented version of the bisimulation algorithm abstracts away from state labels. Thus, it establishes equivalences only for the observable data flow.

Our tool has been applied to different examples. Some of them are text-book examples like the dining philosophers where the highly symmetrical structure of the system allows for huge numbers (ca. 800 philosopher on actual computers, 600MB, 6 minutes of work) of components and therefore large state spaces. Using the implementation of the bisimulation algorithm, we proved the equivalence of two variants of a mutual exclusion protocol. The bisimulation checker of Vereofy has also been used to show the correctness of several "advanced coordination patterns" that have been modeled as Reo circuits using just a small set of basic channels. Currently, we are working on some real-life examples. An initial version of the peer-to-peer system presented in [13] has been specified using RSL and CARML. Vereofy can build the composite system for three peers in about 9 seconds and check for deadlock freedom in half the time. Furthermore, we formalized a mobile sensor network and have been able to check first properties for up to 10 sensor nodes.

We are continuously enhancing our implementation. On the one hand, this includes extensions of the modeling languages and several optimizations to improve the time and space requirements. On the other hand, we are studying other model checking challenges like ASL with observation-based strategies, the synthesis problem for constraint automata and questions regarding compatibility of constraint automata.

References

1. Alur, R., Henzinger, T.: Reactive Modules. Formal Methods in System Design: An Intern. J. 15(1), 7–48 (1999)
2. Alur, R., Henzinger, T., Kupferman, O.: Alternating-Time Temporal Logic. JACM 49, 672–713 (2002)
3. Arbab, F.: Reo: A Channel-Based Coordination Model for Component Composition. Mathematical Structures in Comp. Sci. 14(3), 329–366 (2004)
4. Baier, C., Blechmann, T., Klein, J., Klüppelholz, S.: A Uniform Framework for Modeling and Verifying Components and Connectors. In: Field, J., Vasconcelos, V.T. (eds.) COORDINATION 2009. LNCS, vol. 5521, pp. 247–267. Springer, Heidelberg (2009)
5. Baier, C., Katoen, J.-P.: Principles of Model Checking. MIT Press, Cambridge (2008)
6. Baier, C., Sirjani, M., Arbab, F., Rutten, J.: Modeling Component Connectors in Reo by Constraint Automata. Science of Computer Programming (2006)
7. Blechmann, T., Baier, C.: Checking equivalence for Reo networks. In: FACS 2007. ENTCS, vol. 215, pp. 209–226 (2008)
8. Browne, M., Clarke, E., Grumberg, O.: Characterizing Finite Kripke Structures in Propositional Temporal Logic. In: TAPSOFT, TCS (1988)
9. Clarke, E., Emerson, E., Sistla, A.: Automatic Verification of Finite-State Concurrent Systems Using Temporal Logic Specifications. ACM Transactions on Programm. Languages and Systems 8(2), 244–263 (1986)
10. Clarke, E.M., Emerson, E.A., Sistla, A.P.: Automatic verification of finite-state concurrent systems using temporal logic specifications. In: ACM TOPLAS (1986)
11. Giordano, L., Martelli, A.: Tableau-based automata construction for dynamic linear time temporal logic. Annals of Mathematics and Artificial Intelligence 46(3), 289–315 (2006)
12. Henriksen, J.G., Thiagarajan, P.S.: Dynamic linear time temporal logic. Ann. Pure Appl. Logic 96(1-3), 187–207 (1999)
13. Jaghoori, M.M.: Coordinating object oriented components using data-flow networks. In: de Boer, F.S., Bonsangue, M.M., Graf, S., de Roever, W.-P. (eds.) FMCO 2007. LNCS, vol. 5382, pp. 280–311. Springer, Heidelberg (2008)
14. Kanellakis, P., Smolka, S.: CCS Expressions, Finite State Processes, and Three Problems of Equivalence. Information and Computation 86(1), 43–68 (1990)
15. Klüppelholz, S., Baier, C.: Symbolic Model Checking for Channel-based Component Connectors. Science of Computer Programming (2009)
16. Klüppelholz, S., Baier, C.: Alternating-time stream logic for multi-agent systems. In: Lea, D., Zavattaro, G. (eds.) COORDINATION 2008. LNCS, vol. 5052, pp. 184–198. Springer, Heidelberg (2008)
17. Pnueli, A.: The Temporal Logic of Programs. In: Proc. of 18th FOCS, pp. 46–57. IEEE Computer Society Press, Los Alamitos (1977)
18. Reo website at CWI Amsterdam, http://reo.project.cwi.nl/
19. Vardi, M.: An Automata-Theoretic Approach to Linear Temporal Logic. In: Moller, F., Birtwistle, G. (eds.) Logics for Concurrency. LNCS, vol. 1043, pp. 238–266. Springer, Heidelberg (1996)
20. Vardi, M., Wolper, P.: An Automata-Theoretic Approach to Automatic Program Verification. In: LICS, pp. 332–345. IEEE Computer Society Press, Los Alamitos (1986)

Formal Modular Modelling of Context-Awareness

Mats Neovius[1,2] and Kaisa Sere[1]

[1] Åbo Akademi University, Joukahaisenkatu 3 – 5, 20520 Turku, Finland
[2] Turku Center for Computer Science, Joukahaisenkatu 3 – 5, 20520 Turku, Finland
{mats.neovius,kaisa.sere}@abo.fi

Abstract. Characterising for a context-aware software is its ability to adjust to the prevailing situation. Such software reacts and bases the context-aware decisions upon inputs describing its operating conditions, i.e. on context(s). In this paper, we will seek the roots of context(s) and reason on the methods for deducing information by processing contexts; that is, present a methodology to enhance the relevance from raw data to knowledge. Thus, this paper will point out the relationship between introducing, constructing, serving, gluing and utilising context. Moreover, we show how to in a structured manner construct a context-service that satisfies given requirements and supplement the context-aware utiliser. For the sake of reuse and scalability, we will separate an application's specification from context reasoning and consider them as systems in their own rights. The findings will be motivated on a general level, with an easily conceivable example and formalised with the action system formalism.

1 Introduction

With the electro-mechanical development and the miniaturisation of transistors, the once fictitious deployment scenarios of computerised gadgetry turn into reality. As the computing is being weaved into the very foundations of our society, the domain of applicability extends. The reliance and expectations placed on these computerised gadgets are also ever increasing. Among others, gadgets are expected to be aware of the surrounding conditions and adapt automatically to them as envisioned by Weiser in 1991 [1]; that is, be context-aware. Because this development is likely going to continue, the future will be about navigating the ubiquity of information, being able to select, rely on and process relevant information [2, 3] as well as to reason rigorously with these.

Context in all its aspects complements software. As software alone is algorithmic and bound to operate on mathematical rules; the source of context in all its forms is data relying on some reading that characterise the operating conditions, e.g. temperature, location or identity. However, the contexts are ambiguous due to inherent inaccuracies of the acquiring equipments but are from the system's point of view unambiguous as no more descriptive data is available. Hence, context breaks the algorithmic model down [4] but introduces the possibility to context-awareness. Moreover, the provided contexts must be universal as no obligations on its utiliser aka. context consumer [5] or widgets [6], can be placed at time of creation. On the other hand, even though the application's algorithmic calculations were verifiable correct, misinterpreting a context is similar to

F.S. de Boer et al. (Eds.): FMCO 2008, LNCS 5751, pp. 102–118, 2009.

misinterpreting the operating conditions. Since context typically constitutes a decisive artefact, such misinterpretation can potentially result in faulty behaviour. We will however not consider faulty, absent, timeout or ambiguity of contextual information, as sheer fault tolerance and dependability issues branches to a separate field of research [7, 8, 9].

In paper we argue that a context-aware system cannot be said to be verified unless the construction and integration process of the necessary contextual information is. The sole reason is that discarding the treatment of context is intolerable for the sake of rigour, constituting the motivation of this paper. The main contribution addresses this source of motivation; this paper provides a methodology that will challenge the context (system) engineer to formally specify how the contextual information is constructed and integrated to a context-aware system that is to operate in a continuously changing contextual surrounding. That is, this paper is not about how to use context(s) but on what the context(s) constitute of, what are demanded from them and specifying how they are treated for providing rigorously to the required context-aware functionality.

Our approach takes an abstract view on the continuously changing context in a system. The contexts are considered globally available and thus, modelling the functional behaviour with shared variables suites our purpose well. Hence, we will concentrate on assuring the correct treatment of the provided (deduced) context. We treat context in a modular fashion defining an interface for the utiliser with which to depend on the contextual information through the glue that acquires and prepares contexts. This modularity is fundamental for the sake of adaptability [3], and hence also for scalability and reusability. Consequently, the context can be considered to be provided by a standalone, independent, replaceable and interoperable service. We use the action system formalism [10, 11, 12] to formally specify treatment of context, where the required syntactical language constructs are discussed in greater detail in Section 3.

We build on our earlier work [13, 14, 15] providing a methodology for integrating, depending on and formally treating continuously changing context. The context is represented by modules in separation from its utiliser alike in Context UNITY [3] that relates to our work but having an agent-like view on context-awareness with policies on updating the common context. In process calculi, Braione and Picco [16] consider an approach where inhibiting channels with context enables different implementations satisfying the same basic requirement whilst Zimmer [17] formalises, among others, a remote procedure call. Other approaches we are aware of [18, 19, 20] consider how a specification can be constructed given a rigorously modelled continuously changing environment, yielding a specification on the certain environment that it models.

The outline of this paper is as follows: in Section 2 we provide our definition of context and an example that is used throughout the paper. Section 3 introduces the action system formalism used to formally reason about context. Section 4 ties the context model with the action system formalism presenting how context is utilised, discovered, processed and composed for increasing the informative value. Finally, Section 5 concludes this paper.

2 Concepts Used in This Paper

We start by providing a definition of context and its different appearances. In Section 2.2 we outline an example to support the intuition of the reader when gradually referred to along with the formal definitions to various aspects that are provided throughout this paper.

2.1 Definition of Context and Context Related Matters

Research on context and context-awareness stems from 1992 and Olivetti's Active Badge research [21]. Following this, context has been given many and varying definitions. Pascoe [22] consider context to be subjective and defined by the entity that perceives it. Pascoe's subjectivity however refers to the perception made on the given context, such as 'close to'. Schilt et al. [23] considers aspects of context as "where you are, who you are with and what resources are nearby". Chen and Kotz [24] defines context to be environmental states and settings that affect the application and Yang and Galis [25] add the virtual object to the definition. Hence, according to these definitions context describe the operating conditions that have an impact on the application. As we concur with all, but further add the dictionary interpretations [26, 27] and Dey's and Abowd's [28], we end up in defining context accordingly:

> **Definition 1, context:** *Context is any information that can be used to characterise the situation of entities. An entity is a person, place, object, virtual object or state that is considered relevant to the interaction between a user and an application, including the user and the application themselves.*

Thus, according to the definition, context is a piece of information describing the situation of/in an entity that impacts the output/computations. Such context is typically extracted from either the logical e.g. identity, member of workgroup, time; or from the physical surroundings e.g. temperature, luminosity [29]. We do however not consider context to be cold, high, close, pretty, late or any other perceived matter.

In this paper, we call the source of contextual data *elementary context*. An elementary context is always from the system's point of view, a still-shot of the matter as it was at a specific moment. We call the outcome of composing contexts together and/or processing elementary contexts for providing enhanced information *deduced context*; which covers roles and relations of entities [30]. Consequently, we use the word *context* on a general level, whether it being an elementary or deduced context. The contexts are only updated by the entity introducing them. Given this definition and its interpretations, we define an activity or a system to be *context-aware* whenever any of its functionalities are impacted by some context per definition [28]. In other words, nearly all software reacting on some input could be considered context-aware to some extent [6].

The instance providing for the context is called a *context-service*. Thereby, a context-service is typically a careful composition of elementary context(s) that is considered an entity in its own right. The consumer of a service, the application or an intermediate compositional entity, is called the *utiliser* of this context-service.

In order for a context-service to provide some deduced contextual information, the service's output needs to be published. As an elementary context as such can potentially constitute a context-service in its own right, all context need to be published. Because all contexts are published, one context can provide to several context-services. For example, temperature at location x can be inquired by an utiliser, where translated to a Boolean (<20°C) as well as read to be used in some other service for calculating average temperature.

2.2 The Example: A Fictitious Speed Surveillance System

In order to motivate our ideas, we will construct a fraction of a simplified fictitious context-service providing the necessities for a speed surveillance system. The speed surveillance system is able to decide whether to allow further acceleration, qualifying as a good example encompassing straight forward decision making. The example demonstrate that once the algorithmic functionality of a context utiliser is verified, the hazards relate to the informal acquiring and perception of the information provided by context [31, 32]. It relies on easily conceivable calculations and on three distinct elements of contexts; namely one counting for current speed, one for the speed limit and one for whether the gas pedal position indicates acceleration. As the speed inevitably involves the logical context of time, we will show how to construct and integrate the context-service providing the perceived state of speeding, depicted in Figure 1.

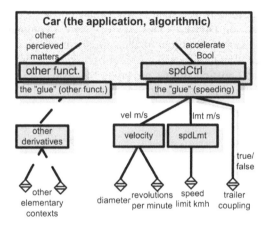

Fig. 1. Speed surveillance context architecture

In Figure 1, the bottommost "diamonds" depicts elementary contexts. The boxes compose and/or process the elementary context. Because the surveillance system is context-aware functioning in a continuously changing conditions where non-algorithmic events occur, exceptions to the functionality are implementable, depicted with the dashed lines and 'other' boxes. We show the adaptability of our approach by introducing the factor of a trailer coupling fixing the maximum speed limit. Examples basing on this surveillance system are clearly distinguishable in the text.

3 The Action System Formalism at a Glimpse

Formal methods facilitate systematic construction of reliable and rigorous software. Even though elementary contexts, as defined in this paper, are not software, formal treatment of them is important as they constitute in a decisive factor in the functionality of the context-aware software. Hence, not only the way contexts are integrated to software, but the methodology of composing deduced contexts from elementary context is of interest.

We model the construction and integration of contextual knowledge in the action system formalism. The action system framework provides means for reasoning about the contextual information in a modular, distributed, manner. For brevity, we omit type checking of the variables. Moreover, we aim at presenting a methodology rather than stepwise development, omitting the supported paradigm of refinement. Readers interested in the powerful methodology of refinement are directed to publications devoted to describing this [10, 11, 13, 33, 34, 35, 36, 37]. However, we feel obliged to stress that since refinement is about preserving correctness on mathematical foundations, it is restricted to the algorithmic part [4, 31, 32] and thereby, refinement as presented in the referenced literature, cannot be directly applied on the physical or logical elementary contexts.

3.1 Action System at a Glimpse

The action system framework is a state based formalism for defining distributed systems [12, 38]. It bases on Dijkstra's language of guarded commands [39, 40] and is defined with the *weakest precondition* predicate transformer, wp. From wp (A, q) we can derive all pre-conditions for which executing *action* A, the post-condition q is satisfied where pre and post-conditions are predicates over state variables. The weakest precondition is defined for various actions as follows:

wp $(abort, q)$	$= false$	*Aborting action*
wp $(magic, q)$	$= true$	*Miraculous action*
wp $(skip, q)$	$= q$	*Stuttering action*
wp $(x \mathrel{\hat{=}} E, q)$	$= q[E/x]$	*Multiple assignment*
wp $(A; B, q)$	$= $ wp $(A,$ wp $(B, q))$	*Sequential composition*
wp $(A~[]~B, q)$	$= $ wp $(A, q) \land$ wp (B, q)	*Nondeterministic choice*
wp $([a], q)$	$= a \Rightarrow q$	*Assumption*
wp $(\{a\}, q)$	$= a \land q$	*Assertion*

The action *abort* is used to model disallowed behaviour, thus q is never satisfied, i.e. the outcome is *false*. Action *magic* always establishes true. Stuttering action *skip* does nothing, thus, the weakest pre-condition for establishing post-condition q is q. Action $x := E$ is multiple assignment where every occurrence of x is substituted with an element from E. $A; B$ is the sequential composition of two actions and $A~[]~B$ the nondeterministic choice between actions A and B. $[a]$ is the assumption and $\{a\}$ is called the assertion. Assumption $[a]$ is assumed true and $\{a\}$ is a predicate needed to evaluate true in order for the execution to proceed to guarantee q. If assumption 'a' is *false*, the action behaves magically whilst if assertion 'a' evaluates false, the action aborts.

The language allows guarded commands, $[g]; A$, for convenience written $g \rightarrow A$, where g is the guard, the predicate and A the action, meaning in the wp-notation:

$$\text{wp} \ (g \rightarrow A, q) \ = g \Rightarrow \text{wp} \ (A, q)$$

that given the guard g, executing A satisfies q. The guard of A, gA is defined so that it does assure the establishment of a valid post-condition.

$$gA \qquad = \neg\text{wp} \ (A, false)$$

Having defined the guarded actions, we can define conditional choice and repetitive construct:

wp (**if** A **fi**, q)   = wp $(A, q) \wedge gA$

wp (**do** A **od**, q)= $(\forall n.\text{wp}\ (A^n, gA \vee q)) \wedge (\exists n.\neg gA^n)$

where $A^0 = skip$ and $A^{n+1} = A^n$; A. The repetitive construct defines that each action enables another or establishes q and that there must exist some that does not enable any other, i.e. partial correctness and termination. Within the repetitive construct, we define an action to only execute whenever its guarding predicate evaluates true.

To start reasoning with action systems, we define the elements of one, here named $\mathcal{A}$:

Definition 2, action system:
$\mathcal{A} = |[\textbf{var}\ v,w^*;\ \textbf{proc}\ P{:}p;\ R^*{:}r\bullet\ Init{:}\ A_0;\ \textbf{do}\ Lbl{:}A\ \textbf{od}]|{:}i$

In $\mathcal{A}$, v and w^* are the variables declared by this action system. Variables v are *local* and w^* constitute the uniquely named *exported* variables (denoted with an asterisk). The clause **proc** defines procedures where $P: p$ is a local procedure p labelled P, only executed if called upon whilst R^* is a uniquely named globally referable procedure. A procedure is substituted for each call on it from an action. Action $Init{:}A_0$ is the initialising action assigning the variables their initial value where $Init$ is the label of this action, A_0. Each action and procedure label belongs to the *Names of labels* in the declaring action system. The **do...od** bracket pair constitutes the repetitive construct within which the action A, labelled Lbl, is repeatedly executed until A aborts or until termination i.e. when gA evaluates false; otherwise it continues infinitely. Whenever gA evaluates true, we say that the action is *enabled*. Of the enabled action(s) within the **do...od** clause, one is chosen non-deterministically for atomic execution. Variables i stand for the optional *imported* variables that are declared and exported by other action systems but referenced from this. Together, import i and export w^* variables constitute a situation resembling shared writable memory between action systems.

This paper considers reactive action systems in which action system $\mathcal{A}$ is a part of a greater system where all other action systems are considered in their own rights but as $\mathcal{A}$'s environment, commonly denoted as $\mathcal{E}$ for environment. As the action atomicity holds on the greater system, an action of $\mathcal{A}$ can be preceded by an action in $\mathcal{E}$ impacting $\mathcal{A}$ by writing to $\mathcal{A}$'s global variable space. Consequently, in a reactive system a component does not terminate by itself as the environment can, through the global variables, enable some actions within this. This makes termination a global property and the formalism comes to showing properties of execution traces.

Distinct action systems can be composed according to Definition 3:

Definition 3, parallel composition '||': Let $\mathcal{A}$ and $\mathcal{B}$ be two action systems
$\mathcal{A} = |[\textbf{var}\ v_a, w_a{}^*;\ \textbf{proc}\ P{:}p \bullet Init{:}A_0;\ \textbf{do}\ LblA{:}\ A\ \textbf{od}]| : i$
$\mathcal{B} = |[\textbf{var}\ v_b, w_b{}^*;\ \textbf{proc}\ R^*{:}r \bullet Init{:}B_0;\ \textbf{do}\ LblB{:}\ B\ \textbf{od}]| : j$
Then, their compositional action system $\mathcal{C} = \mathcal{A} \parallel \mathcal{B}$ is
$\mathcal{C} = |[\textbf{var}\ v_m, w_n{}^*;\ \textbf{proc}\ P{:}p;\ R^*{:}r \bullet Init{:}A_0;\ B_0\ \textbf{do}\ LblA{:}\ A$
$[]\ LblB{:}\ B\ \textbf{od}]|{:}\ h$
Where $h = i \cup j \backslash (w_a \cup w_b)$, $w_c{}^* = w_a \cup w_b$ and $v_c = v_a \cup v_b$ given that $v_a \cap v_b = \emptyset$.

In Definition 3, action system $\mathcal{C}$ is a parallel composition of $\mathcal{A}$ and $\mathcal{B}$. The definition basically states that if a set of action systems operate on disjoint set of local variables, $v_a \cap v_b = \varnothing$, procedure names and action labels, they can be composed to one action system where the actions within the repetitive **do** ... **od** loop are treated non-deterministically and procedures remain intact. If the local variables are not disjoint or the local procedure names coincide, non-interference can be achieved through renaming. This compositionality provides a powerful means to formally compose and decompose action systems for abstraction and refactoring. In total, the action system framework provides us with a well established mathematically verified 'toolbox' with a sound semantic foundation to formally master modularisation, parallel composition, parallel and sequential execution, conditional and repetitive constructs.

3.2   Action Systems for Modelling Context

When modelling context, the import and export clauses do not suffice for passing of context due to the possibility of overwriting. Consequently, we introduce two new variable types for declarations of locally writable and globally readable variables: *read_only* and *publish* respectively denoted by a suffixing ◊, called *sentient* and *impact* variables by Roman et. al. [3]. Hence, advertising and reading the non-writeable context is possible, addressed in Property 1.

Property 1, context passing: Each *read_only* variable has exactly one system publishing it.

In addition, the introduction of elementary contexts motivates declaration of a special clause to the action system called **elemContext**, revising Definition 2 to 2'.

Definition 2', contextual action system:
$\mathcal{A}=|[\text{elemContext } c; \textbf{ var } v,w^*, x\diamond; \textbf{ proc } P{:}p; R^*{:}r\bullet \text{ Init}{:}A_0; \textbf{ do } Lbl{:}Aod]|{:}i, y\diamond$

In Definition 2', **elemContext** denotes the non-writeable elementary context c introduced by this action system whilst variables $x\diamond$ and $y\diamond$ denote the published and *read_only* variables respectively.

One elementary context can contribute to many deduced context. Thus, the action system introducing an elementary context needs to publish it as such, without alternation or processing, addressed in Property 2.

Property 2, introduction of context: Each elementary context is published as such.

The new variable types compel to revision of Definition 3 to 3':

Definition 3', parallel composition of contextual action systems '‖':
Definition 3 with *read_only* variables $v_a\diamond$, $v_b\diamond$, $v_c\diamond$; *publish* variables $w_a\diamond$, $w_b\diamond$, $w_c\diamond$ and elemContext c_a, c_b and c_c for $\mathcal{A}$, $\mathcal{B}$ and $\mathcal{C}$ respectively. Then:
$v_c\diamond = v_a\diamond \cup v_b\diamond \setminus (w_a\diamond \cup w_b\diamond)$, $w_c\diamond = w_a\diamond \cup w_b\diamond$, $c_c\diamond = c_a\diamond \cup c_b\diamond$
provided that $\forall c_a \in w_a$ and $\forall c_b \in w_b$.

Given these definitions and properties, we can denote contextual action systems and encapsulate its algorithmic calculations for verification. We exemplify this in example 1, omitting several pitfalls such as assurance of type checking.

Example 1: Consider three action systems, $\mathcal{F}$, $\mathcal{G}$ and $\mathcal{H}$ calculating velocity based on revolutions in degrees per second (*rps*) and diameter.

$\mathcal{F} = |[\textbf{var } vel\diamond \bullet Init:F_0;$
$\quad \textbf{do } Km/h: true \rightarrow vel\diamond := rpm\diamond \times dia\diamond \times \pi \times 60 \div 1000 \textbf{ od}]| : i_F, rpm\diamond, dia\diamond$

$\mathcal{G} = |[\textbf{elemContext } rps; \textbf{var } rpm\diamond, v\diamond \bullet Init:G_0;$
$\quad \textbf{do } RevPerMin: true \rightarrow v\diamond := rps; rpm\diamond := (rps \div 360 \times 60) \bmod 1 \textbf{ od}]|: i_G$

$\mathcal{H} = |[\textbf{elemContext } diameter; \textbf{var } dia\diamond\bullet Init:H_0;$
$\quad \textbf{do } WheelDia: true \rightarrow dia\diamond := diameter \textbf{ od}]| : i_H$

The action system $\mathcal{F}$ provides a service constituting of the deduced context velocity in km/h through the *publish* variable *vel*$\diamond$. *vel*$\diamond$ is calculated in the action labelled *Km/h*, given that the *read_only* variables are provided. Service $\mathcal{H}$ provides the diameter in meters and publishes this as *dia*$\diamond$ and $\mathcal{G}$ provides the service *rpm*$\diamond$ in revolutions per minute. Here, $\mathcal{H}$ merely maps the elementary context whilst $\mathcal{G}$ processes the elementary context *rps* to *rpm*$\diamond$. Hence, $\mathcal{G}$ and $\mathcal{F}$ function as the algorithmic part that is subjects to verification. Moreover, $\mathcal{G}$ publishes the elementary context *rps* unchanged as *v*$\diamond$. Unit concurrency, absolute vs. relative velocity, tolerance to mention a few are omitted. – *end of example*

In addition to the two types of variables and **elemContext**, we need to define means for the context utiliser to acquire this with unidirectional dependency, the glue. Thereby, we define a language construct called *dependency operator*, \\:

Definition 4, \\ dependency operator: Let A and B be two actions. Then, $A\backslash\backslash B$ is defined as: $A\backslash\backslash B = gA \wedge gB \rightarrow A; B$.

Definition 4 states the definition for \\ language construct denoting a dependency relation between two actions. This dependency relation is unidirectional, where both actions A and B need to be enabled and A guaranteed not to disable B[1] for $A\backslash\backslash B$ to be enabled. Mathematically, action B evaluates its guard gB prior to execution.

We will model the dependency on action/procedure labels in order to avoid confusion of concepts, i.e. $A\backslash\backslash B_{orig}$ in action system $\mathcal{D}$ where B_{orig} is the label of an action.

$\mathcal{D} = |[\textbf{var } w; \textbf{proc } P; \bullet Init: D_0; \textbf{do} \quad LblAdependB: A\backslash\backslash B_{orig} \; [] \; B_{orig}: B \textbf{ od}]| : i$

Declaring dependency between A and B directly restricts the expressiveness of action B to the inclusion of its guard as we cannot differentiate when action B is executed as a dependency reference and when as an action in its own right. Expressiveness is achieved by referencing a procedure instead of action B's label directly i.e. the action labelled $LblAdependB: A\backslash\backslash B_{orig}$ translates to $A\backslash\backslash P$ where P stands for a procedure that enables a specific variant of action B where the procedure action is substituted for the call on it. We label this specific variant B_{wake}. B_{wake} is executed once in the wake of a dependency reference, disables itself with a guard complementing gB_{orig}. Hence, the action labelled B_{orig} split up to two actions, B_{nat} and B_{wake}, making an action specifically

---

[1] The guard for $A\backslash\backslash B$: $\neg wp(A\backslash\backslash B, false) = gA \wedge gB \wedge \neg wp(A, \neg gB)$.

for dependency reference purposes. However, doing so breaks the atomicity of \\ and assurance of no other action disabling B_{wake} needs to be guaranteed, formally defined as atomicity refinement [10, 11].

$\mathcal{X} = |[\ldots$ **do** $LblAdependB$: $A\backslash\backslash B_{orig}$ [] B_{orig}: B **od** $\ldots]|$

-- *translates to* --

$\mathcal{X} = |[\ldots$ **proc** P: $gB \wedge coord = false \rightarrow coord := true$
    do $LblAdependB$: $gA \wedge gP \rightarrow A; P$
    [] B_{wake}: $gB \wedge coord = true \rightarrow B; coord := false$
    [] B_{nat}: $gB \wedge coord = false \rightarrow B$
    od $\ldots]|$

In the operational outline above, notable is that both B_{wake} and B_{nat} assure execution of action B, i.e. B_{orig} and the add-on guards exclude each other. The referenced procedure P's guard must include gB. The Boolean coordination variable *coord* assures that no dependencies are "pending"[2]. Procedure call substitution makes action labelled $LblAdependB$ to execute the following:

$LblAdependB$: $gA \wedge gB \wedge coord = false \rightarrow A; coord := true$

For assurance of the transformation validity, the translation compliance with refinement ought to be shown. Indeed, the refinement calculus provides the conditions for auxiliary functionality to be added to B_{wake} and/or B_{nat}. Consequently, we have reached the situation of Definition 4 where given action $A\backslash\backslash B_{orig}$, A depends on an action labelled B_{wake} through the variables assigned by procedure P that guarantees execution of action B exactly once in the wake of action A.

In addition to \\, we define the @ operator to enable remote references in Definition 5.

Definition 5, @ construct location: Let K label an action or a globally referable procedure and $\mathcal{K}$ an action system where $K \in$ labels of $\mathcal{K}$. Then $K@\mathcal{K}$ refers to action or globally referable procedure labelled K in action system $\mathcal{K}$.

Combining Definitions 4 and 5, writing in action system $\mathcal{A}$: $A\backslash\backslash K@\mathcal{K}$ [3] makes action A depend on an action labelled K in action system $\mathcal{K}$, providing for, for example, some deduced context. Recalling breaking of atomicity above, referring to a remotely available procedure is as follows where $gP*$ is the outcome of $gB \wedge coord = false$ and P is $coord := true$:

$\mathcal{X} = |[\ldots$ **do** $LblAdependB$: $A\backslash\backslash P*@\mathcal{Z}$ **od** $\ldots]|$

-- *translates to* --

$\mathcal{X} = |[\ldots$ **do** $LblAdependB$: $gA \wedge gP* \rightarrow A; P$ **od** $\ldots]|$

$\mathcal{Z} = |[\ldots$ **proc** $P*$: $gB \wedge coord = false \rightarrow coord := true$
    [] B_{wake}: $gB \wedge coord = true \rightarrow B; coord := false$
    [] B_{nat}: $gB \wedge coord = false \rightarrow B$
    od $\ldots]|$

---

[2] Other data structures are implementable as well, such as queues, rings and so forth.

[3] Writing $A\backslash\backslash K*@\mathcal{K}$ refers to a remote procedure.

Definition 3' is applicable for composition. Hence, if $K@\mathcal{K}$ provides a context, we have managed to successfully encapsulate the behaviour and construction of this contextual information and its updates from $A@\mathcal{A}$, just as intended, still complying with Definition 4. In the rest of the paper, we focus on showing how this separation of concerns can be exploited in a sensible manner.

4 Context Modelled with Actions Systems as a Part of a Program

As all software operates algorithmically, reasoning mathematically about its functionality is feasible and software can be shown to satisfy its requirements given that these are provided formally. When a system is formally verified, it explicitly meets with the formal requirements. Consequently, on a theoretical level, formally verified software on formally expressed requirements does not fail; it merely complies with its requirements.

Following the definition of context used in this paper, context and changes in it cannot be modelled formally as we cannot model the behaviour of the elementary contexts. However, putting effort into reasoning with context is motivated, as from a user point of view the reason for failing software, let it be misinterpretation or erroneous algorithm, is irrelevant as the consequences remain.

The aim of treating context in the presented modelling methodology is to reveal the characteristics of context to the designer for specifying them rigorously and verifying the involved algorithmic calculations. Because of this, we start by describing how a context-service is integrated to an utiliser, followed by describing how the elementary contexts are introduced. In Section 4.3 we show how these are formally treated to provide context information and provide a complete view of the characteristics.

4.1 Integrating Contextual Information to an Application

Claiming to have verified a context-aware system inevitably includes verification of its context. As the utiliser's context-aware decisions are impacted by *read_only* variables, a context-service can be treated as a black (white) box. Thereby, a context-service can be independently substituted for another, given that it provides the same verified contextual information on the same *publish* variables. This modularisation of contextual information facilitates reuse and provides comprehensibility through abstraction.

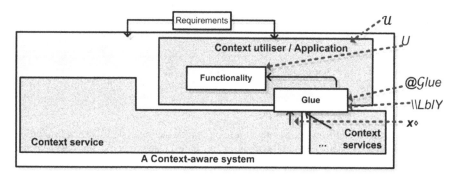

Fig. 2. Context-service - utiliser relation with references to example

A context-aware system can be depicted as in Figure 2, where the context utilising action system $\mathcal{U}$ depends on its glue to perceive matters based on certain context(s). Action U in $\mathcal{U}$ inquires an action or procedure in its glue, $LblY@Glue$ to resolve some matter based on the *read_only* variable $x\diamond$ published by a context-service. The action initiating this, i.e. U, is only enabled given that the guard of $LblY@Glue$ evaluate true. The dotted arrows and the labels in Figure 2 concur with action system $\mathcal{U}$ and $Glue$ action U labelled $LblU$ and action Y labelled $LblY$ respectively, outlined below.

$\mathcal{U}$ =|[**var** w • $Init$:U_0; **do** $LblUdependonY$: $U\backslash\backslash LblY@Glue$
                    [] '*other actions*' **od**]| : j

$Glue$ =|[**var** y • $Init$:Y_0; **do** $LblY$: Y [] '*other actions*' **od**]| : i, $x\diamond$

Considering action system $\mathcal{U}$ to be the utiliser in Figure 2, it relies on action system $Glue$ to glue. When so, guard gY is a predicate on the *read_only* variable(s) $x\diamond$ published by some other context-service. With this, we say that action system $Glue$ perceives a feature of interest to $\mathcal{U}$.

The operators \\ and @ abstract the perception of context from the specific action that decides on it, i.e. $LblUdependonY$. This is essential as the utiliser cannot anticipate all operating conditions it will have to place decisions in throughout its lifetime [3]. Moreover, the *read_only* variable $x\diamond$ can be a prerequisite for several independent gluing action systems, facilitating scalability.

Example 2: Consider a speed surveillance system assembled in a car assuring that speeding will not take place, action system $\mathcal{U}$ in Figure 2. Because speeding is something that bases on speed limit and velocity, the system cannot proceed unless they are provided. Action system $Glue$ counts for the glue, defining its action $LbLY$ as follows:

$Glue$ =|[**var** ; • $Init$:Y_0;
        do $LblY$: $vel\diamond \leq spdLmt\diamond \rightarrow Y$
            [] '*other actions*'
        od]| : i, $vel\diamond$, $spdLmt\diamond$

where $vel\diamond$ refers to velocity as calculated in example 1 and $spdLmt\diamond$ to speed limit that are updated and published by some context-service. According to Definition 4, $U\backslash\backslash LblY@Glue$ is to be enabled if gU is true and speeding is false, resolved in the guard of action labelled $LblY$. As maximum velocity is fixed whenever a trailer is coupled, including the Boolean *trailCpl* according to Figure 1, action labelled $LblY$ must treat this for the whole range of values. Consequently, action system $Glue$ becomes:

$Glue$ =|[**var** ; • $Init$:Y_0;
        do $LblY$: (($vel\diamond \leq spdLmt\diamond \wedge \neg trailCpl\diamond$) $\vee$
                ($vel\diamond \leq spdLmt\diamond \wedge trailCpl\diamond \wedge vel\diamond \leq 80kmh$)) $\rightarrow Y$
            [] '*other actions*'
        od]| : i, $vel\diamond$, $spdLmt\diamond$, $trailCpl\diamond$

Notable is that the utiliser needs only to rely on that the action system $Glue$ indeed provides adequate velocity. Having actions in the glue raising specific flags whenever certain condition are met abstracts the evaluation of sometimes long guards from the utiliser – *end of example*

Because the utiliser $\mathcal{U}$ and the glue $\mathcal{G}lue$ are treated independently from the context-service providing $x\diamond$, the service must not pose any obligations on how its reading is to be perceived. For the context $x\diamond$ we cannot allow confusion between a valid "*context value*" and the absence/timeout of it, i.e. "*do not know*". The absence/timeout refers to erroneous or outdated context that as noted earlier, is out of the scope of this paper.

We define context universality for valid values, Definition 6:

Definition 6, context universality: Let c_n denote the domain of a context and c_m the range decided on, where $c_m \subseteq c_n$ and let c_i be the complement of c_m. Then the context-service must provide for c_i as well.

Since the nature of context, the utiliser becomes a coordinating system that triggers some functionality based on current context(s). The impact of a context can be tuned with non-contextual information in the referencing action $\mathcal{U}$, for example, scheduling action U in action system $\mathcal{U}$ or prioritising it over another [41].

4.2 Composing Information from Elementary Contexts

The elementary contexts constitute the basis for all deduced contexts and context-awareness, making the process of constructing a context-service seemingly hierarchical. Figure 3 depicts any level in the process of constructing a context-service. The input data to this level, the context dependent (CD) segment aka. context provider [5], takes the elementary context c introduced here and/or some *read_only* variables $y\diamond$ as inputs, publishing it as $z\diamond$. $z\diamond$ is then processed in the context refiner/reasoner (CI) segment (aka. context synthesizer [5]). The output is published by the providing (CP) segment [13]. We define the segment interdependencies as follows, omitting type checking:

Definition 7, acquiring context CD: Let CD *read_only* $y\diamond$, introduce elementary context(s) $c \subseteq c_n$ and publish $z\diamond$ and $r\diamond$, then $z\diamond \subseteq y\diamond \cup c$ and $r\diamond = c$.

Definition 8, improving context CI: Let CI *read_only* $z\diamond$ and publish $q\diamond$, then $q\diamond := f(z\diamond)$ according to refiner/reasoner involving optional imported variable conditions i.

Definition 9, providing context CP: Let CP publish $x\diamond$ and *read_only* $q\diamond$, then assuming $q\diamond$ is published by the CI and $r\diamond$ is the set of elementary context(s) introduced by this processing level, $x\diamond := q\diamond \cup r\diamond$ and i be updated.

Hence, the output of this processing level is $x\diamond := f(z\diamond \cup c) \cup r\diamond$ given that the necessary input is provided. Writing this as action systems, the three segments in Figure 3 and Definition 7 through 9 translate into namesake action systems $\mathcal{CD}$, $\mathcal{CI}$ and $\mathcal{CP}$.

$\mathcal{CD}$ =|[**elemContext** c; **var** $z\diamond$, $r\diamond \bullet CD_0$;
    do Get: $true \rightarrow z\diamond := y\diamond \cup c$, $r\diamond := c$ [] '*other actions*' **od**]| : $y\diamond$

$\mathcal{CI}$ = |[**var** $q\diamond$, β; $\bullet$ CI_0; **proc**;
    do $Process$: $true \wedge i \rightarrow q\diamond := f_1(z\diamond, i)$[] '*other actions*' **od**]| : i, $z\diamond$

$\mathcal{CP}$ =|[**var** $x\diamond$; $\bullet$ CP_0; **do** $Provide$: $true \rightarrow x\diamond := q\diamond \cup r\diamond$ [] '*other actions*' **od**]| : i, $q\diamond$, $r\diamond$

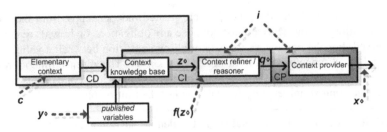

Fig. 3. Processing context

The action system labelled $\mathcal{CD}$ handles the introduction of the variables, the $\mathcal{CJ}$ the actual algorithmic functionality and the $\mathcal{CP}$ the publishing of the deduced context(s) and the possible elementary context(s). The *import* variables i provide the possibility for shared variables, e.g. asynchronous handshaking.

This segmentation defines input and output interfaces and encapsulates the algorithmic part. At the same time, the elementary context(s) is available as measured to be included by other systems. Combined with the *read_only* variables, the processing increases the level of information that is eventually published.

4.3 Processing Context

The task of constructing a context-service providing the context read by the glue reveals the importance of mastering the composition and calculation with context. Recalling Figure 3, one instance of context processing, Figure 4 illustrates the relation of several such instances resulting in context services providing for action system $\mathcal{Glue}$ in Section 4.1.

Figure 4 depicts how the en route context improvers increase the relevance depending on *publish* variables [2, 13] and elementary contexts. Hence, guaranteeing loop freeness of the context variables is necessary; declaring that the *publish* variable(s)

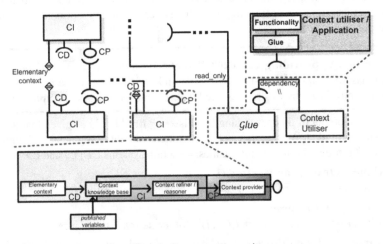

Fig. 4. Context processing

that are *read_only* to a certain level must not include that same level's published variables nor a deduced context depending on such constituting in Property 3.

Property 3, loop avoidance: Let an instance *read_only* $y_n\diamond$ relying on *publish* variables $t_n\diamond$ and $\alpha := y_n\diamond \cup t_n\diamond$. Then α denote all variables this instance relies on. Let c denote elementary contexts introduced by this instance and $x\diamond$ variables it publishes, then $\alpha \cap x\diamond = \emptyset$ and $x\diamond$ comes to rely on $\alpha \cup c$.

In addition to Property 3, in order to provide well defined abstractions and verifiable deduced context, keeping track of the context unit(s) is important.

With these restrictions, processing context is the act of increasing the relevance of information by applying some algorithm or composing several contexts together. Each context processing level, as there might be several (denoted by three dots in Figure 4), is alike the one depicted within the dotted lines down left in Figure 4 and in Figure 3. The context utiliser, in upper right corner Figure 4, is as the dependency references depicted in Figure 2.

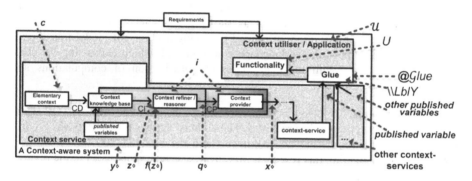

Fig. 5. Construction of a context-service

Example 3: Considering example 1 and 2 and Figure 4, the unit of velocity and speed limit must coincide. The three CI boxes in Figure 4 could stand for action systems $\mathcal{F}$, $\mathcal{G}$ and $\mathcal{H}$ in example 1. The utiliser's names correspond to names used in Section 4.1. Moreover, for the sake of reuse, the system must take a stand on the units and their implementation, such as whether the velocity is absolute or relative – *end of example*.

Figure 5 combines all presented the figures depicting the processing of context to a context-aware system. The Definitions 4 through 9 presented in this paper assure that contexts place no obligation on its utilisers and that it can be reasoned about like if it was a special variable with restricted write access.

5   Conclusions

This paper stresses the importance of processing contextual information systematically as context most certainly constitutes a decisive factor of any context-aware system. Because of this, in order to claim that a system is formally verified, we argue that the decisive matters, including context and its processing, need to be formally expressed and its mathematical matters verified. In this paper, we have presented a methodology and a language construct to the action system formalism that split the contextual characteristics from the software through a gluing system. The contexts are considered to be provided and processed within context-services. We have also outlined and motivated qualities of a context variable that need to hold for facilitating scalability and reuse.

Modelling context in the presented methodology challenges the designer to construct rigorous realistic context-aware systems. This is achieved by revealing the characteristics of the needed context when formally specifying the processing of context utilised by an application. Once these contexts are formalised, the formalisation has fulfilled a purpose of revealing shortcomings to the designer. The action system framework is used for processing and composing contexts where the constraints are placed by the elementary context. Moreover, as this paper consider modularised context, we can foresee that the presented ideas could be extended to formalise other distributed well-defined matters as well.

Being able to express dependencies between actions and services is a first step in modelling services with action systems; future work will address chains of dependencies, unordered dependencies as well as showing characteristics of refinement of inter-dependent actions. We aim at instead of having a library of model transformation rules, to define new simple language construct with which expressing the challenges brought along with the ever increasing distribution of computations and responsibilities are possible.

Acknowledgements. Mr. Neovius wishes to express his gratitude towards TOP-säätiö for the financial support he has received. The authors' wishes to thank to Mr. Fredrik Degerlund for the discussions and comments and the FP7 IST-2007.1.2 DEPLOY-project for partly funding this research. Moreover, a special thank goes to the reviewers for extraordinary extensive and valuable comments on means to improve this paper.

References

1. Weiser, M.: The Computer for the Twenty-First Century. Scientific American (1991)
2. Neovius, M., Yan, L.: A Design Framework for Wireless Sensor Networks. In: Proceedings of the IFIP 19th World Computer Congress (2006)
3. Roman, G.-C., Julien, C., Payton, J.: A formal treatment of context-awareness. In: Wermelinger, M., Margaria-Steffen, T. (eds.) FASE 2004. LNCS, vol. 2984, pp. 12–36. Springer, Heidelberg (2004)
4. Shaw, M., Garlan, D.: Software Architecture, Perspectives on an Emerging Discipline. Prentice-Hall Inc., Englewood Cliffs (1996)
5. Ranganathan, A., Al-Muhtadi, J., Campbell, R.H.: Reasoning about Uncertain Contexts in Pervasive Computing Environments. IEEE Pervasive Computing 3(2) (2004)
6. Dey, A.K., Abowd, G.D., Salber, D.: A conceptual framework and a toolkit for supporting the rapid prototyping of context-aware applications. Human-Computer Interaction 16(2) (2001)
7. Aviziens, A.: Fault-Tolerant Systems. IEEE Transactions on Computers C-25(12) (1976)

8. Randell, B., Lee, P., Treleaven, P.C.: Reliability Issues in Computing System Design. ACM Computer Survey 10(2) (1978)
9. Avizienis, A., Laprie, J.-C., Randell, B.: Dependability and its Threats: A Taxonomy. In: Proceedings of the IFIP 18th World Computer Congress (2004)
10. Sere, K., Waldén, M.A.: Data Refinement and Remote Procedures. In: Ito, T., Abadi, M. (eds.) TACS 1997. LNCS, vol. 1281. Springer, Heidelberg (1997)
11. Sere, K., Waldén, M.A.: Data Refinement of Remote Procedures. Formal Aspects of Computing 12(4) (2000)
12. Back, R.J.R., Kurki-Suonio, R.: Decentralization of Process Nets with Centralized Control. In: Proceedings of the 2nd ACM SIGACT-SIGOPS Symposium on Principles of Distributed Computing (1983)
13. Neovius, M., Sere, K., Yan, L., Satpathy, M.: A Formal Model of Context-Awareness and Context-Dependency. In: Proceedings of the 4th IEEE International Conference on Software Engineering and Formal Methods (2006)
14. Degerlund, F., Sere, K.: A Framework for Incorporating Trust into Formal Systems Development. In: Jones, C.B., Liu, Z., Woodcock, J. (eds.) ICTAC 2007. LNCS, vol. 4711, pp. 154–168. Springer, Heidelberg (2007)
15. Yan, L., Sere, K.: A Formalism for Context-Aware Mobile Computing. In: Proceedings of the Third international Symposium on Parallel and Distributed Computing/Third international Workshop on Algorithms, Models and Tools For Parallel Computing on Heterogeneous Networks (2004)
16. Braione, P., Picco, G.P.: On Calculi for Context-Aware Coordination. In: De Nicola, R., Ferrari, G.-L., Meredith, G. (eds.) COORDINATION 2004. LNCS, vol. 2949. Springer, Heidelberg (2004)
17. Zimmer, P.: A Calculus for Context-Awareness. BRICS Report Series RS-05-27, Denmark (2005) ISSN 0909-0878
18. Petre, L., Qvist, M., Sere, K.: Distributed Object-Based Control Systems. Technical Report 241, TUCS (Feburary 1999)
19. Rönkkö, M., Ravn, A.P., Sere, K.: Hybrid Action Systems. Theoretical Computer Science 290(1) (2003)
20. Hayes, I.J., Jackson, M.A., Jones, C.B.: Determining the specification of a control system from that of its environment. In: Proceedings of the International Symposium of Formal Methods (2003)
21. Want, R., Hopper, A., Falcao, V., Gibbons, J.: The Active Badge Location System. ACM Transactions on Information Systems 10 (1992)
22. Pascoe, J.: Adding Generic Contextual Capabilities to Wearable Computers. In: Proceedings of the Second International Symposium on Wearable Computers (1998)
23. Schilit, B., Adams, N., Want, R.: Context-Aware Computing Applications. In: Proceedings of the IEEE Workshop on Mobile Computing Systems and Applications (1994)
24. Chen, G., Kotz, D.: A Survey of Context-Aware Mobile Computing Research. Technical Report TR2000-381, Dept. of Computer Science, Dartmouth College (2000)
25. Yang, K., Galis, A.: Policy-Driven Mobile Agents for Context-Aware Service in Next Generation Networks. In: Horlait, E., Magedanz, T., Glitho, R.H. (eds.) MATA 2003. LNCS, vol. 2881, pp. 111–120. Springer, Heidelberg (2003)
26. Merriam Webster Online dictionary, Merriam-Webster Inc., Springfield, MA 01102
27. Oxfords Advanced learner's dictionary (2000) CD-ROM
28. Dey, A.K., Abowd, G.D.: Towards a better understanding of context and context-awareness. In: Proceedings of the CHI 2000 Workshop on the What, Who, Where, When, and How of Context-Awareness (2000)

29. Schmidt, A., Aidoo, K.A., Takaluoma, A., Tuomela, U., Van Laerhoven, K., Van de Velde, W.: Advanced interaction in context. In: Gellersen, H.-W. (ed.) HUC 1999. LNCS, vol. 1707, p. 89. Springer, Heidelberg (1999)

30. Coutaz, J., Crowley, J.L., Dobson, S., Garlan, D.: Context is key. Communications of the ACM special issue: The disappearing computer 48(3) (2005)

31. Zemanek, H.: Abstract Architecture, General concepts for systems design. In: Bjorner, D. (ed.) Abstract Software Specifications. LNCS, vol. 86. Springer, Heidelberg (1980)

32. Naur, P.: Intuition in software development. In: Ehrig, H., Floyd, C., Nivat, M., Thatcher, J. (eds.) TAPSOFT 1985 and CSE 1985. LNCS, vol. 186. Springer, Heidelberg (1985)

33. Back, R.J.R., Sere, K.: Stepwise Refinement of Action Systems. Structured Programming 12(1), 17–30 (1991)

34. Back, R.J.R., von Wright, J.: Refinement Calculus: A Systematic Introduction. Graduate Texts in Computer Science. Springer, Heidelberg (1998)

35. Back, R.J.R., von Wright, J.: Trace Refinement of Action Systems. In: Jonsson, B., Parrow, J. (eds.) CONCUR 1994. LNCS, vol. 836. Springer, Heidelberg (1994)

36. Back, R.J.R., von Wright, J.: Compositional Action System Refinement. TUCS technical report no. 464 (June 2002)

37. Back, R.J.R.: Correctness Preserving Program Refinements: Proof Theory and Applications. Mathematical Center Tracts, vol. 131, Mathematical Centre, Amsterdam, The Netherlands (1980)

38. Sere, K.: Stepwise derivation of parallel algorithms, PhD dissertation, Åbo Akademi (1990)

39. Dijkstra, E.W.: A Discipline of Programming. Prentice Hall, Englewood Cliffs (1976)

40. Dijkstra, E.W.: Guarded commands, nondeterminacy and formal derivation of programs. Communications of the ACM 18(8) (1975)

41. Sekerinski, E., Sere, K.: A Theory of Prioritizing Composition. The Computer Journal 39(8) (1996)

Towards Demonstrably Correct Compilation of Java Byte Code*

Michael Leuschel

Institut für Informatik, Universität Düsseldorf, D-40225, Düsseldorf, Germany
leuschel@cs.uni-duesseldorf.de

Abstract. In this paper we investigate the feasibility of a demonstrably correct compiler for Java bytecode. We first examine the suitability of adapting the existing high assurance compiler DECCO for the Pascal-like language PASP, based on a Z formalisation of the compiler manually transcribed to Prolog. During the investigation we have uncovered several problematic issues and argue that these can be avoided by formally deriving the code of the compiler from the formal specification, rather than manually transcribing it. We have conducted a case study, developing a compiler for a subset of Java bytecode to an idealised RISC processor using the B-method. We show that refinement is a natural way to model compilation and that the B-method can in principle be used to develop a demonstrably correct compiler. In particular, the tool support for B turned out to be extremely valuable: animation, automated refinement checking, and proof each uncovered a series of mistakes.

1 Introduction and Motivation

Ensuring the correctness of the compilation process is an important consideration in the construction of reliable software. If the compiler generates code that is not faithful to the original source program code, then all efforts spent in proving the correctness of the system could have been in vain. Proving that target code is correct w.r.t. the program source is especially important for high assurance systems, as unfaithful target code can lead to loss of life and/or property.

In earlier work [38], AWE together with Susan Stepney and the company Logica have developed the DECCO compiler which translates a Pascal-like high-level language (called PASP) into machine code for the ASP (Arming System Processor) processor, an in-house "RISC processor with separate data and program buses, only three registers, and built-in test utilities" [18]. For this, the semantics of PASP and of ASP were specified in Z [3,36]. Also, various intermediate levels such as unlinked, relocatable ASP assembly modules were also formally specified, and the whole compiler and linker process was proven to be meaning preserving and thus correct. The ASP chip itself was also formally specified and verified in [35].

Note that DECCO stands for DEmonstrably Correct COmpiler. There are two reasons why DECCO is only called "demonstrably correct" and not just plain "correct":

---

* This work has been supported by AWE plc. within the JASP project.

F.S. de Boer et al. (Eds.): FMCO 2008, LNCS 5751, pp. 119–138, 2009.
© Springer-Verlag Berlin Heidelberg 2009

1. The compiler was formalised and proven in Z, but was then manually translated into Prolog for execution. While the translation was "straightforward" [38], one cannot exclude errors having been made in the translation.
2. The proof of correctness was performed by hand (i.e., using pencil and paper).

Still, the development of DeCCo was a Herculean task and it provides a degree of assurance that is far beyond what traditional compiler construction techniques provide.

Unfortunately, several major issues are limiting the practical use of DeCCo within AWE:

1. It is difficult to find qualified programmers for the PASP language (based on Pascal).
2. The compiler has performance problems in the presence of complex branching.
3. Maintenance of the DeCCo system is an issue. In particular, it turned out to be difficult to adapt the source code to work on recent hardware.

Contributions of the Paper

To address the first issue, AWE is keen on replacing PASP by (a subset of) Java bytecode as the input language of the compiler. This would allow to produce various front ends (e.g., for ADA [27] or JavaCard), for which programmers can be found. New front ends could be developed as the need arises. In this paper, we investigate whether the existing DeCCo implementation is a suitable starting point for this endeavour and whether the DeCCo approach can be further improved.

Investigation of DeCCo. We have first inspected the Prolog code of the DeCCo system, uncovering some relatively surprising issues. Indeed, while great care went into the Z specifications of DeCCo and the translation to Prolog, the quality of some of the infrastructure code is poor. We have uncovered a series of issues with the current implementation, more precisely with the way the formal compiler specification was transcribed into Prolog. Some of these issues are also the likely cause of the performance problems. This does not put the DeCCo approach itself into question, as it is clearly still better than conventional compiler development. Still, we argue to strengthen the DeCCo approach, by *more rigorously transcribing the formal specification of the compiler into code.*

Formal Compiler Development using B. We have investigated using a DeCCo style approach for compiling Java bytecode, but replacing the use of Z by B [2], which is the successor of Z developed with tool support in mind. This allows us to replace the manual pencil and paper proofs by mechanical proofs, and also allows automated code generation via refinement, closing one of the loopholes of the original DeCCo system. Indeed, the type of errors we uncovered in the existing DeCCo system can be avoided if we succeed to formally derive the whole compiler using the B-method. The use of B also gives us access to powerful tool support, e.g., in the form of animation and model checking.

A Worked-out Compiler for a Subset of Java Bytecode. The development of a compiler from simplified bytecode to a simplified RISC architecture was conducted using the adapted DECCO approach. Our experiment has proven the value of the various B tools (each finding different kind of errors), and has also shown the feasibility and potential of the approach. We have also shown that B refinement is a natural way to express the compilation process and prove it correct.

Note that we were also able to develop part of the compilation process in another language (here, Prolog), ensuring the integrity of the compilation process by validating the output of the subsidiary Prolog programs using properties expressed in B. This may allow us to tap into the vast number of tools developed for Java bytecode (e.g., the tools [7,6,5,19]).

While a number of research advances will certainly be required to develop a fully verified Java bytecode compiler to completion, the fact that we start from intermediate code (and not high-level code) leads us to believe that the overall goal of a verified compiler could be achieved within the medium-term future.

2   Study of the Existing DECCO System

General Architecture and Code Quality. The existing DECCO system is implemented in LPA WinProlog. A interesting discovery we made is that DECCO was accidentally run in a mode where LPA WinProlog does not raise exceptions when encountering errors with built-in predicates, but silently fails, thereby initiating backtracking. This meant that a series of runtime errors, such as calls to built-in predicates of LPA WinProlog which no longer existed in the current version, were not detected.

Also, several predicates were discovered which produced multiple solutions in circumstances where the predicates should behave like a function. Finally, several bugs were uncovered in the infrastructure predicates of the compiler. For example, the predicate, inserting elements into a keyed binary tree, contained a bug whereby elements were sometimes inserted in the wrong position of the tree. The predicate is used at over 120 places in the source code of the compiler, e.g., inserting entries into the symbol table, or for merging environments.

Instantiation of Arguments. To achieve a translation of the Z schemas into executable code, the DECCO project used DCTGs (Definite Clause Translation Grammars; see, e.g., part 3 of paper VI of [38]). Apart from this, very little additional Prolog predicates for Z constructs were required. Indeed, as mentioned in page 3 of part VI of [38], the Z schemas are constructive, and hence the Prolog counterparts of the Z operators behave like functions and it is clearly determined which are the inputs and which the outputs. For example, $x = \{1, 2\} \cup \{3\}$ is a constructive use of the set union operator: the value of x can be computed from the value of its operands $\{1, 2\}$ and $\{3\}$. This allows for a much simpler Prolog counterparts to be used within DECCO than, e.g., within PROB [30], in which predicates can be used in various directions.[1] Within, DECCO the Prolog

---

[1] I.e., PROB also has to deal with, e.g., $\{1, 2, 3\} = x \cup \{3\}$ or $\{1, 2, y\} = x \cup \{z\}$.

cut was also liberally used for those predicates to improve efficiency. The price is that those Prolog predicates are only correct when used in the prescribed way. Indeed, page 12 of part VI of [38] says that correctness of the domRes/3 predicate (representing the Z operator to restrict the relation to a particular domain) requires that the first two arguments are ground. Given that we work in a safety critical environment, it would be advisable that this aspect of the Prolog translation is ensured more formally. Indeed, there are analysis techniques [8,33] which could in principle guarantee that all Z operators are indeed used in a constructive fashion. One could also use runtime supervision to at least detect those errors when they occur.

Moreover, a lot of other DECCO predicates also assume that certain arguments are instantiated when being called (e.g., because of their use of the Prolog cut). Again, these assumptions should be tested, as otherwise unsound compilation may ensue. In our investigation, we have added some runtime supervision to a handful of predicates of the DECCO system, and have indeed uncovered various instances where these assumptions were *not* met (such as when calling the predicate to delete from a keyed binary tree). This is very likely to cause errors in the compilation process.

Summary. Great care went into the underlying formalisation of the DECCO system and the translation of Z schemas into Prolog. The DECCO approach is still superior to convential compiler development in terms of reliability and correctness. Nonetheless, the existing implementation of DECCO still contains bugs and has not enough safeguards against erroneous runtime behaviour.

The most reliable (and interesting) part of the DECCO code is the one derived from the Z schemas. However, PASP is very different from Java bytecode and the whole parsing process of DECCO (which is intertwined with the compilation process) would need to be rewritten anyway.

Thus, given the various findings of our investigation, we argue to strengthen the DECCO approach, by more rigorously establishing the equivalence between the formal compiler specification and the code of the compiler. One way to achieve this is by moving from Z to B and to use B's *code generation* facilities; an approach which we evaluate in the remainder of this paper. The B-method also gives us access to various provers, which can also be used to perform the the compiler correctness proofs mechanically — rather than by hand using pencil and paper — thereby closing another loophole.

One potential problem, however, is that B is not very good at dealing with recursive datastructures, such as trees (often used in compiling algorithms). On the other hand, the notion of refinement is very well suited to compilation: a correctly compiled program can be viewed as a refinement of the original high-level source program. Also, B is reasonably close to Z used in DECCO. Hence, in the remainder of this paper we evaluate the feasibility of using B for a demonstrably correct compiler from a subset of Java Bytecode to an idealised RISC processor.

3   Description of the Subset of Java Bytecode

So as not to be overwhelmed with small details, we have decided in the remainder of this paper to stick to a small subset of the Java bytecode. A precise formalisation of a large part of the Java bytecode can be found in [37]; other formalisations can be found in [29,20]. For the remainder of this paper it is important to know that, for each method, the Java bytecode operates on:

- a set of local variables, which are numbered (from 0..255)
- a local operator stack. Note that this stack must have the important property that for each program point, the stack layout is independent of the way this program point was reached. We will return to this issue later, as it is important for compilation.

We have dealt with the following eleven opcodes, where *Addr* refers to an address in the bytecode, *Var* to the number of a local variable and *Cst* to an immediate constant:

- **nop:** an operation having no effect (apart from increasing the program counter),
- **return:** terminate the execution of the current method,
- **goto *Addr*:** jump to a specific address *Addr* in the bytecode,
- **istore *Var*:** pop the top of the operator stack and write it into local variable numbered *Var*,
- **iload *Var*:** push the contents of variable *Var* on top of the stack,
- **iconst *Cst*:** push the immediate constant *Cst* on top of the stack,
- **pop:** pop the top of the stack and discard it,
- **ifle *Addr*:** pop the top of the operator stack and if it is less or equal to 0 jump to the address *Addr*,
- **iinc *Var*, *Cst*:** add the immediate constant *Cst* to the contents of the local variable *Var*,
- **imul:** pop the two topmost values of the operator stack, multiply them and push the result onto the stack,
- **iadd:** pop the two topmost values of the operator stack, add them and push the result onto the stack.

Note, that we thus do not treat method calls and the ensuing possible recursion; nor do we consider object orientation. For simplicity, we have also assumed that the above opcodes operate on **unbounded** integers.

As it turns out, this subset is complicated enough to exhibit some interesting issues, and allowed us to experiment with several approaches within the confines of this paper.

Example 1. In the remainder of this paper we will use the following example bytecode program to illustrate various points:

```
 0: iconst_2      10: ifle 25
 1: istore_1      13: iinc 3, -1
 2: iconst_5      16: iload 4
 3: istore_2      18: iload_1
 4: iload_2       19: imul
 5: istore_3      20: istore 4
```

```
6: iconst_1          22: goto 9
7: istore 4          25: return
9: iload_3
```

It was obtained by running javap -c Power on the following Java program, and removing method calls and keeping the bytecode for the main method:

```
public class Power {
public static void main(String args[])
  {
    int base = 2; int exp = 5;  int i = exp;   int res = 1;
    while (i>0) {
       i--;  res = res*base;
    }
}}
```

4   Stack Layout Analysis

Java bytecode has the property [34] that at every program point we need to have the same stack layout, irrespective of the particular execution path that has led to this program point. This is crucial for our compiler, as it allows to replace the stack operations by direct register or memory accesses, without requiring to explicitly having to update a stack pointer.

We have implemented a way to obtain the stack layout using abstract interpretation [13] in Prolog. We will see later that the output of the analysis will be formally validated (but not the implementation of the anlysis itself).

The idea of abstract interpretation is to replace the set of concrete values by a set of abstract values, in order to ensure that one can obtain finite representations of all possible program behaviours in finite time. In particular, the state of an abstract interpreter contains abstract values rather than concrete values. Also, instead of applying concrete operations, the abstract interpreter applies abstract counterparts of these operations.

First, we have implemented a Java byte code interpreter in Prolog, which includes a small DCG (Definite Clause Grammar) parser to read in decompiled byte code programs. You may notice that the bytecode from Example 1 actually contains some specialized opcodes, such as istore_2, iconst_5. In the remainder of this paper, we have treated these as an unspecialized opcode taking an argument. Indeed, the parser automatically converts those opcodes into the corresponding more general instructions (e.g., istore_2 gets translated into istore 2).

We have then adapted our Java bytecode interpreter to perform abstract interpretation; the full code can be found in [25]. Note that it replaces concrete arithmetic operations and comparisons by abstract ones. Our abstract interpreter does a little bit more analysis than strictly necessary for our purposes, i.e., it infers additional information about whether values can be zero, positive or negative. For full-blown Java bytecode, we will actually also have to infer types of the values on the stack, so this extension illustrates the way this can be achieved.

Below is a sample output of our abstract interpreter. For every program point, we obtain information about the operand stack and the local variables, where top denotes the abstract value which represents every possible value, pos only denotes strictly positive values.

```
Starting ABSTRACT Interpretation
runtime_ms(0)
ABSTRACT INFORMATION AT PROGRAM POINTS:
 0 : iconst(2)    : env([],        [])
 1 : istore(1)    : env([pos],     [])
 2 : iconst(5)    : env([],        [1/pos])
 3 : istore(2)    : env([pos],     [1/pos])
 4 : iload(2)     : env([],        [1/pos,2/pos])
 5 : istore(3)    : env([pos],     [1/pos,2/pos])
 6 : iconst(1)    : env([],        [1/pos,2/pos,3/pos])
 7 : istore(4)    : env([pos],     [1/pos,2/pos,3/pos])
 9 : iload(3)     : env([],        [1/pos,2/pos,3/top,4/pos])
10 : ifl(<=,0,25): env([top],     [1/pos,2/pos,3/top,4/pos])
13 : iinc(3,-1)   : env([],        [1/pos,2/pos,3/top,4/pos])
16 : iload(4)     : env([],        [1/pos,2/pos,3/top,4/pos])
18 : iload(1)     : env([pos],     [1/pos,2/pos,3/top,4/pos])
19 : imul         : env([pos,pos], [1/pos,2/pos,3/top,4/pos])
20 : istore(4)    : env([pos],     [1/pos,2/pos,3/top,4/pos])
22 : goto(9)      : env([],        [1/pos,2/pos,3/top,4/pos])
25 : return       : env([],        [1/pos,2/pos,3/top,4/pos])
```

As can be seen, we have inferred for every program point the layout of the stack (the first part of the env term). For example for program point 19, performing the imul instruction, we have as stack layout [pos,pos], i.e., there are exactly two values on the stack (which are also guaranteed to be positive). For compilation this means that when generating the compiled code for program point 19 we know exactly how the stack looks like and exactly from which memory location we need to take the two operands for the multiplication.

Soundness of abstract interpretation is an important consideration, and can be established mathematically [13]. However, we could still have made an error in the implementation of the abstract interpreter, deviating from the mathematical theory. Hence, one important question for correct compilation is: *how can we trust the output of this analysis*?

In turns out we do not have to trust the output. In the upcoming formal B specification of Java bytecode, we will introduce properties which will guarantee that a correct stack layout is provided. Hence, the output of our abstract interpreter can be validated formally, either by using a B prover or using the PROB model checker.

Related Work. The CLIP group from the Technical University of Madrid has developed a class file loader Prolog library and analyse Java bytecode using their CiaoPP abstract interpretation engine; see, for example, [7,6,5,19]. Another related work is [17] as well as part of [21]. Also, since Java SE 6 (version 50.0 of the class file format), class files now also contain information about the stack layout (see, e.g., Section 4.8.4 of [11]). Note that Section 4.11 of [11] contains Prolog code as a specification of the type checking verfication procedure for class files.

5   B Formalisation of the Java Bytecode

5.1   B

Both B [2] and Z [3,36] are formal mathematical specification notations, using the same underlying set theory and predicate calculus, providing a wide array of sophisticated data structures (sets, sequences, relations, higher-order functions) and operations on them (set union, difference, function composition to name but a few). Both formalisms are used in industry, mainly for safety-critical applications.

The B-method was derived from Z with the goal of enabling tool support in general and automatic proving and code generation in particular. B formal models are structured into *machines*, each machine having a set of *variables* which can be modified through *operations*. The consistency of a B machine is expressed in terms of an *invariant*: a predicate that should be true in all initial states and preserved by all operations. In addition to variables, B machines can also contain *constants*. One can express assumptions about the constants as *properties*. Another core concept of the B-method is *refinement*, whereby a given abstract machine can be refined by a more concrete one, closer to an actual implementation. Every possible state of the concrete machine should be linked to a corresponding state of the abstract machine; this link is expressed through a *glueing invariant*.

5.2   Formalisation of Java Bytecode Execution

In a first instance we have developed a formal B model of our subset of Java bytecode from Section 3. The B model describes the structure of a bytecode program as well as operations which perform individual bytecode instructions. All B models can be found in [25]. Due to our focus on a small subset of Java bytecode, our formalisation is of course much less ambitious than the one in [37] using abstract state machines [9], the one in [29] using Coq, or the one in [20] using Isabelle/HOL.

First, we use the constant PSIZE to indicate the number of instructions in the bytecode program under consideration. The bytecode program itself is modelled by three total functions: PrgOpcode, PrgArg1, and PrgArg2. The domain of these functions is 1..PSIZE, and as such can be viewed as arrays (see Figure 1). The functions indicate for each instruction the opcode, the value of the first and second argument respectively. (In case an opcode takes less than two arguments the value of PrgArg2 is irrelevant. The same applies to PrgArg1 in case the opcode takes no arguments.)

In addition, we include another total function StackLayout, which contains the statically computed stack layout information (see Figure 1), using, e.g., the technique described in Section 4. Note that we encode a certain number of properties of the stack layout in B, and will later prove that these ensure that the statically computed information is correct for all possible runtime executions.

In addition to the bytecode program, the B model also contains constants for the number of local variables (MAXVAR), the set of all local variables (VARS), the integer range of a byte (BYTE), and the maximum positive number representable by a signed byte (MAXBYTE).

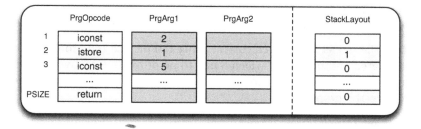

Fig. 1. B Data Representation of the Bytecode Program

Let us now look more precisely at the properties of our model:

```
PROPERTIES
...
   PSIZE : NATURAL1 &
   PrgOpcode: 1..PSIZE --> Opcodes &
   PrgArg1: 1..PSIZE --> VARS &
   PrgArg2: 1..PSIZE --> BYTE &
...
   StackLayout: 1..PSIZE --> VARS
   /* for each Program Point: indicate size of stack */
      &
   StackLayout(1) = 0 & /* Initially stack is empty */
...
   !pc1.(pc1:1..PSIZE =>
      ((PrgOpcode(pc1)/=goto & PrgOpcode(pc1)/=return)=> pc1+1 <= PSIZE ))
&
      !pc2.(pc2:1..PSIZE & PrgOpcode(pc2) = goto
               => (PrgArg1(pc2):1..PSIZE &
                              StackLayout(PrgArg1(pc2))= StackLayout(pc2)) )
   ...
```

As an example, the universially quantified[2] formula over pc1 stipulates that any address following an opcode instruction different from a goto and return must be within the scope of the program. The universally quantified formula over pc2 expresses the fact that a jump does not alter the stack layout.

The state of the B model contains the current program counter PC, the state of the stack Stack, the values of the defined variables Vars, as well as a boolean Finished indicating whether execution of the bytecode program has terminated. The full invariant of the model is the following, which also establishes a link between the statically computed StackLayout and the dynamic state of the stack:

```
INVARIANT
   PC: 1..PSIZE &              /* PC remains in the bounds of the program */
   Stack: seq(INTEGER) &
   Vars: VARS +->INTEGER &
```

---

[2] Universal quantification is expressed in B as $\forall x.(P \Rightarrow Q)$ or !x.(P => Q) in ASCII, where the predicate P must be sufficient to give x a type.

```
Finished: BOOL &
size(Stack) = StackLayout(PC)          /* StackLayout is correct for PC */
```

Note that the model was proven correct using B4Free [12] (44 proof obligations were generated and proven, of which 8 had to be proven interactively). Correctness in this case means that, given the assumptions about the Java bytecode expressed in the properties,

- the program counter PC will always remain within the boundaries of the bytecode and
- that the statically established StackLayout is a correct description of all possible dynamic stack layouts encountered while executing the bytecode.

Note that in order to prove the model, we had to decompose the representation of the bytecode into three total functions (PrgOpcode, PrgArg1, PrgArg2) rather than one function to tuples (as the prover was having difficulty with the projection functions prj1 and prj2). The prover also uncovered assumptions which were missing in earlier versions of our model (e.g., StackLayout(1) = 0), which were not uncovered by animation and model checking (as this was done for our particular sample bytecode, which satisfied those properties).

The model can be animated and model checked using PROB, which is important as this formal specification is a starting point for our compiler; any error here would also lead to an erroneous compiler. Figure 2 shows a screenshot of PROB, animating the model for our bytecode from Example 1 for inputs 2 and 5. As can be seen, variable 4 contains $2^5 = 32$ as expected.

Here is an example operation of the JavaBC0 machine, implementing the iload opcode:

```
ex_iload(A1)= PRE PrgOpcode(PC) = iload & A1=PrgArg1(PC) & A1:dom(Vars)
THEN PC := PC+1 ||  Stack := Stack <- Vars(A1) END;
```

This is quite succinct and readable, thus also allowing easy human inspection. Let us look at one construct which we can compare with a corresponding construct in DECCO, the ifle opcode of the Java bytecode. First, the B operation to execute this opcode is:

```
ex_ifle(A1) = PRE PrgOpcode(PC) = ifle  & A1=PrgArg1(PC) THEN
    IF Stack(1) <= 0 THEN   PC := A1
    ELSE PC := PC+1 END ||
    Stack := tail(Stack) END;
```

This is arguably more readable than the corresponding DCTG formalisation in part VI of [38] (see also appendix of [25]) or the Z schemas in [38]. The B specification is relatively succinct and clear, and can of course be formally reasoned upon.

6   B Description of the RISC Processor

In order to formalise the compilation process, we also need to describe the target architecture. To avoid distracting from central issues, we have chosen the

Fig. 2. Animating the Power bytecode using PROB

simple RISC Instruction set from the Dragon book [4] chapters on code generation. Note, exactly as in the Java bytecode, we furthermore assume the use of unbounded integers for simplicity. The following are the instructions of the processor:

- LDI Reg, Cst:
- LDM Reg, Mem
- STM Reg, Mem
- ADD Reg, Reg, Reg
- MUL Reg, Reg, Reg
- res := ISPOS Reg

Note that this model of the processor contains no conditional or unconditional jumps yet. This will be added later; for the moment the control flow will be handled by the abstract specification.

Maybe the semantics is best explained using B, which we believe to be easily readable. Readiblity is important, as this is a specification of the target hardware and as such needs to be validated independently:

```
MACHINE RISC
CONSTANTS
  NrReg,  /* Number of registers */
  MSize,   /* Memory Size */
  RBYTE, MAXRBYTE
PROPERTIES
  MAXRBYTE = 31 & /* 127 & */
  NrReg:INT & NrReg>1 &  MSize:INTEGER & MSize>1 &
  RBYTE = (-MAXRBYTE-1)..MAXRBYTE &
  NrReg =2 & MSize = 4*(MAXRBYTE+1)-1
VARIABLES
  R, /* Register Contents */  MEM /* Memory Contents */
INVARIANT
  R: 1..NrReg --> INTEGER &
  MEM: 0..MSize --> INTEGER
INITIALISATION
  R := %x.(x:1..NrReg | 0) || MEM := %y.(y:0..MSize | 0)
OPERATIONS
  LDI(r,imm) = PRE r:1..NrReg & imm:RBYTE THEN
    R(r) := imm
  END;
  LDM(r,mem) = PRE mem:0..MSize & r:1..NrReg THEN
    R(r) := MEM(mem)
  END;
  STM(r,mem) = PRE mem:0..MSize & r:1..NrReg THEN
      MEM(mem) := R(r)
  END;
  ADD(r1,r2,r3) = PRE r1: 1..NrReg & r2: 1..NrReg & r3: 1..NrReg THEN
      R(r1) := R(r2)+R(r3)
  END;
  MUL(r1,r2,r3) = PRE r1: 1..NrReg & r2: 1..NrReg & r3: 1..NrReg THEN
      R(r1) := R(r2)*R(r3)
  END;
  SUBT(r1,r2,r3) = PRE r1: 1..NrReg & r2: 1..NrReg & r3: 1..NrReg THEN
      R(r1) := R(r2)-R(r3)
  END;
  res <-- ISPOS(r) = PRE r:1..NrReg THEN
    IF R(r)> 0 THEN    res := TRUE
      ELSE  res := FALSE END
    END
END
```

In order to get closer to the ASP processor used in the DECCo project, we have fixed in the remainder the number of registers to two.

7   Compiling Data Operations by Refinement

The main idea of our compiler is to refine every opcode in the JavaBC0 model into a sequence of calls of the operations of the RISC machine. If we can prove

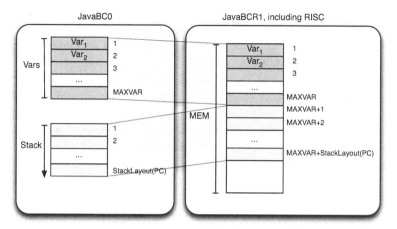

Fig. 3. Illustrating the Gluing Invariant

that this results in a correct refinement, we have proven correctness of our translation patterns for the opcodes. Hence, our new machine `JavaBCR1` refines the
machine `JavaBC0` from Section 5 and includes the machine `RISC` from Section 6.

Also, part of the memory of the RISC processor is allocated for the local
variables and a separate part is used to hold the stack's contents. More precisely,
memory locations 0 to `MAXVAR` hold the values of the (defined) local variables
0 to `MAXVAR` respectively. The stack starts at memory location `MAXVAR+1` and
grows upwards. In other words, memory location `MAXVAR+1` contains the bottom
element of the stack (if the stack is non-empty). Note that there is no stack
pointer: for every Java bytecode instruction the compiler knows the exact size of
the stack through the B constant `StackLayout`. Hence, if we are at instruction
PC, the top of the stack can be found at `MAXVAR+StackLayout(PC)`.

To make our model more readable, we use the following DEFINITIONS:

```
AdvancePC == BEGIN PC := PC+1 END;
TOP == (MAXVAR + StackLayout(PC));
```

The link between the state of the Java bytecode program and the state of the
compiled RISC program is specified by the following gluing invariant, which is
also illustrated in Figure 3:

```
!v.(v:dom(Vars) => Vars(v) = MEM(v)) &
!sv.(sv:dom(Stack) => Stack(sv) = MEM(MAXVAR+sv))
```

Let us look at how one particular opcode, `iload` which we have already seen
earlier, is refined into two assembly language instructions:

```
ex_iload(A1) = PRE  PrgOpcode(PC)=iload & PrgArg1(PC)=A1 THEN
       LDM(1,A1); STM(1,TOP+1); AdvancePC
    END;
```

Note that `AdvancePC` advances the program counter of the Java bytecode program, *not* the assembly program. The control flow inside the assembly program
is dealt with in the Section 8.

Before attempting a formal proof that JavaBCR1 is indeed a correct refinement of JavaBC0, we have first used the PROB automated refinement checker (using the bytecode of Example 1). This has already uncovered a number of errors in the first versions of our model:

- it caught two mistakes in the translation of the ifle opcode. Firstly, the refinement operation was checking for >= 0 while it should have checked for > 0. Secondly, the refinement incorrectly took two arguments (only one argument is provided; the other value is popped from the stack).
- ProB animation revealed an error in one of the preconditions.

After the refinement checker found no more errors, we switched to using B4Free [12] to formally prove the refinement. This process allowed us to catch a few more errors:

- We discovered an error in our definition of the top of the stack. Note that this error did not lead to an erroneous behaviour (and hence was not caught by the PROB trace refinement checker), only to the gluing invariant being false.
- We found a subtle error in the translation of **iconst**: the argument provided to a RISC operation was in the range 0..63 whereas the RISC machine expected -32..31.
- There was an error in **imul**, it was pulling off the second operand from the wrong side of the stack. This was not detected earlier, as we only have one type of operand for the stack and for all animation examples there were exactly two elements on the stack when **imul** was called.
- There was an error in the abstract version of **ifle**, where again the bottom element rather than the top element was checked and removed. During animation this was not detected, as the stack was always of size 1 at the point **ifle** was executed.

After correcting the above errors, we have started interactively proving the refinement. We have fully proven the translation for all opcodes (overall all 58 proof obligations were discharged, of which 28 interactively).

The proof effort was sometimes relatively laborious, mainly because the prover had trouble dealing with operations upon the stack (modelled as a sequence). After proving lemmas about the stack (such as size(Stack)>0 => last(Stack) = Stack(size(Stack))), proof became easier and the last proof obligations were discharged in about 10 minutes each. If we wish to scale up our approach to a larger subset of Java bytecode and more detailed models of the hardware, it is likely that the development of a lot of custom proof rules will be required to keep the proof effort under control.

In summary, the combination of animation, refinement checking and proof was extremely useful to uncover problems with our compiler model. Some problems are easier to uncover using animation, while for other aspects proof was better.

8   Compiling Control Flow

In the above we have developed and proven correct the compilation of the data-manipulation aspects of Java bytecode. We now turn our attention to the control flow. First, we have extended the RISC Machine to include its own program counter and to include branching instructions. All instructions always advance the program counter RPC of the RISC machine by one, except for the branching instructions:

```
BLEZ(r,Lbl) = PRE r:1..NrReg & Lbl:NATURAL THEN
  IF R(r)<=0 THEN RPC := Lbl ELSE  RPC := RPC+1 END
END
```

Note that we now need an additional gluing invariant linking the Java bytecode program counter PC to the RISC program counter RPC. For this we have defined the constant function `patsize` defines for each opcode the size of the RISC translation as well as the constant function `loc`, which gives for every Java bytecode instruction the corresponding location in the RISC machine:

```
CONSTANTS patsize,loc
PROPERTIES
  patsize = { istore|->2, iconst|->2, iload|->2, imul|->4,
              iadd|->4, iinc |->4, ifle|->2, nop|->1,
              goto|->2, return |->1, pop |-> 1} &
  patsize: Opcodes --> NATURAL &
  MAXRBYTE = MAXBYTE &
  loc: 1..PSIZE >-> NATURAL &  /* location of Java PC in RISC RPC */
  loc(1) = 0 &
  !x.(x:2..PSIZE => loc(x) = loc(x-1)+patsize(PrgOpcode(x-1)))
```

In the invariant, we can now write `loc(PC) = RPC` to establish the link between the abstract and refined program counters. Note that the constant `loc` could be computed by a subsidiary B development or by a subsidiary program. In the latter case, one could use the B properties to validate the output of the subsidiary program. Below, we have simply used PROB to compute the solution for `loc` for us.

In the next step we have performed animation and refinement checking with PROB, which again found two interesting errors. One error was found in the translation of **ifle**, where the branch was going the wrong way. Another was that RISC instructions in the middle of a translation pattern were accessing the wrong stack layout information. No interactive proof has been attempted so far, but the automatic prover of B4Free has proven 57 of 91 proof obligations.

Note that we have not constructed an *explicit* represenation of the compiled program, but it is possible to do so (e.g., using our PROB validation tool).

Optimisations

So far we have basically looked at a non-optimising compiler: apart from getting rid of stack management, we have not tried to optimise the generated machine code and have tried to keep the compiler as simple as possible, in the hope of proving it correct.

Indeed, introducing compiler optimisations poses further challenges for correctness. There is, however, one kind of optimisation that can be introduced with reasonable effort into our approach. The idea is to provide optimised translations for certain combinations of Java bytecodes. For this, we would need to specify these combinations of opcodes in our abstract model JavaBC0, and then refine these combinations differently. E.g., one could specify the recurring pattern of an iload followed by an istore as follows:

```
ex_iload_istore(CA1,SA1) = PRE PrgOpcode(PC)=iload & CA1=PrgArg1(PC) &
        PrgOpcode(PC+1) = istore & SA1=PrgArg1(PC+1) THEN
      PC := PC+2  || Vars(SA1) := Vars(CA1)
    END;
```

Now, in case there is no jump to the istore opcode location, we can use shorter translation for this combination: LDM(1, CA1) ; STM(1,SA1).

9   Related Work: Overview of Alternative Approaches

Considerable research has been done in the area of verified compilers, starting from the work of McCarthy [26]. Most efforts directed at proving compiler correctness fall into three categories:

Proof. Those that treat the compiler as just another program and use standard verification techniques to manually or semi-automatically establish its correctness (e.g., [14,15,16]). Even with semi-automation this is a very labour intensive and expensive undertaking, which has to be repeated for every new language, or if the compiler is changed.

Nonetheless, Xavier Leroy and his group are very active developing formally certified compilers using Coq, see, e.g., [39,24,31] as well as the Compcert compiler (http://gallium.inria.fr/~xleroy/compcert/). In [23] Leroy reports on a formally certified compiler from Cminor to PowerPC assembly code.

Program Transformation. Those that use program transformation systems to transform source code into target code [22,28]. The disadvantage in this approach is that specifying the compiler operationally can be quite a lengthy process. Also, the compilation time can be quite large.

Validating Compilers. Recently, Pnueli et al have taken the approach of verifying a given run of the compiler rather than a compiler itself [1]. This removes the burden of maintaining the compiler's correctness proof; instead each run is proved correct by establishing a refinement relationship. However, this approach is limited to very simple languages. As the authors themselves mention, their approach "seems to work in all cases that the source and target programs each consist of a repeated execution of a single loop body ."

Automatic Compiler Generation. Those that *generate* the compiler automatically from the mathematical semantics of the language. Typically the semantics used is denotational (see for example Chapter 10 of [32]). The so automatically generated compilers, however, have not been used in practice due to their slowness and/or inefficiency/poor quality of the code generated. In more recent work [40] we have presented a compilation approach based on formal semantics, Horn logic, and *partial evaluation* for obtaining provably correct compiled code. We showed that not only the syntax specification, but also the semantic specification can be coded in the DCG notation.

More precisely, we adapted our interpreter in such a way that it calls a lower-level layer, which itself is implemented in terms of Prolog predicates, mimicking the RISC's instruction set. On the one hand, this experiment was successful; the compiler was very fast and the stack layout analysis was actually performed automatically by the partial evaluator. On the other hand, the correctness of the approach relies on the correctness of the partial evaluator and of the interpreter. The latter is probably the most problematic, because in order for partial evaluation to be effective the interpreter had to be rewritten in a certain style. This actually means that the compilation is actually not fully done by partial evaluation, part of the compilation is hidden in the way the interpreter is written. We believe that for a more realistic subset of Java bytecode and more realistic processor, a substantial part of the compilation process will be encoded in the way the interpreter is written. Hence, it is not obvious that the automatic code generation provided by the partial evaluator will be a big benefit.

10   Conclusion

We have examined the existing DECCo system for compiling PASP to a RISC processor, based on a Z formalisation of the compiler then manually transcribed into Prolog. The goal was to investigate whether the system or approach could be adapted for a compiler from Java bytecode to a RISC processor, with the aim of making the compiler more widely applicable. In the investigation we have uncovered several issues with the DECCo implementation, and have argued that the DECCo approach should be strengthened for a new high assurance compiler, by more rigorously transcribing the compiler specification into code. This can be achieved for instance by using the B-method instead of Z.

We have then conducted a case study, whereby we developed a compiler for a small subset of Java bytecode to an idealised RISC processor using the B-method. All in all, the outcome of this case study is very positive. We have shown that refinement is a natural way to model compilation and that the B-method can in principle be used to develop a demonstrably correct compiler. In particular, the tool support for B turned out to be extremely valuable: animation, automated refinement checking, and proof each uncovered a series of errors. Of course, considerable effort and further research will be required to tackle a translation of a larger subset of Java bytecode to a realistic processsor with carry bits, overflows and a much larger instruction set.

In summary, compared to the DECCo approach based on Z schemas manually translated to Prolog, the B approach provides following benefits:

– animation and model checking tools to validate the semantic specifications of the Java bytecode and the target processor,

- proof support for proving properties of the abstract models, and proving that the compiled code is a refinement of the Java bytecode semantics,
- potential test-case generation from the abstract model,
- execution of the compiler either via code generation using a B code generator or even using PROB animation, obliviating the need for hand-translation of Z schemas and hand-writing infrastructure predicates for the Z operators. One can also use subsidiary programs written in arbitrary programming languages (e.g, Haskell or Prolog), and then validate the output using B.

The drawbacks are that:

- the model will have to be written with automated proof in mind (such as the way we had to replace one function representing the bytecode by three functions),
- the additional effort for mechanical proof; mechanical proof will probably be more labour intensive than paper and pencil proofs in DECCO, but also provides a much higher assurance of correctness.

Given that our starting point (Java bytecode) is already at a relatively low-level, and given that we are not aiming to produce an optimizing compiler, the goal of achieving demonstrably correct compilation of a subset of Java bytecode to a RISC processor seems achievable in the near to mid-term future.

Acknowledgements. We would like to thank Colin Marsh, Neil Evans, and Alun Lewis for extremely useful information and feedback and for supporting this research project. We are grateful to Stefan Hallerstede, Susan Stepney, anonymous referees and the FMCO participants for their feedback. My thanks also go to Marc Fontaine, Ivaylo Dobrikov as well as Jens Bendisposto. This paper is dedicated to the memory of Martha Stemmer.

References

1. Pnueli, E.S.A., Siegel, M.: Translation validation. In: Steffen, B. (ed.) TACAS 1998. LNCS, vol. 1384, p. 151. Springer, Heidelberg (1998)
2. Abrial, J.-R.: The B-Book. Cambridge University Press, Cambridge (1996)
3. Abrial, J.-R., Schuman, S.A., Meyer, B.: Specification language. In: McKeag, R.M., Macnaghten, A.M. (eds.) On the Construction of Programs: An Advanced Course, pp. 343–410. Cambridge University Press, Cambridge (1980)
4. Aho, A.V., Lam, M.S., Sethi, R., Ullman, J.D.: Compilers. Principles, Techniques, and Tools, 2nd edn. Addison-Wesley, Reading (2007)
5. Albert, E., Arenas, P., Genaim, S., Puebla, G., Zanardini, D.: Cost analysis of java bytecode. In: De Nicola, R. (ed.) ESOP 2007. LNCS, vol. 4421, pp. 157–172. Springer, Heidelberg (2007)
6. Albert, E., Genaim, S., Gómez-Zamalloa, M.: Heap space analysis for java bytecode. In: Morrisett, G., Sagiv, M. (eds.) ISMM, pp. 105–116. ACM Press, New York (2007)
7. Albert, E., Gómez-Zamalloa, M., Hubert, L., Puebla, G.: Verification of java bytecode using analysis and transformation of logic programs. In: Hanus, M. (ed.) PADL 2007. LNCS, vol. 4354, pp. 124–139. Springer, Heidelberg (2006)

8. Apt, K.R., Marchiori, E.: Reasoning about Prolog programs: from modes through types to assertions. Formal Aspects of Computing 6(6A), 743–765 (1994)
9. Börger, E.: Abstract State Machines. Springer, Heidelberg (2003)
10. Bowen, J.P.: Formal Specification and Documentation using Z. International Thomson Computer Press (1996)
11. Buckley, A.: Jsr-000202 JavaTM class file specification update evaluation 1.0 final release. Technical report (December 2006),
    http://jcp.org/en/jsr/detail?id=202
12. ClearSy, Aix-en-Provence, France. B4Free: Tool and Manuals (2006),
    http://www.b4free.com
13. Cousot, P., Cousot, R.: Abstract interpretation: A unified lattice model for static analysis of programs by construction of approximation of fixed points. In: Proceedings of the 4th ACM Symposium on Principles of Programming Languages, Los Angeles, pp. 238–252. ACM Press, New York (1977)
14. Dold, A., Gaul, T., Vialard, V., Zimmermann, W.: Asm-based mechanized verification of compiler back-ends. In: Workshop on Abstract State Machines, pp. 50–67 (1998)
15. Dold, A., Vialard, V.: Formal verification of a compiler back-end generic checker program. In: Bjørner, D., Broy, M., Zamulin, A.V. (eds.) PSI 1999. LNCS, vol. 1755, pp. 470–480. Springer, Heidelberg (2000)
16. Dold, A., von Henke, F.W., Goerigk, W.: A completely verified realistic bootstrap compiler. Int. J. Found. Comput. Sci. 14(4), 659 (2003)
17. Eichberg, M., Kahl, M., Saha, D., Mezini, M., Ostermann, K.: Automatic incrementalization of prolog based static analyses. In: Hanus, M. (ed.) PADL 2007. LNCS, vol. 4354, pp. 109–123. Springer, Heidelberg (2006)
18. Evans, N., Ifill, W.: Hardware verification and beyond: Using B at AWE. In: Julliand, J., Kouchnarenko, O. (eds.) B 2007. LNCS, vol. 4355, pp. 260–261. Springer, Heidelberg (2006)
19. Gómez-Zamalloa, M., Albert, E., Puebla, G.: Improving the decompilation of java bytecode to prolog by partial evaluation. Electr. Notes Theor. Comput. Sci. 190(1), 85–101 (2007)
20. Klein, G., Nipkow, T.: A machine-checked model for a Java-like language, virtual machine and compiler. ACM Trans. Prog. Lang. Syst. 28(4), 619–695 (2006)
21. Klose, K., Ostermann, K., Leuschel, M.: Partial evaluation of pointcuts. In: Hanus, M. (ed.) PADL 2007. LNCS, vol. 4354, pp. 320–334. Springer, Heidelberg (2006)
22. Leonard, E.I., Heitmeyer, C.L.: Program synthesis from formal requirements specifications using apts. Higher-Order and Symbolic Computation 16(1-2), 63–92 (2003)
23. Leroy, X.: Formal certification of a compiler back-end, or: programming a compiler with a proof assistant. In: 33rd symposium Principles of Programming Languages, pp. 42–54. ACM Press, New York (2006)
24. Leroy, X., Blazy, S.: Formal verification of a C-like memory model and its uses for verifying program transformations. Journal of Automated Reasoning 41(1), 1–31 (2008)
25. Leuschel, M.: Towards demonstrably correct compilation of java byte code. Technical report, Institut für Informaitk, Universität Düsseldorf (2009),
    http://www.stups.uni-duesseldorf.de/~leuschel/publication.php
26. McCarthy, J., Painter, J.: Correctness of a compiler for arithmetic expressions. Technical report, MIT AI Lab Memo (1967)

27. Nettleton, C., Ifill, W., Marsh, C.: Towards a demonstrably-correct Ada compiler. In: Srivastava, A., Baird III, L.C. (eds.) SIGAda, pp. 89–96. ACM, New York (2007)

28. Paige, R.: Viewing a program transformation system at work. In: Rodríguez-Artalejo, M., Levi, G. (eds.) ALP 1994. LNCS, vol. 850, p. 5. Springer, Heidelberg (1994)

29. Pichardie, D.: Bicolano – Byte Code Language in Coq. Summary appears in Mobius Deliverable 3.1 (2006), http://mobius.inria.fr/bicolano

30. Plagge, D., Leuschel, M.: Validating Z Specifications using the ProB Animator and Model Checker. In: Davies, J., Gibbons, J. (eds.) IFM 2007. LNCS, vol. 4591, pp. 480–500. Springer, Heidelberg (2007)

31. Rideau, L., Serpette, B.P., Leroy, X.: Tilting at windmills with Coq: formal verification of a compilation algorithm for parallel moves. Journal of Automated Reasoning 40(4), 307–326 (2008)

32. Schmidt, D.: Denotational Semantics: a Methodology for Language Development. W.C. Brown Publishers (1986)

33. Smaus, J.-G., Hill, P.M., King, A.: Mode analysis domains for typed logic programs. In: Bossi, A. (ed.) LOPSTR 1999. LNCS, vol. 1817, pp. 82–101. Springer, Heidelberg (2000)

34. Smith, J., Nair, R.: Virtual Machines: Versatile Platforms for Systems and Processes. Morgan Kaufmann, San Francisco (2005)

35. Sorensen, I.: A mathematical AMN state based description of the ASP. Technical report, AWE (1998)

36. Spivey, J.M.: The Z Notation: A Reference Manual, 2nd edn. Prentice Hall International Series in Computer Science (1992)

37. Stärk, R.F., Schmid, J., Börger, E.: Java and the Java Virtual Machine. Springer, Heidelberg (2001)

38. Stepney, S., Nabney, I.T.: The DeCCo project papers I-VI. Technical Report YCS-2002-358 – YCS-2002-363, Department of Computer Science, University of York (June 2003)

39. Tristan, J.-B., Leroy, X.: Formal verification of translation validators: A case study on instruction scheduling optimizations. In: 35th symposium Principles of Programming Languages, pp. 17–27. ACM Press, New York (2008)

40. Wang, Q., Gupta, G., Leuschel, M.: Towards provably correct code generation via horn logical continuation semantics. In: Hermenegildo, M.V., Cabeza, D. (eds.) PADL 2004. LNCS, vol. 3350, pp. 98–112. Springer, Heidelberg (2005)

Incremental System Modelling in Event-B*

Stefan Hallerstede

University of Düsseldorf
Germany
`halstefa@cs.uni-duesseldorf.de`

Abstract. A reasonable approach to formal modelling is to start with a specification that captures the requirements of a system and then use formal refinement to implement it.

The problem with this approach is that for complex systems the specification itself is complex. It becomes a challenge to say whether the specification is the right one for the given requirements. Sometimes requirements also concern features of a system closely related to its implementation. This would make an abstract specification necessarily incomplete.

We believe that it is better not to follow the rigid approach to modelling described above. Instead, we argue that the specification itself should be elaborated by refinement. Ultimately, the distinction between specification and implementation is no longer made in the strict sense above. There is only one model of the system that is connected by successive refinements. Using Event-B, we demonstrate how this can be applied to cope with the complexity of specifications. On the one hand we benefit from the reduced number of detail to consider at different times. On the other hand we are encouraged to reason about the formal model since the beginning and to rethink it occasionally to capture better its intended behaviour and match the requirements.

1 Introduction

When we create a complex model, usually, our understanding of it is incomplete at first; and a modelling method should help to improve our understanding of the model. During initial phases in the modelling process, we use refinement to manage the many details of a complex model. Refinement is seen as a technique to introduce detail gradually at a rate that eases understanding. We do not assume that we have one most abstract model, the specification, that could serve as point of reference for all further refinements. Instead, the model is completed by refinement until we are satisfied that the model captures all important requirements and assumptions. In this article we concern ourselves only with what is involved in coming up with an abstract model of some system. Refinement can also be used to produce implementations of abstract models, for instance, in terms of a sequential program [1,16]. But this is not discussed in this article.

---

* This research was carried out as part of the EU research project DEPLOY (Industrial deployment of system engineering methods providing high dependability and productivity) http://www.deploy-project.eu/

F.S. de Boer et al. (Eds.): FMCO 2008, LNCS 5751, pp. 139–158, 2009.

Event-B [2] is a formal modelling method for discrete systems based on refinement [4,5,6]. Event-B and its predecessor, the B Method, have been used in large scale industrial projects [7,8,19]. In Event-B formal modelling serves primarily for reasoning: reasoning is an essential part of modelling because it is the key to understanding complex models. Reasoning about complex models should not happen accidentally but needs systematic support within the modelling method. This thinking lies at the heart of the Event-B method. It gives a prominent rôle to proof obligations. Proof obligations serve to reason about a model and to provide meaning [11].

We briefly contrast the incremental refinement-based modelling approach to two well-known approaches, TLA+ [14] and ASM [9]. In TLA+ modelling begins with a *specification*, in ASM with a *ground model*. In both methods there are guidelines on how to begin. This is a difficult and serious problem as an inadequate model may not provide the kinds of insight we seek or may be plainly wrong (as a starting point for an implementation). Among the hints on how to begin we find: (1) choose the appropriate abstraction level; (2) be as abstract as possible yet complete; (3) be simple and concise. This article addresses (1) and (2) by effectively avoiding the precise choice of an initial abstraction level. We begin with some simple abstract model and introduce detail gradually. Guideline (3) remains, being the key to comprehensibility.

We understand incremental modelling in two ways. The first way is by formal refinement. An existing model is proved to be refined by another: all properties of the existing model are preserved in the refined model. The second way is by alteration of an existing model: properties of the existing model may be broken. When a model is shown to be not consistent, it needs to be modified in order to make it consistent. This reflects a learning process supported by various forms of reasoning about a model, for instance, proof, animation, or model-checking. This way of thinking about a model is common in mathematical methodology [13,17,18]. The first way is commonly used in formal methods, whereas the second is at least not acknowledged. We believe both ways are crucial for formal modelling.

The incremental approach is only feasible in the presence of software tools that make reasoning easy and modifications to a model painless. We have relied on the Rodin modelling tool [3] for Event-B for proof obligation generation and proof support and on the ProB tool [15] for animation and model-checking. Both tools are integrated in the Rodin platform and can be used seamlessly. In later sections we do not further specify the tools used, though, as this should be clear from the context. Also note that we present proof in an equational style [10,20] whereas the Rodin tool uses sequents as in [2].

Overview. In Section 2 we introduce Event-B. The following sections are devoted to solving a concrete problem in Event-B. In Section 3 the problem is stated. A first model is produced and discussed in Section 4. In Sections 5 and 7 we elaborate the model by refinement. Section 6 contains a small theory of transitive closures that is needed in the refinement. In Section 8 some further improvements of the model are made and limitations of formal modelling discussed.

2   Event-B

Event-B models are described in terms of the two basic constructs: *contexts* and *machines*. Contexts contain the static part of a model whereas machines contain the dynamic part. Contexts may contain *carrier sets*, *constants*, *axioms*, where carrier sets are similar to types [4]. In this article, we simply assume that there is some context and do not mention it explicitly. Machines are presented in Section 2.1, and proof obligations in Section 2.2 and Section 2.3. All proof obligations in this article are presented in the form of sequents: "premises" ⊢ "conclusion".

For the purpose of this article, we have reduced the Event-B notation used so that only a little notation suffices and formulas are easier to comprehend, in particular, concerning the relationship between formal model and proof obligations. We have also reduced the amount of proof obligations associated with a model. We have done this for two reasons: firstly, it is easier to keep track of what is to be proved; secondly, it permits us to make a point about a limitation of formal methods later on.

2.1 Machines

Machines provide behavioural properties of Event-B models. Machines may contain *variables, invariants, theorems, events*, and *variants*. Variables $v = v_1, \ldots, v_m$ define the state of a machine. They are constrained by invariants $I(v)$. Theorems are predicates that are implied by the invariants. Possible state changes are described by means of events $E(v)$. Each event is composed of a *guard* $G(t, v)$ and an *action* $x := S(t, v)$, where $t = t_1, \ldots, t_r$ are *parameters* the event may contain and $x = x_1, \ldots, x_p$ are the (distinct) variables it may change[1]. The guard states the necessary condition under which an event may occur, and the action describes how the state variables evolve when the event occurs. We denote an event $E(v)$ by

$$
E(v) \;\widehat=\; \begin{array}{l} \text{any} \quad t \quad \text{when} \\ \qquad G(t, v) \\ \text{then} \\ \qquad x := S(t, v) \\ \text{end} \end{array}
\qquad \text{or} \qquad
E(v) \;\widehat=\; \begin{array}{l} \text{begin} \\ \qquad x := S(v) \\ \text{end} \end{array}
$$

The short form on the right hand side is used if the event does not have parameters and the guard is true. A dedicated event of the latter form is used for *initialisation*. All assignments of an action $x := S(t, v)$ occur simultaneously; variables y that do not appear on the left-hand side of an assignment of an action are not changed by the action, yielding one simultaneous assignment

$$
x_1, \ldots, x_p, y_1, \ldots, y_q := S_1(t, v), \ldots, S_p(t, v), y_1, \ldots, y_q \quad , \tag{1}
$$

where $x_1, \ldots, x_p, y_1, \ldots, y_q$ are the variables v of the machine. The action $x := S(t, v)$ of event $E(v)$ denotes the formula (1), whereas in the proper model we only specify those variables x_ℓ that may change.

2.2 Machine Consistency

Invariants are supposed to hold whenever variable values change. Obviously, this does not hold a priori for any combination of events and invariants $I(v) = I_1(v) \wedge \ldots \wedge I_i(v)$

---

[1] Note that, as x is a list of variables, $S(t, v) = S_1(t, v), \ldots, S_p(t, v)$ is a corresponding list of expressions.

and, thus, needs to be proved. The corresponding proof obligations are called *invariant preservation* ($\ell \in 1 .. i$):

$$
\begin{array}{l}
I(v) \\
G(t,v) \\
\vdash \\
\quad I_\ell\left(S(t,v)\right) \quad ,
\end{array}
\tag{2}
$$

for every event $E(v)$. Similar proof obligations are associated with the initialisation event of a machine. The only difference is that neither an invariant nor a guard appears in the premises of proof obligation (2), that is, the only premises are axioms and theorems of the context. We say that a machine is consistent if all events preserve all invariants.

2.3   Machine Refinement

Machine refinement provides a means to introduce more details about the dynamic properties of a model [4]. The refinement theory of Event-B originates in the Action System formalism [6]. We present some important proof obligations for machine refinement that are used in this article.

A machine N can refine at most one other machine M. We call M the *abstract* machine and N a *concrete* machine. The state of the abstract machine is related to the state of the concrete machine by a *gluing invariant* $J(v,w) = J_1(v,w) \wedge \ldots \wedge J_j(v,w)$, where $v = v_1, \ldots, v_m$ are the variables of the abstract machine and $w = w_1, \ldots, w_n$ the variables of the concrete machine.

Each event $E(v)$ of the abstract machine is *refined* by a concrete event $F(w)$. Let abstract event $E(v)$ with parameters $t = t_1, \ldots, t_r$ and concrete event $F(w)$ with parameters $u = u_1, \ldots, u_s$ be

$$
\begin{array}{llll}
E(v) & \widehat{=} & \text{any } t \text{ when} \\
& & \quad G(t,v) \\
& & \text{then} \\
& & \quad v := S(t,v) \\
& & \text{end}
\end{array}
\qquad \text{and} \qquad
\begin{array}{ll}
F(w) & \widehat{=} & \text{any } u \text{ when} \\
& & \quad H(u,w) \\
& & \text{with} \\
& & \quad t = W(u) \\
& & \text{then} \\
& & \quad w := T(u,w) \\
& & \text{end}
\end{array}
$$

Informally, concrete event $F(w)$ refines abstract event $E(v)$ if the guard of $F(w)$ is stronger than the guard of $E(v)$, and the gluing invariant $J(v,w)$ establishes a simulation of the action of $F(w)$ by the action of $E(v)$. The corresponding proof obligations are called *guard strengthening* ($\ell \in 1 .. g$):

$$
\begin{array}{l}
I(v) \\
J(v,w) \\
H(u,w) \\
\vdash \\
\quad G_\ell\left(W(u),v\right) \quad ,
\end{array}
\tag{3}
$$

with the abstract guard $G(t,v) = G_1(t,v) \wedge \ldots \wedge G_g(t,v)$, and (again) *invariant preservation* ($\ell \in 1 .. j$):

$$I(v)$$
$$J(v, w)$$
$$H(u, w)$$
$$\vdash$$
$$J_\ell\left(S(W(u), v), T(u, w)\right) \quad . \tag{4}$$

The term $W(u)$ denotes *witnesses* for the abstract parameters t, specified by the equation $t = W(u)$ in event $F(w)$, linking abstract parameters to concrete parameters. It describes how $F(w)$ refines $E(v)$ just as the gluing invariant describes how concrete machine N refines abstract machine M^2.

(The variable lists v and w do not need to be disjoint. If a variable name gets reused in a refined machine, equality between the abstract and the concrete variable is postulated implicitly, corresponding to a gluing invariant "$v_{abs} = v_{con}$". Similarly, equality for common parameters of abstract and concrete events is postulated with a witness "$t_{abs} = t_{con}$".)

3   Problem Statement

In the following sections we develop a simple model of a secure building equipped with access control. The problem statement is inspired by a similar problem used by Abrial [2]. Instead of presenting a fully developed model, we illustrate the process of how we arrive at the model. We can not follow the exact path that we took when working on the model: we made changes to the model as a whole several times. So we would soon run out of space. We comment on some of the changes without going too much into detail in the hope to convey some of the dynamic character of the modelling process.

The model to be developed is to satisfy the following properties:

P1 : The system consists of persons and one building.
P2 : The building consists of rooms and doors.
P3 : Each person can be at most in one room.
P4 : Each person is authorised to be in certain rooms (but not others).
P5 : Each person is authorised to use certain doors (but not others).
P6 : Each person can only be in a room where the person is authorised to be.
P7 : Each person must be able to leave the building from any room where the person is authorised to be.
P8 : Each person can pass from one room to another if there is a door connecting the two rooms and the person has the proper authorisation.
P9 : Authorisations can be granted and revoked.

Properties P1, P2, P8, and P9 describe environment assumptions whereas properties P3, P4, P5, P6, and P7 describe genuine requirements. It is natural to mix them in the description of the system. Once we start modelling, the distinction becomes important. We have to prove that our model satisfies P3, P4, P5, P6, and P7 assuming we have P1, P2, P8, and P9.

---

[2] In full Event-B, instead of an equation $t = W(u)$ a witness can be any predicate. It can also have more free variables than just the abstract parameters u.

4   Getting Started with a Fresh Model

Our aim is to produce a faithful formal model of the system described by the properties P1 to P9 of Section 3. The first decision we need to make concerns the use of refinement. We have decided to introduce the properties of the system in two steps. In the first step we deal only with persons and rooms, in the second also with doors. This approach appears reasonable. At first we let persons move directly between rooms. Later we state how they do it, that is, by passing through doors. In order to specify doors we need to know about rooms they connect. It is a good idea, though, to reconsider the strategy chosen for refinement when it turns out to be difficult to tackle the elements of the model in the planned order. For now, we intend to produce a model with one refinement:

(i) the *abstract machine* (this section) models room authorisations;
(ii) the *concrete machine* (sections 5 and 7) models room and door authorisations.

In Event-B we usually begin modelling by stating invariants that a machine should preserve. (For an alternative approach see, for instance, [12].) When events are introduced subsequently, we think more about how they preserve invariants than about what they would do. The focus is on the properties that have to be satisfied. We declare two carrier sets for persons and rooms, $Person$ and $Room$, and a constant O, where $O \in Room$, modelling the outside. We choose to describe the state by two variables for authorised rooms and locations of persons, arm and loc, with invariants

$inv1 \; : \; arm \in Person \leftrightarrow Room^3$ $\qquad\qquad$ Property P4

$inv2 \; : \; Person \times \{O\} \subseteq arm$

$inv3 \; : \; loc \in Person \to Room$ $\qquad\qquad$ Property P3

$inv4 \; : \; loc \subseteq arm$ $\qquad\qquad\qquad$ Property P6

Invariant $inv2$, that *each person is authorised to be outside*, is necessary because we decided to model location by a total function making the outside a special room. In a first attempt, we made loc a partial function from $Person$ to $Room$ expressing that a person not in the domain of loc is outside. However, this turned out to complicate the gluing invariant when introducing doors into the model later on. (Because of property P7 we need an explicit representation of the outside in the model.) As a consequence of our decision we had to introduce invariant $inv2$. It corresponds to a new requirement that is missing from the list in Section 3 but that we have uncovered while reasoning formally about the system. In the following we focus on how formal reasoning is used to improve the model of the system.

In order to satisfy $inv2$, $inv3$ and $inv4$ we let

```
initialisation
   begin
      act1 : arm := Person × {O}
      act2 : loc := Person × {O}
   end
```

---

[3] The term $A \leftrightarrow B$ denotes the set of relations from A to B.

We model passage from one room to another by event *pass*,

> *pass*
>   any p, r when
> $grd1 : p \mapsto r \in arm$ p is authorised to be in r
> $grd2 : p \mapsto r \notin loc$ but not already in r
>   then
> $act1 : loc := loc \domres\!\!\!\!- \{p \mapsto r\}$
>   end

(For relations a and b relational overwriting $\domres\!\!\!\!-$ is defined by $a \domres\!\!\!\!- b = \mathrm{dom}(b) \domsub a \cup b$, and, for a set s, domain subtraction $\domsub$ by $x \mapsto y \in s \domsub a \Leftrightarrow x \notin s \wedge x \mapsto y \in a$.)
Event *pass* preserves the invariants. For instance, it preserves $inv4$:

$$
\frac{
\begin{array}{ll}
loc \subseteq arm & \textit{Invariant } inv4 \\
p \mapsto r \in arm & \textit{Guard } grd1 \\
p \mapsto r \notin loc & \textit{Guard } grd2
\end{array}
}{
\begin{array}{ll}
loc \domres\!\!\!\!- \{p \mapsto r\} \subseteq arm & \textit{Modified invariant } inv4
\end{array}
}
$$

We prove,

$$
\begin{array}{lll}
& loc \domres\!\!\!\!- \{p \mapsto r\} & \{\text{ def. of } \domres\!\!\!\!- \} \\
= & \{p\} \domsub loc \cup \{p \mapsto r\} & \{ \{p\} \domsub loc \subseteq loc \} \\
\subseteq & loc \cup \{p \mapsto r\} & \{ inv4 \text{ and } grd1 \} \\
\subseteq & arm \quad .
\end{array}
$$

Granting and revoking authorisations for rooms is modelled by the two events

> *grant*
>   any p, r when
> $grd1 : p \in Person$
> $grd2 : r \in Room$
>   then
> $act1 : arm := arm \cup \{p \mapsto r\}$
>   end

> *revoke*
>   any p, r when
> $grd1 : p \in Person$
> $grd2 : p \mapsto r \notin loc$
>   then
> $act1 : arm := arm \setminus \{p \mapsto r\}$
>   end

The two events do not yet model all of P9 which refers to authorisations in general, including authorisations for doors. Events *grant* and *revoke* appear easy enough to get them right. But it is as easy to make a mistake. This is why we have specified invariants: to safeguard us against mistakes. If the proof of an invariant fails, we have the opportunity to learn something about the model and improve it. The two events preserve all invariants except for *revoke* which violates invariant $inv2$,

$$
\frac{
\begin{array}{ll}
Person \times \{O\} \subseteq arm & \textit{Invariant } inv2 \\
p \in Person & \textit{Guard } grd1 \\
p \mapsto r \notin loc & \textit{Guard } grd2
\end{array}
}{
\begin{array}{ll}
Person \times \{O\} \subseteq arm \setminus \{p \mapsto r\} & \textit{Modified invariant } inv2
\end{array}
}
$$

In an instance of the model with two different rooms I and O and one person P we find a counter example:

$$arm \ = \ \{P \mapsto I, P \mapsto O\}, \quad loc \ = \ \{P \mapsto I\}, \quad p = P, \quad r = O \ .$$

In fact, we must not remove O from the set of authorised rooms of any person. To achieve this, we add a third guard to event *revoke*:

$$grd3 \ : \ r \neq O \ .$$

A counter example provides valuable information, pointing to a condition that it does not satisfy. It may not always be as simple to generalise but at least one can obtain an indication where to look closer.

The model we have obtained thus far is easy to understand. Ignoring the doors in the building, it is quite simple but already incorporates properties P3, P4, and P6. Its simplicity permits us to judge more readily whether the model is reasonable. We can inspect it or animate it and can expect to get a fairly complete picture of its behaviour. Way may ask: Is it possible to achieve a state where some person can move around in the building? We have only partially modelled the assumptions P1, P2, P8, and P9. We could split them into smaller statements that would be fully modelled but have decided not to do so. Instead, we are going to document how they are incorporated in the refinement that is to follow.

5   Elaboration of More Details

We are satisfied with the abstract model of the secure building for now and turn to the refinement where doors are introduced into the model. In the refined model we employ two variables adr for authorised doors and loc for the locations of persons in the building (as before). The intention is to keep the information contained in the abstract variable arm implicitly in the concrete variable adr. That is, in the refined model variable arm would be redundant. We specify

$$inv5 \ : \ adr \in Person \ \to \ (Room \leftrightarrow Room) \qquad \text{Property P5}$$
$$inv6 \ : \ \forall q \cdot \mathsf{ran}(adr(q)) \ \subseteq \ arm[\{q\}] \,^{4} \qquad\qquad \text{Property P4}$$

5.1   Moving between Rooms

Let us first look at event *pass*. Only a few changes are necessary to model property P8,

> *pass*
> any p, r when
> $grd1 \ : \ loc(p) \mapsto r \in adr(p)$
> then
> $act1 \ : \ loc := loc \mathbin{\vartriangleleft\mkern-9mu-} \{p \mapsto r\}$
> end

---

[4] The term $R[A]$ denotes the relational image of the set A under the realtion R, that is, $R[A] = \{y \mid \exists x \cdot x \in A \wedge x \mapsto y \in R\}$.

We only have to show guard strengthening, because loc does not occur in $inv5$ and $inv6$. For the abstract guard $grd1$ we have to show:

$$\vdash \begin{array}{l} \forall q \cdot \text{ran}(adr(q)) \subseteq arm[\{q\}] \\ loc(p) \mapsto r \in adr(p) \\ \hline p \mapsto r \in arm \end{array} \qquad \begin{array}{l} \textit{Invariant inv6} \\ \textit{Concrete guard grd1} \\ \textit{Abstract guard grd1} \end{array}$$

which holds because $r \in \text{ran}(adr(p))$. The second guard strengthening proof obligation of event $pass$ is:

$$\vdash \begin{array}{l} loc \in Person \to Room \\ loc(p) \mapsto r \in adr(p) \\ \hline p \mapsto r \notin loc \end{array} \qquad \begin{array}{l} \textit{Invariant inv3} \\ \textit{Concrete guard grd1} \\ \textit{Abstract guard grd2} \end{array}$$

Using $inv3$ we can rephrase the goal,

$$\begin{array}{ll} & p \mapsto r \notin loc & \{ inv3 \} \\ \Leftrightarrow & loc(p) \neq r \end{array}$$

Neither concrete guard $grd1$ nor the invariants $inv1$ to $inv6$ imply this. The invariant is too weak. We do not specify that doors connect *different* rooms. In fact, our model of the building is rather weak. We decide to model the building by the doors that connect the rooms in it. They are modelled by a constant $Door$. We make the following three assumptions about doors:

$$\begin{array}{lll} axm1 & : Door \in Room \leftrightarrow Room & \textit{Each door connects two rooms.} \\ axm2 & : Door \cap \text{id}_{Room} = \varnothing & \textit{No door connects a room to itself.} \\ axm3 & : Door \subseteq Door^{-1} & \textit{Each door can be used in both directions.} \end{array}$$

These assumptions are based on our domain knowledge about properties of typical doors. They were omitted from the problem description because they seemed obvious. However, the validity of our model will depend on them. As such they ought to be included. We began to think about properties of doors because we did not succeed proving a guard strengthening proof obligation. If axiom $axm2$ would hold for all relations $adr(p)$, for $p \in Person$, we should succeed. Hence, we add a new invariant $inv7$. We realise that it captures much better property P5 than invariant $inv5$,

$$inv7 \ : \ \forall q \cdot adr(q) \subseteq Door \ . \qquad \qquad \textit{Property P5}$$

We prove,

$$\begin{array}{lll} & x \mapsto y \in adr(p) & \{ inv7 \text{ with ``}q := p\text{''} \} \\ \Rightarrow & x \mapsto y \in Door & \{ axm2 \} \\ \Rightarrow & x \mapsto y \notin \text{id}_{Room} & \{ \text{def. of id}_{Room} \} \\ \Leftrightarrow & x \neq y \ , \end{array}$$

thus, $\forall x, y \cdot x \mapsto y \in adr(p) \Rightarrow x \neq y$, and with "$x, y := loc(p), r$" we are able to show:

$$
\begin{array}{ll}
Door \cap id_{Room} = \varnothing & \text{Axiom } axm2 \\
loc \in Person \rightarrow Room & \text{Invariant } inv3 \\
\forall q \cdot adr(q) \subseteq Door & \text{Invariant } inv7 \\
loc(p) \mapsto r \in adr(p) & \text{Concrete guard } grd1 \\
\hline
p \mapsto r \notin loc & \text{Abstract guard } grd2
\end{array}
$$

6   Intermezzo on Transitive Closures

Property P7 is more involved. It may be necessary to pass though various rooms in order to leave the building. We need to specify a property about the transitive relationship of the doors. We can rely on the well-known mathematical theory of the transitive closure of a relation.

A relation x is called *transitive* if $x\,;x \subseteq x$. In other words, any composition of elements of x is in x. The transitive closure of a relation x is the least relation that contains x and is transitive. We define the *transitive closure* x^+ of a relation x by

$$\forall x \cdot x \subseteq x^+ \tag{5}$$

$$\forall x \cdot x^+\,;x \subseteq x^+ \tag{6}$$

$$\forall x, z \cdot x \subseteq z \wedge z\,;x \subseteq z \Rightarrow x^+ \subseteq z \ . \tag{7}$$

That is, x^+ is the least relation z satisfying $x \cup z\,;x \subseteq z$. Furthermore, the order in which the transitive closure is formed does not matter,

$$\forall x \cdot x \cup x^+\,;x = x^+ \tag{8}$$

$$\forall x \cdot x \cup x\,;x^+ = x^+ \ . \tag{9}$$

The transitive closure is monotonic and maps identity and empty relation to themselves,

$$\forall x, y \cdot x \subseteq y \Rightarrow x^+ \subseteq y^+ \tag{10}$$

$$\forall w \cdot id_w^+ = id_w \tag{11}$$

$$\varnothing^+ = \varnothing \ . \tag{12}$$

A relation x is called *symmetric* if $x \subseteq x^{-1}$. For a symmetric relation we can prove more laws about its transitive closure: it is symmetric too and the identity is contained in it,

$$\forall x \cdot x \subseteq x^{-1} \Rightarrow (x^+)^{-1} \subseteq x^+ \tag{13}$$

$$\forall x \cdot x \subseteq x^{-1} \Rightarrow id_{dom(x)} \subseteq x^+ \ . \tag{14}$$

7   Towards a Full Model of the Building

Using the transitive closure of authorised rooms we can express that every person can at least reach the authorised rooms from the outside,

$$inv8 \; : \; \forall q \cdot arm[\{q\}] \subseteq adr(q)^+[\{\boldsymbol{O}\}] \quad .$$

This invariant is weaker than property P7. However, given the discussion about properties of doors in Section 5 we should be able to prove that all invariants jointly imply property P7 which we formalise as a theorem,

$$thm1 \; : \; \forall q \cdot (arm[\{q\}] \setminus \{\boldsymbol{O}\}) \times \{\boldsymbol{O}\} \subseteq adr(q)^+ \quad . \qquad \text{Property P7}$$

We proceed like this because we expect that proving $inv8$ to be preserved would be much easier than doing the same with $thm1$. Let us continue working with $inv8$ for now and return to $thm1$ later.

7.1   Initialisation

In the abstract model all persons can only be outside initially. This corresponds to them not being authorised to use any doors,

```
initialisation
  begin
    act1 : adr := Person × {∅}
    act2 : loc := Person × {O}
  end
```

The invariant preservation proof obligations for $inv5$ and $inv6$ hold, as can easily be seen letting "$arm, adr := Person \times \{\boldsymbol{O}\}, Person \times \{\varnothing\}$" in $inv5$, $inv6$, and $inv7$,

$$\vdash \quad Person \times \{\varnothing\} \in Person \rightarrow (Room \leftrightarrow Room)$$
$$\vdash \quad \forall q \cdot \mathrm{ran}((Person \times \{\varnothing\})(q)) \subseteq (Person \times \{\boldsymbol{O}\})[\{q\}]$$
$$\vdash \quad \forall q \cdot (Person \times \{\varnothing\})(q) \subseteq Door$$

For invariant $inv8$ there is more work to do. We have to show:

$$\vdash \quad \forall q \cdot (Person \times \{\boldsymbol{O}\})[\{q\}] \subseteq (Person \times \{\varnothing\})(q)^+[\{\boldsymbol{O}\}]$$

We prove,

	$(Person \times \{\varnothing\})(q)^+[\{\boldsymbol{O}\}]$	{ set theory }
$=$	$\varnothing^+[\{\boldsymbol{O}\}]$	{ law (12) }
$=$	$\varnothing[\{\boldsymbol{O}\}]$	{ set theory }
$=$	$\varnothing$	
$\not\supseteq$	$\{\boldsymbol{O}\}$	{ set theory }
$=$	$(Person \times \{\boldsymbol{O}\})[\{q\}]$	.

Invariant $inv8$ is too strong! Because of invariant $inv7$ we cannot initialise adr to $Person \times \{\{\boldsymbol{O} \mapsto \boldsymbol{O}\}\}$ and because of $inv6$ we cannot use any other door. Thus, we must weaken invariant $inv8$. We replace it by:

$$inv8' \; : \; \forall q \cdot arm[\{q\}] \subseteq adr(q)^{+}[\{\boldsymbol{O}\}] \cup \{\boldsymbol{O}\}$$

After analysing initialisation and event *pass* of the refined machine, the gluing invariants of the refined machine have become

$$inv5 \quad : \; adr \in Person \rightarrow (Room \leftrightarrow Room)$$
$$inv6 \quad : \; \forall q \cdot \mathsf{ran}(adr(q)) \subseteq arm[\{q\}]$$
$$inv7 \quad : \; \forall q \cdot adr(q) \subseteq Door$$
$$inv8' \quad : \; \forall q \cdot arm[\{q\}] \subseteq adr(q)^{+}[\{\boldsymbol{O}\}] \cup \{\boldsymbol{O}\} \quad .$$

7.2   Granting Door Authorisations

A new door authorisation can be granted to a person if (a) it has not been granted yet and (b) authorisation for one of the connected rooms has been granted to the person. We introduce constraint (a) to focus on the interesting case and constraint (b) to satisfy invariant *inv8'*. Thus,

> *grant*
> any   *p, s, r*   when
>   grd1 : $s \mapsto r \notin adr(p)$
>   grd2 : $s \in \mathsf{dom}(adr(p))$
> then
>   act1 : $adr := adr \mathbin{\lhd\mkern-9mu-} \{p \mapsto adr(p) \cup \{s \mapsto r, r \mapsto s\}\}$ [5]
> end

Invariant *inv5* is preserved by event *grant* by definition of relational overwriting $\mathbin{\lhd\mkern-9mu-}$. For invariant *inv6* we have to prove:

$\forall q \cdot \mathsf{ran}(adr(q)) \subseteq arm[\{q\}]$	Invariant *inv6*
$s \mapsto r \notin adr(p)$	Concrete guard *grd1*
$s \in \mathsf{dom}(adr(p))$	Concrete guard *grd2*

$$\vdash$$
$$\mathsf{ran}((adr \mathbin{\lhd\mkern-9mu-} \{p \mapsto adr(p) \cup \{s \mapsto r, r \mapsto s\}\})(q))$$
$$\subseteq (arm \cup \{p \mapsto r\})[\{q\}] \qquad \textit{Modified invariant } inv6$$

for all *q*. For $q \neq p$ the proof is easy. For the other case $q = p$ we prove, letting $D = \{s \mapsto r, r \mapsto s\}$,

	$\mathsf{ran}(adr(p) \cup D) \subseteq (arm \cup \{p \mapsto r\})[\{p\}]$	{ set theory, def. of D }
$\Leftrightarrow$	$\mathsf{ran}(adr(p)) \cup \{r, s\} \subseteq arm[\{p\}] \cup \{r\}$	{ *inv6* with "$q := p$" }
$\Leftrightarrow$	$\{r, s\} \subseteq arm[\{p\}] \cup \{r\}$	{ $\{r\} \subseteq \{r\}$ }
$\Leftrightarrow$	$\{s\} \subseteq arm[\{p\}] \cup \{r\}$	{ set theory }
$\Leftrightarrow$	$s \in arm[\{p\}] \lor s = r$	{ *inv6* with "$q := p$" }
$\Leftarrow$	$s \in \mathsf{ran}(adr(p))$	

---

[5] Event-B has the shorter (and more legible) notation $adr(p) := adr(p) \cup \{s \mapsto r, r \mapsto s\}$ for this. We do not use it because we can use the formula above directly in proof obligations. We also try as much as possible to avoid introducing more notation than necessary.

We would expect $s \in \mathrm{ran}(adr(p))$ to hold because doors are symmetric and because of concrete guard $grd2$, that is, $s \in \mathrm{dom}(adr(p))$. We specified symmetry in axiom $axm3$ but this property is not covered by invariant $inv7$. We have to specify it explicitly,

$$inv9 \;:\; \forall q \cdot adr(q) \subseteq adr(q)^{-1} \quad . \qquad\qquad \text{(see axiom } axm3)$$

We can continue the proof where we left off

$$
\begin{array}{ll}
\quad s \in \mathrm{ran}(adr(p)) & \{\, inv9 \text{ with ``}q := p\text{''} \,\} \\
\Leftarrow \quad s \in \mathrm{dom}(adr(p)) &
\end{array}
$$

It is easy to show that invariant $inv9$ itself is preserved by event $grant$:

$$
\begin{array}{ll}
\forall q \cdot adr(q) \subseteq adr(q)^{-1} & \text{Invariant } inv9 \\
s \mapsto r \notin adr(p) & \text{Concrete guard } grd1 \\
s \in \mathrm{dom}(adr(p)) & \text{Concrete guard } grd2 \\
\vdash & \\
\quad (adr \Leftarrow \{p \mapsto adr(p) \cup \{s \mapsto r, r \mapsto s\}\})(q) & \text{Modified invariant } inv9 \\
\quad \subseteq (adr \Leftarrow \{p \mapsto adr(p) \cup \{s \mapsto r, r \mapsto s\}\})(q)^{-1} &
\end{array}
$$

for all q. Let $D = \{s \mapsto r, r \mapsto s\}$. The interesting case is $q = p$ as above,

$$
\begin{array}{ll}
\quad adr(p) \cup D & \{\, inv9 \text{ with ``}q := p\text{''} \,\} \\
\subseteq \quad adr(p)^{-1} \cup D & \{\, D^{-1} = D \,\} \\
= \quad adr(p)^{-1} \cup D^{-1} & \{\, \text{set theory} \,\} \\
= \quad (adr(p) \cup D)^{-1} \quad . &
\end{array}
$$

Invariants $inv8'$ and $inv7$ remain to be analysed. We begin with the proof obligation for the preservation of invariant $inv7$:

$$
\begin{array}{ll}
\forall q \cdot adr(q) \subseteq Door & \text{Invariant } inv7 \\
s \mapsto r \notin adr(p) & \text{Concrete guard } grd1 \\
s \in \mathrm{dom}(adr(p)) & \text{Concrete guard } grd2 \\
\vdash & \\
\quad (adr \Leftarrow \{p \mapsto adr(p) \cup \{s \mapsto r, r \mapsto s\}\})(q) & \\
\quad \subseteq Door & \text{Modified invariant } inv7
\end{array}
$$

for all q. For $q = p$,

$$
\begin{array}{lll}
\quad adr(p) \cup \{s \mapsto r, r \mapsto s\} \subseteq Door & \{\, inv7 \text{ and set theory} \,\} \\
\Leftarrow \quad \{s \mapsto r, r \mapsto s\} \subseteq Door & \{\, inv9 \text{ and set theory} \,\} \\
\Leftarrow \quad s \mapsto r \in Door \quad . & & (15)
\end{array}
$$

The guard of event $grant$ needs to be strengthened; we replace $grd1$ by $grd1'$,

$$grd1' \;:\; s \mapsto r \in Door \setminus adr(p) \quad ,$$

which implies $s \mapsto r \in Door$, that is, (15). With $grd1'$ in place of $grd1$ the proof succeeds. For invariant $inv8'$ we have some more work to do:

$$\forall q \cdot arm[\{q\}] \subseteq adr(q)^+[\{O\}] \cup \{O\} \qquad \text{Invariant } inv8'$$
$$s \mapsto r \in Door \setminus adr(p) \qquad \text{Guard } grd1'$$
$$s \in \mathrm{dom}(adr(p)) \qquad \text{Guard } grd2$$
$$\vdash$$
$$(arm \cup \{p \mapsto r\})[\{q\}] \qquad \text{Modified invariant } inv8'$$
$$\subseteq (adr \mathbin{\lhd\mkern-9mu-} \{p \mapsto adr(p) \cup \{s \mapsto r, r \mapsto s\}\})(q)^+[\{O\}] \cup \{O\}$$

for all q. Let $D = \{s \mapsto r, r \mapsto s\}$. For $q = p$ we have to prove:

$$arm[\{p\}] \cup \{r\} \subseteq (adr(p) \cup D)^+[\{O\}] \cup \{O\},$$

given that $(arm \cup \{p \mapsto r\})[\{p\}] = arm[\{p\}] \cup \{r\}$. We begin with the case "$arm[\{p\}] \subseteq (adr(p) \cup D)^+[\{O\}] \cup \{O\}$":

$$arm[\{p\}] \qquad \{ inv8' \text{ with "}q := p\text{" } \}$$
$$\subseteq adr(p)^+[\{O\}] \cup \{O\} \qquad \{ \text{law (10) with "}x, y := adr(p), adr(p) \cup D\text{" } \}$$
$$\subseteq (adr(p) \cup D)^+[\{O\}] \cup \{O\} \quad .$$

Before proving the second case "$\{r\} \subseteq (adr(p) \cup D)^+[\{O\}] \cup \{O\}$", we have a closer look at guard $grd2$,

$$s \in \mathrm{dom}(adr(p)) \qquad \{ inv9 \text{ with "}q := p\text{" } \}$$
$$\Rightarrow s \in \mathrm{ran}(adr(p)) \qquad \{ inv6 \text{ with "}q := p\text{" } \}$$
$$\Rightarrow s \in arm[\{p\}] \qquad \{ inv8' \text{ with "}q := p\text{" } \}$$
$$\Rightarrow s \in adr(p)^+[\{O\}] \cup \{O\} \qquad \{ \text{set theory} \}$$
$$\Leftrightarrow s \in adr(p)^+[\{O\}] \lor s = O \quad . \qquad\qquad (16)$$

Now we can conclude the proof, letting $AD = adr(p) \cup D$:

$$AD^+[\{O\}] \cup \{O\} \qquad \{ \text{set theory} \}$$
$$\supseteq AD^+[\{O\}] \qquad \{ \text{law (8) with "}x := AD\text{", set theory} \}$$
$$= AD[\{O\}] \cup (AD^+ ; AD)[\{O\}] \qquad \{ \text{set theory} \}$$
$$\supseteq D[\{O\}] \cup (AD^+ ; D)[\{O\}] \qquad \{ \text{law (10) with "}x, y := adr(p), AD\text{" } \}$$
$$\supseteq D[\{O\}] \cup (adr(p)^+ ; D)[\{O\}] \qquad \{ \text{set theory} \}$$
$$= D[\{O\}] \cup D[adr(p)^+[\{O\}]] \qquad \{ \text{(16) and def. of } D \}$$
$$\supseteq \{r\} \quad .$$

Having specified invariant $inv9$ we would now succeed proving theorem $thm1$ postulated in the beginning of this section. This shows that our model satisfies property P7. We do not carry out the proof but turn to the last event not yet refined.

7.3 Revoking Door Authorisations

We model revoking of door authorisations symmetrically to granting door authorisations. A door authorisation can be revoked if (a) there is an authorisation for the door, (b) the corresponding person is not in the room that could be removed, and (c) the room is not the outside. Condition (a) is just chosen symmetrically to $grd1$ of refined event $revoke$ (for the same reason). The other two conditions (b) and (c) are already present in the abstraction. The two refined events $grant$ and $revoke$ together model property P9.

> $revoke$
>   any p, s, r when
> $grd1 : s \mapsto r \in adr(p)$
> $grd2 : p \mapsto r \notin loc$
> $grd3 : r \neq O$
>   then
> $act1 : adr := adr \lessdot \{p \mapsto adr(p) \setminus \{s \mapsto r, r \mapsto s\}\}$
>   end

We expect that the guard of event $revoke$ will be to weak to preserve invariant $inv8'$. We are going to search for it in the corresponding proof. But we can get started without it, in particular, proving guard strengthening of the abstract guards $grd1$ to $grd3$ and preservation of $inv5$, $inv6$, $inv7$, and $inv9$. For instance, preservation of $inv6$:

$$\forall q \cdot \mathsf{ran}(adr(q)) \subseteq arm[\{q\}] \qquad \text{\textit{Invariant} } inv6$$
$$s \mapsto r \in adr(p) \qquad \text{\textit{Concrete guard} } grd1$$
$$p \mapsto r \notin loc \qquad \text{\textit{Concrete guard} } grd2$$
$$r \neq O \qquad \text{\textit{Concrete guard} } grd3$$
$$\vdash$$
$$\mathsf{ran}((adr \lessdot \{p \mapsto adr(p) \setminus \{s \mapsto r, r \mapsto s\}\})(q))$$
$$\subseteq (arm \setminus \{p \mapsto r\})[\{q\}] \qquad \text{\textit{Modified invariant} } inv6$$

for all q. For $q = p$ we have to prove

$$\mathsf{ran}(adr(p) \setminus \{s \mapsto r, r \mapsto s\}) \subseteq arm[\{p\}] \setminus \{r\} \quad ,$$

thus,

$$r \notin \mathsf{ran}(adr(p) \setminus \{s \mapsto r, r \mapsto s\}) \quad .$$

This does not look right. Indeed, we find a counter example with one person P and three different rooms H, I, O:

$$adr = \{P \mapsto \{O \mapsto H, H \mapsto O, O \mapsto I, I \mapsto O, I \mapsto H, H \mapsto I\}\}$$
$$arm = \{P \mapsto H, P \mapsto I, P \mapsto O\}$$
$$loc = \{P \mapsto O\} \quad p = P \quad s = I \quad r = H$$

In order to resolve this problem we could remove all doors connecting to r. But this seems not acceptable: we grant door authorisations one by one and we should revoke them one by one. We could also strengthen the guard of the concrete event requiring, say, $adr(p)[\{r\}] = \{s\}$. But then we would not be able to revoke authorisations once there are two or more doors for the same room. The problem is in the abstraction! The abstract event $revoke$ should not always remove r. We weaken the guard of the abstract event,

> $revoke$
>> **any** $p,\ R$ **when**
>>> $grd1 : p \in Person$
>>> $grd2 : loc(p) \notin R$
>>> $grd3 : R \in \mathbb{S}(Room \setminus \{O\})$
>> **then**
>>> $act1 : arm := arm \setminus (\{p\} \times R)$
>> **end**

where for a set X by $\mathbb{S}(X)$ we denote all subsets of X with at most one element:

$$Y \in \mathbb{S}(X) \ \ \widehat{=} \ \ Y \subseteq X \wedge (\forall x, y \cdot x \in Y \wedge y \in Y \Rightarrow x = y) \ \ .$$

With this the proof obligation for invariant preservation of $inv6$ becomes:

$$
\begin{array}{ll}
\forall q \cdot ran(adr(q)) \subseteq arm[\{q\}] & \text{Invariant } inv6 \\
s \mapsto r \in adr(p) & \text{Concrete guard } grd1 \\
p \mapsto r \notin loc & \text{Concrete guard } grd2 \\
r \neq O & \text{Concrete guard } grd3 \\
\vdash \\
ran((adr \mathbin{\lhd\mkern-9mu-} \{p \mapsto adr(p) \setminus \{s \mapsto r, r \mapsto s\}\})(q)) \\
\quad \subseteq (arm \setminus (\{p\} \times R))[\{q\}] & \text{Modified invariant } inv6
\end{array}
$$

for all q. For $q = p$ we have to prove,

$$ran(adr(p) \setminus \{s \mapsto r, r \mapsto s\}) \subseteq arm[\{p\}] \setminus R \ \ . \tag{17}$$

Before we can continue we need to make a connection between r and R. We need a witness for R. After some reflection we decide for

$$R = \{r\} \setminus ran(adr(p) \setminus \{s \mapsto r, r \mapsto s\}) \ \ . \tag{18}$$

Witness (18) explains how the concrete and the abstract event are related. If there is only one door s connecting to room r, then $R = \{r\}$ and the authorisation for room r is revoked. Otherwise, $R = \varnothing$ and the authorisation for room r is kept. Now we are ready to prove (17). In case $r \in ran(adr(p) \setminus \{s \mapsto r, r \mapsto s\})$, that is $R = \varnothing$ by (18),

$$
\begin{array}{ll}
& ran(adr(p) \setminus \{s \mapsto r, r \mapsto s\}) & \{ \text{ set theory } \} \\
\subseteq & ran(adr(p)) & \{ inv6 \text{ with ``} q := p\text{'' } \} \\
\subseteq & arm[\{p\}] & \{ R = \varnothing \} \\
= & arm[\{p\}] \setminus R \ \ ,
\end{array}
$$

otherwise, that is in case $r \notin \mathrm{ran}(adr(p) \setminus \{s \mapsto r, r \mapsto s\})$,

$$
\begin{array}{lll}
 & \mathrm{ran}(adr(p) \setminus \{s \mapsto r, r \mapsto s\}) & \{\, r \notin \mathrm{ran}(\ldots) \,\} \\
\subseteq & \mathrm{ran}(adr(p)) \setminus \{r\} & \{\, R = \{r\} \text{ by } (18) \,\} \\
= & \mathrm{ran}(adr(p)) \setminus R & \{\, inv6 \text{ with “} q := p\text{” } \} \\
\subseteq & arm[\{p\}] \setminus R & .
\end{array}
$$

We note without showing the proofs that guard strengthening of the abstract guards $grd1$ to $grd3$ and preservation of $inv5$, $inv7$, and $inv9$ all hold. Only preservation of invariant $inv8'$ remains:

$$
\begin{array}{ll}
\quad \forall q \cdot arm[\{q\}] \subseteq adr(q)^{+}[\{\boldsymbol{O}\}] \cup \{\boldsymbol{O}\} & \text{Invariant } inv8' \\
\quad s \mapsto r \in Door \setminus adr(p) & \text{Guard } grd1' \\
\quad s \in \mathrm{dom}(adr(p)) & \text{Guard } grd2 \\
\vdash & \\
\quad (arm \setminus (\{p\} \times R))[\{q\}] & \text{Modified invariant } inv8' \\
\qquad \subseteq (adr \mathbin{\vartriangleleft\mkern-9mu-} \{p \mapsto adr(p) \setminus \{s \mapsto r, r \mapsto s\}\})(q)^{+}[\{\boldsymbol{O}\}] \cup \{\boldsymbol{O}\}
\end{array}
$$

for all q. Let $D = \{s \mapsto r, r \mapsto s\}$. For $q = p$ we have to show

$$
(arm \setminus (\{p\} \times R))[\{p\}] \subseteq (adr(p) \setminus D)^{+}[\{\boldsymbol{O}\}] \cup \{\boldsymbol{O}\} \quad . \tag{19}
$$

We have seen above that the term on term on the left hand side is either $arm[\{p\}]$ or $arm[\{p\}] \setminus \{r\}$. So we won't succeed proving (19) unless we add a guard to event *revoke*. We cannot use $arm[\{p\}]$ in the guard because the refined machine does not contain variable arm. If $inv6$ was an equality, we could use $\mathrm{ran}(adr(p))$ instead of $arm[\{p\}]$, obtaining the guard

$$
grd4 \; : \; \mathrm{ran}(adr(p)) \setminus \{r\} \subseteq (adr(p) \setminus D)^{+}[\{\boldsymbol{O}\}] \cup \{\boldsymbol{O}\} \quad .
$$

It says that all rooms except for r must still be reachable from the outside after revoking the authorisation for door D leading to room r. This sounds reasonable. We find that it is not possible to turn the set inclusion into an equality in invariant $inv6$. However, we can still prove the weaker theorem

$$
thm2 \; : \; \forall q \cdot \mathrm{ran}(adr(q)) \cup \{\boldsymbol{O}\} = arm[\{q\}] \quad ,
$$

using $inv2$, $inv6$, $inv8'$, and property (8) of the transitive closure. The authorised rooms are maintained precisely by means of the authorised doors. As a matter of fact, initially we used $thm2$ as invariant instead of $inv6$ but then weakened the invariant to $inv6$ and proved $thm2$ as a theorem. This is a useful strategy for reducing the amount of proof necessary while keeping powerful properties such as $thm2$. Similarly, we get the theorem

$$
thm3 \; : \; \forall q \cdot arm[\{q\}] = adr(q)^{+}[\{\boldsymbol{O}\}] \cup \{\boldsymbol{O}\} \quad .
$$

We prove (19) by case distinction similarly to (17). In case $r \in \text{ran}(adr(p) \setminus D)$, letting $AD = adr(p) \setminus D$,

$$
\begin{array}{lll}
& (arm \setminus (\{p\} \times R))[\{p\}] \subseteq AD^+[\{\boldsymbol{O}\}] \cup \{\boldsymbol{O}\} & \{\, R = \varnothing \,\} \\
\Leftrightarrow & arm[\{p\}] \subseteq AD^+[\{\boldsymbol{O}\}] \cup \{\boldsymbol{O}\} & \{\, thm2, \text{``}q := p\text{''} \,\} \\
\Leftrightarrow & \text{ran}(adr(q)) \subseteq AD^+[\{\boldsymbol{O}\}] \cup \{\boldsymbol{O}\} & \{\, grd4 \,\} \\
\Leftarrow & AD^+[\{\boldsymbol{O}\}] \cup \{\boldsymbol{O}\} \cup \{r\} \subseteq AD^+[\{\boldsymbol{O}\}] \cup \{\boldsymbol{O}\} & \{\, \text{set theory} \,\} \\
\Leftarrow & r \in AD^+[\{\boldsymbol{O}\}] & \{\, (8), \text{``}x := AD\text{''} \,\} \\
\Leftrightarrow & r \in (AD \cup AD^+ ; AD)[\{\boldsymbol{O}\}] & \{\, \text{set theory} \,\} \\
\Leftarrow & r \in AD[\{\boldsymbol{O}\}] \cup AD[AD^+[\{\boldsymbol{O}\}]] & \{\, AD^{-1}[\{r\}] \neq \varnothing \,\} \\
\Leftarrow & AD^{-1}[\{r\}] \subseteq \{\boldsymbol{O}\} \cup AD^+[\{\boldsymbol{O}\}] & \{\, inv9, \text{def. of } D \,\} \\
\Leftrightarrow & AD[\{r\}] \subseteq \{\boldsymbol{O}\} \cup AD^+[\{\boldsymbol{O}\}] & \{\, \text{set theory} \,\} \\
\Leftarrow & adr(p)[\{r\}] \subseteq \{\boldsymbol{O}\} \cup AD^+[\{\boldsymbol{O}\}] & \{\, r \notin adr(p)[\{r\}] \,\} \\
\Leftarrow & \text{ran}(adr(p)) \setminus \{r\} \subseteq AD^+[\{\boldsymbol{O}\}] \cup \{\boldsymbol{O}\} & ,
\end{array}
$$

and in case $r \notin \text{ran}(adr(p) \setminus D)$,

$$
\begin{array}{lll}
& (arm \setminus (\{p\} \times R))[\{p\}] & \{\, R = \{r\} \,\} \\
= & arm[\{p\}] \setminus \{r\} & \{\, thm2 \text{ with ``}q := p\text{''} \,\} \\
= & (\text{ran}(adr(p)) \cup \{\boldsymbol{O}\}) \setminus \{r\} & \{\, r \neq \boldsymbol{O} \,\} \\
= & (\text{ran}(adr(p)) \setminus \{r\}) \cup \{\boldsymbol{O}\} & \{\, grd4 \,\} \\
\subseteq & (adr(p) \setminus D)^+[\{\boldsymbol{O}\}] \cup \{\boldsymbol{O}\} & .
\end{array}
$$

Now we have taken into account all important properties P1 to P9 and we have proved that the abstract and the concrete model are consistent. We have proved that all invariants $inv1$ to $inv9$ are preserved by the initialisation and the events $pass$, $grant$ and $revoke$.

8   Towards a Better Model

Assuming we have one person P and three different rooms $\boldsymbol{H}$, $\boldsymbol{I}$, and $\boldsymbol{O}$ we can inspect how the modelled system would behave.

Initially variables adr and loc have the values

$$
\begin{aligned}
adr &= Person \times \{\varnothing\} \\
loc &= Person \times \{\boldsymbol{O}\} \quad .
\end{aligned}
$$

Event $pass$ is disabled as expected; $grd1$, that is, $loc(p) \mapsto r \in adr(p)$ cannot be satisfied for any p and r. Similarly, event $revoke$ is disabled, but also event $grant$: guard $grd2$, $s \in \text{dom}(adr(p))$, cannot be satisfied for any s, leading to a deadlock. We have not proved all properties we would expect from our model. This property seems to be implicitly contained in properties P8 and P9, but we have missed it. We have to weaken $grd2$,

grant
  any p, s, r when
    $grd1' : s \mapsto r \in Door \setminus adr(p)$
    $grd2' : s \in \text{dom}(adr(p)) \cup \{O\}$
  then
    $act1 : adr := adr \Leftarrow \{p \mapsto adr(p) \cup \{s \mapsto r, r \mapsto s\}\}$
  end

As a consequence, we have to check again that concrete event *grant* preserves all invariants. Fortunately, our proof of preservation of $inv8'$ can is easily adaptable because we have first inferred (16) from $grd2$; it is still implied by $grd2'$.

The proof obligations shown in Section 2 have been restricted not to take into account deadlock-freedom to emphasise the problem that we only verify properties where we expect difficulties but not more. This is a problem of formal modelling in general. But it is more visible in the incremental approach.

9   Conclusion

We have demonstrated how a model in Event-B is created incrementally by refinement and alteration. Refinement permits to structure a complex model thus to cope better with complexity. While reasoning formally about the model developed in this article as a whole we found some problems. These led us to alter the model, both the abstraction and the refinement. Although this is only mentioned in the introduction it should be clear how much this depends on good tool support [3,15]. Modifying a model is encouraged by these tools that that have been developed expressly to facilitate changes. Without such tools the approach would fail in practice. In this article we have focused more on methodological benefits than on how to use the respective tools because this is where the principal gain of using them is to be found. The techniques we have used are not meant to be comprehensive. For instance, we have not made use of temporal logic, behaviour specification, or testing.

We have not solved the problem of how to come up with a perfect specification. That is not our aim. We are content with achieving a model of good quality that captures required behaviour reasonably well and reasonably complete. By serious reasoning about the model we have gone some way towards a meticulous validation of the intended behaviour of the model. Some required properties are usually linked to the implementation. They would be difficult to incorporate into a more abstract model. Our solution would be not to incorporate them but to deal with them at the appropriate level.

Acknowledgment. I am grateful to Michael Leuschel and the STUPS group at the University of Düsseldorf for their suggestions and stimulating discussions.

References

1. Abrial, J.-R.: The B-Book: Assigning Programs to Meanings. CUP (1996)
2. Abrial, J.-R.: Modeling in Event-B: System and Software Engineering. Cambridge University Press, Cambridge (2008)

 3. Abrial, J.-R., Butler, M., Hallerstede, S., Voisin, L.: An open extensible tool environment for event-B. In: Liu, Z., He, J. (eds.) ICFEM 2006. LNCS, vol. 4260, pp. 588–605. Springer, Heidelberg (2006)
 4. Abrial, J.-R., Hallerstede, S.: Refinement, Decomposition and Instantiation of Discrete Models: Application to Event-B. Fundamentae Informatica 77(1-2) (2007)
 5. Abrial, J.-R., Mussat, L.: Introducing dynamic constraints in B. In: Bert, D. (ed.) B 1998. LNCS, vol. 1393, pp. 83–128. Springer, Heidelberg (1998)
 6. Back, R.-J.: Refinement Calculus II: Parallel and Reactive Programs. In: de Bakker, J.W., de Roever, W.-P., Rozenberg, G. (eds.) REX 1989. LNCS, vol. 430, pp. 67–93. Springer, Heidelberg (1990)
 7. Badeau, F., Amelot, A.: Using B as a high level programming language in an industrial project: Roissy VAL. In: Treharne, H., King, S., Henson, M.C., Schneider, S. (eds.) ZB 2005. LNCS, vol. 3455, pp. 334–354. Springer, Heidelberg (2005)
 8. Behm, P., Desforges, P., Meynadier, J.-M.: MéTéOR: An industrial success in formal development. In: Bert, D. (ed.) B 1998. LNCS, vol. 1393, pp. 26–26. Springer, Heidelberg (1998)
 9. Börger, E., Stärk, R.: Abstract State Machines: A Method for High-Level System Design and Analysis. Springer, Heidelberg (2003)
10. Gries, D., Schneider, F.B.: A Logical Approach to Discrete Math. Springer, Heidelberg (1994)
11. Hallerstede, S.: On the purpose of event-B proof obligations. In: Börger, E., Butler, M., Bowen, J.P., Boca, P. (eds.) ABZ 2008. LNCS, vol. 5238, pp. 125–138. Springer, Heidelberg (2008)
12. Hoang, T.S., Kuruma, H., Basin, D.A., Abrial, J.-R.: Developing topology discovery in event-B. In: Leuschel, M., Wehrheim, H. (eds.) IFM 2009. LNCS, vol. 5423, pp. 1–19. Springer, Heidelberg (2009)
13. Lakatos, I.: Proofs and Refutations. Cambridge University Press, Cambridge (1976)
14. Lamport, L.: Specifying Systems, The TLA+ Language and Tools for Hardware and Software Engineers. Addison-Wesley, Reading (2002)
15. Leuschel, M., Butler, M.: ProB: an automated analysis toolset for the B method. International Journal on Software Tools for Technology Transfer 10(2), 185–203 (2008)
16. Morgan, C.C.: Programming from Specifications: Second Edition. Prentice-Hall, Englewood Cliffs (1994)
17. Pólya, G.: Mathematics and Plausible Reasoning. Induction and Analogy in Mathematics, vol. 1. Princeton University Press, Princeton (1954)
18. Pólya, G.: How to Solve It: A New Aspect of Mathematical Method, 2nd edn. Princeton Science Library. Princeton University Press, Princeton (1957)
19. Pouzancre, G.: How to diagnose a modern car with a formal B model? In: Bert, D., Bowen, J.P., King, S. (eds.) ZB 2003. LNCS, vol. 2651, pp. 98–100. Springer, Heidelberg (2003)
20. van Gasteren, A.J.M.: On the Shape of Mathematical Arguments. LNCS, vol. 445. Springer, Heidelberg (1990)

An Asynchronous Distributed Component Model and Its Semantics

Ludovic Henrio[1], Florian Kammüller[2], and Marcela Rivera[1]

[1] INRIA – CNRS – I3S – Université de Nice Sophia-Antipolis
{lhenrio,mrivera}@sophia.inria.fr
[2] Institut für Softwaretechnik und Theoretische Informatik – TU-Berlin
flokam@cs.tu-berlin.de

Abstract. This paper is placed in the context of large scale distributed programming, providing a programming model based on asynchronous components. It focuses on the semantics of asynchronous invocations and component synchronisation. Our model is precise enough to enable the specification of a formal semantics. A variant of this model has been implemented, together with tools for managing components.

This paper explains why we consider that our component model is efficient and provides a convenient programming model. We show how futures play a major role for such asynchronous components, and provide a reduction semantics for the component model. This reduction semantics has been specified in the Isabelle theorem prover, and will be used to prove properties on the component model and its implementations.

1 Introduction

Component models provide a structured programming paradigm, and ensure a better re-usability of programs. Indeed application dependencies are defined together with provided functionalities by the means of provided/required ports; this improves the program specification and thus its re-usability. In distributed systems, this takes even more importance as the structure of components can also be used at runtime to discover services or adapt component behaviour. Several effective distributed component models have been specified, developed, and implemented in the last years [1, 2, 3, 4] ensuring different kinds of properties to their users. To be able to prove such properties, one must rely on some well defined semantics for the underlying programming language or middleware. This paper provides such a background for a category of component models.

This work is a study of asynchrony in component models. We present here a model for distributed components. This model is based on one key principle: *Components are the unit of concurrency*. More precisely, components only communicate by sending requests or results for those requests. We say that this model is asynchronous because requests can be treated in an asynchronous manner thanks to the introduction of *futures* (place-holders for request results). In order to prevent other communications or concurrency to occur, we require that *components do not share memory*, which ensures that components really are the

F.S. de Boer et al. (Eds.): FMCO 2008, LNCS 5751, pp. 159–179, 2009.
© Springer-Verlag Berlin Heidelberg 2009

concurrency units. From a computational point of view, components are loosely coupled: the only strong synchronisation consists in waiting for the result of a request, and can be performed only when and where this result is really needed thanks to the use of futures.

Such components can then provide a convenient abstraction for distribution: each component can be placed on a different (virtual) machine. Indeed, the abstractions suggested above imply that each memory location is only accessible by one component, and thus it is easy to place each component on a different independent location. This makes our component model adapted to distribution.

This component model is closely related to the Grid Component Model (GCM). Indeed, this work can be considered as the GCM model, where communication is chosen to be a request / reply mechanism with futures. ProActive/GCM is a reference implementation of the GCM. Our objective is to provide a programming model more general than the one adopted in ProActive/GCM, but more precise than the strict GCM definition. Indeed, GCM provides a structural description of components. From this definition, we precise component composition and communication semantics; more precisely we define composite component behaviour and an asynchronous communication mechanism using futures. ProActive/GCM can also be considered as *a possible* implementation of our model where components are implemented as active objects. Our definition of components being both precise and formalised, we expect it to be a strong guide and a reliable basis for both component system implementation and formal tools.

Our components are loosely coupled, with a data-flow oriented synchronisation. While being a very convenient way of parallelising computations, loose coupling can raise issues when one wants to synchronise the management of several components. We will show in this paper some of the issues that can arise for synchronising the management of components, and some possible solutions.

We first detail the component model we suggest and explain why we think the proposed constructs are efficient (Section 2). After this introduction of our major concepts, we offer a comparison by summarising the main component models found in the literature (Section 3). Next, we introduce our formal model of asynchronous components (Section 4), and we present several implementation and component management issues (Section 5). Finally, we conclude this paper.

2   An Asynchronous Component Model

The GCM [4] is a component model defined by the European Network of Excellence CoreGrid. It extends the Fractal component model, by addressing Grid computing: it supports deployment, scalability, autonomic behaviour, and asynchronous communications. The GCM relies on the following aspects:

- *Fractal as the basis for the component architecture:* the main characteristics GCM benefits from Fractal are its hierarchical structure, the enforcement of separation between functional and non-functional concerns, its extensibility, and the separation between interfaces and implementation.

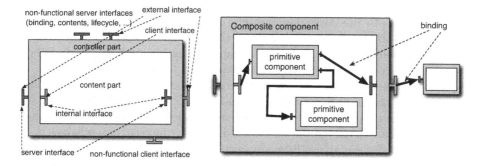

Fig. 1. A GCM component   **Fig. 2.** A component system

- Communication Semantics: GCM components should allow for any kind of communication semantics (e.g., streaming, file transfer, event-based) either synchronous or asynchronous. However, for dealing with latency, asynchronous communication is preferred, and considered as the default.
- GCM supports collective communications – one-to-many, many-to-one, but also many-to-many.
- GCM also comes with a support for autonomic aspects and better separation of concerns (functional vs. non-functional).

In this section, we will first recall precisely the component structure of GCM components; then we will refine this model to define the semantics of our asynchronous components.

2.1 Component Structure

Let us start by the structure of the component model that is inherited from Fractal [5]. GCM is a hierarchical and reflective component model. A GCM component can be either *composite* (i.e. composed of subcomponents), or *primitive* (a basic element encapsulating the business code). A component comprises a content (providing the functional code) and a membrane (a container managing non-functional operations).

The interfaces are the access points to components. The components have *client interfaces* – emitting messages/invocations– and *server interfaces* – able to receive messages/invocations. A *binding* connects a client interface to a server interface (shown in Figure 2), with the implicit semantics that the message emitted by the client will be received by the server interface. Each client interface is bound to a single server interface. For composite components, if the interface is exposed to subcomponents this is an *internal* interface. If, on the contrary, the interface is exposed to other components this interface is an *external* interface. All the external interfaces of a component as well as its internal interfaces must have distinct names. Depending on its functionality, each interface is either functional or non-functional. Each internal functional interface must have a corresponding external interface of the same name. The implicit semantics is that

a call received on a server external (resp. internal) interface will be transmitted
– unchanged – to the corresponding internal (resp. external) client interface.
Among those notions, only non-functional client interfaces have been introduced
in GCM compared to Fractal. A GCM component architecture can be described
using an architecture description language (ADL).

A GCM component and its different parts are shown in Figure 1. Functional
interfaces are shown horizontally, and non-functional ones vertically. Client interfaces are on the right (or bottom) and server on the left (or top). Note that
each external functional interface has a corresponding internal one, whereas non-
functional interfaces may not have any corresponding internal ones in case non-
functional requests are treated by the membrane. Figure 2 shows a component
assembly composed of two main components, the left one is a composite composed of two primitives; the figure also illustrates all the kind of bindings that
can be encountered in a GCM component assembly.

Adaptation mechanisms are triggered by the control part of the components;
we call this part *non-functional* (NF). This NF part, named *membrane*, is composed of controllers that implement NF concerns. The membrane is a set of (controller) components that can be (re)configured. These controllers can manage
configurations and reconfigurations. Compared to Fractal, GCM gives a component structure to the membrane; moreover in GCM controllers inside the membrane can interact with the membranes of other components through bindings
between NF interfaces.

Interface Cardinality. The interface cardinality indicates how many bindings
can be made from or to this interface. We have three kinds of cardinalities:
singleton, collection, and collective. Collection interfaces were defined in Fractal
to let an interface be instantiated as many times as necessary. GCM defines
collective interfaces: multicast (one-to-many) and gathercast (many-to-one).

A *multicast* interface is a client interface that transforms a single invocation
into a list of invocations, forwarded in parallel to a set of connected interfaces.
The result of an invocation on a multicast interface is a list of results. Invocation
parameters can be distributed according to a distribution policy: for example,
broadcast sends the same parameter to each of the connected server interfaces;
and *scatter* strips the parameter so that the bound components work on different
data. Distribution policy can also be customized.

Symmetrically, a *gathercast* interface is a server interface that synchronises a
set of invocations toward the same destination. A gathercast interface coordinates a set of incoming invocations before continuing the invocation flow, for-
warding a single invocation. This interface may define synchronisation barriers
and may gather incoming data.

Formalising collection and collective interfaces is outside the scope of this
paper and we will focus on singleton interfaces. Singleton cardinality is to our
mind sufficient to express the crucial points of asynchrony, and many-to-many
communications can be studied as an extension to this work.

2.2   Informal Semantics

We focus now on the semantics of our component model; for this we make a few additional assumptions compared to the GCM component model. First of all, we start from the point of view presented in the introduction: "components are the unit of concurrency" and components do not share memory. This way interaction between components is limited to communication.

Communication. The basic communication paradigm we consider is asynchronous message sending: upon a communication the message is enqueued at the receiver side in a queue. To prevent shared memory between components, messages can only transmit parameters which are copied at the receiver side; no object or component can be passed by reference.[1] This communication semantics is similar to requests in an active object model like ASP [6], but also to communication in Actors [7], where messages are enqueued in the message delivery system of the destination.

We call *requests* the messages that are transmitted between components, and that can contain parameters also transmitted (copied) between components.

References to components cannot be passed between components, for example, method parameters cannot contain references to components. More precisely, in order to allow non-functional features to be aware of component structure and manage the component system, we restrict component manipulations to non-functional concerns.

Returning Results. We call our component model asynchronous because communication does not trigger computation on the receiver side immediately, it just enqueues a request. Such a mechanism can be implemented with synchronous or asynchronous communications. As in ASP and ProActive, the model defined in Section 4 relies on a rendez-vous (enqueueing a request is done synchronously but the receiver component is always ready to enqueue a request). Asynchronous invocations could be performed by enforcing request results to be returned by an explicit call-back mechanism, but we prefer handling results automatically in order to prevent business code from dealing with communication purposes.

To allow for transparent asynchronous requests with results, we use *futures*, first introduced in [8, 9]. A future is an empty object that represents the result of a computation and will be updated when the result is available. In our case, futures are a transparent and natural way to handle asynchronous requests: a future is automatically created when sending a request from a component to another, it represents the result of this request. Transparent futures come with a natural and automatic synchronisation called *wait-by-necessity*: futures can be safely transmitted between components or stored while the real value of the result is not needed. When the value is really needed the thread accessing the future is automatically blocked until the result is available.

---

[1] To be precise, only futures are passed by reference, because their value will be finally transmitted by a copy semantics.

Transmitting a future between components is not considered as an operation requiring the value. Consequently, the result or the parameters of a request can contain a future, or even can simply be a future. Consequently, several components in the system may have a reference to the same future, the component platform will then be in charge of updating all those references. *Updating* a future consists in replacing a future reference by the result for the corresponding request. We call those futures *first-class* because they can be transmitted between components as any other value.

Primitive Component Behaviour. Let us now detail a behaviour for primitive components that will ensure asynchronous communications and future handling.

The primitive components encapsulate the business code, thus in our model we consider they can have, internally, any behaviour. They will serve requests in the order they wish, providing answer for all the requests they receive. They can call other components by emitting a request on one of the client interface. However, each primitive component must always be able to accept a request (that will just be enqueued in its request queue), and to receive a result (that will replace a future reference by the received value).

Figure 3 illustrates a primitive component and its behaviour. A primitive component consists of a request queue, a content, a membrane, and a result list. Its content contains the business code that serves the requests; requests arrive from the server interfaces on the left and are emitted by the client interface on the right. An incoming request is enqueued immediately, associated with its future identifier. Later this request is served and treated by the component content, possibly emitting new requests to the clients. When the service is finished and a value is calculated for its result, this value is stored in the result list, stating that the future for the request is mapped to this calculated value. The calculated value can itself contain references to other futures. Later, the result will be sent from the result list to the components that hold a reference to the corresponding future. As future references can spread in all the components, including requests, results, and current component states, received results are used to update future references in all parts of the component.

Mono-threaded Components. In our model, a given thread manipulates a single component, but nothing prevents our components from being multi-threaded. Even, a component can serve several requests at the same time.

However, like in ProActive/GCM, components can be chosen to be mono-threaded; this simplifies concurrency, as each component has a sequential behaviour but can create deadlocks. For example, if there is a cycle of dependencies between results of requests: in a subsystem with two components, C1 and C2, a request A, computed by C1 depends on the result of a request B to component C2, itself depending on the result of another request C, but awaited from C1. In that case, C1 will be indirectly waiting for itself, which could only be resolved by a second thread in C1. Fortunately, most applications can be written without such cyclic dependencies, especially thanks to first-class futures.

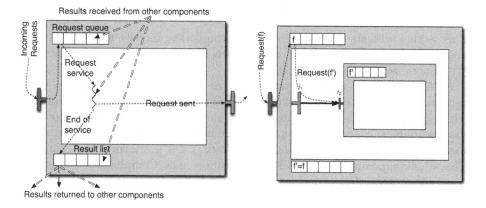

Fig. 3. Component behaviour   **Fig. 4.** Request delegation

Composite Component Behaviour. To summarise, the behaviour of the primitive components is highly parameterised. We have just specified the handling of requests and futures in the preceding paragraphs. By contrast, composite components have a predefined behaviour.[2] Composite components serve requests in a FIFO order, delegating request to the bound components or to the external ones in a much transparent and natural way. Globally, a request emitted by the client interface of a primitive component will be sent unchanged to the server interface of the primitive component that is linked by a binding. More precisely, several bindings may be used and several composite components may be crossed.

This request transmission can rely on a mechanism similar to the handling of requests by primitive components; this mechanism is illustrated by Figure 4. Requests are dequeued in a FIFO order from the request queue. Consider one request (associated with the future f), suppose the request has been received from the outside of the composite, i.e., it was received on an external server interface. There is necessarily an internal client interface matching this external one. Handling the requests consists in sending another request from the internal client interface matching the interface that receives the request ($i1$). This request is sent to the interface bound to $i1$, that is $i2$ in the figure; this interface necessarily belongs to an inner component. This new request corresponds to a future f', and the result for the first one is just a reference to f', i.e. $f = f'$. In case the request was received from the inside of the composite, the mechanism is similar, with a new request sent from the matching external client interface.

An alternative approach would consist in implementing a delegation mechanism, like in allowing a component to delegate the calculation of a result to another component, like handlers of [10]. However, we did not choose this technique in order to avoid introducing a new mechanism, but also to ensure that the component calculating a value for a given future will not change along time.

---

[2] In the future, we want to study how the behaviour of the composite component could be changed safely but this is not the purpose of this paper.

3   Comparison with Some Component Models

This section presents the main distributed component models, focusing on their main characteristics with respect to structure, distribution, and synchronisation. We summarise this comparison in Table 1.

CCA [1] aims at a minimal specification of component architecture for high-performance computing. CCA builds on core concepts, defining a component (the software entity), a framework (the container), and ports (the access towards the environment). The components are assembled at runtime connecting ports together, thanks to scripts that interact with the CCA framework. The container allows building, connecting and running components. Component composition is not hierarchical. CCA considers parallelism and distribution of data.

CCM (CORBA Component Model) [11, 2] is a specification for business components which can be distributed, heterogeneous, and implemented over different programming languages or operating systems. CCM components communicate through ports that can be interconnected. Also, the OMG D&C specification [12] supports hierarchical assemblies. All component instances are handled at runtime by their container. A fortitude of CCM is to provide a clear separation between functional and non-functional concerns.

SCA (Service Component Architecture) [3] provides a component-oriented programming model for building applications and solutions based on a Service Oriented Architectures. SCA provides a model for both the composition of services and the creation of service components, including the reuse of existing application functions within SCA composites. SCA is a hierarchical component model, but its component structure is not specified at runtime. Additionally, SCA components can be implemented with different languages such as Java, BPEL, and state machines.

ASP [6, 13] is the computation model behind ProActive. This calculus of active objects starts from ς_{imp}-calculus [14] extending it with explicit commands for activating an object and for serving requests. Activities contain an active object, possibly several passive objects, and are managed by only one thread. Communication is realized using an asynchronous request reply mechanism with futures. A request is associated to each future, and the request service aims at providing a result value to the future. Using a translational semantics, ASP components are defined as hierarchical combinations of activities.

Creol [15, 16] is a programming and modelling language for distributed systems based on active objects communicating via asynchronous method calls using futures. Creol's base language is – at least in more recent publications, e.g. [17] – an extended version of the functional ς-calculus [14]. Besides explicit distinction between fields and methods of objects the authors introduce classes and threads as first class citizens. Classes contain implementation of methods; threads are sequences of method calls referenced by futures; objects' fields contain the values resulting from thread evaluation. Concurrent access to objects is controlled by an explicit lock mechanism. The operational semantics is a reduction style structural operational semantics based on rewriting logic implemented in Maude which enables testing of model specifications [18]. Interfaces are integral part of the Creol language. They describe the observable behaviour of objects using assumption guarantee specifications [19]. Traces of communication events between the object and its environment specify input and output behaviour based on visible parts of an object's features. More recently, [17] defines Creol components, and a framework for describing and testing them. The authors use a simple specification language over communication labels enabling the expression of component behaviour as a set of traces at the interfaces.

A Creol component is a collection of classes, objects, and threads where the threads are simply composed in parallel. Thus, components are not hierarchical. Threads – or sets of threads – define concurrent components. A thread never leaves the object in which it is defined. Thus objects are the unit of concurrency. Distribution is not given by explicit locations but using independent object evaluation and asynchronous method call invocations. In comparison to Creol, our approach is hierarchical. We use a separate level of component specification with an abstract behaviour model. We separate the structural component level from the program semantics.

FOCUS [20] is a framework for the systematic formal specification and development of distributed components communicating by asynchronous messages. Contrarily to other models, in this framework the basic notion is the stream. There are two types of streams: streams of actions (traces) and streams of messages. Streams of messages are used to represent *communication histories* of channels. The behaviour of a component is described by logical formulas specifying stream processing functions. Compared to this approach, our formalization focuses on components that could be imperative and can have a much richer behaviour, more difficult to specify, but more expressive. We expect to be able to prove automatically properties on component composition and component behaviour.

The Relational Calculus of Object and Component Systems (rCOS) [21] is based on the Unifying Theory of Programming by He and Hoare supporting concurrency and relational refinement. In the rCOS component model [22] components are aggregations of objects; it uses required and provided interfaces together with contracts. rCOS has a rich and fine-grained object model but lacks – in comparison to our approach – the variety of hierarchical composition at the component level and consequently the explicitness of component interaction.

Fractal [5] and GCM [4] were presented in the preceding section. Let us simply recall their main differences. Contrary to Fractal, GCM specifies distribution aspects of the component model, and defines one-to-many and many-to-one communication, which are particularly efficient for distributed components. The GCM model also refines the structure of the membrane, and defines some controllers for autonomic behaviour.

A GCM reference implementation is based on ProActive [23]. In this implementation each component and each composite membrane is an active object. The controllers are encapsulated in the membrane which also dispatches functional calls to inner components. In this implementation, components communicate through asynchronous method calls with futures. Futures can be

Table 1. Comparison of component models

Component Model	Hierarchy	Distribution Unit	Concurrency	Communication
CCA	no	Application dependent	Unspecified	Synchronous
CCM	yes	Application dependent	Unspecified	Synchronous or Asynchronous
SCA	yes	Unspecified	Unspecified	Call-and-return messages
ASP- component	yes	Active Object	Monothreaded Active Objects	Asynchronous, implicit futures
Creol	no	Object	Multi-threaded Active Objects	Asynchronous, explicit futures
Fractal(Julia)	yes	Unspecified	Multi-threaded Components	Synchronous
GCM	yes	Primitive Component	Unspecified	Request-Reply Paradigm
GCM (ProActive)	yes	Primitive Component	Unique control thread per component	Asynchronous, implicit futures

forwarded to any component in a non-blocking manner. A property inherent to this implementation is the absence of shared memory between components, this leads to constraints but also greatly simplifies the reasoning about concurrency. The primitive components act as the unit of distribution and concurrency (each thread is isolated in a component).

In order to formalise Fractal components, several models and calculi have been designed, addressing different aspects. The Kell-calculus was introduced as a very general calculus able to represent component containment, control and passivation [24]. Then, this work was extended and adapted in order to deal with shared components [25]. In Fractal, a component is shared if it is the subcomponent of several different composite components. The formalism we present does not deal with component sharing. More recently, the Fractal component model has been formalised in Alloy [26]. This paper gives a very precise and unambiguous formalisation of Fractal component's structure and control. Compared to this framework, our work focuses on the asynchronous aspects of components, and somehow takes the decision of giving a less general semantics to components and component communications in order to provide a formal model of the interplay between component communication, component behaviour, their control and their structure.

Amongst the formal models for distributed computing, our work relies on the notion of futures and requests that have already been formalised, outside the context of components, see for example [27] in the context of Creol or [10] in the context of functional programming.

4   Formal Model

This section defines a semantics for our component model. It is being formalised in Isabelle/HOL [28].[3] This explains some design choices made here.

4.1   Structure and Notations

We let v_j, p_j range over values, f_j range over futures, i_j range over interfaces, N range over component names, and C over components. A list is denoted $[a_i]^{i \in 1..n}$. The operator $\#$ is the list append operation. $l \setminus f$ removes f from the list l, whatever its position is.

Component definition. We build requests as triples (future identifier, parameter value, invoked interface): $R_j ::= [f_j, v_j, i_j]$. A result maps a value to an identified future: $F_j ::= [f_j, v_j]$. A component is either a primitive or a composite, each one has a state and a set of interfaces, a composite has additionally bindings and subcomponents ($subCp$): Prim[$itfs$, $PrimState$], Comp[$itfs$, $subCp$, $bindings$, $CompState$]. Enqueue(C, R) enqueues a request R in the request queue of the component C.

States. Each state (*PrimState*, *CompState*) is a record containing a *queue*, and a list of computed results (*results*); additionally a primitive component state (*PrimState*) contains an internal state (*intState*), and a behaviour (*behaviour*). A behaviour is a labelled transition system between internal states where labels are actions defined below. An internal state contains a set of current requests (*currRq*), and a state referencing a set of futures.

  $s.queue$ returns the current queue of state s. The constituents of a state s, e.g. its queue, can be updated individually, for example $s(\!queue := Q\!)$ denotes a new state obtained by changing the queue of s to Q.

Subcomponents. The set of subcomponents of a composite is a mapping from component names to components: $SubCp ::= [N \mapsto C]^{i \in 1..n}$. The subcomponent named N of the composite component Comp[$itfs$, $subCp$, $bindings$, $CompState$] is denoted $subCp[N]$, and $subCp[N \mapsto C]$ denotes a new set of subcomponents where C is the new component associated to the name N.

Bindings. Each binding is of the form $[N.i_1, N'.i_2]$, if interface i_1 of component named N is plugged to the interface i_2 of N' (where N and N' can be *This* if the plugged interface is the composite component that defines the bindings).

Futures. For any value, state, or component, futs(v) (resp. futs(s), futs(C)) represents the set of futures referenced by this element. We use a function *UpdFut* that is applied to values; *UpdFut*(v_i, f, v) replaces the future f – if present – in value v_i by v. Note that futs(*UpdFut*(v_i, f, v)) $\subseteq$ futs(v) $\cup$ futs(v_i) $\setminus \{f\}$ ($\setminus$ is the set subtraction). findRes(S, f) looks inside a component system S and returns the value which is the result corresponding to future f, if it is already computed.

---

[3] Prototype specification available at www.inria.fr/oasis/Ludovic.Henrio/misc

4.2 Local Actions

The behaviour of the primitive components is greatly customisable. For the purpose of the component model, we suppose this behaviour is specified by an (infinite) labelled transition system, it is denoted by $\mathcal{B}_C$ for a given primitive C. The actions of the primitive components are the labels of the transitions, and states are those of the primitive component. Actions of interest are the following:

NewService itfs p f dequeues a request on an interface of the set *itfs* and starts serving it; f receives the future identifier and p the request parameter.

Tau is a non-observable action allowing to encapsulate internal behaviour.

Call i p f sends a request on interface i with parameter p; f receives the future identifier that corresponds to the request. i must be one of the client interfaces of the primitive component.

EndService f v finishes a service associating value v to future f; this action adds a new entry in the result list.

ReceiveResult f v receives a result value: future f is updated with value v. A primitive component must always be able to receive a future (if $f \notin \text{futs}(s)$ this action has no effect):

$$(\forall f, s, v.\, \exists s'.\, (s, ReceiveResult\ f\ v, s') \in \mathcal{B}_C)$$

Constraints on Current Requests. The set *currRq* of requests currently handled by the primitive component changes only when a request is served (one current request added), or a service is finished (one current request removed). Additionally, one can only finish a service for a request that is current; this leads to the following constraints:

$$(s, NewService\ itfs\ p\ f, s') \in \mathcal{B}_C) \Rightarrow s'.currRq = f \# s.currRq$$

$$(s, EndService\ f\ v, s') \Rightarrow (f \in s.currRq \wedge s'.currRq = s.currRq \setminus f)$$

For all the other actions we have $(s, action, s') \in \mathcal{B}_C \Rightarrow s'.currRq = s.currRq$.

Constraints on Referenced Futures. Futures referenced by the internal state of a primitive component are also constrained. In general $(s, action, s') \in \mathcal{B}_C$ implies $\text{futs}(s') \subseteq \text{futs}(s)$, except when a new request is served or a result is received. In those cases, the request parameter or the result may contain new futures. Additionally, when a result is received, the future updated should not be referenced any more.

$$(s, NewService\ itfs\ p\ f, s') \in \mathcal{B}_C) \Rightarrow \text{futs}(s') \subseteq \text{futs}(s) \cup \text{futs}(p)$$

$$(s, ReceiveResult\ f\ v, s') \in \mathcal{B}_C) \wedge f \in \text{futs}(s) \Rightarrow \text{futs}(s') \subseteq (\text{futs}(s) \setminus \{f\}) \cup \text{futs}(v)$$

Moreover, sent values can only reference futures known by the internal state:

$$(s, Call\ i\ p\ f, s') \in \mathcal{B}_C) \Rightarrow \text{futs}(p) \subseteq \text{futs}(s)$$

$$(s, EndService\ f\ v, s') \Rightarrow \text{futs}(v) \subseteq \text{futs}(s)$$

Handling Received Values. When an action receives a value, for example, *NewService itfs p f* receives p, the action must accept any value for parameter p and alter the internal state accordingly; p is, in fact, a variable that will, in turn, receive a value from the request queue. Similarly, f will receive the identifier of the future to handle. Instead of introducing variables and scoping, we simply chose to state that some of the parameters must be able to receive any value:

$$(s, NewService\ itfs\ p\ f, s') \in \mathcal{B}_C \Rightarrow \forall p', f'. \exists s'. (s, NewService\ itfs\ p'\ f', s') \in \mathcal{B}_C$$

This applies also for f in *Call i p f*: the future must be chosen fresh, and v in *ReceiveResult f v*: the received result is given by another component.

4.3   Semantics of the Component Model

The formal semantics of the component model defines a reduction relation $\rightarrow_R$ by a set of inductive rules. $S \vdash C \rightarrow_R C'$ if, in the component system S, the component C can be reduced to the component C'; S is the composite component containing all the components of the system. It is necessary to know the whole component system to retrieve request results and update futures. From $\rightarrow_R$, a reduction for the global component system can then be defined: $S \rightsquigarrow S' \Leftrightarrow S \vdash S \rightarrow_R S'$.

There is a second parameterised relation $\dashv i_1, f, v \mapsto$ allowing to express that a component is willing to emit a request, and must be matched with a reception action; statements of the form $\dashv i_1, f, v \mapsto$ used as hypotheses to the rules for composite components lead back to statements of $\rightarrow_R$. If $\vdash C \dashv i_1, f, v \mapsto C'$, then C emits a request on the interface i_1, with parameter v, and associated to a future f; after the emission, C becomes C'.

There are two kinds of reduction rules: the ones for primitive components (Figure 5), and the ones dealing with composite components (Figure 8).

In detail, the behaviour defined in primitive components determines the following rules of reduction.

TAU: If the state s of a primitive component Prim[*itfs, s*] contains a *Tau* transition from the internal state *s.intState* to another state s_2 then the component's internal state can be replaced by s_2. In Figure 3, this rule corresponds to internal transitions inside the content of the composite.

RCVRESULTPRIM: The primitive component's behaviour always contains a transition defining the reception of value v for future f, i.e. *ReceiveResult f v*, changing the internal state into the result state s_2 defined in the behaviour. The result value is found in the component system S; it is returned by the function findRes(S, f). The future is also updated in the request queue and the result list by the function *UpdFut*. After such a reception, the future f is not referenced anymore by the primitive. In Figure 3, this rule corresponds to the three thick arrows with "results received from other components".

CALL: The call to an interface i_1 with future f and parameter value v presupposes that the future f is fresh. Such a call transition in the behaviour of a primitive component creates now a parameterised reduction $\dashv i_1, f, v \mapsto$

TAU
$$(s.intState, Tau, s_2) \in s.behaviour$$
$$S \vdash Prim[itfs, s] \rightarrow_R Prim[itfs, s(\!|intState := s_2|\!)]$$

RCVRESULTPRIM
$$(s.intState, ReceiveResult\ f\ v, s_2) \in s.behaviour$$
$$findRes(S, f) = v \qquad s.queue = [f_j, v_j, i_j]^{j \in 1..n} \qquad Q = [f_j, UpdFut(v_j, f, v), i_j]^{j \in 1..n}$$
$$s.results = [f_k, v_k]^{k \in 1..n'} \qquad R = [f_k, UpdFut(v_k, f, v)]^{k \in 1..n'}$$
$$S \vdash Prim[itfs, s] \rightarrow_R Prim[itfs, s(\!|intState := s_2, queue := Q, results := R|\!)]$$

CALL
$$(s.intState, Call\ i_1\ v\ f, s_2) \in s.behaviour \qquad f \notin futs(S)$$
$$\vdash Prim[itfs, s] \dashv i_1, f, v \mapsto Prim[itfs, s(\!|intState := s_2|\!)]$$

ENDSERVICE
$$(s.intState, EndService\ f\ v, s_2) \in s.behaviour$$
$$S \vdash Prim[itfs, s] \rightarrow_R Prim[itfs, s(\!|intState := s_2, results := s.results\#[f, v]|\!)]$$

SERVENEXT
$$(s.intState, NewService\ itfs\ v\ f, s_2) \in s.behaviour$$
$$[f', v', i'] \in Q \Rightarrow i' \notin itfs \qquad s.queue = Q\#[f, v, i]\#Q'$$
$$S \vdash Prim[itfs, s] \rightarrow_R Prim[itfs, s(\!|intState := s_2, queue := Q\#Q'|\!)]$$

Fig. 5. Primitive Component Semantics

of the primitive component because this call is passed on to the enclosing composite component. Upon synchronisation with the component bound to this one, the reduction will occur, modifying the internal state and storing locally the future f. In Figure 3, this rule corresponds to the "request sent" arrow sent to the client interface.

ENDSERVICE: The end of a service denotes that one of the current requests of a primitive component is finalised yielding value v. Hence, the respective primitive component's result list is extended by the pair $[f, v]$ where f is the future that corresponds to the finalised current request. After reduction the primitive component's current requests does not contain f anymore (see above). In Figure 3, this rule corresponds to the arrow.

SERVENEXT: Finally, a *NewService itfs v f* transition in a primitive component's behaviour leads to the creation of a new current request in the internal state of the component. The oldest request on the interface i is served. The parameter v matches the parameter of the first request in the request queue, and f, its corresponding future. The reduction updates the internal state by plugging in the target state s_2 of the behaviour's transition, and by popping off the head of the request queue. In Figure 3, this rule corresponds to the "end of service" arrow.

The inductive rules for *composite components* determine how the service communication distributes on properly assembled systems. The first rule embeds

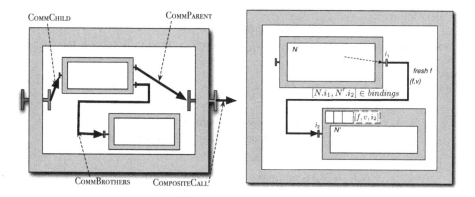

Fig. 6. Component Communications   **Fig. 7.** Subcomponents communicate

subcomponent reduction in composite contexts; the second performs future updates inside composite components. The three COMM-rules, in the middle, define the communications transmitted by the different kinds of bindings inside the composite component; finally the last rule allows composite components to emit requests on their external client interfaces. In detail, the rules finalise the formal semantics as follows. Figure 6 illustrates the different kinds of communications expressed by the four last rules.

HIERARCHY: This rule is a compositionality rule; it expresses that if a subcomponent $subCp[N]$ reduces in isolation to a component C then it does so as well in the context of a component hierarchy – given by updating $SubCp$ with $SubCp[N \mapsto C]$ in the context $Comp[itfs, SubCp, bindings, s]$.

RCVRESULTCOMP: This rule is very similar to the RCVRESULTPRIM rule for primitive components. However, this one is simpler because the composite component does not have any internal state; only the request queue and the result list are updated by the received result.

COMMBROTHERS, illustrated by Figure 7: a subcomponent N can pass a call to subcomponent N' inside the set of subcomponents $subComp$ of a composite component. The respective client interface of N, on which the call was emitted – $N.i_1$ – must be bound to the interface i_2 of the destination component – $N'.i_2$ – this binding must be stored in $bindings$. The call parameters f, v – parameterised in the request emission relation – are passed to interface i_2 of subcomponent N'. The operator $Enqueue$ denotes that the request $[f, v, i_2]$ is properly added onto the request list of subcomponent N'. N is reduced simultaneously, sending a request.

COMMPARENT, illustrated by Figure 9: if a subcomponent – a child – N of a composite component utters a request i_1, f, v to its parent component, then – similar to the previous rule – N is reduced simultaneously as it sends a request, and the request is added to the composite component's request queue. The bindings must bind the component N interface to the (inner server) interface of the parent.

HIERARCHY
$$S \vdash subCp[N] \rightarrow_R C$$
$$S \vdash Comp[itfs, subCp, bindings, s] \rightarrow_R Comp[itfs, (subCp[N \mapsto C]), bindings, s]$$

RCVRESULTCOMP
$$findRes(S, f) = v \qquad s.queue = [f_j, v_j, i_j]^{j \in 1..n} \qquad Q = [f_j, UpdFut(v_j, f, v), i_j]^{j \in 1..n}$$
$$s.results = [f_k, v_k]^{k \in 1..n'} \qquad R = [f_k, UpdFut(v_k, f, v)]^{k \in 1..n'}$$
$$S \vdash Comp[itf, subCp, bindings, s] \rightarrow_R$$
$$Comp[itf, subCp, bindings, s(\!|queue := Q, results := R|\!)]$$

COMMBROTHERS
$$[N.i_1, N'.i_2] \in bindings \qquad \vdash subCp[N] \dashv i_1, f, v \mapsto C$$
$$SubCp' = subCp[N \mapsto C] \qquad C' = Enqueue(subCp'[N'], [f, v, i_2])$$
$$S \vdash Comp[itfs, subCp, bindings, s] \rightarrow_R Comp[itfs, SubCp'[N' \mapsto C'], bindings, s]$$

COMMPARENT
$$[N.i_1, This.i2] \in bindings; \vdash subCp[N] \dashv i_1, f, v \mapsto C$$
$$S \vdash Comp[itfs, subCp, bindings, s] \rightarrow_R$$
$$Enqueue(Comp[itfs, subCp[N \mapsto C], bindings, s], [f, v, i_2])$$

COMMCHILD
$$s.queue = [f, v, i_1] \# Q \qquad [This.i_1, N'.i_2] \in bindings \qquad f' \notin futs(S)$$
$$C' = Enqueue(subCp[N'], [f', v, i_2]) \qquad s' = s(\!|queue := Q, results := s.results \# [f, f']|\!)$$
$$S \vdash Comp[itfs, subCp, bindings, s] \rightarrow_R Comp[itfs, subCp[N' \mapsto C'], bindings, s']$$

COMPOSITECALL
$$s.queue = [f, v, i_1] \# Q \qquad i_1 \text{ is a client interface}$$
$$f' \notin futs(S) \qquad s' = s(\!|queue := Q, results := s.results \# [f, f']|\!)$$
$$\vdash Comp[itfs, subCp, bindings, s] \dashv i_1, f', v \mapsto Comp[itfs, subCp, bindings, s']$$

Fig. 8. Semantics of the component composition

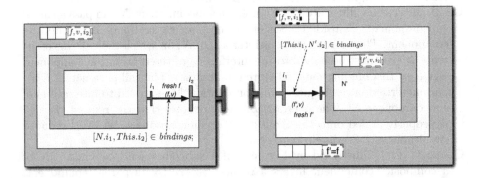

Fig. 9. COMMPARENT rule   **Fig. 10.** COMMCHILD rule

COMMCHILD, illustrated in Figure 10: this rule is the inverse case of the preceding one – a component communicates to a child – corresponds to a delegation of a request to subcomponents as shown in Figure 4. The parent component's request queue is reduced by its first element, a new future f' for the result of this request is created and added to the result list of the parent component, and the request – with the new future – is queued into the respective subcomponent. The subcomponent is determined using the bindings: if the original request was on the (external server) interface i_1 and **This.i_1** is bound to $N.i_2$ then the request will be sent to the interface i_2 of the subcomponent N. The composite component records in its request queue that the result for the future f is in fact the newly created future f'.

COMPOSITECALL: This rule explains how a call received by a subcomponent is emitted on the external client interface onto the context of the enclosing component. This rule corresponds to the CALL rule for the primitive components. The first request f, v received on (internal server) interface i_1 is sent on the matching external client interface (with same name). This call will be matched against a COMM rule that will enqueue this request. A fresh future f' is found for this new request and the composite records that the value of f is in fact the future f'.

Figure 11 illustrates a sequence of rules allowing a client component Cli to send, on interface c, a request to the interface s of a component Srv; Srv is encapsulated in a composite component Cmp, thus the request transits by the interface i. The first reduction sends a request from Cli to the composite, then the request is delegated to Srv by the composite, with a new future f' aliased to f. Finally, Cli obtains a direct reference to future f' while Srv starts serving the request. The original configuration is of the following form (for the sake of exposition, we only mention internal states of primitives, and interface descriptions are omitted).

$$\text{Comp}[\emptyset, \text{Cli} \mapsto \text{Prim}[\{c\}, s_0^c],$$
$$\text{Cmp} \mapsto \text{Comp}[\{i\}, \text{Srv} \mapsto \text{Prim}[\{s\}, s_0^s], \{[\textbf{\textit{This.i}}, \text{Srv.s}]\}, s_0]$$
$$\{[\text{Cli.c}, \text{Cmp.i}]\}, s_0']$$

5   Tools/Middleware

This section presents component management tools which are necessary to provide adaptation mechanism for distributed components. Proving the correctness of these tools could be a great opportunity for using the formal component model presented in the preceding section. We focus below on two aspects: stopping components, and component reconfiguration; tools for dealing with these two aspects have been implemented in the ProActive/GCM component platform, thus showing already their practical impact.

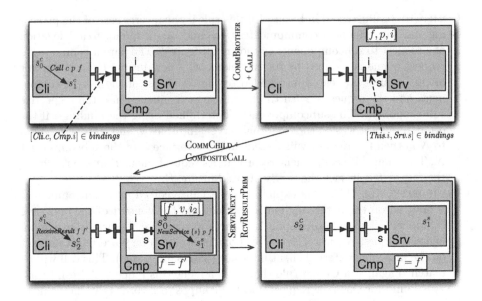

Fig. 11. Example of a Reduction (Hierarchy not mentioned)

5.1 Synchronisation and Stop

Fractal component lifecycle proposes a *stop* action, and a stopped state. Existing frameworks for Fractal and GCM sometimes consider recursively stopping a component assembly. However, safely stopping asynchronous components cannot be addressed by stopping procedures proposed so far.

The paper [29] proposes an algorithm for stopping a GCM component system. This algorithm recursively stops a component together with all its subcomponents, and reaches a *safe state* where the component is idle and has no request to serve. This algorithm defines as *master component* the component that receives initially a stop request. The algorithm is split into two phases. In the first phase the master component marks all the requests it sends. This phase lasts until all the requests, for which the master awaits the results, are marked. In the second phase the master component blocks all the requests it receives (except the marked ones) and the inner components continue processing their requests. When all the components are idle, and all inner components have empty request queues, the components are stopped. Let us only focus here on the request marking mechanism. This mechanism is useful to identify re-entrant requests, and to avoid deadlocks involving such requests. Roughly, the algorithm relies on a propagation of marks: each request sent during the service of a marked request is marked too. The master does not propagate marks to its subcomponents; thus only requests outside the master component are marked.

The formal component model presented in this paper allows, for example, the identification of waiting states, of deadlocks, and of re-entrant requests; it will allow us to reason about such requests, and to prove the correctness of the algorithm sketched above. This model also could verify properties on the algorithm termination and the state of the components when stopped.

5.2 Adaptation and Reconfiguration

One of the main purposes of stopping a component system is to be able to reconfigure it in order to adapt it to a different execution context, or to provide new functionalities. Indeed, for safely reconfiguring a component system, a component assembly must be in a state where components are stopped, and considered as easily reconfigurable.

In Fractal and GCM, adaptation is performed by dynamic reconfiguration. For adaptivity purposes, the GCM extends the reconfiguration capabilities of Fractal to the non-functional aspects: the control part of a component can be reconfigured dynamically. Moreover, the GCM specifies interfaces for the autonomic management and adaptation of components. *Autonomicity* is the ability for a component to adapt to situations without relying on the outside. By default, support for some autonomicity concerns are implemented by GCM components with precise non-functional interfaces, but the model being extensible, autonomic behaviour can easily be improved, adapted, and extended.

The formal model presented above enables reasoning on the interplay between the component configuration and the communications. To our mind, it is a crucial tool to prove correctness of autonomic adaptation procedures. Also, in order to ease the development of adaptation procedures, we are developing a scripting reconfiguration language that can be interpreted in a distributed manner, and that can synchronise with communication events or component state.

6   Conclusions

In this paper we presented a model for asynchronous components. Compared to existing component models and language specifications, our work is focused on the interaction between the programming model and the component model. More precisely, we defined the structure of our component model: it relies on the notion of interfaces, separation of non-functional and functional aspects, hierarchy, and bindings transmitting communications. Then, we presented a coherent model for allowing components to communicate asynchronously through a request/reply mechanism, but also through the use of futures. The semantics of our model is flexible enough to allow for multiple implementations and design choices, like multi-threaded versus mono-threaded components, choice of a future update strategy, choice of one of several local programming models, etc. On the contrary the interplay between hierarchy, asynchrony, and communication is quite precisely defined.

The definition of the component model's semantics is precise enough for a formal specification of this semantics to be written, for example in a theorem prover like Isabelle/HOL. We expect this formal specification to allow us to prove properties on component systems, management protocols for those components, or design choices of the different implementations of the model. Such a framework will provide a consequent step toward safe compositions of components, design of verification frameworks for asynchronous components, and safety of their management procedures.

On the other hand, we have taken care that the component model stays sufficiently abstract to be refined to different execution models. Since our component model abstracts from a concrete execution model it can be instantiated to others. One suitable execution model could be ASP, but also Creol is a candidate that could thereby be extended by hierarchical components. Even in the context of SOA, our model could enable SCA to be extended with a precise semantics for asynchronous communications.

References

[1] CCA-Forum: The Common Component Architecture (CCA) Forum home page (2005), http://www.cca-forum.org/

[2] Object Management Group, Inc. (OMG): CORBA Component Model Specification. Omg headquarters edn. (April 2006),
http://www.omg.org/cgi-bin/apps/doc?formal/06-04-01.pdf

[3] Beisiegel, M., Blohm, H., Booz, D., Edwards, M., Hurley, O.: SCA service component architecture, assembly model specification. Technical report (March 2007),
http://www.osoa.org/display/Main/
Service+Component+Architecture+Specifications

[4] Baude, F., Caromel, D., Dalmasso, C., Danelutto, M., Getov, V., Henrio, L., Pérez, C.: GCM: A Grid Extension to Fractal for Autonomous Distributed Components. Annals of Telecommunications (accepted for publication) (2008)

[5] Bruneton, E., Coupaye, T., Stefani, J.B.: Recursive and dynamic software composition with sharing. In: Proceedings of the 7th ECOOP International Workshop on Component-Oriented Programming, WCOP 2002 (2002)

[6] Caromel, D., Henrio, L.: A Theory of Distributed Objects. Springer, New York (2005)

[7] Agha, G., Mason, I.A., Smith, S.F., Talcott, C.L.: A foundation for actor computation. Journal of Functional Programming 7(1), 1–72 (1997)

[8] Yonezawa, A., Briot, J.P., Shibayama, E.: Object-oriented concurrent programming in ABCL/1. In: Proceedings OOPSLA 1986, November 1986, pp. 258–268 (1986); Published as ACM SIGPLAN Notices, 21

[9] Halstead Jr., R.H.: Multilisp: A language for concurrent symbolic computation. ACM Transactions on Programming Languages and Systems (TOPLAS) 7(4), 501–538 (1985)

[10] Niehren, J., Schwinghammer, J., Smolka, G.: A concurrent lambda calculus with futures. Theoretical Computer Science 364(3), 338–356 (2006)

[11] omg.org team: CORBA Component Model, V3.0 (2005),
http://www.omg.org/technology/documents/formal/components.htm

[12] OMG: Deployment and configuration of component-based distributed applications, v4.0. Document formal/2006-04-02 Edition (April 2006)

[13] Caromel, D., Henrio, L., Serpette, B.P.: Asynchronous and deterministic objects. In: Proceedings of the 31st ACM SIGACT-SIGPLAN symposium on Principles of programming languages, pp. 123–134. ACM Press, New York (2004)

[14] Abadi, M., Cardelli, L.: A Theory of Objects. Springer, New York (1996)

[15] Johnsen, E.B., Owe, O.: An asynchronous communication model for distributed concurrent objects. In: Proc. 2nd Intl. Conf. on Software Engineering and Formal Methods (SEFM 2004), pp. 188–197. IEEE press, Los Alamitos (2004)

[16] Johnsen, E.B., Owe, O., Yu, I.C.: Creol: a types-safe object-oriented model for distributed concurrent systems. Journal of Theoretical Computer Science 365(1-2), 23–66 (2006)

[17] Grabe, I., Steffen, M., Torjusen, A.B.: Executable interface specifications for testing asynchronous creol components. Technical Report Research Report No. 375, University of Oslo (July 2008)

[18] Meseguer, J.: Conditional reqriting logic as a unified model of concurrency. Journal of Theoretical Computer Science 96, 73–155 (1992)

[19] Jones, C.B.: Development Methods for Computer Programs Including a Notion of Interference. PhD thesis, Oxford University, UK (June 1981)

[20] Broy, M., Dederich, F., Dendorfer, C., Fuchs, M., Gritzner, T., Weber, R.: The design of distributed systems - an introduction to focus. Technical Report TUM-I9202, Technische Univerität München (1992)

[21] He, J., Li, X., Liu, Z.: rcos: A refinement calculus for object systems. Theoretical Computer Science 365(1-2), 109–142 (2006)

[22] Chen, X., He, J., Liu, Z., Zhan, N.: A model of component-based programming. In: Arbab, F., Sirjani, M. (eds.) FSEN 2007. LNCS, vol. 4767, pp. 191–206. Springer, Heidelberg (2007)

[23] Caromel, D., Delbé, C., di Costanzo, A., Leyton, M.: ProActive: an integrated platform for programming and running applications on grids and P2P systems. Computational Methods in Science and Technology 12(1), 69–77 (2006)

[24] Schmitt, A., Stefani, J.-B.: The kell calculus: A family of higher-order distributed process calculi. In: Priami, C., Quaglia, P. (eds.) GC 2004. LNCS, vol. 3267, pp. 146–178. Springer, Heidelberg (2005)

[25] Hirschkoff, D., Hirschowitz, T., Pous, D., Schmitt, A., Stefani, J.-B.: Component-oriented programming with sharing: Containment is not ownership. In: Glück, R., Lowry, M. (eds.) GPCE 2005. LNCS, vol. 3676, pp. 389–404. Springer, Heidelberg (2005)

[26] Merle, P., Stefani, J.B.: A formal specification of the Fractal component model in Alloy. Research Report RR-6721, INRIA (2008)

[27] de Boer, F.S., Clarke, D., Johnsen, E.B.: A complete guide to the future. In: De Nicola, R. (ed.) ESOP 2007. LNCS, vol. 4421, pp. 316–330. Springer, Heidelberg (2007)

[28] Nipkow, T., Paulson, L.C., Wenzel, M.T.: Isabelle/HOL. LNCS, vol. 2283. Springer, Heidelberg (2002)

[29] Henrio, L., Rivera, M.: Stopping safely hierarchical distributed components: application to gcm. In: CBHPC 2008: Proceedings of the 2008 compFrame/ HPC-GECO workshop on Component based high performance, pp. 1–11. ACM, New York (2008)

Specification and Verification for Grid
Component-Based Applications: From Models to Tools

Antonio Cansado and Eric Madelaine

INRIA – CNRS – I3S – Université de Nice Sophia-Antipolis
2004 Route des Lucioles, Sophia Antipolis - France
{acansado,madelain}@sophia.inria.fr

Abstract. Computer Grids offer large-scale infrastructures for computer intensive applications, as well as for new service-oriented paradigms. Programming
such applications brings a number of difficulties due to asynchrony and dynamicity, and require specific verification methods. We define a behavioural model
called pNets for describing the semantics of distributed component systems.
pNets (for parameterized networks of synchronised automatas) are hierarchical
assemblies of labelled transition systems, with data parameters expressing both
value-passing and parameterized topology. We use pNets for building models for
Fractal (hierarchical) and GCM (distributed) components. We present the Ver-
Cors platform, that implements these model generation procedures, but also abstraction mechanisms and connections with the model-checking engines of the
CADP toolset.

1 Introduction

Software components [1] are the de facto standard in many information technology
industries. Component-based frameworks and languages are seen as the natural succes-
sors of object-oriented languages for obtaining applications which are more modular,
composable and reusable. Many solutions have been proposed during the past 10 years,
with EJB being certainly the most well-known and used one. However, these promises
are often considered from a software engineering perspective and are at best only em-
pirically verified. We want to build development methods and environments that allow
application designers to specify the external behaviour of software components in a
black-box fashion, assemble them to build bigger components while guaranteeing that
the parts will behave smoothly together, and check that such an assembly implements
the overall behaviour expected by the user requirements. Beyond interoperability between components constituting large modern systems, e.g. in grid computing applications, or in large scale distributed software services, raise additional problems. In
particular distributed and asynchronous components require more complex behaviour
models, and the complexity of the analysis is higher. The analysis of properties related
with reconfiguration and dynamicity brings new aspects to check, e.g. defining evolving
systems, or checking substitutability.

Among the existing component models, *Fractal* [2] provides the following crucial
features: the explicit definition of provided/required interfaces for expressing dependencies between components; a hierarchical structure allowing to build components

F.S. de Boer et al. (Eds.): FMCO 2008, LNCS 5751, pp. 180–203, 2009.

by composition of smaller components; and the definition of non-functional features through specific interfaces, providing a clear separation of concerns between functional and non-functional aspects. The *Grid Component Model (GCM)* [3], extends Fractal by addressing large scale distributed aspects of components, providing structures for asynchronous method calls with implicit futures[1], and NxM communication mechanisms. Both Fractal and GCM models provide means to specify and implement management and reconfiguration operations.

The objective of our work is to provide tools to the programmer of distributed components systems in order to verify the correct behaviour of programs. We require those tools to be intuitive and user-friendly to be usable by non-experts of formal methods. To this end we build an analysis toolset, including graphical editors for defining the architecture and the behaviour of components, and state-of-the-art model-checking tools. At the heart of this platform lie the behaviour semantics of our component systems, and the model generation tools that are the subject of this article. In this context the choice of the behavioural model is crucial: it has to be compact, expressive enough to represent the behavioural semantics, but not too much, that could prevent us to map the models to the input formats of automatic verification tools. Some recent approches, for example π-ADL [4], are using formalisms based on the π-calculus, others, like μ-CRL [5] or STS [6] use algebraic descriptions of data domains. In both cases, such foundations give them powerful primitives for describing dynamic or mobile architectures, but also strong limitations for using automatic verification.

Most established approaches, on the other side, are using intermediate formats with data, that can be unfolded to finite-state structures. This is the case e.g. for the CADP toolbox [7], or for the SPIN model-checker and its specification language PROMELA, whose data values are instantiated (on bound domains) by the state exploration engines.

Our choice is to use an intermediate approach with a compositional semantic model including data called pNets [8]. It is different from previous approaches in the sense that we want a low-level model able to express various mechanisms for distributed systems, and that we do not limit ourselves to finite systems: we shall be able to define mappings to various classes of systems, finite or not. At the same time, the structure of our parameterized model is closer to the programming language or the specification language structure. Consequently, parameterized models are more compact, and easier to produce, than classical internal models. Typically, our pNets model is lower level than Lotos and Promela, but more flexible for expressing different synchronisation mechanisms. On the other hand, it has no recursive constructs, in order to better control the finiteness of encodings.

The second half of this work is a set of software tools called VerCors [9] for specifying and verifying GCM component systems. In the middle term, it will include both a textual and a graphical specification languages, unifying the architectural and the behavioural description of components [10]. It provides tools for defining abstractions of the system, and for computing their behaviour model in term of pNets. Finally it

---

[1] This is in contrast with languages like MultiLisp or Creol, where futures are explicit in the code. Having implicit futures in GCM/ProActive allows us to automatically provide optimal asynchrony.

has bridges with the CADP verification toolset, allowing efficient (explicit) state-space construction, and model-checking.

In the next section we describe the context of this work, namely the formalisms and models that we use for hierarchical distributed components: Fractal and GCM, and the communication mechanisms of the GCM implementation ProActive. In section 3 we recall the definitions of the parameterized networks of synchronised automatas (pNets), and we give the definition of the behavioural semantics of distributed components, starting with active objects, then modelling hierarchical components, Fractal components, and finishing with the specific features of GCM components, including multicast and gathercast interfaces, and first-class futures. In section 4, we describe the VerCors specification and verification platform, with a glimpse at its architecture, a description of the graphical editors, of the model generation tool, and some results obtained with the platform.

2 Context: Asynchronous Component Model, Active Objects, Grids

2.1 ASP and Active Objects

The ASP calculus [11] is a distributed object calculus with futures featuring:

- asynchronous communications: by a request-reply mechanism,
- futures, that are promised replies of remote method invocations,
- sequential execution within each process: each object is manipulated by a single thread of control,
- imperative objects: each object has a state.

An essential design decision is the absence of sharing: objects live in disjoint activities. An activity is a set of objects managed by a unique process and a unique active object. Active objects are accessible through global/distant references. They communicate through asynchronous method calls with futures. A future is a global reference representing a result not yet computed. The main result consists in a confluence property and its application to the identification of a set of programs behaving deterministically. This property can be summarized as follows: future updates can occur at any time; execution is only characterized by the order of requests; programs communicating over trees are deterministic.

From the proposed framework, we have shown a path that can lead to a component calculus [12]. It demonstrates how we can go from asynchronous distributed objects to asynchronous distributed components, including collective remote method invocations (group communications), while retaining determinism.

The impact of this work on the development of the ProActive library on one hand, and on the building of the behavioural semantics on the other hand, is probably one of our strongest achievements.

2.2 Fractal and GCM

Fractal [2] is a flexible and extensible component model. Its main features are: a hierarchical structure, in which everything can be built from components (including bindings and membranes), a generic description of non-functional concerns (e.g. life-cycle, binding, attribute management) through specific control interfaces, a strong separation of concerns between functional and non-functional aspects, a well-defined architecture description language (ADL), and several implementations [13, 14].

The Grid Component Model (GCM) [3] is a novel component model that has been defined by the European Network of Excellence CoreGrid and implemented by the EU project GridCOMP. The GCM is based on Fractal, and extends it to address Grid concerns.

Grids consider thousands of computers all over the world; programming Grids involve dealing with latency in communications between computing nodes, and optimizing whenever possible the parallelism of the computation. For that, GCM extends Fractal using asynchronous method calls. Grid applications usually have numerous similar components, so the GCM defines collective interfaces which ease design and implementation of such parallel components by providing synchronisation and distribution capacities. There are two kinds of collective interfaces in the GCM: multicast (client) and gathercast (server).

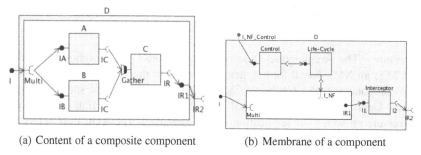

(a) Content of a composite component   (b) Membrane of a component

Fig. 1. GCM components

One to N and N to one interfaces. Typically a multicast interface (such as the interface Multi in Fig. 1(a)) is bound to the service interfaces of a number of parallel components, and a method call toward this interface is distributed, as well as its parameters, to several or all of them. GCM provides various policies for the request parameters, that can be broadcast, or scattered, or distributed in a round-robin fashion; additional policies can be specified by the user. The computation on the remote components will eventually terminate and send back, asynchronously, their results; Then the results of the invocations have to be assembled back with different possible policies (gather the results in a list, return the sum of the results, compute the maximum, or just pick the first that arrives and discard others...).

Symmetrically, gathercast interfaces (e.g. Gather in Figure 1(a)) are bound to a number of client components, and various synchronisation policies are provided. This corresponds to synchronisation barriers in message-based parallel programming, though here you may also have to specify how you redistribute the result on the client interfaces.

This treatment of collective communications provides a clear separation of concern between the programming of each component, and the management of the application topology: within a component code, method calls are addressed simply to the component local interfaces. The management of bindings of clients (on a gathercast interface) or services (on a multicast interface) is separated from the functional code.

Membranes and Non-functional interfaces. The component's non-functional (NF) aspects are handled by the component's membrane. The membrane is structured as a component system defining so-called *NF components*. Moreover, the GCM specifies interfaces for the autonomic management and adaptation of components. The membrane is also in charge of controlling the interaction between the component's content and the environment: the membrane decides how requests entering or leaving the component are to be treated.

The simplest binding one can define in a membrane is a binding from an external interface to an internal interface (e.g server interface I to internal interface Multi in Figure 1(b)): requests will simply be forwarded to a subcomponent server interface. But a NF component called Interceptor can be inserted between an external and an internal functional interface that will perform some non-functional processing (e.g. encrypting, logging, etc); an example is the Interceptor component between interfaces IR1 and IR2 in Fig. 1(b)).

More complex NF components can be used for introspection, reconfiguration, or autonomic management. Those will typically lie between the external and internal NF interfaces of the composite component.

Architecture. The Architecture Description Language (ADL) of both Fractal and the GCM is an XML-based format, that contains both the structural definition of the system components (subcomponents, interfaces and bindings), and some deployment concerns. Deployment relies on *virtual nodes* that are an abstraction of the physical infrastructure on which the application will be deployed. The ADL only refers to an abstract architecture, and the mapping between the abstract architecture and a real one is given separately as a deployment descriptor.

The Fractal/GCM ADL descriptions are static. Dynamicity of component applications, and the ability to reconfigure them, is gained through specific operations of their APIs. Several aspects of GCM, including its ADL, API, deployment description, application resources description, are now standardized by the European Telecommunication Standards Institute ETSI [15].

2.3   A GCM Reference Implementation: GCM/ProActive

The GCM reference implementation is based on ProActive [16], an Open Source middleware implementing the ASP calculus. In this implementation, an active object is used to implement each primitive component and each composite membrane. Although composite components do not have functional code themselves, they have a membrane that encapsulates controllers, and dispatches functional calls to inner subcomponents. As a consequence, this implementation also inherits some constraints and properties w.r.t. the programming model:

- components communicate through asynchronous method calls with transparent futures (place-holders for promised replies): a method call on a server interface adds a request in the server's *request queue*;
- communication semantics use a "rendez-vous" ensuring the causal ordering of communications;

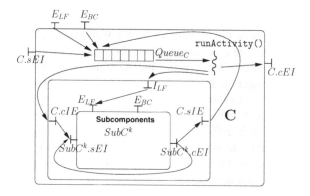

Fig. 2. *ProActive* composite component

- synchronisation between components is ensured with a data-flow synchronisation called *wait-by-necessity*: futures are first order objects that can be forwarded to any component in a non-blocking manner, execution is only blocked if the concrete value of the result is needed (accessed), while the result is still unavailable;
- there is no shared memory between components, and a single thread is available for each component.

Each primitive component is associated with an active object written by the programmer. Some methods of this active object are exported as the methods of the component's interfaces. The active object managing a composite is generic and provided by the GCM/ProActive platform; it forwards the functional requests it receives to its subcomponents. Primitive component functionalities are addressed by the encapsulated active object. For primitive components, it is possible to define the order in which requests are served by writing a specific method called runActivity(); we call this the service policy. If no runActivity() is given, a default one implements a FIFO policy (excepted for non-functional requests, see below). Composite components always use a FIFO policy. Note that futures create some kinds of implicit return channels, which are only used to return one value to a component that might need it.

Life-Cycle of GCM/ProActive Components. GCM/ProActive implements the membrane of a composite as an active object, thus it contains a unique request queue and a single service thread. The requests to its external server interfaces (including control requests) and from its internal client interfaces are dropped to its request queue. A graphical view of a composite is shown in Fig. 2.

Like in Fractal, when a component is stopped, only control requests are served. A component is started by invoking the non-functional request: start(). Because threads are non-interruptible in Java, a component necessarily finishes the request it is treating before being stopped. If a runActivity() method is specified by the programmer, the stop signal must be taken into account in this method.

Note that a *stopped* component will not emit functional calls on its required interfaces, even if its subcomponents are active and send requests to its internal interfaces.

2.4   Example

We will use the example in Fig. 3 to illustrate the various aspects of this paper. It is formed from one composite component B and three primitive components A, C, D. Component B has a number of subcomponents, and requests on its server interface S are dispatched to them through the multicast interface MC. Component D has two server interfaces W and R, and is supposed to host some shared resource (e.g. a database); its role in the example is to show the possible race-conditions or deadlocks that could arise, e.g, if a request on interface W has a side effect on the shared resource. Component A plays the client role, and will send requests to B, creating futures containing their promised responses, and transmitting these futures as parameters to requests to C. Component B also has two non-functional interfaces NF1 and NF2 that may be used e.g. to reconfigure its content.

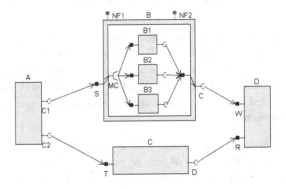

Fig. 3. Running example

3   Semantic Model

In this section, we recall the main definitions of the *parameterized Networks of synchronised automatas* (pNets, [8]). We use pNets as a general low level behaviour model for encoding different variants of our languages or component models. We start with the formal definitions of the model. Then we use pNets to define the behavioural semantics of two basic and important formalisms in the domain of distributed components: the ProActive "Active Objects" on one hand, and Fractal hierarchical components on the other hand (both examples are excerpts from [8]). Finally, we give an encoding for GCM components, including the management of request queues in primitives and composite components, and the encoding of future proxies, in presence of first class futures.

3.1   Parameterized Networks of Synchronised Automata (pNets)

The following definitions are taken from [8]. We start with classical labelled transition systems and structure them using synchronisation networks. Then we extend these definitions to include parameters, both as arguments in communication and in state definitions (à la "value-passing CCS"), and in synchronisation operators, obtaining a model powerful enough to describe parameterized and dynamic topologies.

We model the behaviour of a process as a Labelled Transition System (**LTS**) in a classical way [17]. The LTS transitions encode the actions that a process can perform in a given state.

Definition 1. LTS. *A labelled transition system is a tuple* $\langle S, s_0, L, \rightarrow \rangle$ *where S (possibly infinite) is the set of states,* $s_0 \in S$ *is the initial state, L is the set of labels,* $\rightarrow$ *is the set of transitions :* $\rightarrow \subseteq S \times L \times S$. *We write* $s \xrightarrow{\alpha} s'$ *for* $(s, \alpha, s') \in \rightarrow$.

We define **Nets** in a form inspired by the *synchronisation vectors* of Arnold and Nivat [18], that we use to synchronise a (potentially infinite) number of processes.

In the following definitions, we frequently use indexed vectors: we note $\tilde{x}_I$ the vector $\langle ..., x_i, ... \rangle$ with $i \in I$, where I is a countable set.

Definition 2. Network of LTSs.[2] *Let Act be an action set. A* **Net** *is a tuple* $\langle A_G, J, \tilde{O}_J, \overrightarrow{V} \rangle$ *where* $A_G \subseteq Act$ *is a set of global actions, J is a countable set of argument indexes, each index* $j \in J$ *is called a* hole *and is associated with a sort* $O_j \subset Act$. $\overrightarrow{V} = \{\overrightarrow{v}\}$ *is a set of synchronisation vectors of the form:* $\overrightarrow{v} = \langle a_g.\tilde{\alpha}_I \rangle$ *where* $a_g \in A_G$, $I \subseteq J \wedge \forall i \in I, \alpha_i \in O_i$

Fig. 4 gives a naive representation of the Net representing component B, with four subcomponents. Here the semantics has been configured so that call requests are going through a MC policy component, and are made visible (to the next level) as "?call(m,args)" for requests received by B, and "B[i].call(m,args)" for the requests dispatched to the respective B[i]. As an example, the second synchronisation vector in $\overrightarrow{V}$ reads as: action "!call(m,x1)" of the first hole (here MC) can occur synchronised with action "?call(m,x1)" of B1, and the corresponding global action is "B[1].call(m,x1)". There should be one such vector for each possible value of x1.

Note that the specific syntax (and meaning) of the actions is not important here: it depends on the specific formalism that has been translated into Nets. The synchronisation vectors are the only means that we use to express the synchronisation mechanisms. This way we can express traditional message passing (matching emission/reception), as well as other mechanisms like one to N synchronisation. In this first non parameterized version, we may need a infinite number of vectors to express the synchronisations occuring in a Net.

Definition 3. *A* **System** *is a tree-like structure whose nodes are* **Nets**, *and leaves are* **LTSs**. *At each node a partial function maps holes to corresponding* **subsystems**. *A system is* **closed** *if all holes are mapped, and* **open** *otherwise.*

Definition 4. *The* **Sort** *of a system is the set of actions that can be observed from outside the system. It is determined by its top-level node, with:*

$$Sort(\langle S, s_0, L, \rightarrow \rangle) = L \qquad\qquad Sort(\langle A_G, J, \tilde{O}_J, \overrightarrow{V} \rangle) = A_G$$

---

[2] This definition is simpler than the one we gave in [8], from which we have removed the *transducer* element in the pNet structure. It is possible to obtain an expressiveness similar to pNets with transducers by adding an extra argument to each pNet, and specifying this "Controller" as an argument pLTS.

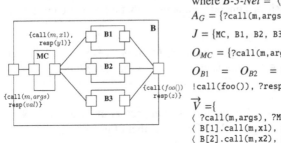

where $B\text{-}3\text{-}Net = \langle A_G, J, \tilde{O}_J, \vec{V} \rangle$ with:

$A_G = \{?\texttt{call(m,args)}, \,!\texttt{resp(val)}, \texttt{B1.call(m,x)}, \ldots\}$

$J = \{\texttt{MC, B1, B2, B3}\}$

$O_{MC} = \{?\texttt{call(m,args)}, \,!\texttt{resp(val)}, \,!\texttt{call(m,x1)}, \ldots\}$

$O_{B1} \;=\; O_{B2} \;=\; O_{B3} \;=\; \{?\texttt{call(m,x)}, \,!\texttt{resp(val)},$
$!\texttt{call(foo())}, ?\texttt{resp(z)}\}$

$\vec{V} = \{$
$\langle \; ?\texttt{call(m,args)}, ?\texttt{MC.call(m,args)}, -, -, - \rangle$
$\langle \; \texttt{B[1].call(m,x1)}, !\texttt{B1.call(m,x1)}, ?\texttt{call(m,x1)}, -, - \rangle$
$\langle \; \texttt{B[2].call(m,x2)}, !\texttt{B2.call(m,x2)}, -, ?\texttt{call(m,x2)}, - \rangle$
$\ldots \}$

Fig. 4. Example of Net

Next we enrich the above definitions with parameters in the spirit of Symbolic Transition Graphs [19]. We start by giving the notion of parameterized actions. We leave unspecified here the constructors and operators of the action algebra, they will be defined together with the encoding of some specific formalism.

Definition 5. Parameterized Actions. *Let P be a set of names, $\mathcal{L}_{A,P}$ a term algebra built over P, including at least a distinguished sort Action, and a constant action τ. We call $v \in P$ a parameter, and $a \in \mathcal{L}_{A,P}$ a parameterized action, $\mathcal{B}_{A,P}$ the set of boolean expressions (guards) over $\mathcal{L}_{A,P}$.*

Definition 6. pLTS. *A parameterized LTS is a tuple $\langle P, S, s_0, L, \rightarrow \rangle$ where:*

- *P is a finite set of parameters, from which we construct the term algebra $\mathcal{L}_{A,P}$,*
- *S is a set of states; each state $s \in S$ is associated to a finite indexed set of free variables $fv(s) = \tilde{x}_{J_s} \subseteq P$,*
- *$s_0 \in S$ is the initial state,*
- *L is the set of labels, $\rightarrow$ the transition relation $\rightarrow \subset S \times L \times S$*
- *Labels have the form $l = \langle \alpha, e_b, \tilde{x}_{J_{s'}} := \tilde{e}_{J_{s'}} \rangle$ such that if $s \xrightarrow{l} s'$, then:*
  - *α is a parameterized action, expressing a combination of inputs $iv(\alpha) \subseteq P$ (defining new variables) and outputs $oe(\alpha)$ (using action expressions),*
  - *$e_b \in \mathcal{B}_{A,P}$ is the optional guard,*
  - *the variables $\tilde{x}_{J_{s'}}$ are assigned during the transition by the optional expressions $\tilde{e}_{J_{s'}}$*

  with the constraints: $fv(oe(\alpha)) \subseteq iv(\alpha) \cup \tilde{x}_{J_s}$ and $fv(e_b) \cup fv(\tilde{e}_{J_{s'}}) \subseteq iv(\alpha) \cup \tilde{x}_{J_s} \cup \tilde{x}_{J_{s'}}$.

Example: Fig. 5 represents a possible behaviour of the body of component A from our example. The action alphabet used here reflects the active object communication schema: each remote request sent by the body has the form "$!\texttt{call}(f, M(a\vec{r}g))$", where M is the method name, eventually with parameters $a\vec{r}g$, and f is the identifier of the future proxy instance. Thus in this example, the action expressions are built from variables f and val, from the constants M_1 and M_2, and from the binary action constructors $\texttt{call}$ and $\texttt{getValue}$. These actions allow the component to perform a remote method call, and

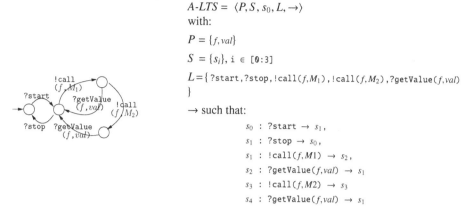

$$A\text{-}LTS = \langle P, S, s_0, L, \rightarrow \rangle$$

with:

$$P = \{f, val\}$$

$$S = \{s_i\},\ i \in [0:3]$$

$$L = \{\, ?\mathtt{start}, ?\mathtt{stop}, !\mathtt{call}(f, M_1), !\mathtt{call}(f, M_2), ?\mathtt{getValue}(f, val) \}$$

$\rightarrow$ such that:

$$s_0\ :\ ?\mathtt{start} \rightarrow s_1,$$
$$s_1\ :\ ?\mathtt{stop} \rightarrow s_0,$$
$$s_1\ :\ !\mathtt{call}(f, M1) \rightarrow s_2,$$
$$s_2\ :\ ?\mathtt{getValue}(f, val) \rightarrow s_1$$
$$s_3\ :\ !\mathtt{call}(f, M2) \rightarrow s_3$$
$$s_4\ :\ ?\mathtt{getValue}(f, val) \rightarrow s_1$$

Fig. 5. Behavioural model of component A

access the return value resp.; more details on how the component communicates with its environment are given later in Fig. 7.

Now, we define pNets as Nets where the holes can be indexed by a parameter, to represent (potentially unbounded) families of similar arguments.

Definition 7. *A pNet is a tuple* $\langle P, pA_G, J, \tilde{p}_J, \tilde{O}_J, \overrightarrow{V} \rangle$ *where: P is a set of parameters, $pA_G \subset \mathcal{L}_{A,P}$ is its set of (parameterized) external actions, J is a finite set of holes, each hole j being associated with (at most) a parameter $p_j \in P$ and with a sort $O_j \subset \mathcal{L}_{A,P}$. $\overrightarrow{V} = \{\overrightarrow{v}\}$ is a set of synchronisation vectors of the form:* $\overrightarrow{v} = \langle a_g, \{\alpha_t\}_{i \in I, t \in B_i} \rangle$ *such that: $I \subseteq J \wedge B_i \subseteq \mathcal{D}om(p_i) \wedge \alpha_i \in O_i \wedge fv(\alpha_i) \subseteq P$*

Explanations: Each hole in the pNet has a parameter p_j, expressing that this "parameterized hole" corresponds to as many actual arguments as necessary in a given instantiation of its parameter (we could have, without changing the expressiveness, several parameters per hole). In other words, the parameterized holes express *parameterized topologies* of processes synchronised by a given Net. Each parameterized synchronisation vector in the pNet expresses a synchronisation between some instances ($\{t\}_{t \in B_i}$) of some of the pNet holes ($I \subseteq J$). The hole parameters being part of the variables of the action algebra, they can be used in communication and synchronisation between the processes.

Fig. 6 is the parameterized version of the pNets for component B, in which the second hole (B) has a parameter n. The second synchronisation vector in the examples synchronises one (parameterized) action of the first hole MC, with an action (?call(m,x)) of the nth instance of B. The comparison with the instantiated version in Fig. 4 shows clearly the benefits of parameterization, in term of compactness, and of generality. Note that this is still a very simplified and naive version of the pNet for B, the full semantics of GCM composite components will be given later.

A pNet by itself is stateless, but it has state variables that encode some notion of internal memory that can influence the synchronisation. pNets have the nice property that they can be easily represented graphically, e.g. using the Autograph editor [20].

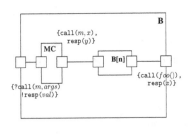

where $B\text{-}param\text{-}Net = \langle P, pA_G, J, \tilde{p}_J, \tilde{O}_J, \vec{V} \rangle$ with:

$P = \{$n, args, val, x$\}$

$pA_G = \{$?call(m,args), !resp(val), B[n].call(m,x), ...$\}$

$J = \{$MC, B$\}$

$p_{MC} = \{\}, p_B = \{$n$\}$

$O_{MC} = \{$?call(m,args), !resp(val), !call(m,x), ?resp(y)$\}$

$O_B = \{$?call(m,x), !resp(val), !call(foo()), !resp(z)$\}$

$\vec{V} = \{$
$\langle$?call(m,args), ?call(m,args), - $\rangle$
$\langle$ B[n].call(m,x), !B(n).call(m,x), n&?call(m,x)$\rangle$

... $\}$

Fig. 6. Example of a pNet

Building hierarchical pNets. Once a pNet hierarchical system is built, you need operations to transform it, and, at least:

– a product operation for reducing a pNets hierarchy to a flat pLTS,
– a way of instantiating a parameterized pNet system with respect to a given domain for one or several of its parameters.

In [8], we gave the definition of pNets instantiation, and we defined the product operation only for fully instantiated systems. This is enough for instantiating a pNet system for some finite abstraction of the parameter domains, and building the global state-space of the system.

3.2   Model Generation for Active Objects

The first application of pNets that we have published was for defining the behavioural semantics of active objects of the ProActive library. In [21, 22] we presented a methodology for generating behavioural models for active objects (AOs), based on static analysis of the Java/ProActive code. The pNets model fits well in this context, and allows us to build compact models, with a natural relation to the code structure: we associate a hierarchical pNet to each active object of the application, and build a synchronisation network to represent the communication between them.

Fig. 7 illustrates the structure of the pNets expressing an asynchronous communication between two active objects. A method call to a remote activity goes through a proxy, that encodes the creation of the local future object, while the request goes to the remote request queue. Note that for each program point pp corresponding to a remote method call in the source code, a series of futures, indexed by a counter c, can be created. The request arguments include the references to the caller and callee objects, but also to the future. Later, the request may eventually be served, and its result value will be sent back and used to update the future value.

This method is composed of two steps: first the source code is analysed by classical compilation techniques, with a special attention to tracking references to remote objects in the code, and identifying remote method calls. This analysis produces a graph including the method call graph and some data-flow information. The second step consists in

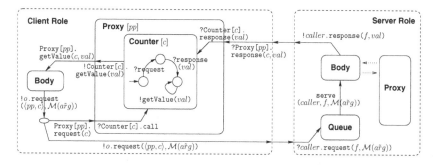

Fig. 7. Communication between two Active Objects

applying a set of structured operational semantics (SOS) rules to the graph, computing the states and transitions of the behavioural model.

The construction of the extended graphs by static analysis is technically difficult, and fundamentally imprecise. Imprecision comes from classical reasons (having only static information about variables, types, etc), but also from specific sources: it may not be decidable statically whether a variable references a local or a remote object. Furthermore, the middleware libraries include a lot of dynamic code generation, and the analysis would not be possible for Java code relying on introspection, classically used to manage some types of "dynamic topologies" in ProActive.

3.3 Model Generation for Hierarchical Components

Going from active objects to distributed and hierarchical components allows us to gain precision in the generated models. The most significant difference is that required interfaces are explicitly declared, and active objects are statically identified by components, so we always know whether a method call is local or remote. Moreover, the pNets's formalism expresses naturally the hierarchical structure of components, and will allow to scale up better, using compositional verification methods,

The pNet construction here may apply to any kind of hierarchical component model that features:

- Components with a set of interfaces and a content.
- Interfaces typed by a set of methods with their signature.
- Bindings between sibling subcomponents, or between a component and one of its subcomponent.
- Composite content composed of subcomponents, internal interfaces, and bindings.
- Empty content for primitive components.

We leave here undefined the code of a primitive component. It will depend on the framework, and will be used to generate a pLTS representing the primitive behaviour. We also leave undefined the data domains used for specifying indexes within the parameterized structure, and for building the arguments of the method calls.

From the information in a Component structure, it is straightforward to generate a pNet representing the communication between the interfaces and the subcomponents, from the following elements:

- the pNet has one hole for each (parametric) subcomponent;
- the global actions pA_G and hole sorts $\tilde{O}_J$ of the pNets are sets of actions of the form $[!|?]\, C_i.Itf.\mathcal{M}(\overrightarrow{arg})$ for invoking/serving a method $\mathcal{M}$ on the interface Itf.
- for each binding, and for each method in the signature of the source interface of the binding, it has two parameterized synchronisation vectors, one for sending the request, and one for receiving the response.

3.4   Hierarchical Components + Management Interfaces = Fractal

In the Fractal model, and in Fractal implementations, the ADL describes a static view of the architecture (used to build the initial component system through a *component factory*), and non-functional (NF) interfaces are used to control dynamically the evolution of the system. In this section we consider the core of the Fractal model, containing the hierarchical structure from the previous section, plus the basic non-functional interfaces and controllers, namely the Life-Cycle Controller (LF) and the Binding Controller (BC). We defined the behavioural semantics of Fractal applications in terms of pNets, giving the overall structure of the pNets encoding primitive and composite components, and the pLTS defining the LF and BC controllers.

A life controller pLTS (see Fig. 8) is attached to each component. Control actions (start/stop) are synchronised with the parent component and with all of its subcomponents. Status actions (started/stopped) are synchronised with the component's functional behaviour and with the BC, because the BC may only allow rebinding of interfaces when stopped.

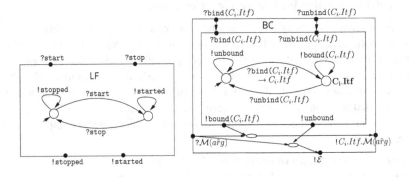

Fig. 8. pLTS of Fractal Life Cycle and Binding Controllers

A binding controller pLTS (see Fig. 8) is attached to each interface. Control actions (bind/unbind) are synchronised up to the higher level (Fractal defines a white-box definition for NF actions) and with the affected interface; status actions (bound/unbound) are used to allow method calls $\mathcal{M}(\overrightarrow{arg})$, to forward the call to the appropriate bound interface and to signal errors. The latter is a distinguished action $\mathcal{E}(unbound, C, Itf)$, visible to the higher level of hierarchy, and triggered whenever a method call is performed over an unbound interface.

Fig. 9 sketches the structure of the synchronisation of a component with its subcomponents. In this drawing, the behaviour of subcomponents is represented by the box

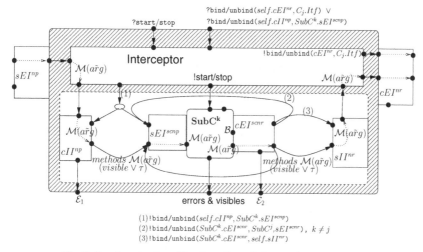

$(1) !\texttt{bind/unbind}(self.cII^{np}, SubC^{k}.sEI^{scnp})$
$(2) !\texttt{bind/unbind}(SubC^{k}.cEI^{scnr}, SubC^{j}.sEI^{scnr}),\ k \neq j$
$(3) !\texttt{bind/unbind}(SubC^{k}.cEI^{scnr}, self.sII^{nr})$

Fig. 9. Synchronisation pNet for a Fractal Composite Component

named $SubC^{k}$. For each interface defined in the component's ADL description, a box encoding the behaviour of its internal (cII and sII) and external (cEI and sEI) views is incorporated. The dotted lines inside the boxes indicate a causality relation induced by the data flow through the box. Primitive components have a similar automaton without subcomponents and internal interfaces.

3.5   Model Generation for GCM

In Figure 10, we show the behavioural model of a GCM primitive component. There is a pLTS for dealing with the component's life-cycle (**LF**), and a pLTS for serving functional and non-functional requests (**Service**). The behavioural model for a composite component is an instance of the model of Figure 9, in which the interceptor itself is a primitive component.

Service implements the treatment of control requests. It interacts with the **LF** controller through the !start and !stop actions. The action !start fires the process representing the runActivity() method in the **Body**, and at the same time changes the LF state to "started". The !stop action is more complicated: it is sent by **Service** to the **Body**, but a running body may not be able to stop immediately upon reception of a stop request (because Java is non-interruptible). If the service policy of the component is the default FIFO, this stop request will be executed when all previous requests will be served. If the developer has specified his own runActivity() method, she/he has the responsibility for testing the presence of a stop request, and terminate the runActivity() method. At this point the !stop action will be transmitted to the **LF** controller, while the **Body** will be back in its initial state, ready for receiving a !start action.

The **Queue** pNet encodes an unbounded Fifo queue, containing requests composed by a method name and its arguments, and a selection mode (typically oldest or younguest request matching a predicate). It is always ready to perform any of the three actions numbered (1) to (3) in Fig. 10:

- (1) serve the first functional method obeying the selection mode;
- (2) serve a control method only at the head of the queue;
- (3) serve only control methods in FIFO order, bypassing the functional ones.

Depending on the state of the life-cycle controller, these actions may or may not synchronise with the Body and the Service pNets. This is encoded through the emission of the !started or !stopped actions by the LF pNet.

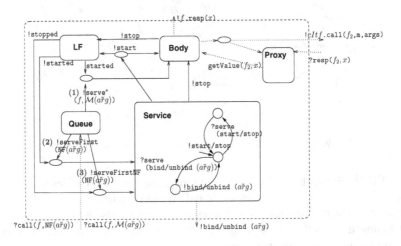

Fig. 10. Behavioural model of a primitive component

Modelling Collective Interfaces. Collective interfaces are responsible of distributing and gathering request calls and responses. Therefore, we provide a particular kind of proxy pLTS and N-ary synchronisation vectors encoding the control and data flow of these interfaces.

In Fig. 3, the multicast interface MC broadcasts request calls to all B's subcomponents and gathers the results. We gave incomplete views of its pNet model, in Figures 4 and 6, and we show now its complete model in Figure 11. The proxy Multicast(f) pLTS is in charge of distributing the requests to all bound interfaces (in this case the server interfaces of B's subcomponents). We use N-ary synchronisation vectors for broadcasting the call (!call(args)). This ensures that the call will be enqueued in every subcomponent at the same time. On the contrary, the response values of each component (?resp(val)) are sent back to the proxy individually and in any order. The proxy is in charge of gathering the result values in a vector. Later, when all results have arrived (guaranteed by the guard [rep==N]), it allows the component to access the result (!getValue(f,x)).

Modelling First-Call Futures. In Fig. 7 we depicted a simple proxy structure for ProActive futures. In GCM, futures can be transmitted in the parameters of a method call, or in the return value of a method call. In a naive approach, this requires knowing statically the flow of futures for each component because a future may have been created locally or by a third-party. This requires the analysis of the complete system. Instead, a better approach is to assign locally in each component an identifier f_{id} for

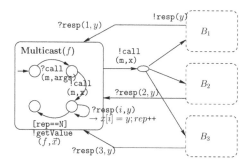

Fig. 11. Behavioural model of a multicast interface

each future, which permits the construction of behavioural models independently from the environment. Later, when the environment is known, the data-flow between components will determine which identifiers represent the same future object. At this point, these identifiers will be put in correspondence, and will be matched in the corresponding synchronisation vectors. This approach yields a compositional model.

In [23] we have shown the technical details of how to address different scenarios depending whether (i) a component transmits a locally created future; (ii) a component receives a future; and (iii) a component receives a future and retransmits it to a third-party. Here we define a new generic proxy that is able to deal with any combination of the 3 scenarios above. The proxy model has additional transitions w.r.t. the model presented in Figure 7 to allow futures to be transmitted. Figure 12 depicts this proxy[3].

When the local component is the creator of the future, the proxy starts by a transition `?call`. This allows the component to perform the remote remote call. In this case the proxy will wait for the `?response` transition to synchronise on the response value. Then there is a transition `!forward` for transmitting the future value to all components (if any) that may receive the future reference. Finally, the component body may access the content of the future through a `!getValue` transition.

Complementarily, if the local component did not create the future, the first transition of the proxy is a `?forward` which receives the value of the future. Afterward, the proxy behaves as in the previous case: it transmits the value to the remote components, and allows the component to access the future value.

Example: Sending a future created locally as a method call parameter. In Figure 12, the Client performs a method call M_1 on Server-A, and creates a Proxy(f) for dealing with the result. Then the Client sends the future to a third activity (Server-B) in the parameter of the method $M_2(f)$ (this call should eventually create another future f_2, but we have omitted it for simplicity).

---

[3] In this modelisation, we have an unbounded number of proxy instances, that live forever, and don't need to be terminated/destroyed. In the implementation, we may want to be more efficient: based on static analysis, the implementation can decide that some futures have a limited life-time, and that they can be destroyed or recycled at some point. Then we may want to prove correctness of such an optimisation.

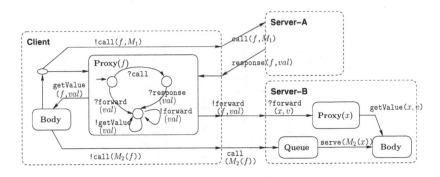

Fig. 12. Model for sending a future created locally as a method call parameter

From Server-B's point of view, there is no way of knowing if a parameter is (or contains) a future, so every parameter in a method call must be considered as a potential future. Server-B includes, therefore, a proxy for dealing with the parameter x of the method call M_2.

This example concludes the construction of pNets models for GCM components, incorporating non-functional controllers, request queues, future proxies, and NxM communication. In the current implementation, described in the next sections, the NxM communication and the proxies for first class futures are not yet supported.

4   VerCors: A Toolset for Specification and Verification

In this section, we report on the tool developments ongoing within our VerCors platform, implementing the behaviour model generation explained in the first half of this paper. We start with a description of the current and middle term functionalities of the platform, and we explain briefly the software tools used for the construction of the platform. Then we give more details on the graphical editors, on the model generation tool, and the model instantiation tools. Finally, we discuss some pragmatic aspects of various verification strategies for using the tools, and give some figures on typical case-studies.

4.1   Vercors Architecture

Fig. 13 sketches the architecture of VerCors. This toolset is available as free software, from our web site [9]. The platform has two goals: the verification of designs, and the generation of safe-by-construction code. In the following description of the VerCors modules, we shall indicate which functionalities are already available in the distribution (V0.2, spring 2009), and which are still under construction.

Front-End. VCE (for Vercors Component Editor) is our graphical component editor for designing components. It provides diagrams for defining the component architecture (see Section 4.3), and diagrams for defining the component behaviour (see Section 4.4). The latter is not yet available in V0.2. The Java Distributed Components specification language (JDC) is a textual language more expressive than our graphical diagrams, but is not yet implemented. It has been described in [10, 24].

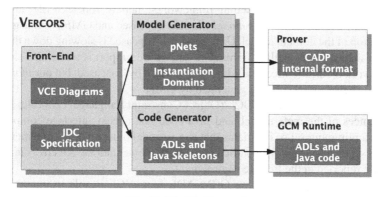

Fig. 13. The VerCors toolset

Model Generator. The model generator is the kernel of the platform. It is fed with specifications given by VCE diagrams or JDC specifications. It includes tools for data abstraction (from user-defined classes in JDC to Simple Types in pNets), tools for building the parameterized models from the specifications, and tools for manipulating and instantiating pNets (see section 4.5).

Code Generator. Another central part of the platform will be the code generator that is not (yet) currently developed. We will generate code capable of running under the standard GCM specification. It has an architecture definition based on the GCM ADL and Java code based on GCM / ProActive framework. The latter must be refined by the user by filling-in the business code.

External Tools. Externally to the platform, we interact with model-checking engines and with the GCM runtime. For now, VerCors uses the CADP toolset [25] for distributed state-space generation, hierarchical minimization, on-the-fly verification, and equivalence checking (strong/weak bisimulation). The connection with CADP is done through various textual input formats, that we generate from (fully instantiated) pNet models. A better approach would be to use a more generic and standardized intermediate format, like the FIACRE format [26], that would allow us to represent directly many (parameterized) constructs from the pNet model.

Verification is done by verifying regular μ-calculus formula encoding the user requirements. In the future, we would like to specify these properties within JDC, which would be subject to the same abstractions, and finally be translated into regular μ-calculus formula. We also plan to use other state-of-the-art provers, and in particular apply so-called "infinite system" provers to deal directly with certain types of parameterized systems.

4.2   Building Tools Using Eclipse Meta-modelling Framework

From a practical point of view, VCE consists of graphical editors for specifying the architecture and the behaviour of distributed components. It is built as an Eclipse plug-in based on EMF and GEF.

We use two similar meta-modelling frameworks, namely Topcased [27] and GMF. EMF plays the role of the *domain model* whereas Topcased and GMF provide graphical editors on top of the domain model. Unfortunately, Topcased is slowing down the development of their meta-modelling framework and future support is uncertain. Therefore, our early work on the architectural editor is generated by Topcased, but our more recent work on the behavioural editor is generated by GMF.

Model validation is based on OCL (Object Constraint Language) [28] rules that validate instances of the meta-model, and Java code that checks interface compatibility. There are a minimum set of invariants that every model must hold. Complementary, an additional set of rules cope with particular GCM implementations. All errors in the user models are reported in the Eclipse environment.

There is also compatibility with GCM ADL files. VCE is able to import and export GCM ADL files, though this is limited to functional components since there is no standard definition of NF components in the GCM ADL.

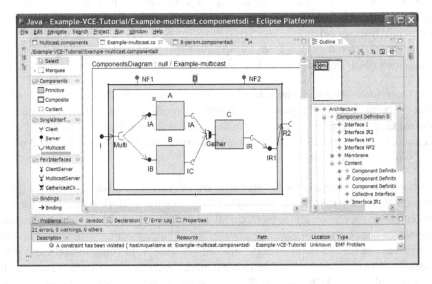

Fig. 14. Vercors Component Editor

4.3   Graphical Diagrams for Component Architecture

The kernel of the graphical language is a meta-model that reflects the GCM component structure. As these graphical constructions have already been used throughout this paper, we will only comment here on the main design choices that we have made.

At the top-level, the designer defines the root component that sets the services to be provided and required by the application to the environment. A component has a *content* that implements the business code, and a *membrane* that contains the non-functional code.

Components in the content are called *functional* components and those in the membrane are called *non-functional* (NF) components. The content is represented as a white rectangle inside the component, and the membrane is the grey area that surrounds the content. Nevertheless, the content of primitive components is not depicted; therefore, primitive components are distinguished as grey rectangles. We colour blue the "usual" functional interfaces, and green the NF interfaces.

Interface icons are inspired by the ones used in UML component diagrams. Server interfaces are drawn as filled circles (e.g. interfaces I, IA, ... in Figure 14), and client interfaces as semi-circles (e.g. interfaces IC, IR, ...). GCM's *collective interfaces* are not defined in UML and hence we adopted our own icons. Figure 14 also shows the icons we provide for *multicast* and *gathercast* interfaces, labelled Multi and Gather respectively. In the example, the interface Multi broadcasts incoming requests to components A and B, and the interface Gather gathers and synchronises requests coming from interfaces IC of components A and B towards the component C.

4.4 Diagrams for Behaviour Specification

The diagrams for behaviour specification have been defined in [29], but the diagram editors are not yet available in the toolset. They are based on a variant of UML 2 State Machine diagrams, with a number of State Machines used to specify respectively: the component service policy, each service method and each local method, the interface policies, etc.

4.5 Model Generation

The role of the ADL2N tool is to:

- build an abstract version of the component system, in which the user-defined Java classes used for the parameter domains are abstracted by some Simple Types from the pNets library.
- use the behaviour semantics defined in sections 3.3 to 3.5 to build the pNet model for each piece of the system.

The first step of the model generation deals with data abstraction: data types in a JDC specification are standard, user-defined Java classes, but they must be mapped to Simple Types before generating the behavioural models and running the verification tools. The result is an abstract specification with the same structure than the initial ADL.

In practice the user of ADL2N uses a GUI to specify at the same time the methods that will be visible, the arguments that are significant for the proofs, and finite domains for these arguments. This is shown in Fig. 15. Here some tool guidance would be very helpful to reduce the amount of user input required, and to guarantee the coherency of the abstraction with the dataflow within the system. This kind of guidance is not yet available in the toolset.

Such an Abstract Specification will then be given as input to the model generator. This tool builds a model in terms of pNets, including all necessary controllers for non-functional and asynchronous capabilities of the components. The only missing part is the functional behaviour (Body) of primitive components for which ADL2N only defines their sorts.

The second usage of the abstraction module of ADL2N is to specify a *finite* abstraction of the parameters domains (from Simple Types to finite Simple Types), so that the

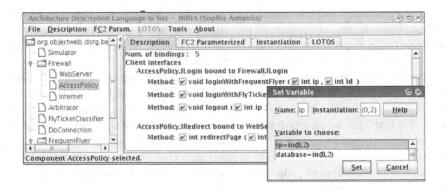

Fig. 15. Screenshot of ADL2N

final pNet system is finite, and suitable for analysis with finite-state model-checkers. In practice ADL2N produces two files, one file with the parameterized system, the other file with the definitions of the finite instantiations for the parameter domains.

pNets instantiations and export formats. The textual notation we use currently in the platform to encode pNets is called FC2 [30]. We provide two tools, FC2INSTANTIATE and FC2EXP [31], that create finite instantiations of the models and transform the files into the input formats of CADP, namely BCG for transition systems, and Exp for synchronisation vectors [32].

4.6 Model-Checking: Engineering, Pragmatic Complexity

Having produced our models in a structured and hierarchical format allows us to use many pragmatic strategies to master as much as possible the state-space complexity of model-checking. The main tool is compositionality: as we use a bisimulation-based verification toolset, it is essential that each intermediate subsystem is reduced (by branching or weak minimization) before being synchronized with others. If we are careful to reduce as much as possible the visibility of actions, then state-space explosion can be contained (to some extent) within the model of composite components. Additionally, a number of advanced features of the CADP toolset can help us to fight state-explosion, and to scale up. Typically, we can build the state-space at each level of the hierarchy using the distributed state-space generation of CADP, including on-the-fly hiding and tau-reduction, but also behaviour generation constrained by the environment. Then the minimization has to take place on a single machine, because the bisimulation engine is not implemented in a distributed way. And the next cycle of construction can be distributed again... This way your state-space construction can scale up to any system in which the largest intermediate structure will be in the range of 10^8 states. The model-checker engine itself has an experimental version working in a distributed fashion.

Using this kind of strategy, we have done some middle-size case studies, including for example the Common Component Modeling Example (CoCoME, [33]). This is a system of 17 components structured in 5 levels of hierarchy, with more than 10 data parameters, and some broadcast communication. We have treated this case using the

Fractal model generation (3.4), with very small abstract domains for the variables (typically 2 or 3 values). The brute force state space for this would be approximately 2.10^8, while the biggest intermediate structure that we generate is lower than 10000 states. We have shown in [33] a number of properties and problems verified on this model.

Such models can be used to check the satisfiability of safety or liveness formulas in branching time logics, or to check the bisimulation equivalence with respect to an abstract specification. In practice, we want to provide non-expert users with simple "press button" verification functions. This is easy for some families of reachability properties, like correct termination of deployment, or occurrence of some predefined sets of error actions. Deadlock detection is also a popular "push button" function, but explaining to the user the reasons of a deadlock can be challenging; it often involves some "missed synchronisation", that may be difficult to show, especially in presence of abstraction and instantiation.

The type of properties we can check on our models are more versatile than in most approaches, because we do not only encode the usual functional interactions between the components, but also their reconfiguration operations. So we can prove properties of applications in which one would change bindings, or remove and update subcomponents, while the rest of the system keeps running. This kind of properties typically depends on the behaviour of the system parts, and is not a general property of the middleware.

5   Conclusion and Perspectives

In this paper we have presented the models and tools we have been implementing to assist the development of Grid component-based applications. The approach is based on the modelling of the component behaviour using parameterized networks of automata. In addition, we have presented tools that generate these models, and tools for the specification of the component system.

This paper makes a step forward towards the verification of Grid applications. It provides novel models for multicast interfaces and generic proxies for transmitting futures. Moreover, one of the strong original aspects of this work is the focus put on non-functional properties, and the results we provide on the interleaving between functional and non-functional concerns. Thus, the programmer should be able to prove the correct behaviour of his distributed component system in presence of evolution (or reconfiguration) of the system.

We are currently developing additional tools in the VerCors platform to support our methodology. This includes the front-ends for textual and graphical specification languages, a tool for helping the user to build correct abstractions, and tools for providing readable explanations of the provers diagnostics.

Finally, we have presented techniques to master state-space explosion. The key aspect is the use of compositionality to reduce the system at each level of hierarchy. Nevertheless, in some cases, particularly when queues are unbounded, state-space explosion is inevitable when using explicit-state model-checkers. Therefore, our latest work focuses on the development of an infinite-state model-checker that verifies automata endowed with unbounded FIFO queues.

References

[1] Szyperski, C.: Component Software, 2nd edn. Addison-Wesley, Reading (2002)

[2] Bruneton, E., Coupaye, T., Leclercq, M., Quema, V., Stefani, J.-B.: An open component model and its support in java. In: Crnković, I., Stafford, J.A., Schmidt, H.W., Wallnau, K. (eds.) CBSE 2004. LNCS, vol. 3054, pp. 7–22. Springer, Heidelberg (2004)

[3] CoreGRID, Programming Model Institute: Basic features of the grid component model (assessed). Technical report, CoreGRID, Programming Model Virtual Institute, Deliverable D.PM.04 (2006),
http://www.coregrid.net/mambo/images/stories/Deliverables/d.pm.04.pdf

[4] Oquendo, F.: π-ADL: An Architecture Description Language based on the Higher Order Typed π-Calculus for Specifying Dynamic and Mobile Software Architectures. ACM Software Engineering Notes 26(3) (2004)

[5] Groote, J., Mathijssen, A., Reniers, M., Usenko, Y., van Weerdenburg, M.: The Formal Specification Language mCRL2. In: Proc. Methods for Modelling Software Systems (2007)

[6] Poizat, P., Royer, J.-C., Salaün, G.: Bounded Analysis and Decomposition for Behavioural Descriptions of Components. In: Gorrieri, R., Wehrheim, H. (eds.) FMOODS 2006. LNCS, vol. 4037, pp. 33–47. Springer, Heidelberg (2006)

[7] Garavel, H., Lang, F., Mateescu, R.: An overview of CADP 2001. European Association for Software Science and Technology (EASST) Newsletter 4, 13–24 (2002)

[8] Barros, T., Boulifa, R., Cansado, A., Henrio, L., Madelaine, E.: Behavioural models for distributed Fractal components. Annals of Telecommunications 64(1-2) (January 2009); also Research Report INRIA RR-6491.

[9] OASIS team: VerCors: a Specification and Verification Platform for Distributed Applications (2007-2009), http://www-sop.inria.fr/oasis/index.php?page=vercors

[10] Cansado, A., Henrio, L., Madelaine, E., Valenzuela, P.: Unifying architectural and behavioural specifications of distributed components. In: International Workshop on Formal Aspects of Component Software (FACS 2008), Malaga, Electronic Notes in Theoretical Computer Science (ENTCS) (September 2008)

[11] Caromel, D., Henrio, L.: A Theory of Distributed Objects. Springer, Heidelberg (2005)

[12] Caromel, D., Henrio, L.: Asynchonous distributed components: Concurrency and determinacy. In: Proceedings of the IFIP International Conference on Theoretical Computer Science 2006 (IFIP TCS 2006), Santiago, Chile, August 2006. Springer Science (2006); 19th IFIP World Computer Congress

[13] Bruneton, E., Coupaye, T., Leclercq, M., Quema, V., Stefani, J.-B.: An open component model and its support in java. In: Crnković, I., Stafford, J.A., Schmidt, H.W., Wallnau, K. (eds.) CBSE 2004. LNCS, vol. 3054, pp. 7–22. Springer, Heidelberg (2004)

[14] Seinturier, L., Pessemier, N., Coupaye, T.: AOKell: an Aspect-Oriented Implementation of the Fractal Specifications (2005),
http://www.lifl.fr/~seinturi/aokell/javadoc/overview.html

[15] European Telecommunication Standards Institute, http://portal.etsi.org

[16] Caromel, D., Delbé, C., di Costanzo, A., Leyton, M.: ProActive: an integrated platform for programming and running applications on grids and P2P systems. Computational Methods in Science and Technology 12(1), 69–77 (2006)

[17] Milner, R.: Communication and Concurrency. Prentice-Hall, Englewood Cliffs (1989)

[18] Arnold, A.: Finite transition systems. Semantics of communicating sytems. Prentice-Hall, Englewood Cliffs (1994)

[19] Lin, H.: Symbolic transition graph with assignment. In: Sassone, V., Montanari, U. (eds.) CONCUR 1996. LNCS, vol. 1119. Springer, Heidelberg (1996)

[20] Madelaine, E.: Verification tools from the CONCUR project. EATCS Bull. 47 (1992)
[21] Barros, T., Boulifa, R., Madelaine, E.: Parameterized models for distributed java objects. In: de Frutos-Escrig, D., Núñez, M. (eds.) FORTE 2004, Madrid. LNCS, vol. 3235, pp. 43–60. Springer, Heidelberg (2004)
[22] Boulifa, R.: Génération de modèles comportementaux des applications réparties. PhD thesis, University of Nice - Sophia Antipolis – UFR Sciences (December 2004)
[23] Cansado, A., Henrio, L., Madelaine, E.: Transparent first-class futures and distributed component. In: International Workshop on Formal Aspects of Component Software (FACS 2008), Malaga, Electronic Notes in Theoretical Computer Science, ENTCS (September 2008)
[24] Cansado, A.: Formal Specification and Verification of Distributed Component Systems. PhD thesis, Université de Nice - Sophia Antipolis – UFR Sciences (December 2008)
[25] Garavel, H., Lang, F., Mateescu, R., Serwe, W.: CADP 2006: A Toolbox for the Construction and Analysis of Distributed Processes. In: CAV (2007)
[26] Berthomieu, B., Bodeveix, J.P., Filali, M., Garavel, H., Lang, F., Peres, F., Saad, R., Stoecker, J., Fran, C.V.: The Syntax and Semantics of FIACRE V2.0. Technical report (Feburary 2009)
[27] Pontisso, N., Chemouil, D.: Topcased combining formal methods with model-driven engineering. In: ASE, pp. 359–360. IEEE Computer Society, Los Alamitos (2006)
[28] Object Management Group: UML 2.0 Object Constraint Language (OCL) Specification. formal/03-10-14 edn, version 2.0 (2003)
[29] Ahumada, S., Apvrille, L., Barros, T., Cansado, A., Madelaine, E., Salageanu, E.: Specifying Fractal and GCM Components With UML. In: Proc. of the XXVI International Conference of the Chilean Computer Science Society (SCCC 2007), Iquique, Chile, Nov 2007, IEEE, Los Alamitos (2007)
[30] Ressouche, A., de Simone, R., Bouali, A., Roy, V.: The FC2Tool user manuel (1994), http://www-sop.inria.fr/meije/verification/
[31] Barros, T.: Formal specification and verification of distributed component systems. PhD thesis, University of Nice - Sophia Antipolis (November 2005)
[32] Lang, F.: Exp.Open 2.0: A flexible tool integrating partial order, compositional, and on-the-fly verification methods. In: Romijn, J.M.T., Smith, G.P., van de Pol, J. (eds.) IFM 2005. LNCS, vol. 3771, pp. 70–88. Springer, Heidelberg (2005)
[33] Rausch, A., Reussner, R., Mirandola, R., Plášil, F.: The Common Component Modeling Example. LNCS, vol. 5153. Springer, Heidelberg (2008)

Semi-formal Models to Support Program Development: Autonomic Management within Component Based Parallel and Distributed Programming

M. Aldinucci[1], M. Danelutto[2], and P. Kilpatrick[3]

[1] Dept. Computer Science, Univ. of Torino
[2] Dept. Computer Science, Univ. of Pisa
[3] Dept. Computer Science, Queen's Univ. Belfast

Abstract. Functional and non-functional concerns require different programming effort, different techniques and different methodologies when attempting to program efficient parallel/distributed applications. In this work we present a "programmer oriented" methodology based on formal tools that permits reasoning about parallel/distributed program development and refinement. The proposed methodology is *semi-formal* in that it does not require the exploitation of highly formal tools and techniques, while providing a palatable and effective support to programmers developing parallel/distributed applications, in particular when handling non-functional concerns.

Keywords: program modelling, rewriting, non-functional concerns, performance tuning, autonomic computing.

1 Introduction

Modern distributed systems including grids, clouds and, more generally, service oriented architectures, are characterized by heterogeneity and dynamism in the sense of failure, delays and the varying availability of services. They therefore pose new challenges to the programmer of parallel/distributed applications.

In particular, when developing a parallel/distributed application, a programmer has to deal with two distinct kinds of concern: functional and the non-functional (a.k.a. extra-functional) concerns. Functional concerns are those related to *what* has to be computed, i.e. to the algorithm defining the result as a function of the input data. Non-functional concerns are those related to *how* the result has to be computed, i.e. to the techniques needed to implement the algorithm in an efficient way on the parallel/distributed architecture at hand. Examples of typical non-functional concerns include performance tuning, fault tolerance, security and power management.

In fact, programming the non-functional part of a distributed application is frequently much more demanding than programming the functional part. Programming the functional part of these applications requires sound knowledge of

F.S. de Boer et al. (Eds.): FMCO 2008, LNCS 5751, pp. 204–225, 2009.
© Springer-Verlag Berlin Heidelberg 2009

the application field and of the algorithms that can be used to solve the problem at hand. This knowledge is normally in the repertoire of the application programmer. The situation is significantly different for non-functional concerns. In this case, specific knowledge related to the target architecture is required in order to develop efficient solutions/implementations solving the problems related to non-functional concern management. For example, if load balancing is to be achieved in the computation of some embarrassingly parallel application, the overall architecture of the target machine (shared memory vs. distributed memory, high vs. low bandwidth (latency) interconnection network, etc.) must be known to tackle effectively the load balancing. Also, the techniques used to manage non-functional concerns are often significantly different from those used to address functional concerns. The "normal" application programmer, however, usually has in his background neither specific knowledge related to the target architecture nor knowledge related to the particular techniques needed to tackle non-functional concerns.

It is therefore commonly recognized that, ideally, functional concerns should be the responsibility of the application programmer, i.e. the programmer with specific knowledge on the application field, whereas the non-functional concerns should be addressed by system programmers, i.e. the programmers with specific knowledge of the target architecture and of the techniques and peculiarities of particular non-functional concerns. In the terminology of Aspect-Oriented Programming, non-functional concerns represent cross-cutting concerns w.r.t. functional ones, and thus typically require orthogonal techniques and experience.

The remainder of the paper is structured as follows: Sec.2 further discusses the functional/non-functional aspects in parallel and distributed programming and Sec. 3 introduces behavioural skeletons and GCM, the Grid Component Model by CoreGRID where these concepts were first introduced. Then Sec. 4 introduces Orc, the formal model we use in our semi-formal program development support methodology. Finally, Sections 5 to 7 discuss how the semi-formal methodology supports reasoning about alternative implementations (5), autonomic management strategy design (6) and metadata usage to evaluate again alternative implementations (7).

2   Addressing Functional and Non-functional Concerns

In this work we consider some typical non-functional concerns that have to be managed when developing parallel and distributed applications on modern architectures and we propose a methodology based on semi-formal use of formal models and tools to support design, refinement, improvement and in general reasoning about non-functional concerns in parallel and distributed applications. However, as will be seen, here we do not take a classical approach to non-functional concern management.

In both sequential and concurrent programming, coding for a specific non-functional behaviour to achieve a given QoS goal was evident three decades ago. The software engineering solution to achieve it was to introduce levels of

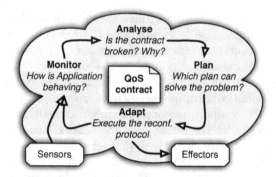

Fig. 1. Basic control loop for autonomic management

abstraction, effectively yielding a tree of refinements, from the problem specification to alternative target programs [1]. The derivation of a target program
then follows a path down this tree. The transition from one node to the next
can be described formally by a semantics-preserving program transformation or
refinement. Conceptually, porting a program to a different execution platform
configuration and/or QoS specification means backtracking to a previous node
on the path and then following another path to a different target program. Typically, the goal is achieved according to the spiral model by way of a number of
tuning iterations [2]. In this, the real extent of non-functional flexibility is often
experienced ex-post. Commonly, the cost of some of those iterations turns out
to be unacceptably high, thus reducing the potential market of the applications.
Traditionally, the design backtracking happens off-line because it requires the
partial re-design of the code. This makes the approach completely unsuited to
capturing variation points modelling run time events or dynamic changes in the
required QoS. Moreover, the design backtracking cost is directly related to the
frequency of non-functional adaptations.

An alternative approach consists in moving the non-functional concern han-
dling into an autonomic manager associated with the functional application code.
This autonomic manager, implementing a control loop such as that depicted in
Fig. 1, moves the choice of different design alternatives to launch or run time.
These alternatives may have been either fully or partially abstracted out during
the static design of the application.

In this work we assume this latter approach. Thus we consider that non-
functional concerns are dealt with within autonomic managers as is the case in
behavioural skeletons – introduced in Sec. 3 – which can be considered as code
factories in the form of high-order, parametric components that can be dynamically adapted along a predefined schema that is dynamically instantiated by a
previously unknown QoS contract. Having restricted the domain to autonomic
management of non-functional concerns *á la behavioural skeleton*, we introduce
semi-formal reasoning, i.e. a semi-formal way to use formal models [3,4,5] and
we demonstrate how several semi-formal techniques can be used to support
the design, development and refinement of autonomic managers dealing with
non-functional concerns in parallel and distributed applications.

3   Components and Behavioural Skeleton

Behavioural skeletons are component abstractions that capture both the functional and non-functional behaviour of some component assemblies, each of them specialised to solve one or more management goals, such as configuration, optimisation, healing and protection. Given a component model, these paradigms can be represented as parametric schema of wiring and/or nesting. The concept of behavioural skeleton was originally introduced to bring autonomic features within the *Grid Component Model* (GCM); however, since it is more abstract than the component model itself, it can be used in any component model admitting the dynamic reconfiguration of component assemblies.

3.1   The Grid Component Model (GCM)

The *Grid Component Model* (GCM) is a hierarchical component model explicitly designed to support component-based autonomic applications in distributed contexts. GCM allows component interactions to take place with several distinct mechanisms. In addition to classical "RPC-like" use/provide ports, GCM allows streaming ports and collective interaction patterns to be used in component interaction. GCM disciplines the life-cycle of components, which can be dynamically created, destroyed, bound to and unbound from assemblies. These distinguished features makes GCM particularly suitable for modelling distributed and dynamically adaptable applications. The full specification of GCM can be found in [6].

GCM is assumed to provide several levels of autonomic managers in components; they monitor and steer the non-functional features of the component programs. GCM components thus have two kinds of interfaces: functional and non-functional ones. The functional interfaces host those ports concerned with implementation of the functional features of the component. The non-functional interfaces host those ports needed to support the component management activity in the implementation of the non-functional features, i.e. those features contributing to the efficiency of the component in obtaining the expected (functional) results but not directly involved in result computation. Each GCM component contains an *Autonomic Manager* (AM), interacting with other managers in other components via the non-functional interfaces.

In this vision, the AM can reconfigure the assembly of its managed components to pursue a QoS goal. This typically happens if one of its *plans* is foreseen to be effective in re-establishing the validity of the QoS contract. Alternatively, the AM can contact a number of the other AMs in order to set up a cooperative reconfiguration plan, which will involve the union of managed components. In both cases, the AM may induce a structural reconfiguration of the component assembly through a number of *functionally equivalent* component assemblies.

The design of those plans is clearly a critical step for the effectiveness of the whole process. Two key aspects come into play:

1. the "creative" exploration of possible equivalent design alternatives, their aggregation and variation points, and their non-functional profile;
2. the checking of their functional equivalence.

While formal tools are useful for the second aspect, they are not very effective for addressing the first. The use of behavioural skeletons also address the second point since they represent, by definition, families of functionally equivalent assemblies. In this case the issue is raised at the skeleton design time, i.e. reduced to the first aspect. In this paper we advocate the use of a semi-formal methodology to address the first aspect. The methodology uses Orc as specification tool.

3.2 Behavioural Skeletons

Behavioural skeletons represent a specialisation of the algorithmic skeleton concept for component management [7]. Algorithmic skeletons have been traditionally used as a vehicle to provide efficient implementation templates of parallel paradigms. Behavioural skeletons, as algorithmic skeletons, represent patterns of parallel computations (which are expressed in GCM as graphs of components), but in addition they exploit the inherent skeleton semantics to design sound self-management schemes of parallel components.

As shown in Fig. 2, behavioural skeletons are composed of an algorithmic skeleton together with an autonomic manager and provide the programmer with a component that can be turned into a running application by providing the code parameters needed to instantiate the algorithmic skeleton parameters (e.g. the different stages in a pipeline or the workers in a farm) and some kind of Service Level Agreement (SLA, e.g. the expected parallelism degree or the expected throughput of the application). The choice of the skeleton to be used as well as the code parameters provided to instantiate the behavioural skeleton are functional concerns, while the autonomic management itself is a nonfunctional concern. In turn, the implementation of both the algorithmic skeleton and the autonomic manager is in the charge of the "system" programmer, i.e. the one providing the behavioural skeleton framework to the application user, while the instantiation of the behavioural skeleton is in the charge of the application programmer.

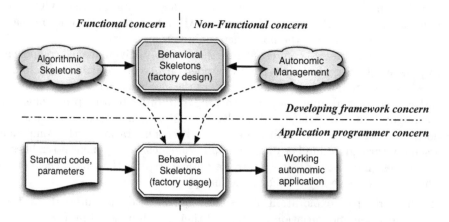

Fig. 2. Behavioural skeleton rationale

Autonomic management of non-functional concerns is based on the concurrent execution (with respect to the application "business logic") of a basic control loop such as that shown in Fig. 1. In the *monitor* phase, the application behaviour is observed, then in the *analyse* and *plan* phases the observed behaviour is examined to discover possible malfunctioning and corrective actions are planned. The corrective actions are usually taken from a library of known actions and the chosen action is determined by the result of the analysis phase. Finally, the actions planned are applied to the application during the *execute* phase [8,9,10,4].

Component technology, promotes the engineered development of distributed autonomic applications by enabling the co-design of autonomic management of non-functional concerns (performance tuning, in particular) and parallelism exploitation, which can be just-in-time derived from well-known, efficient patterns, such as behavioural skeletons [11].

In a component assembly, the autonomic management ultimately aims to induce non-functional alterations of the component assembly, which may translate into structural alterations of the component assembly. This means that an application is really described by an *evolving assembly* of components, i.e. an initial assembly and all its possible evolutions across the iterations of the adaptation phase. These reconfigurations of the assembly should be *formally* specified (at least) because they should be encoded in the manager. In addition, since in an autonomic system the management is inherently non-centralized, these reconfiguration should be *locally* specified, whereas the *global* evolution of the system is distributively realized via the cooperation of managers.

The formal description of evolving assemblies of processes, services and components has been the subject of active research in the global computing community [12]. Some of the results achieved in that community have also been cast to formal specification of the evolving assembly of autonomic components (see Sec. 8). However, the fully-fledged formal treatment of them requires enrichment of the model with many details that rapidly bring the complexity beyond reasonable (human) limits.

For this reason, we advocate the idea of *semi-formal* reasoning, i.e. a semi-formal way to reason about the equivalence of formal specifications [3,4,5]. Here, the main idea is to develop a, possibly partial, formal specification of a component assembly described using some formal tool such as Orc [13]. The specification provides the developer with a representation of the assembly and management overlay which allows exploration of their properties and the development of what-if scenarios while hiding the inessential detail. By studying the communication patterns present within the Orc process traces, the designer is able to derive for some paradigmatic assemblies (e.g. behavioural skeletons) an alternative structure which maintains core functionality, while allowing variation of non-functional behaviour, and thus different QoS. The derivation proceeds in a series of semi-formally justified steps, with incorporation of insight and experience as exemplified by the inclusion of expressions such as "reasonable to transfer this functionality" and "such modification makes sense".

4   Tools to Support Reasoning about Autonomic Management

As stated above, in modern parallel and, in particular, distributed systems much of the challenge lies in composing the various units of core functionality, rather than in implementation of the core functionality itself. Typically non-functional properties of an application depend on the overall "shape" of the system and this has led to an increased emphasis on orchestration: different designs of an application may be used to obtain different non-functional properties. A developer may, at design time, wish to explore the nature of different designs in terms of non-functional properties. Moreover, it is increasingly the case that *dynamic* adaption of the system design is required in response, for example, to differing resource availability, differing security considerations and so on. (Indeed, functional properties may lead to demand for architecture change: the occurrence of a hot-spot in processing data may require the addition of further resources, for example, to maintain a throughput requirement). In essence, this requirement for dynamic change is the raison d'être for autonomic management. The development of such dynamic systems requires means to describe both functional and non-functional concerns in relation to different designs; and means to support argument that the change induced by an autonomic system in response to, for example, environmental change, maintains functionality while adapting non-functional properties to the new conditions.

The need to explore different designs and their relation to differing non-functional properties motivates the search for a notation to be used as a vehicle for such investigation. We sought a notation which would

1. be oriented toward orchestration of components providing core functionality, rather than the core functionality itself;
2. allow an operational-style description of a system so that different designs could be described;
3. ideally, have a simple syntax and well-defined semantics so that properties of systems could be described and reasoned about with relative ease.

To this end we identified Orc [13] by Misra and Cook as a suitable candidate: Orc is an orchestration language which abstracts core functionality as site calls (see Sec. 4.1); it is operational in nature and provides a very small range of constructs and these are oriented toward describing the key aspects of concurrent/distributed systems. Thus it fits with our philosophy and lends itself to the level of reasoning that we wished to pursue: that is, a semi-formal style of reasoning in which one benefits from the clean, abstract, semantically well-founded description mechanism provided, but shies away from fully-formal proofs of general properties. Generally, we are content to prove properties that hold in particular situations and to draw upon insight and experience to allow conclusions to be drawn that are not fully supported by formal argument.

4.1 Orc

Orc is a language for distributed and concurrent programming that is targeted at the description of systems where the challenge lies in organising a set of computations, rather than in the computations themselves. Orc has, as primitive, the notion of a site call, which is intended to represent basic computations. A site, which represents the simplest form of Orc expression, either returns a *single* value or remains silent. Three operators (plus recursion) are provided for the orchestration of site calls:

1. operator $>$ (sequential composition)
   $E_1 > x > E_2(x)$ evaluates E_1, receives a result x, calls E_2 with parameter x. If E_1 produces two results, say x and y, then E_2 is evaluated twice, once with argument x and once with argument y. The abbreviation $E_1 \gg E_2$ is used for $E_1 > x > E_2$ when evaluation of E_2 is independent of x.
2. operator $|$ (parallel composition)
   $(E_1 \mid E_2)$ evaluates E_1 and E_2 in parallel. Both evaluations may produce replies. Evaluation of the expression returns the merged output streams of E_1 and E_2.
3. where (asymmetric parallel composition)
   E_1 where $x :\in E_2$ begins evaluation of both E_1 and $x :\in E_2$ in parallel. Expression E_1 may name x in some of its site calls. Evaluation of E_1 may proceed until a dependency on x is encountered; evaluation is then delayed. The first value delivered by E_2 is returned in x; evaluation of E_1 can proceed and the thread E_2 is halted.

Orc has a number of special sites:

- 0 never responds (0 can be used to terminate execution of threads);
- if b returns a signal if b is true and remains silent otherwise;
- *RTimer(t)*, always responds after t time units (can be used for time-outs);
- *let* always returns (publishes) its argument.

The notation
$$(\mid i : 1 \leq i \leq 3 : worker_i)$$
is used as an abbreviation for
$$(worker_1 \mid worker_2 \mid worker_3).$$
In Orc processes may be represented as expressions which, typically, name channels which are shared with other expressions. In Orc a channel is represented by a site [13]. *c.put(m)* adds m to the end of the (FIFO) channel and publishes a signal. If the channel is non-empty *c.get* publishes the value at the head and removes it; otherwise the caller of *c.get* suspends until a value is available.

5 Sample "Semi-formal" Usage of Orc

As an example of the way Orc can be used to support reasoning about parallel/distributed programs we consider the reverse engineered model of the muskel interpreter as derived in [3].

$$system(pgm, tasks, contract, G, t) \triangleq$$
$$taskpool.add(tasks)$$
$$| \; discovery(G, pgm, t)$$
$$| \; manager(pgm, contract, t)$$

$$discovery(G, pgm, t) \triangleq (|_{g \in G} \; (\; \text{if } remw \neq false \gg rworkerpool.add(remw)$$
$$\textbf{where } remw :\in$$
$$(\; g.can\_execute(pgm)$$
$$| \; Rtimer(t) \gg let(false) \;)$$
$$)$$
$$) \gg discovery(G, pgm, t)$$

$$manager(pgm, contract, t) \triangleq$$
$$|i : 1 \leq i \leq contract : (rworkerpool.get > remw > ctrlthread_i(pgm, remw, t))$$
$$| \; monitor$$

$$ctrlthread_i(pgm, remw, t) \triangleq taskpool.get > tk >$$
$$(\; \text{if } valid \gg resultpool.add(r) \gg ctrlthread_i(pgm, remw, t)$$
$$| \; \text{if } \neg valid \gg (\; taskpool.add(tk)$$
$$| \; alarm.put(i) \gg c_i.get > w > ctrlthread_i(pgm, w, t)$$
$$)$$
$$)$$
$$\textbf{where } (valid, r) :\in$$
$$(\; remw(pgm, tk) > r > let(true, r) \; | \; Rtimer(t) \gg let(false, 0) \;)$$

$$monitor \triangleq alarm.get > i > rworkerpool.get(remw) > remw > c_i.put(remw)$$
$$\gg monitor$$

Fig. 3. Reverse engineering of the `muskel` prototype

`muskel` is a full Java skeleton programming environment under development at the University of Pisa[1] since the early '00s [9]. The `muskel` environment can execute in parallel stream-parallel skeleton programs on networks/clusters/grids of Java enabled workstations. A simple autonomic manager maintains "best effort"—a performance contract (parallelism degree) provided by the user—in the presence of faulty or malfunctioning processing elements. In fact, autonomic managers were first implemented in `muskel` and then moved and greatly extended in the behavioural skeleton research framework.

When a `muskel` skeleton program is run, the `muskel` framework scans the available network looking for processing nodes hosting a `muskel` runtime system and recruits a number of these resources to execute the program. The number of resources recruited is as close as possible to the parallelism degree requested by the user via a *performance contract* provided with the program code. Then, the recruited resources are used to compute tasks appearing on the program input stream. In particular, an instance of the distributed macro data flow interpreter used in `muskel` to execute skeleton programs is used on each of the resources recruited.

---

[1] See http://cotognata.di.unipi.it/~marcodanelutto/wiki/doku.php?id=muskel

The muskel prototype is written in Java and uses RMI to interact with remote interpreter instances and UDP multicast to discover available resources in the network. The full muskel environment amounts to some 5K lines of code.

In Fig. 3 we show the "reverse engineering" of the muskel prototype in Orc. The Orc code here presents all the significant features of the actual prototype. This code has been manually derived from the actual Java code of the muskel prototype. A first version of the Orc code was written, which was much more complex than that of Fig. 3. This version was then refined to produce that of Fig. 3. No specific tools were used in this process, but most of the techniques outlined in this work relating to transformation and manipulation of Orc programs were used.

The discovery process, performed in parallel with the complete execution of the skeleton program, is modelled by the process behind the $discovery(G, pgm, t)$ expression. G represents the **grid** environment on which the program executes, *pgm* is the skeleton program itself, and t is the timeout delay before initiating another discovery action.

The autonomic manager action is modelled by the *manager(pgm,contract,t)* term. The manager starts a pool of *contract* control threads. Each of the control threads is in charge of fetching fireable macro data flow instructions[2] from the task pool and executing them on the remote interpreter instance (*remw* in the control thread) associated with the control thread. The manager also starts a *monitor* process in charge of getting a new remote resource from the discovery process and launching a new control thread when a previously running control thread terminates upon discovery of failure of the associated remote interpreter.

This Orc code can be understood much more readily than the actual Java muskel implementation and can be used to investigate properties of the implementation. In fact, in [3] it has been used to derive a new version of muskel where the potential bottleneck represented by the centralized discovery service has been removed. The new version was derived in three steps:

- First, the Orc code was analysed looking for possible modifications that may be used to remove the bottleneck. In fact we first analysed process traces to aid understanding of the interactions involved and, using insight gleaned from this, identified functionality that could be shifted between processes to achieve the desired non-functional goal—removal of the bottleneck—while retaining the functional behaviour.
- Then a new Orc model was written with the bottleneck removed—with a discovery service distributed among the control threads.
- Finally, the actual muskel code was modified in accordance with the model redesign to produce a new decentralized discovery version.

The whole process allowed us to postpone all Java related coding until a feasible solution had been identified and modelled in Orc. The modified version of the Java muskel prototype fulfilled the expectations of its Orc model.

---

[2] That in turn derive from the compilation of the muskel skeleton program.

The technique used to derive the new Orc model of autonomic management and discovery in `muskel` uses *traces* derived from Orc computations. In particular, the approach followed to derive the new manager/discovery structure in the `muskel` interpreter is the following:

- we take the Orc description of the `muskel` interpreter and expand terms so as to obtain *traces* modelling the evolution of the different parallel/distributed computations involved;
- we match traces by identifying matching pairs of send receive statements;
- we try to merge these traces into a single trace by collapsing send/receive pairs and moving item generation accordingly;
- we finally reverse-engineer an Orc expression that generates the resulting trace.

This process is effectively the application of a rule such as:

$$a > x > ch.put(x) > R) \mid (\ldots \gg ch.get() > y > S)$$
$$R \mid \ldots \gg a > y > S \tag{1}$$

where R should be a term with no occurrence of x. Rule 1 states that part of process A leading to the generation of a value x eventually sent to process B can be moved to process B in place of the actions receiving the x value from A, provided x is not needed in the continuation of A.

The same procedure will be used in Sec. 6 to validate skeleton transformation rules used within behavioural skeleton autonomic managers in a completely different context. It is worth pointing out the kind of usage made of Orc here: we use a formal notation to develop an abstract version of the code needed to implement the application at hand. The programmer can then reason on the abstract version in terms of mechanisms and tools close to his background: computations, traces, pairing of communication primitives, etc. Eventually, when something satisfactory from the viewpoint of the goal he had in mind has been achieved in the abstract code, this solution can be programmed with the actual programming tools at hand, that are much more difficult to manage properly and require a significantly more substantial effort than "programming" with Orc.

6   Demonstrating the Validity of Autonomic Management Policy with Semi-formal Reasoning in Orc

In this section we illustrate in more detail the kind of reasoning we have found useful with models expressed in Orc. We first introduce a model of the autonomic managers used in GCM behavioural skeletons (as discussed in Sec. 3). Then we introduce the skeleton structured programming model defined through behavioural skeletons and we provide an Orc modelling of the skeletons used. Finally, we show how we can justify the source-to-source transformations applied by autonomic managers of behavioural skeletons taking care of the performance tuning of an application.

6.1   Modelling Autonomic Management

We introduce an Orc model of the autonomic management activities in behavioural skeletons. Any autonomic manager in a GCM behavioural skeleton can be modelled by the following Orc code:

$$
\begin{aligned}
Mgr(Sk, SLA) = {} & distribute(Sk, SLA) > s > \\
& monitor(s) > m > analyse(s, m) > (b, p, v) > \\
& ((if(b) \gg adapt(s, p) > s1 > Mgr(s1, SLA)) \\
& \mid (if(\sim b) \gg raise(v) > Mgr(s, SLA))
\end{aligned}
$$

where Sk is the skeleton program derived from the behavioural skeleton nesting used by programmers to model their application and SLA is the contract the user specifies/requires to be ensured. The manager structure clearly reflects the control cycle outlined in Fig.1. During the *adapt* phase, a new version of the original Sk program may be produced to adapt the program to the dynamic change in either the target architecture or in the computation, as perceived from the *monitor* phase. This new version may differ from the pervious one, either by some non-functional feature (e.g. a varied number of workers in the implementation of a task farm skeleton) or by some functional feature (e.g. a varied parallelism exploitation pattern). In this latter case, the varied pattern will be one among the possible rewritings of the original skeleton program Sk that preserve the functionality of the application while (possibly) improving some non-functional feature. The new version of the program—$s1$—is eventually used to call recursively the Mgr. If the *analyse* phase does not succeed in finding a corrective plan for a malfunction perceived through the *monitor* phase, a violation is raised to the upper levels of management (upper level autonomic managers in the case of a hierarchy of behavioural skeletons, or to the user if this is the top level manager).

For example, if in the *analyse* phase the manager discovers that the user defined SLA cannot be guaranteed due to the too fine grain of two consecutive pipeline stages in Sk it may consequently decide to apply a stage merging rule (i.e. a rule merging the computation of two consecutive pipeline stages at the same computing element)[3] in the *adapt* phase, and therefore restart with deployment (*distribute*) of the (possibly new) SLA related to the new program version $s1$ with the collapsed stages.

Another notable case of *adapt*ation is represented by the variation of non-functional features of the skeleton program in execution—typically, variations of the parallelism degree used when implementing task farms. If in the *analyse* phase the manager discovers that there is a farm with a small inter arrival time for input tasks and a longer service time, its parallelism degree can be increased—new workers can be added—to improve the overall program efficiency [14].

Once more, the Orc model allows system designers to reason about the logical behaviour of the system at hand without needing to resort to analyzing the actual implementation code. In the following sections, we will show how Orc

---

[3] This rule will be better explained and demonstrated in Sec. 6.2.

based reasoning can be used in the application of one of the transformation rules used within the manager.

6.2 Reasoning about Program Transformation Rule Correctness with Orc

We assume the availability of behavioural skeletons modelling the more common patterns of stream parallel computations, namely pipeline and task farm computations (i.e. computations organised in stages, and embarrassingly parallel computations over streams of input tasks). We also assume the availability of a skeleton modelling sequential composition of other skeletons onto the same processing resources (aka "in place" pipeline, henceforth named *comp*).

An application parallel program will thus be structured as a hierarchical tree of skeletons with pipeline, farm and comp skeletons in the nodes of the tree, and sequential components in the leaves providing the sequential code to be computed in the lowest level pipeline stages or task farm workers. Here we will assume that the structure of the parallel application, in terms of the skeleton used, can be represented with terms derived using the following grammar:

$$Sk ::= farm(Sk) \mid pipeline(Sk, Sk) \mid comp(Sk, Sk) \mid seq(f)$$

where **seq** models a sequential component implementing some function f[4]. The task farm and pipeline skeletons can be modelled in Orc as follows:

$$
\begin{aligned}
\mathsf{pipeline}(A, B, ch_{in}, ch_{out}) &= \mathsf{stage}(A, ch_{in}, ch_{new}) \mid \mathsf{stage}(B, ch_{new}, ch_{out}) \\
\mathsf{farm}(W, nw, ch_{in}, ch_{out}) &= \mid i = 1, nw \ : \ \mathsf{stage}_i(W, ch_{in}, ch_{out}) \\
\mathsf{seq}(A, ch_{in}, ch_{out}) &= \mathsf{stage}_i(A, ch_{in}, ch_{out}) \\
\mathsf{comp}(A, B, ch_{in}, ch_{out}) &= \mathsf{cBody}(A, B, ch_{in}, ch_{out}) \gg \\
&\quad \mathsf{comp}(A, B, ch_{in}, ch_{out}) \\
\mathsf{cBody}(A, B, ch_{in}, ch_{out}) &= ch_{in}.get() > task > A(task) > y > \\
&\quad B(y) > result > ch_{out}.put(result) \\
\mathsf{stage}(A, ch_{in}, ch_{out}) &= \mathsf{body}(A, ch_{in}, ch_{out}) \gg \mathsf{stage}(A, ch_{in}, ch_{out}) \\
\mathsf{body}(A, ch_{in}, ch_{out}) &= ch_{in}.get() > task > A(task) > \\
&\quad result > ch_{out}.put(result)
\end{aligned}
$$

In the algorithmic skeleton framework it has been demonstrated that suitable rewriting can be performed at the skeleton tree level to obtain differently performing applications.

For example, pipeline computations with sequential stages can be collapsed to sequential computations to provide higher grain stages/workers and therefore to improve efficiency of the parallel computation:

$$pipeline(seq(f), seq(g)) \equiv comp(seq(f); seq(g))$$

---

[4] That is represents the skeleton wrapping of sequential code modelling a function (i.e. code with no side effects).

This result can be easily demonstrated using the Orc modelling of the skeletons presented above, and we will use this example to illustrate the Orc-based semi-formal reasoning that underpins our methodology.

The approach followed to demonstrate the equivalence above is the same as that used to derive the new version of the muskel manager in Sec. 5: we generate traces relative to the execution of Orc code, we look for matching *put* and *get* pairs, and we try to collapse traces using rule 1 of Sec. 5.

Applying this rule to our sample equation gives the following transformation:

$\mathsf{pipe}(A, B, c_1, c_3) =$

$\qquad \mathsf{stage}(A, c_1, c_2) \mid \mathsf{stage}(B, c_2, c_3)$

$= \qquad \mathsf{body}(A, c_1, c_2) \gg \mathsf{stage}(A, c_1, c_2) \mid \mathsf{body}(B, c_2, c_3) \gg \mathsf{stage}(B, c_2, c_3)$

$= \qquad c_1.get() > t > A(t) > y > \mathbf{c_2.put(y)} \gg \mathsf{stage}(A, c_1, c_2) \mid$
$\qquad\quad \mathbf{c_2.get}() > t > B(t) > y > c_3.put(y) \gg \mathsf{stage}(B, c_2, c_3)$

$\equiv \qquad \mathsf{stage}(A, c_1, c_2) \mid$
$\qquad\quad c_1.get() > t > A(t) > y > B(y) > z > c_3.put(z) \gg \mathsf{stage}(B, c_2, c_3)$

$= \qquad \mathsf{stage}(A, c_1, c_2) \mid$
$\qquad\quad \mathsf{comp}(A, B, c_1, c_3) \gg \mathsf{stage}(B, c_2, c_3)$

and unfolding another iteration we get:

$= c_1.get() > t > A(t) > y > \mathbf{c_2.put(y)} \gg \mathsf{stage}(A, c_1, c_2) \mid$
$\quad \mathsf{comp}(A, B, c_1, c_3) \gg \mathbf{c_2.get}() > t > B(t) > y > c_3.put(y) \gg \mathsf{stage}(B, c_2, c_3)$

$\equiv \mathsf{stage}(A, c_1, c_2) \mid \mathsf{comp}(A, B, c_1, c_3) \gg$
$\quad c_1.get() > t > A(t) > y > B(y) > z > c_3.put(z) \gg \mathsf{stage}(B, c_2, c_3)$

$= \mathsf{stage}(A, c_1, c_2) \mid \mathsf{comp}(A, B, c_1, c_3) \gg \mathsf{comp}(A, B, c_1, c_3) \gg \mathsf{stage}(B, c_2, c_3)$

It is clear that $\mathsf{pipe}(A, B, c_1, c_3)$ unfolds to an iterated sequence of $\mathsf{comp}(A, B, c_1, c_3)$ when rule 1 is applied. The parallelism degree of the original program schema ($\mathsf{pipe}(A, B, c_1, c_3)$) is clearly higher than that of the derived schema ($\mathsf{comp}(A, B, c_1, c_3)$). The original schema allows A and B to be computed in parallel on two consecutive tasks appearing on the pipeline input stream. The derived schema allows only computation of one item at a time, but this computation has clearly a higher computation grain[5] and therefore is more suitable for use in conditions where communication overheads are not negligible. In other words, the two schemas can be considered functionally equivalent but they differ non-functionally in that they offer different grains of computation and thus are suitable for differing execution platforms.

Although the result emerging here from transformation of the Orc model is well-known (pipeline stage collapsing to coarsen granularity) the intent here is to illustrate the way in which we use Orc descriptions supported by semi-formal reasoning to investigate design alternatives for non-functional properties. In the

---

[5] Ratio between the time spent to compute and the time spent to communicate, i.e. the time spent to receive the input task and to deliver the result.

case of the earlier `muskel` example, no such well-known pattern underpinned the design, but reasoning at a similar level allowed redesign to achieve the desired non-functional property—bottleneck removal.

7   Extending Orc with Metadata

In the previous sections we showed how an Orc based framework can be used to described parallel/distributed programs, to analyze their features and possibly to compare different versions of the same parallel/distributed applications with respect to some well defined features (e.g. number of actual parallel activities, kind of synchronizations involved, etc.).

The next step in the methodology is aimed at extending the amount and the kind of information within the Orc based framework, in such a way that further applications of the methodology presented so far can be investigated.

The kind of enrichment of the Orc framework we consider is *adding metadata* to the Orc expressions and terms used to model the parallel application [15]. By metadata we mean any data associated with Orc terms and expressions to represent non-functional concerns of the computation. Metadata are therefore *annotations* associated with Orc terms.

We will demonstrate how metadata can be used by considering a simple case: metadata representing *locations* of the computation where the associated Orc terms are actually computed. Other typical kinds of metadata modelling information on the non-functional concerns include those related to security (e.g. whether a given computation described by an Orc term has to be considered confidential or not), to performance (e.g. actual and predicted performance values relative to computations performed by the Orc term/expression) or to fault tolerance (e.g. MTBF of a node). Using *location* metadata we will eventually be able to evaluate the best implementation among a set of functionally equivalent implementations differing only with respect to their non-functional features.

7.1   Introducing *location* Metadata

According to our methodology, metadata is associated to Orc terms in a formal way. We assume that each Orc expression has one or more metadata associated. We also assume that metadata are represented by using names (functors) and parameters (parameters of the functors). As an example, the term $location(E, a)$ represents the fact that $location(a)$ is associated with the Orc expression E.

Location metadata can be formally associated to complex Orc expressions in a completely formal way. For example, consider Orc expressions using the farm and pipeline skeletons presented in Sec. 6. Location metadata can be associated as follows:

- explicit association of user supplied metadata with expressions/terms in the Orc code;
- a rule rewrite method is defined to derive location metadata from the user supplied metadata in such a way that location information is propagated along the entire skeleton tree.

Several policies can be defined to propagate *location* metadata along the skeleton tree. We consider, at the extremes:

conservative placement policy the location of the root skeleton nodes are propagated unchanged to *all* the immediate descendant nodes, unless differently specified by the user/programmer. The process is applied recursively.

speculative placement policy independent of the location of the root node, a fresh location is assigned to each of the immediate descendant nodes, unless differently specified by the user/programmer. The process is applied recursively.

What usually will happen is that the user supplies location metadata for a few, notable expressions, and then the other metadata location can be derived with one of the available policies, possibly the one identified by appropriate metadata provided by the user/programmer. For example, consider the code:

$$prog(f, g, h) \equiv pipeline(seq(f), pipeline(seq(g), seq(h)))$$

In our example, the programmer may be interested in expressing the maximum parallelism degree possible, and to keep the root of the tree on his own workstation. Therefore the program sketched above can be *user* annotated as follows: `location(prog,my_workstation)`, `locPropagPolicy(speculative)`. This in turn, will lead to the following annotation of the skeleton tree:

$$\langle \; location(prog, my\_workstation), location(seq(f), fresh\_loc()),$$
$$location(pipe(seq(f), pipe(seq(g), seq(h))), fresh\_loc()),$$
$$location(pipe(seq(g), seq(h)), fresh\_loc()),$$
$$location(seq(g), fresh\_loc()), location(seq(h), fresh\_loc()) \quad \rangle$$

where the $fresh\_loc()$ function will query a resource manager and return the name of a fresh location.

7.2   Exploiting *location* Metadata

The annotation of a skeleton tree with location metadata can be used for different purposes. First (and obviously) it can be used to drive the deployment of the skeleton program on the distributed architecture at hand (the one represented by the resource manager answering the $fresh\_loc()$ calls. Then, it can be used to analyse those non-functional concerns that depend on (relative) location of computations: communication cost analysis, for example.

If we wish to evaluate the communication cost of our sample computation, we can keep expanding the relevant Orc terms and adding/deriving location metadata in such a way that we eventually get the locations of the sites involved in sends and receives. In turn, this information can be used to derive the cost of all the communications involved, assuming we know some constant T_{lc} and T_{rc} for communications having partners on the same node (T_{lc} local communication) and those having the involved partners on different nodes (T_{rc} remote communication), respectively[6].

Traces may also be considered, associated to *location* metadata. In this case, the cost derived using metadata represents the overall amount of time spent communicating in the parallel/distributed application generating the trace.

These results, however, are not so interesting of themselves. The ability to take a program model and come up with a figure stating that the communication cost is $k \times T_{lc} + h \times T_{rc}$ is not so meaningful, independent of the ks and hs involved.

A much more interesting result stems from the ability to compare two **alternative** implementations. Let us assume that the parallel/distributed computation at hand can be implemented with two different algorithms/applications, modelled by Orc terms $OrcAppl_a$ and $OrcAppl_b$

In this case, we can proceed with the same user supplied initial metadata and location propagation policies and evaluate the final **ground** location labelling of our program (or, better, of the corresponding traces). Once this is done, we can compute the communication costs in terms of T_{lc} and T_{rc}. This time, however, by getting the two resulting terms giving the communication costs of traces relative to the same computation in $OrcAppl_a$ and $OrcAppl_b$, we can **compare** them and therefore determine which is the better of the computations with respect to communication costs.

More formally, this example of exploitation of Orc associated metadata can be expressed by:

- a grammar of terms over Orc expressions and metadata values is defined. For example:

$$E ::= \dots Orc\ expressions \dots$$
$$LocationMetadata ::= location(E, M) \mid locPropPolicy(M)$$
$$M ::= fresh\_loc() \mid loc(\langle literal \rangle) \mid \dots$$

  The grammar is used to denote all the "admissible" metadata for our Orc code.
- a set of rewriting rules are defined that provide a rewriting system propagating metadata along the Orc expressions modelling the computations: As an example, the following rule will belong to the set, denoting propagation of location in case of a conservative policy within a pipeline program:

$$\frac{location(pipe(A, B), L)}{location(A, L), location(B, L)} \quad \text{CONS.1}$$

- an abstract interpreter that computes the Orc expressions with respect to the associated metadata only and exploiting the rewriting rule set mentioned above.

---

[6] More realistically, we may consider functions of the sizes d of transmitted data $T_{lc}(d) = d/memory\_bandwidth$ and $T_{rc}(d) = latency + d/bandwidth$, with the same kind of results.

7.3 Exploiting *location* Metadata within Autonomic Managers

In previous sections, we have shown how *location* metadata can be used to evaluate which is the best implementation—with respect to a particular aspect, e.g. communication cost—among a set of equivalent, alternative implementations.

Such a result can be exploited in the manager described in Sec. 6.1. In particular, the result can drive choices made during the $analyse(s, m) > (b, p, v)$ phase, i.e. when analyzing a particular skeleton implementation s and the corresponding monitored behaviour m to determine whether some corrective action can be planned (b:boolean), which is the relative actuation plan p and, if necessary, which violation v has to be reported to the upper level manager. If alternative, feasible plans p' and p'' exist the result of $analyze(s, m)$ will be (b, p^x, v) with $p^x \in \{p', p''\}$ being the plan that in the subsequent $adapt(s, p) > s1$ phase will generate the improved new skeleton configuration, $s1$.

8 Related Work

In this work we concentrated on various issues relating to autonomic management of non-functional features in parallel/distributed computations. Although there is extensive work demonstrating how various aspects of parallel and distributed programming can be modelled using formal tools, there is much less work on exploitation of *semi*-formal techniques to support reasoning about non-functional concerns in parallel and distributed programs. We mention here a few research areas where reasoning schemas similar to that discussed in this work can be adopted.

The Service Component Architecture (SCA) [16] focuses on policies and implementation aspects of services but does not natively support dynamic reconfiguration of service assembly. However, the model can be extended to support dynamic reconfiguration. For example, the *Spatio-Temporal sKeleton Model* (STKM) [17,18], which can be defined in term of SCA, supports model reconfiguration by way of behavioural skeletons [4]. The STKM does not provide any specific methodology to reason about functionally equivalent assemblies or workflows of components.

An alternative approach is based on UML models. The work of [19] proposes the use of modes to address dynamic reconfiguration of service-oriented architectures and extends the UML to visualise such reconfiguration. The UML extension sticks to the mode terminology and does not include a visualisation of the transformation rules. The OMG is also working to standardize a UML profile and metamodel for services (UPMS) [20]. The current version does not support reconfigurations. Those approaches also propose a non-formalised approach (i.e. neither formal nor semi-formal). The only exception is the UML extension for service-oriented architectures that can be found in [21], which proposes refinement issues based on architectural styles formalised by graph transformation systems.

Architectural styles are the basis of the *Architectural Design Rewriting* (ADR) approach, which has been inspired mainly by graph-based approaches [22,23].

The use of graphs and graph transformations to model architectural styles has been proposed by several authors (e.g [24]) who based their approaches on the concept of shapes in programming languages. ADR shares also concepts with approaches based on process calculi with reconfigurable components (e.g. [25]). iADR is also related to approaches that deal with reconfigurations in software architectures defined by an ADL [26], and by graph transformation such as the *Synchronised Hyperedge Replacement* (SHR)[27]. Models in this family typically support the fully-fledged formal reasoning on assembly reconfiguration and equivalence; they have been proved effective in proving the correctness of single adaptations and simple sequences of them [28]. However, to be checked, these abstract models should be mapped down into concrete models describing a specific implementation enormously increasing the complexity of the description. As a matter of a fact, this complexity often prevents the designer from reasoning about the expected long-term evolution of the distributed system.

Model Driven Architecture [29] concepts look close to the idea of using Orc as the modelling language for actual application code. In this perspective, Orc can be intended as the PIM (platform independent model) to be used to derive, with some kind of automatic or semi-automatic tools, the PSM (platform specific model) and eventually an actual implementation.

Aspect Oriented Programming techniques have been taken into account in different frameworks to model and handle non-functional concerns (see, for example, [30,31]). We believe this approach is complementary to the behavioural skeleton idea adopted here. However, AOP techniques and mechanisms could probably be exploited in the autonomic manager implementation to further relieve system programmers of non-functional concern handling details, providing a finer grain of "separation of concerns" within the non-functional ones.

Finally, we chose Orc as our modelling language for two reasons. First, our interest was in *management* of functionality, and Orc's emphasis on orchestration of computations made it thus a perfect fit; second we wished to have a very compact language that allowed us to develop constructive representations of different designs, and reason about them at a high (but not too high) level of abstraction: this caused us to steer away from, on the one hand, very abstract notations such as π-calculus [32] which support a more abstract level of reasoning than we desired; and, on the other hand, parallel programming languages such as Erlang [33] and Oz [34] which are suitable for implementation rather than design.

9   Conclusions

In this paper we have discussed the challenge of non-functional concern management in parallel/distributed systems and emphasized the desirability of separation of functional and non-functional concerns. We have presented behavioural skeletons as a means of extending component-based parallel/distributed skeletons with autonomic managers taking care of non-functional concerns. The suitability and use of Orc (and its extension with metadata) to specify such autonomic management has then been argued and, to this end, we have emphasized a semi-formal style in which the specifications are treated as designs and an informal style of reasoning, drawing heavily upon insight and experience, is used to compare non-functional properties of alternative designs. While the experience has suggested the efficacy of the approach, much more experimentation is needed to determine the extent to which aspects of the methodology such as, for example, the rule identified in section 5 are transferable across different applications within a domain and even across domains of application. Ideally, rules of thumb of this sort would be identified at a level consistent with the approach, that is, an approach in which one gains benefit from the curt, well-founded definitions without resort to onerous formal reasoning.

References

1. Parnas, D.L.: On the design and development of program families. IEEE Trans. on Software Engineering SE-2(1), 1–9 (1976)
2. Boehm, B.W.: A spiral model of software development and enhancement. Computer 21(5), 61–72 (1988)
3. Aldinucci, M., Danelutto, M., Kilpatrick, P.: Management in distributed systems: A semi-formal approach. In: Kermarrec, A.-M., Bougé, L., Priol, T. (eds.) Euro-Par 2007. LNCS, vol. 4641, pp. 651–661. Springer, Heidelberg (2007)
4. Aldinucci, M., Campa, S., Danelutto, M., Vanneschi, M., Dazzi, P., Laforenza, D., Tonellotto, N., Kilpatrick, P.: Behavioural skeletons in GCM: autonomic management of grid components. In: Baz, D.E., Bourgeois, J., Spies, F. (eds.) Proc. of Intl. Euromicro PDP 2008: Parallel Distributed and network-based Processing, Toulouse, France, pp. 54–63. IEEE, Los Alamitos (2008)
5. Aldinucci, M., Danelutto, M., Kilpatrick, P., Dazzi, P.: From Orc models to distributed grid Java code. In: Gorlatch, S., Fragopoulou, P., Priol, T. (eds.) Grid Computing: Achievements and Prospects. CoreGRID, pp. 13–24. Springer, Heidelberg (2008)
6. CoreGRID NoE deliverable series, Institute on Programming Model: Deliverable D.PM.04 – Basic Features of the Grid Component Model (assessed) (2007), http://www.coregrid.net/mambo/images/stories/Deliverables/d.pm.04.pdf
7. Cole, M.: Bringing skeletons out of the closet: A pragmatic manifesto for skeletal parallel programming. Parallel Computing 30(3), 389–406 (2004)
8. Kephart, J.O., Chess, D.M.: The vision of autonomic computing. IEEE Computer 36(1), 41–50 (2003)
9. Danelutto, M.: QoS in parallel programming through application managers. In: Proc. of Intl. Euromicro PDP: Parallel Distributed and network-based Processing, Lugano, Switzerland, pp. 282–289. IEEE, Los Alamitos (2005)
10. Aldinucci, M., Danelutto, M.: Algorithmic skeletons meeting grids. Parallel Computing 32(7), 449–462 (2006)
11. Aldinucci, M., Danelutto, M., Kilpatrick, P.: Co-design of distributed systems using skeletons and autonomic management abstractions. In: César, E., et al. (eds.) Euro-Par 2008 Workshops. LNCS, vol. 5415, pp. 403–414. Springer, Heidelberg (2009)
12. Sensoria Project: Software Engineering for Service-Oriented Overlay Computers (2008), http://sensoria.fast.de/
13. Misra, J., Cook, W.R.: Computation orchestration: A basis for a wide-area computing. Software and Systems Modeling (2006), doi:10.1007/s10270-006-0012-1

14. Aldinucci, M., Danelutto, M., Kilpatrick, P.: Autonomic management of non-functional concerns in distributed and parallel application programming. In: Proc. of Intl. Parallel & Distributed Processing Symposium (IPDPS), Rome, Italy. IEEE, Los Alamitos (2009)

15. Aldinucci, M., Danelutto, M., Kilpatrick, P.: Adding metadata to orc to support reasoning about grid programming. In: Priol, T., Vanneschi, M. (eds.) Towards Next Generation Grids (Proc. of the CoreGRID Symposium 2007). CoreGRID, Rennes, France, pp. 205–214. Springer, Heidelberg (2007)

16. IBM: Service Component Architecture (SCA),
    `http://www.ibm.com/developerworks/library/specification/ws-sca/`
    (last accessed 2008)

17. Aldinucci, M., Danelutto, M., Bouziane, H.L., Pérez, C.: Towards software component assembly language enhanced with workflows and skeletons. In: Proc. of the ACM SIGPLAN Component-Based High Performance Computing (CBHPC), pp. 1–11. ACM, New York (2008)

18. Bouziane, H.L., Pérez, C., Priol, T.: A software component model with spatial and temporal compositions for grid infrastructures. In: Luque, E., Margalef, T., Benítez, D. (eds.) Euro-Par 2008. LNCS, vol. 5168, pp. 698–708. Springer, Heidelberg (2008)

19. Foster, H., Uchitel, S., Kramer, J., Magee, J.: Leveraging modes and UML2 for service brokering specifications. In: CEUR 2008. LNCS, vol. 389, pp. 76–90. Springer, Heidelberg (2008)

20. Object Management Group (OMG): UML Profile and Metamodel for Services (2008)

21. Baresi, L., Heckel, R., Thöne, S., Varró, D.: Style-based modeling and refinement of service-oriented architectures. SOSYM 5(2), 187–207 (2006)

22. Hirsch, D., Montanari, U.: Shaped hierarchical architectural design. In: ENTCS, vol. 109 (2004)

23. Bruni, R., Bucchiarone, A., Gnesi, S., Hirsch, D., Lluch Lafuente, A.: Graph-based design and analysis of dynamic software architectures. In: Degano, P., De Nicola, R., Meseguer, J. (eds.) Concurrency, Graphs and Models. LNCS, vol. 5065, pp. 37–56. Springer, Heidelberg (2008)

24. Shaw, M., Garlan, D.: Software Architecture: Perspectives on an Emerging Discipline. Prentice-Hall, New Jersey (1996)

25. Aguirre, N., Maibaum, T.S.E.: Hierarchical temporal specifications of dynamically reconfigurable component based systems. In: ENTCS, vol. 108, pp. 69–81 (2004)

26. Bruni, R., Lluch-Lafuente, A., Montanari, U., Tuosto, E.: Architectural design rewriting as an architecture description language (position paper). Technical Report MSR-TR-2008-61, Microsoft Research Cambridge, Proceedings of R2D2, Workshop on the Rise and Rise of Declarative Datacentre (2008)

27. Ferrari, G.-L., Hirsch, D., Lanese, I., Montanari, U., Tuosto, E.: Synchronised hyperedge replacement as a model for service oriented computing. In: de Boer, F.S., Bonsangue, M.M., Graf, S., de Roever, W.-P. (eds.) FMCO 2005. LNCS, vol. 4111, pp. 22–43. Springer, Heidelberg (2006)

28. Aldinucci, M., Tuosto, E.: Towards a formal semantics for autonomic components. In: Priol, T., Vanneschi, M. (eds.) From Grids To Service and Pervasive Computing (Proc. of the CoreGRID Symposium 2008). CoreGRID, Las Palmas, Spain, pp. 31–45. Springer, Heidelberg (2008)

29. Kleppe, A., Warmer, J., Bast, W.: MDA Explained: The Model Driven Architecture–Practice and Promise. Addison-Wesley Professional, Reading (2003)

30. Jingjun, Z., Furong, L., Yang, Z., Liguo, W.: Non-functional attributes modeling in software architecture. In: SNPD 2007: Proceedings of the Eighth ACIS International Conference on Software Engineering, Artificial Intelligence, Networking, and Parallel/Distributed Computing, Washington, DC, USA, pp. 149–153. IEEE Computer Society, Los Alamitos (2007)
31. Lohmann, D., Spinczyk, O., Schröder-Preikschat, W.: On the configuration of non-functional properties in operating system product lines. In: Proceedings of the 4th AOSD Workshop on Aspects, Components, and Patterns for Infrastructure Software (AOSD-ACP4IS 2005), Chicago, IL, USA, Northeastern University, Boston (NU-CCIS-05-03), 19–25 (2005)
32. Milner, R.: Communicating and Mobile Systems: the Pi-Calculus. Cambridge University Press, Cambridge (1999)
33. Cesarini, F., Thompson, S.J.: Erlang Programming, A Concurrent Approach to Software Development. O'Reilly, Sebastopol (2009)
34. Van Roy, P. (ed.): MOZ 2004. LNCS, vol. 3389. Springer, Heidelberg (2005)

Session-Based Compilation Framework for Multicore Programming

Nobuko Yoshida[1], Vasco Vasconcelos[2], Hervé Paulino[3], and Kohei Honda[4]

[1] Department of Computing, Imperial College London
[2] Lasige, Department of Computer Science, University of Lisbon
[3] CITI, Departamento de Informática, Universidade Nova de Lisboa
[4] Department of Computer Science, Queen Mary, University of London

Abstract. This paper outlines a general picture of our ongoing work under EU Mobius and Sensoria projects on a type-based compilation and execution framework for a class of multicore CPUs. Our focus is to harness the power of concurrency and asynchrony in one of the major forms of multicore CPUs based on distributed, non-coherent memory, through the use of type-directed compilation. The key idea is to regard explicit asynchronous data transfer among local caches as typed communication among processes. By typing imperative processes with a variant of session types, we obtain both type-safe and efficient compilation into processes distributed over multiple cores with local memories.

1 Introduction

This paper presents a brief overview of our ongoing work under EU Mobius and Sensoria projects on a type-based compilation and execution framework for distributed-memory multicore CPUs. Our aim is to obtain a new level of understanding on the effective shape of compilation and runtime architecture for distributed-memory chip-level multiprocessing. We take the viewpoint that communication and concurrency are a natural and fundamental structuring principle for modern applications. We identify typed processes exchanging messages through asynchronous communication as a basic model of computation, which we reify as a typed intermediate language. This intermediate language acts both as the target of translation from high-level programming languages and as the source of compilation to distributed memory chip-level multiprocessors. In both translation processes, types for communicating processes are used for ensuring key correctness properties for the resulting low-level code.

The background of this project is a recent fundamental change in the internal environment of computing machinery, driven by limiting physical parameters in VLSI manufacturing process [13, 34, 36], from monolithic Von Neumann architectures to chip-level multiprocessing (CMP), or CPUs with multiple cores. In the present work we are mainly interested in the CMP architectures based on distributed memory [24, 35], which offer the hardware interface analogous to distributed memory parallel computers [8] (in contrast to SMP/ccNUMA-like cache coherent CMP architectures [25, 27, 44]). This choice reflects our belief that a major factor for maximally exploiting the physical potential of future microprocessors is how one can harness asynchrony and latency in intra-chip data transfer.

F.S. de Boer et al. (Eds.): FMCO 2008, LNCS 5751, pp. 226–246, 2009.
© Springer-Verlag Berlin Heidelberg 2009

A non-uniform access to memories inside a chip can be realised by different methods, such as cache-line locking, eviction hints and pre-fetching. One method, often used for distributed memory CMP, employs direct asynchronous memory-to-memory data transfer, or Direct Memory Access (DMA), to share data among cores' on-chip local memories. A central observation underlying this approach is that trying to annihilate distance (i.e. to maintain global coherence) can be too costly, just as maintaining hardware interface for coherent distributed shared memory over a large number of nodes is unfeasible. This observation favours the use of explicit operations for directly transferring data from one part of a chip to another, and one of the efficient methods for doing so, effectively exploiting intra-chip communication bandwidth, is DMA operations. In a high-level view, this approach regards CMP as distributed parallel machines with explicit remote data transfer among them, making the framework close to computing models such as the LogP model [7] and parallel hierarchical memories [1]. The direct, asynchronous memory-to-memory transfer as a means of data exchange is flexible and can potentially make the most of on-chip network bandwidth [26], which is many-fold larger than intra-host computer networks [9], promoting concurrent, asynchronous use of communication and computing elements inside a chip. As has been studied in the literature [15–17, 30, 31], message passing concurrency can flexibly and generally represent the diverse forms of control and data flows found in sequential and concurrent applications. At the same time, the very nature of DMA operations, in particular asynchronous, direct rewrite of local memory of a distributed core, makes it hard to harness their power with safety assurance and controllability comparable to the traditional sequential hardware (for further discussions on this model, see §2.1).

In future, high-level applications will be designed and programmed using many different abstractions, especially regarding concurrency [6, 28, 39, 40, 42]. To understand the programming potential of distributed memory CMP, we need to examine whether these diverse abstractions, with associated data and control flow, can be mapped to this hardware model with efficiency, precision and fundamental safety assurance. One of the central concerns in this regard is to find an effective, disciplined method for using the DMA operations, making the most of their raw, asynchronous nature for flexibility and expressiveness while ensuring their correct usage. The desirable correctness properties include the freedom from synchronisation and racing errors (in the sense that data is remotely written only when a receiver is expecting it and at an expected region, and no other simultaneous writes can corrupt the data), the freedom from type errors (only data of a expected type and size is written), and progress of ongoing conversations (interaction sequences take place following the expected structure: in particular, a receiver will eventually obtain an expected datum).

In this paper we discuss one approach to the general compilation framework for distributed memory CMP. The framework is intended to offer a general, uniform and flexible basis for realising efficient translations of diverse (concurrent) programming abstractions to CMP executable code, with a formal guarantee of the aforementioned key correctness properties. The basic idea of our approach is to stipulate *typed communicating processes* as a representation for an intermediate compilation step from high-level abstractions, and, after a type-based analysis of this intermediate representation, perform a *type-directed compilation* [32] onto executable binary code for distributed memory CMP. Schematically:

High-level concurrent languages (L2)

$\Downarrow$

Typed imperative processes (L1)

$\Downarrow$

CMP executable (L0)

Above L0, L1, L2 refer to abstraction levels. Each $\Downarrow$ stands for one or more type-preserving compilations. At L1, we use an intermediate concurrent imperative language with types for channel-based conversations. The preceding studies on types for communicating processes, many centring on the π-calculus, have shown that they can offer fundamental articulation and basic safety guarantee for diverse communication patterns. As communication types for the compilation framework, we use a variant of session types [19, 41] for multiparty interactions [3, 5, 20], into which various high-level abstractions can be translated and which allows their efficient and safety-preserving compilation to distributed CMP primitives. The session types at L1 are generated from the interaction structures implicit in the high-level abstractions in L2, as we shall illustrate with a concrete example in the subsequent sections. The resulting typed communicating processes are amenable to uniform program analyses for safety assurance, and can be directly mapped to efficient code in L0, with a formal guarantee of the aforementioned key correctness properties.

2   Preliminaries

In this section we first clarify our assumptions on a hardware model, followed by a brief illustration of essential features of DMA operations. Then we present a running example for our type-preserving compilation framework, a simple streaming application. In particular we focus on the behaviour of the *double-buffering algorithm* used for compiling the running example. The algorithm is the standard method for stream and media processing to make the best of high-performance, multicore computing [21, 37].

2.1   A Hardware Model and DMA Primitives

Hardware Model. We assume an idealised model where a chip consists of multiple cores of the same Instruction Set Architecture (ISA), each with a local memory. Cores may or may not allow preemptive threads. Data sharing among distributed cores is performed via asynchronous data transfer from one local memory to another (DMA), as illustrated in the following diagram.

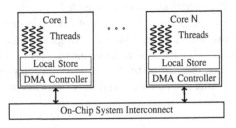

Our focus in the present inquiry is on the DMA-based data sharing among distributed memories: we do *not* consider other issues in distributed memory CMP such as the size of local memory, hierarchical memory organisation, capability control, security and heterogeneity. These are relatively orthogonal issues whose analysis may benefit from the understanding of the factor studied in the present paper.

DMA Primitives. Two versions of DMA primitives are known, an asynchronous write ("put"), and an asynchronous read ("get"). We mainly focus on *put* for brevity. The semantics of the *put* does not demand the sender to know the arrival of data for its sending action to complete: it is a non-blocking write. This asynchronous nature is essential for efficiency. Since a remote operation is anyway relatively expensive (even inside a chip [26]), we amortise the cost by sending a block or blocks of words, which can total hundreds of thousands of bytes. A sender can block until the data is sent out, or can be asynchronously notified. The DMA gains further efficiency by sending (even contiguous) words out-of-order. The receiver can be notified either asynchronously by a different messaging/interrupt mechanism or by a subsequent locally ordered *put* to an associated flag: for example one can place a memory fence [23] between the first *put* for data transfer and the subsequent *put* for a flag, so that the write to the flag (say turning 0 to 1) takes place *after* all the writes for the first *put*. Since consecutive writes are often cheap, this is an efficient method for checking the delivery.

Throughout the present paper, we assume a "macro" command for *put*, which includes initiating a send operation (including, if we use the scheme discussed above, a subsequent fenced flag) and waiting for the data to be sent out from the sender's local memory, but *not* for its arrival (and writing) at the receiver's remote memory. Thus, as soon as the data has been sent out, the CPU will become free. This is the standard usage of *put* [26], based on which we can easily accommodate an asynchronous notification as simple optimisation. Dually we assume a single macro command *wait* for the receiving side of *put*, which can, for example, consist of waiting for a fenced flag to be turned from 0 to 1, as discussed above. Each of these macros can be realised by a few hardware instructions [23], with different schemes depending on the mechanisms offered by a given hardware/software environment.

Observations on DMA Primitives. Because of its efficiency and flexibility, DMA is often used (partially or wholly) in multiprocessor system-on-chips. One of the prominent recent examples include Cell microprocessor [35]. This model considers CMP as a microscopic form of distributed computing, and is capable of making the most of on-chip interconnect, suggesting its potential scalability when the number of cores per chip increases and a relative wire delay inside a chip takes effect [9]. It can realise arbitrary forms of data sharing among cores' local memories, and in that sense it is general-purpose. Being efficient and general-purpose, however, the DMA operations are also extremely hard and unsafe to program in their raw form: the very element that makes the DMA operations fast and flexible — asynchronous, direct rewrites of memory — also makes them unwieldy and dangerous. The direct writes of one memory area to another, asynchronously issued and asynchronously performed, can easily destroy the works being conducted by applications. The danger of programming using these asynchronous operations may be compared to that of bare machine-level programming in sequential computers, without assistance of high-level language constructs such as procedures and data types and the associated compilation infrastructure, aggravated by the presence of concurrency and asynchrony.

2.2   Stream Processing and Double-Buffering

A Simple Stream Program. We take a simple stream program for data encryption as an illustration of our compilation framework [38]. Consider the following stream graph.

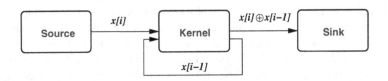

A data producer *Source* continuously feeds data to a *Kernel*, which calculates the XOR of each element with a key and writes the result on a stream to a consumer *Sink*. *Sink* may also have its own processing on the resulting data. The key used at each turn comes from (except for the first time) the Kernel's own output through a feedback, for a cipher block chaining. Such a stream algorithm can be easily expressed in stream programming languages [4, 12, 39, 43], whose program consists of transformers (called *kernels* or *actors*) connected through directed streams: each actor gets data from its incoming streams, processes them and places the results to its outgoing streams. For example, in the application above, a stream program for Kernel will be specified as a transformer which receives (say) an integer x from an incoming stream, calculates the XOR $x \oplus p$ where p is a variable storing the preceding value of x (where the initial value of p would be set to be some encryption key), and places the resulting value to an outgoing stream as well as assigning it to the new value for p. Stream programming has applications in DSP, multimedia and scientific computing and enables natural exploitation of parallelism at various levels, starting from high-level transformation of stream graphs to DMA-based multicore execution.

Double Buffering. In order to execute such a stream graph in a distributed memory CMP, the first step is to enlarge data granules, through the standard strip mining technique [29]: for example we may decide to treat these streams by units of say 16kB. This allows actors to exchange data in large blocks, instead of byte by byte (which would incur high overheads). We then program these three actors to exchange data strips (each of size 16kB) through an interactional algorithm called *double buffering* [37], illustrated in Figure 1, which is often found at the heart of implementations of stream programs in CMP.[1] Kernel uses two 16kB arrays, or *buffers*, named A and B in the picture: while Source uses a single 16k array (in practice it can use a large cyclic buffer), fed by, say, a byte stream from an external channel. The central idea of the algorithm is to repeat the following procedure.

---

[1] An effective method to allocate/schedule actors in a CMP environment is an interesting problem: we do not address this issue here because it involves runtime resource management, which is outside the focus of our present discussions.

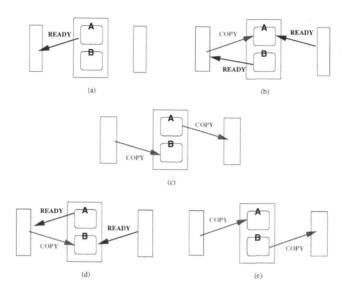

Fig. 1. Double-Buffering

While Kernel is receiving data into array A from Source, it processes data in array B and sends the result to Sink; it then repeats the process by exchanging the roles of A and B.

The five steps in Figure 1 materialise this idea:

(a) Kernel tells Source it is ready to receive an initial strip at buffer A;

(b) Source starts sending to A; asynchronously Kernel tells Source it is *also* ready to receive at buffer B, and again asynchronously Sink tells Kernel it is ready to receive at its own 16kB array;

(c) Kernel finishes processing its A-strip and sends the resulting data to Sink, while Source is sending a strip to B;

(d) Source continues sending to B; Kernel asynchronously tells Source it is ready to receive at A (since Kernel has now sent out its A-strip); again asynchronously Sink tells Kernel it is ready to receive the next strip;

(e) Now the situation is symmetric with respect to **(c)**: Source writes to A and Kernel writes from B. We now go back to **(b)**.

The algorithm allows asynchrony among computations and communications with minimal synchronisation to prevent data pollution. By overlapping computation and communication [7, 14], it makes the most of the available hardware resources, allowing concurrent and asynchronous execution of computation and communication. This allows the effective usage of available communication bandwidth in code execution, the tenet of effective network programming.

3   The Intermediate Language with Multiparty Session Types

This section introduces imperative processes with multiparty session types [41] as an intermediate language using the double-buffering example. This intermediate language serves two purposes. First, it provides an effective *source* language for compilation into a typed assembly language for CMP. Second, it offers an expressive *target* language into which we can efficiently and flexibly translate different kinds of high-level programs. This latter aspect is based on the observation that many concurrent and potentially concurrent programs (such as a streaming example above) can be represented as a collection of structured conversations, where we can abstract the structure of data movement in their programs as types for conversations. Through the use of these types and associated program analyses, we can formally ensure communications in programs are free from synchronisation and type errors, and satisfy progress.

3.1   Double Buffering in the Intermediate Language

The double buffering algorithm is both imperative and interactional, with highly structured communication structures. Asynchrony between sending and receiving is fundamental for its efficiency. The aim of the design of the intermediate language L1 (for *Session-typed Intermediate Language*) is to allow a precise and flexible typed description of such interactional imperative programs with precision and flexibility, in a form directly translatable to the execution mechanisms of distributed CMP.

```
Main Program :                  Kernel(a) :                       Sink(a) :
newPlace p0,p1,p2;              a[1](r1 r2 s1 s2 t1 t2 u1 u2).     a[2](r1 r2 s1 s2 t1 t2 u1 u2).
newChan a;                      newVar xA,xB : int[n];            newVar z : int[n];
spawn(Source(a))@p0;           newVar key : int = KEY;           μX.(
spawn(Kernel(a))@p1;           r1!(); r2!();                        //receive & print xA
spawn(Sink(a))@p2              μX.(                                 t1!(); u1?z;
                                  //process xA                       foreach(i : 1..n){
                                  s1?xA;                                print z[i];
Source(a) :                       foreach(i : 1..n){                  };
a[0](r1 r2 s1 s2 t1 t2 u1 u2).        xA[i] := xA[i] ⊕ key;         //receive & print xB
newVar y : int[n];                    key := xA[i];                 t2!(); u2?z;
μX.(                              };                                 foreach(i : 1..n){
   //send to xA                  t1?(); u1!(xA); r1!();               print z[i];
   foreach(i : 1..n){            //process xB                        };
     y[i] = get_int();           s2?xB;                            X
   }                             foreach(i : 1..n){
   r1?(); s1!(y);                  xB[i] := xB[i] ⊕ key;           )
   //send to xB                     key := xB[i];
   foreach(i : 1..n){            };
     y[i] = get_int();           t2?(); u2!(xB); r2!(); X
   }                           )
   r2?() ; s2!(y);X
)
```

Fig. 2. Double-Buffering Algorithm in L1

Figure 2 shows the description of the double buffering algorithm in L1. Program Main first finds three idle (virtual) cores denoted p_0 to p_2 (newPlace) and creates a new service channel a (newChan) to be used for the session initialisation by programs Source, Kernel, and Sink, running at different cores (spawn). Each "place" denotes an abstract unit of processing and memory resources, which may as well be considered as a virtual notion of a core with local memory in a distributed CMP chip.

The first line in Source represents session initialisation (on channel a); this is the point where Source receives the channels shared by all participants. The asynchronous session types in L1 require distinct channels to be used for distinct communications (except for communications iterated in a loop, which use the same channels), essential for translation into DMA operations. Thus we use four channels r_1, r_2, s_1, s_2 between Source and Kernel, and another four between Kernel and Sink. Now Source starts a conversation: after feeding its array through a for-loop (foreach($i : 1..n$) denotes the *pointwise iterator* for processing arrays which allows us to work with non-trivial programs without addressing array-bound checks [6]), it waits for an "A-ready" signal through r_1 ("?" denotes input), sends the data in the array through s_1 ("!" for output); repeats the same for r_2 and s_2, and returns to the main loop. Communication is purely asynchronous—the sending order is not guaranteed to be preserved at arrival.

Kernel, after allocating its variables (including the initial key value), signals Source that its buffers are both empty, via channels r_1 and r_2; then enters the main loop, where it proceeds as follows: first receives a datum at buffer x_A via s_1, goes through the buffer taking the XOR element-wise, after which it waits for Sink's cue via t_1 (which may have already arrived asynchronously), and finally sends out the buffer contents to Sink via u_1, and tells Source via r_1 that it is ready to receive at buffer A. It then works similarly for the second buffer. Sink acts in a way symmetric to Source (print prints a datum).

The three programs precisely describe the interactional behaviour informally illustrated in Figure 1.

3.2 L1 with Multiparty Session Types

We now outline how these structured dialogues can be abstracted as *types for conversations* in the form of multiparty session types [20], where pure asynchrony in communication is captured by a subtyping relation [33]. For example, in Figure 2, we see Source interacting with Kernel through channels r_1, s_1, r_2 and s_2 in this order, which is *different* from what we read from Kernel which starts by interacting at r_1 and r_2. How can we make sure that the Source's behaviour correctly matches that of the Kernel?

The theory of multiparty session types can type-abstract and verify the structure of a whole conversation. In the present context, the most notable feature of these types is that they can formally guarantee communication-safety and progress (deadlock-freedom). From a design viewpoint, developing a distributed program including a compilation framework demands a clear formal design as to how multiple participants communicate and synchronise with each other. These are the reasons why we start from a *global type* G, which plays the role of a type signature for distributed communications. These global types present an abstract high-level description of the protocol that all participants have to honour when an actual conversation takes place [20].

Once this signature G is agreed upon by all parties as the global protocol to be followed, a local protocol from each party's viewpoint, *local type T_i*, is generated as a projection of G to each party. If the global signature is too rigid, an individual party might wish to change their implementation locally. In this case, each local type T_i can be *locally refined* to, say, T_i', possibly yielding *optimised* protocols that are realised by programs P_i. If all the resulting local programs $P_1,..,P_n$ can be type-checked against refined $T_1',..,T_n'$, then they are automatically guaranteed to interact properly, without incurring in communication mismatch or getting stuck inside sessions, while precisely following the intended scenario.

Global Types. The development of type-safe programs for a double-buffering algorithm starts from designing the global type G,

$$\mu\mathbf{t}.($$

Kernel $\rightarrow$ Source : $r_1\langle\rangle$;	Kernel $\rightarrow$ Source : $r_2\langle\rangle$;
Source $\rightarrow$ Kernel : $s_1\langle U\rangle$;	Source $\rightarrow$ Kernel : $s_2\langle U\rangle$;
Sink $\rightarrow$ Kernel : $\quad t_1\langle\rangle$;	Sink $\rightarrow$ Kernel : $\quad t_2\langle\rangle$;
Kernel $\rightarrow$ Sink : $\quad u_1\langle U\rangle$;	Kernel $\rightarrow$ Sink : $\quad u_2\langle U\rangle$; $\mathbf{t})$

where Source, Kernel and Sink denote participant names, identified as p_0, p_1 and p_2 in the program in Figure 2.

A global type $p \rightarrow p' : k\langle U\rangle; G'$ means that participant p sends participant p' a message of type U on channel k, and then interactions described in G' take place. In this example, U denotes an int-array type. Type $\mu\mathbf{t}.G$ is use for recursive protocols where $\mathbf{t}, \mathbf{t}', \ldots$ are type variables.

The global type G uses recursion to describe an infinite loop where Kernel first notifies Source via r_1, r_2 that it is ready to receive data in its two channels s_1, s_2 (a signal at r_i says s_i is ready); Source complies, sending two chunks of data sequentially via s_1, s_2. Then Kernel (internally processes data and) waits for Sink to inform (via t_1, t_2) that Sink is ready to receive data via u_1, u_2; upon receiving the signals, Kernel sends the two chunks of processed data to Sink. This global protocol specifies a safe and deadlock-free scenario.

Local Session Types and Refinement. Once given global types, a programmer can develop code, one for each participant, incrementally validating its conformance to the projection of G onto each participant by efficient type-checking. When programs are executed, their interactions are guaranteed to follow the stipulated scenario. The type specification also serves as a basis for maintenance and upgrade.

Local session types abstract sessions from each endpoint's view. For example, Type $k!\langle U\rangle$ expresses the sending of a value of type U on channel k. Type $k?\langle U\rangle$ is its dual input. The relation between global and local types is formalised by *projection*, written $G \upharpoonright p$ and called *projection of G onto p*, defined as in [20].

Now we give the local types of Source, Kernel and Sink.

$$T_{\text{source}} = \mu\mathbf{t}.r_1?\langle\rangle; s_1!\langle U\rangle; r_2?\langle\rangle; s_2!\langle U\rangle; \mathbf{t}$$

$$T_{\text{kernel}} = \mu\mathbf{t}.r_1!\langle\rangle; s_1?\langle U\rangle; t_1?\langle\rangle; u_1!\langle U\rangle; r_2!\langle\rangle; s_2?\langle U\rangle; t_2?\langle\rangle; u_2!\langle U\rangle; \mathbf{t}$$

$$T_{\text{sink}} = \mu\mathbf{t}.t_1!\langle\rangle; u_1?\langle U\rangle; t_2!\langle\rangle; u_2?\langle U\rangle; \mathbf{t}$$

The local type of the program Kernel in Figure 2 is given below but it does not match the local type T_{kernel}, which is directly projected from global type G.

$$T^\star = r_1!\langle\rangle; r_2!\langle\rangle; \mu\mathbf{t}.s_1?\langle U\rangle; t_1?\langle\rangle; u_1!\langle U\rangle; r_1!\langle\rangle; s_2?\langle U\rangle; t_2?\langle\rangle; u_2!\langle U\rangle; r_2!\langle\rangle; \mathbf{t}$$

Our purpose is to refine T_{kernel} so that the new local protocol allows further asynchrony by overlapping communication and computation while still conforming to G [7, 14]; this allows us to start from a sequential global type, which is easily checked to be correct and deadlock-free, and refine it to a more optimised protocol, while guaranteeing that all participants still safely interact, e.g., that Kernel can interact with Source and Sink safely so that their interactions as a whole conform to the original global type G.

In the refined protocol $T^\star$, Kernel notifies Source via both r_1, r_2 *before* entering the loop, allowing Source to start its work. Now inside the loop, the refined protocol dictates that Kernel first receives data from Source via its first channel s_1, processes the data and sends out the result to Sink via its first channel u_1 and *immediately notifies Source via r_1 that it is ready on its first channel*, allowing Source to start sending data early. Kernel then repeats the same procedure for its second set of channels shared with Source and Sink. In this way, the refined local type says that Kernel can process data it has already received in one channel while still receiving data in the other, noting that sending, transferring and receiving large pieces of data can be time consuming.

We now summarise how this optimised local protocol is in fact safe with respect to the other participants conforming to G, through the notion of asynchronous communication subtyping. The justification is non-trivial: it uses a combination of a partial commutativity of the input and output actions and nested unfolding of recursive types [33]. The two key subtyping rules for permuting finite actions we use are as follows:

$$k!\langle U\rangle; k'?\langle U'\rangle; T_0 \;\ll\; k'?\langle U'\rangle; k!\langle U\rangle; T_0 \qquad (k \neq k')$$
$$k!\langle U\rangle; k'!\langle U'\rangle; T_0 \;\ll\; k'!\langle U'\rangle; k!\langle U\rangle; T_0 \qquad (k \neq k')$$

In the first rule, the left-hand type allows for more asynchrony (optimal) than the right-hand side type since the output action on k can be performed without waiting for the input on k'. The second rule permutes the two outputs at distinct names since they are sent asynchronously. The rule $\ll$ are applied to only finite length of the session types (hence $\ll$ is decidable). We write $T \gg T'$ for $T' \ll T$.

To define the subtyping for recursive types, we need to combine $\ll$ with unfolding. We call a relation $\Re \in Type \times Type$ an *asynchronous subtype simulation* if $(T_1, T_2) \in \Re$ implies the following conditions.

1. If $T_1 = \text{end}$, then $\text{unfold}^n(T_2) = \text{end}$.
2. If $T_1 = k!\langle U_1\rangle; T_1'$, then $\text{unfold}^n(T_2) \gg k!\langle U_2\rangle; T_2'$, $(T_1', T_2') \in \Re$ and $(U_1, U_2) \in \Re$.
3. If $T_1 = k?\langle U_1\rangle; T_1'$, then $\text{unfold}^n(T_2) = k?\langle U_2\rangle; T_2'$, $(T_1', T_2') \in \Re$ and $(U_2, U_1) \in \Re$.
4. If $T_1 = \mu\mathbf{t}.T$, then $(\text{unfold}^1(T_1), T_2) \in \Re$.

where $\text{unfold}^n(T)$ is the result of inductively unfolding the top level recursion up to a fixed level of nesting. The coinductive subtyping relation $T_1 <: T_2$ (read: T_1 is an *asynchronous subtype* of T_2) is defined when there exists a type simulation $\Re$ with $(T_1, T_2) \in \Re$. An output of T_1 can be simulated after applying asynchronous optimisation $\gg$ to the unfolded T_2. We also need to ensure object type U_1 is a subtype of U_2. This subtyping relation $T <: T'$ is decidable if all channels under each recursive prefix are distinct. $T^\star$ and T_{kernel} satisfy this condition since $r_1, s_1, t_1, u_1, r_2, s_2, t_2$ and u_2 are distinct under the recursive prefix.

To show that $T^\star <: T_{kernel}$, we start by unfolding T_{kernel} once to obtain

$$T_0 = r_1!\langle\rangle; s_1?\langle U\rangle; t_1?\langle\rangle; u_1!\langle U\rangle; r_2!\langle\rangle; s_2?\langle U\rangle; t_2?\langle\rangle; u_2!\langle U\rangle; T_{kernel}$$

Then $r_1!\langle\rangle$ matches the initial part of $T^\star$. To simulate the $r_2!\langle\rangle$ part of $T^\star$, $r_2!\langle\rangle$ is permuted by applying the asynchronous subtyping rules above, together with transitivity.

$$T_0 \gg T'_0 = r_1!\langle\rangle; r_2!\langle\rangle; s_1?\langle U\rangle; t_1?\langle\rangle; u_1!\langle U\rangle; s_2?\langle U\rangle; t_2?\langle\rangle; u_2!\langle U\rangle; T_{kernel}.$$

Let $T^\star = r_1!\langle\rangle; r_2!\langle\rangle; T_R^\star$. Thus the unfold of $T_R^\star$ must be simulated by T'.

$$T' = s_1?\langle U\rangle; t_1?\langle\rangle; u_1!\langle U\rangle; s_2?\langle U\rangle; t_2?\langle\rangle; u_2!\langle U\rangle; T_{kernel}.$$

Next we unfold $T_R^\star$ as:

$$s_1?\langle U\rangle; t_1?\langle\rangle; u_1!\langle U\rangle; r_1!\langle\rangle; s_2?\langle U\rangle; t_2?\langle\rangle; u_2!\langle U\rangle; r_2!\langle\rangle; T_R^\star$$

The first three types $s_1?\langle U\rangle; t_1?\langle\rangle; u_1!\langle U\rangle$ can be simulated by T' in this order. However to simulate $r_1!\langle\rangle$ in above $T_R^\star$, T_{kernel} must be unfolded again since the type in front of T' does *not* include $r_1!\langle\rangle$ outside the recursive prefix. Hence we apply the asynchronous subtyping rule to solve the following relation:

$$r_1!\langle\rangle; s_2?\langle U\rangle; t_2?\langle\rangle; u_2!\langle U\rangle; r_2!\langle\rangle; T_R^\star <: s_2?\langle U\rangle; t_2?\langle\rangle; u_2!\langle U\rangle;$$
$$r_1!\langle\rangle; s_1?\langle U\rangle; t_1?\langle\rangle; u_1!\langle U\rangle;$$
$$r_2!\langle\rangle; s_2?\langle U\rangle; t_2?\langle\rangle; u_2!\langle U\rangle; T_{kernel}$$

By applying $\gg$ to the r.h.s., $r_1!\langle\rangle$ can be permuted to the top. Then we can use the input and output subtyping simulation rules in order to achieve the original pair $(T_R^\star, T')$ again. This concludes the verification of the double-buffering example.

Subject reduction for L1 is proved as in [33], just by replacing the standard branching subtyping relation in [20] to the one which incorporates asynchronous commutative subtyping in [33]. We can also obtain the three key correctness properties, communication safety, type safety and progress, as stated in [20, §5]. Hence we can formally show that the double-buffering example in L1 is correct with respect to these properties — neither deadlock, type-error nor communication mismatch can happen in the interactions among the three participants.

3.3   Further Safety Analysis

One of the key merits of the use of type signatures for interactions, multiparty session types, in the present compilation framework is that they enable and facilitate various safety analyses pertaining to communication actions (hence their DMA translations). One of such analyses is the following race freedom analysis, where we guarantee that, when communication operations in L1 are compiled into DMA primitives, no local writes will interfere with remote writes. This analysis is done at the L1 level. The net consequence is that, as far as the compiled code from L2 to L1 is statically checked to be safe by this analysis, its further compilation into L0 is ensured to be race-free.

We illustrate the basic idea via an example. Assume given three participants, (say) Alice, Bob and Carol, where Alice sends a boolean value to Bob, Bob sends an integer to Carol, and Carol sends another integer to Alice. Note there is a causal chain from the initial output by Alice to the final input, again at Alice.[2] Now assume the following is the program for Alice, with s_b its initial output channel to Bob and s_a its final input channel from Carol:

$$s_b!\langle\text{true}\rangle; \ldots; s_a?\langle x\rangle; \text{print}(x); \qquad (3.1)$$

Now let us fill "..." in (3.1) as follows.

$$s_b!\langle\text{true}\rangle; \boxed{x := 5;} s_a?\langle x\rangle; \text{print}(x); \qquad (3.2)$$

Assuming x is private, the coloured command can have a local write at x in parallel with the remote write at the same variable x, the latter represented as communication through the channel s_a but which is in effect carried out, in the compiled code, as a DMA write on x. This asynchronous remote write at x can take place concurrently as the local write at x by the command $x := 5$. Thus we do not know whether 5 or a different number by the remote write will get printed in the final print command.

Next we consider the following variation of the program above:

$$\boxed{x := 5;} s_b!\langle\text{true}\rangle; \boxed{y := 5;} s_a?\langle x\rangle; \text{print}(x); \qquad (3.3)$$

In this case, assuming the causally chained communications among Alice, Bob and Carol as specified above, we have no racing at x (as far as x and y are not aliased). This is because we know Carol will write only after this program does the first output above, via s_b: as far as x is used for reading or writing *after* this prompting output via s_b — which will eventually initiate the asynchronous write at x via s_a — there can be no interference. Let us summarise this principle:

> If a participant's output action is the cause of its subsequent input for a variable x, then using x between *the prompting output and the subsequent input is dangerous. We want to prevent such dangerous occurrences of variables.*

Several observations are due:

- The safety property crucially depends on causality information (i.e. the relationship between an input and its prompting output) derived from session types.
- Once given this causality information, the standard control flow analysis can quickly check the existence/lack of such a dangerous path (modulo e.g. dead branches).
- This analysis can be done regardless of high-level languages in L2: it can be uniformly performed on all typable programs in L1.

---

[2] Such causal chains can be altered by permutations discussed in the previous subsection. Thus these chains need be extracted from the minimal local types of programs (which coincide with the principal types algorithmically inferred from untyped processes [33]).

This analysis is crucial for ensuring safety in the use of DMA operations. Note the analysis does not have to be performed for each L1 program: it suffices to ensure, once and for all, that a compilation from a given high-level language at L2 never induce dangerous processes in L1 in the above sense.

Another significant program analysis which can exploit the session type structures in L1 is the guarantee of the progress property, or of the lack of a deadlocked input. This property is immediately ensured when no two sessions interleave with each other, or no other blocking operations are present, which may often be the case in the compiled code. When two or more sessions can interleave, we can use many type-based and other analyses which can ensure the lack of deadlocks in communication, exploiting session type structures including its linearity.

There are other useful analyses depending on execution environments and kinds of applications, which will be discussed elsewhere.

4   Compiling Typed Processes to Distributed CMP

4.1   Basic Ideas

Processes with session types are guaranteed to follow rigorous communication structures, given as types. By tracing a session type, we know beforehand what and when processes will send and receive messages: we can even statically determine the target remote addresses of these communications. Such addresses can be exchanged at the time of session initiation.

Using this information, we can replace each message passing in a typed process with a direct remote write to the address of a variable in a core's local memory in a distributed memory CMP chip. As noted, the addresses of many of these variables can be known statically, hence can be exchanged at the time of session initiation. This allows an efficient execution of a conversation code, especially when a loop (iteration) is included inside a session. When one does need to treat dynamically generated data structures such as trees and graphs, whose size may not be able to be determined statically, one may also need to have dynamically allocated addresses communicated at runtime, for their use in subsequent communications. Note such addresses can be piggybacked in preceding messages in the same session.

Since our purpose is to have type-safe compilation, we use a (prototypical) typed low-level programming language targeted at distributed memory CMP and NoC [2, 10], which we call L0 for brevity. L0 is based on the C programming language, and features, among others:

- A two-level code structure where the outer level (called a section) encompasses all the code to run at a (virtual) core, and the inner level conventional C functions and variable/data declarations;
- a new type, **place**, denoting a core (that can be virtualised and mapped into available physical cores); and
- primitives to obtain an idle place (**newPlace**), to launch a new thread at some place (**spawn**), to obtain the current place (**here**), to asynchronously copy an array into some other place via DMA (**put**), and to wait for the completion of an incoming DMA operation (**wait**).

These constructs, together with the safety conditions for L1 programs, allow a direct translation from L1 programs to L0 programs. By the type-based analyses on L1 discussed in the preceding section, the resulting compiled code is guaranteed to satisfy key correctness properties such as synchronisation/type safety, race freedom, and progress, as far as we assume a correct compilation. Also note that the type annotations on the DMA operations in L0 coming from those in the original L1 programs enable us to perform type-based analyses on L0 programs independently.

Type information for multiparty sessions can be used not only at compile time from L1 to L0, but also at runtime. For example, process migration will become necessary from various needs for reconfiguration including load balancing. For this purpose, sound treatment of pending messages are essential, which can be assisted by precise information on the type signatures of involved conversations. In the following, we focus on the most basic usage of session type information in compilation to L0, i.e. compilation of session communications to safe and efficient DMA operations. Other usage of type information will be reported elsewhere.

4.2 Compilation

Figures 3 and 4 present a compilation of our running example into L0. As we have already observed, all typed message passing is replaced by DMA primitives, using addresses of the variables in the local memory of a target place for remote asynchronous write operations, where the addresses are shared by the *session initiation protocol* adapted for distributed memory CMP, as described below.

Section Main defines a program comprising a single procedure, necessarily named main. The program is uploaded at some (virtual) core and the execution of the main function starts. The first **spawn** instruction in Main.main copies section Kernel into the (virtual) core obtained previously via a call to the **newPlace** primitive (we assume this operation will block if no core is available), and launches the execution of Kernel.main.

The *session initiation* protocol works as follows: Kernel writes in variable a0 (received from Main at spawn time) a data-structure with two fields to be filled by the producer and the consumer. These fields are then passed to the respective places at **spawn** time. At this point both the producer and the consumer know the remote address of a variable in the kernel. They can now write in these variables the addresses of the data structures to be shared later, so that these components can communicate by writing to these addresses.

Section Producer comprises a local buffer to hold the produced data, two variables of type Sync (syncA, and syncB) used as a notification for safe DMA operation, and the variables for the target of the remote addresses of the communication. After the session initiation, the place running this section continuously fills the local buffer and puts it in one of the kernel's target buffers with a **put** instruction. A clearance, e.g., **wait**(&syncA), stating that the target buffer is ready must precede the actual placing of the data in the kernel's memory.

The Kernel section declares two incoming/outgoing buffers. After session initiation, it signals the producer that its buffers can now be written (the two instructions that precede the loop). It then waits for the completion of the DMA operation regarding the first of its buffers (bufferA), fills it with the XOR of each data element with the

```
typedef int[4096] Buffer;   // 16KBytes buffer
typedef struct {} Sync;
typedef struct {Buffer *bufferA, Buffer *bufferB} Buffers;
typedef struct {Sync *syncA, Sync *syncB} Syncs;

typedef struct {Syncs *syncs, Buffers buffers} ConsumerInit;
typedef struct {Buffers *buffers, Syncs syncs} ProducerInit;
typedef struct {ProducerInit *prod, ConsumerInit *cons} SessionInit;
section Main () {
  void main () {
    place mainPlace = here();
    place producer = newPlace();
    place consumer = newPlace();
    SessionInit a0;
    spawn Kernel(&a0, mainPlace, producer, consumer) at mainPlace;
    wait(&a0); // session initiation
    spawn Producer(a0.prod, mainPlace) at producer;
    spawn Consumer(a0.cons, mainPlace) at consumer;
}}

section Producer (ProducerInit *a1, place kernel) {
  Buffer buffer;
  Sync syncA; Sync syncB;
  Buffers kernelBuffers;

  void main () {
    put({&kernelBuffers, {&syncA, &syncB}}, a1, kernel); // session initiation
    wait(&kernelBuffers); // end session initiation
    produce: {
      // Produce buffer A
      foreach (i: 0..4095) buffer[i] = get_int();
      wait(&syncA);
      put(buffer, kernelBuffers.bufferA, kernel);
      // Produce buffer B
      foreach (i: 0..4095) buffer[i] = get_int();
      wait(&syncB);
      put(buffer, kernelBuffers.bufferB, kernel);
      loop produce;
    }}
}
```

Fig. 3. L0 code for the double buffering example (Main and Producer sections)

defined key and proceeds to write in the consumer memory, following the same wait-put protocol used by the producer before writing on the kernel's memory. Once the operation is completed, the kernel signals the producer that bufferA is ready to be re-written, proceeding to process bufferB.

Consumer should be easy to understand, it simply waits for the arrival of each buffer at the time, printing their contents.

The resulting code is in direct correspondence with the original typed processes in its operational structure, and, thanks to the well-typedness of the original process in L1 with respect to the declared session types, together with the static analysis for race freedom outlined in §3.3, we can show that the DMA operations in the resulting L0 code faithfully captures all and only communication and other behaviours as found in the original L1 program, modulo the translation of the original session initiation into a protocol realising the equivalent functionality (which distribute remote addresses used for performing DMA writes: note these addresses in effect act as channel ends in the

```
section Kernel(SessionInit *a0, place mainPlace, place producer, place consumer){
  ProducerInit a1;
  ConsumerInit a2;
  Buffer bufferA; Sync syncA;
  Buffer bufferB; Sync syncB;
  int key = KEY;

  void main () {
    put({&a1, &a2}, a0, mainPlace);  // session initiation
    wait(&a1);
    wait(&a2);
    put({&bufferA, &bufferB}, a1.buffers, producer);
    put({&syncA, &syncB}, a2.syncs, consumer); // end session initiation
    put({}, a1.syncs.syncA, producer);
    put({}, a1.syncs.syncB, producer);
    process: {
      // Process buffer A
      wait(&bufferA);
      foreach (i: 0..4095) bufferA[i] = bufferA[i] ^ key;
      wait(&syncA);
      put(bufferA, a2.buffers.bufferA, consumer);
      put({}, a1.syncs.syncA, producer);
      // Process buffer B
      wait(&bufferB);
      foreach (i: 0..4095) bufferB[i] = bufferB[i] ^ key;
      wait(&syncB);
      put(bufferB, a2.buffers.bufferB, consumer);
      put({}, a1.syncs.syncB, producer);
      loop process;
  }}
}

section Consumer (ConsumerInit *a2, place kernel) {
  Buffer buffer;
  Syncs syncs;

  void main () {
    put({&syncs, {&buffer, &buffer}}, a2, kernel); // session initiation
    wait(&sync); // end session initiation
    consume: {
      // Consume buffer A
      put({}, syncs.syncA, kernel);
      wait(&buffer);
      printf("\nBuffer:\n");
      foreach (i: 0..4095) printf("%d ", buffer[i]);
      // Consume buffer B
      put({}, syncs.syncB, kernel);
      wait(&buffer);
      printf("\nBuffer:\n");
      foreach (i: 0..4095) printf("%d ", buffer[i]);
      loop consume;
  }}
}
```

Fig. 4. L0 code for the double buffering example (Kernel and Consumer sections)

original process representation). In fact, the type-directed translation from L1 to L0 can annotate the resulting L0 code with types which closely correspond to those in the original L1 program. This type annotations make the resulting L0 code amenable to the type-based analyses isomorphic to those for L1 programs. This ensures, for the resulting L0 code, the aforementioned three key correctness properties, the synchronisation and race-error freedom, type-error freedom and progress.

We have developed a prototype compiler targeting for a IBM Cell Broadband Engine processor [14], so that we can compile high-level code to low-level code as in Figures 3 and 4, which can further be compiled and executed on Cell. More discussions on this implementation are given in Section 5.

4.3   Further Features

There are several key features of our intermediate language which we do not discuss in the present paper. In particular, although the example under consideration does not use shared session initialisation channels, we often need a component which accepts possibly concurrent requests for session initialisation at a shared channel from multiple clients. Such a channel may be located at main memory or at local memory of a distributed core. The shared server receives a request, at which point (for example) it may fork a thread to one of the available cores for serving the client's needs. Such a framework is especially important for realising shared services used by an unknown number of client processes, either inside an application or across applications, and demands an efficient treatment of possibly concurrent requests arriving at a same channel.

We can treat the arrival of such an indeterminate number of requests through several methods. As a simple way, each core may run a supervisor-mode process to which each user-level process may ask for communication to a shared channel in a remote core (note such requests tend to be relatively fewer than communications inside a session, so that a slightly higher cost for a shared request may be justified). Then a supervisor can put the request to its own queue in a remote or shared memory, which can be polled by a receiver of these requests. Putting a request in a queue can be followed by a simple notification. Such a scheme may be combined with mutual exclusion primitives (lock and/or compare and swap, see [45]) by multiple threads at the service process.

5   Conclusion

Conclusion and Further Topics.   The translation from the initial simple stream application to the low-level code based on double buffering, through intermediate representation as typed processes, suggests flexibility in compilation and execution of concurrent programs in distributed CMP and other extremely concurrent computing environments, opening new opportunities and challenges. We already mentioned the use of our recent work [33] in our compilation framework, which is based on a subtyping relation on multiparty session types which are generalised to capture asynchrony as found in the double buffering process above. Further development of the compilation framework will necessitate new compilation and static analysis techniques for inherently concurrent code, a new, scalable runtime framework for dynamic allocations of hardware resources to communicating processes making the best of their type structures, a formal guarantee of correctness properties for such a runtime, an effective threads scheduling mechanism in each local core, protection and security mechanisms, and integration and management of different abstractions for concurrency.

Related Work. There are several recent works which are closely related and will complement the approaches taken in the presented research direction: research from multiple directions will be needed to explore the rich field of structured concurrent programming. Among these related works, we list only a few. Occam-Pi [46] offers a highly efficient language architecture for channel-based concurrency with potentially millions of light-weight processes. Sing#, a derivative of C# developed for Singularity OS [11], uses a variant of session types called *contracts* to specify the interfaces between OS components, which communicate via channel-based message passing in shared memory environments. X10 [6] presents an advanced language constructs for structured, typed concurrent imperative programming for partitioned shared memory with high-performance computing as its application domain. Kilim [40] is an actor framework for Java based on cooperatively-scheduled lightweight threads which communicate by message-passing. StreamFlex [39] is a real-time stream API for Java guaranteeing sub-millisecond response times and type safety, using a type-based classification of heap objects to obtain a high throughput. In all these languages, high-level structuring constructs play an essential role not only for clean description of concurrency but also for efficient program execution.

A preliminary version of this paper was presented in [18].

Implementation Status. We are currently working on the experiments of the general framework proposed in the present paper. It centres on a simple imperative concurrent language equipped with multiparty session communications and their types, which is close to the language we discussed in Section 3. The language, combined with two other associated languages, is intended to serve as an intermediate language (roughly of level L1 in Section 1), to which typed high-level concurrent languages such as X10 [6], StreamIt [42] and others are compiled into.

The current framework implements a series of type-directed translation steps from high-level typed concurrent languages into C-code targeted at the Cell Broadband Engine architecture. Our experiments so far have been restricted to a single Cell processor. Current efforts focus on, among others, providing support for the deploying of applications across processors on the same blade and across blades. For that purpose we are using a cluster of three IBM QS21 bladecenters [22] and their compiler architecture.

Acknowledgements. The work is partially supported by the EU IST proactive initiative FET-Global Computing (projects Sensoria and Mobius), as well as the Treaty of Windsor Anglo-Portuguese Joint Research Programme B–4/08. The first and the last authors are partially supported by EPSRC GR/T03208, GR/T03215, EP/F002114 and EP/F003757. They thank Francisco Martins for advice and suggestions on the intermediate languages and compilation scheme.

References

1. Alpern, B., Carter, L., Ferrante, J.: Modeling parallel computers as memory hierarchies. In: Proceedings of Programming Models for Massively Parallel Computers, pp. 116–123. IEEE Computer Society Press, Los Alamitos (1993)
2. Benini, L., De Micheli, G.: Networks on chip: a new SoC paradigm. IEEE Computer 35, 1 (2002)

3. Bettini, L., Coppo, M., D'Antoni, L., De Luca, M., Dezani-Ciancaglini, M., Yoshida, N.: Global Progress in Dynamically Interleaved Multiparty Sessions. In: van Breugel, F., Chechik, M. (eds.) CONCUR 2008. LNCS, vol. 5201, pp. 418–433. Springer, Heidelberg (2008)

4. Bilsen, G., Engels, M., Lauwereins, R., Peperstraete, J.A.: Cyclo-static dataflow. IEEE Transactions on Signal Processing 44(2), 397–408 (1996)

5. Bonelli, E., Compagnoni, A.B.: Multipoint Session Types for a Distributed Calculus. In: Barthe, G., Fournet, C. (eds.) TGC 2007 and FODO 2008. LNCS, vol. 4912, pp. 240–256. Springer, Heidelberg (2008)

6. Charles, P., Grothoff, C., Saraswat, V., Donawa, C., Kielstra, A., Ebcioglu, K., von Praun, C., Sarkar, V.: X10: an object-oriented approach to non-uniform cluster computing. In: OOPSLA 2005, pp. 519–538. ACM Press, New York (2005)

7. Culler, D., Karp, R., Patterson, D., Sahay, A., Schauser, K.E., Santos, E., Subramonian, R., von Eicken, T.: Logp: towards a realistic model of parallel computation. SIGPLAN Not. 28(7), 1–12 (1993)

8. Culler, D.E., Gupta, A., Singh, J.P.: Parallel Computer Architecture: A Hardware/Software Approach. Morgan Kaufmann Publishers Inc., San Francisco (1997)

9. Dally, W.J.: Enabling technology for on-chip interconnection networks. In: NOCS 2007, p. 3. IEEE Computer Society Press, Los Alamitos (2007)

10. Dally, W.J., Towles, B.: Route packets, not wires: On-chip interconnection networks. In: DAC 2001, pp. 684–689. IEEE Computer Society Press, Los Alamitos (2001)

11. Fähndrich, M., Aiken, M., Hawblitzel, C., Hodson, O., Hunt, G., Larus, J.R., Levi, S.: Language support for fast and reliable message-based communication in singularity OS. In: EuroSys 2006, pp. 177–190. ACM Press, New York (2006)

12. Fatahalian, K., Horn, D.R., Knight, T.J., Leem, L., Houston, M., Park, J.Y., Erez, M., Ren, M., Aiken, A., Dally, W.J., Hanrahan, P.: Sequoia: Programming the Memory Hierarchy. In: SC 2006, p. 83. ACM Press, New York (2006)

13. Gelsinger, P., Gargini, P., Parker, G., Yu, A.: Microprocessors circa 2000. In: IEEE SPectrum, pp. 43–47 (1989)

14. Gschwind, M.: The Cell Broadband Engine: Exploiting multiple levels of parallelism in a chip multiprocessor. International Journal of Parallel Programming 35(3), 233–262 (2007)

15. Hewitt, C., Bishop, P., Steiger, R.: A universal modular actor formalism for artificial intelligence. In: IJCAI, pp. 235–245 (1973)

16. Hoare, C.A.R.: Communicating sequential processes. Commun. ACM 26(1), 100–106 (1983)

17. Hoare, T.: Communicating Sequential Processes. Prentice-Hall, Englewood Cliffs (1985)

18. Honda, K., Vasconcelos, V., Yoshida, N.: Type-directed compilation for multicore programming. In: PLACES 2008. ENTCS. Elsevier, Amsterdam (2009)

19. Honda, K., Vasconcelos, V.T., Kubo, M.: Language primitives and type discipline for structured communication-based programming. In: Hankin, C. (ed.) ESOP 1998. LNCS, vol. 1381, pp. 122–138. Springer, Heidelberg (1998)

20. Honda, K., Yoshida, N., Carbone, M.: Multiparty Asynchronous Session Types. In: POPL 2008, pp. 273–284. ACM Press, New York (2008)

21. IBM. ALF double buffering, http://www.ibm.com/developerworks/blogs/page/powerarchitecture?entry=ibomb_alf_sdk30_5

22. IBM. IBM BladeCenter QS21, http://www-03.ibm.com/systems/bladecenter/hardware/servers/qs21/index.html

23. IBM. Cell broadband engine programming tutorial version 2.0 (2006)
24. Kapasi, U.J., Dally, W.J., Rixner, S., Owens, J.D., Khailany, B.: The imagine stream processor. In: ICCD 2002, pp. 282–288 (2002)
25. Keltcher, C.N., McGrath, K.J., Ahmed, A., Conway, P.: The AMD Opteron processor for multiprocessor servers. IEEE Micro 23(2), 66–76 (2003)
26. Kistler, M., Perrone, M., Petrini, F.: Cell multiprocessor communication network: Built for speed. IEEE Micro 26(3), 10–23 (2006)
27. Kongetira, P., Aingaran, K., Olukotun, K.: Niagara: A 32-way multithreaded Sparc processor. IEEE Micro 25(2), 21–29 (2005)
28. Lin, C.-k., Black, A.P.: DirectFlow: A domain-specific language for information-flow systems. In: Ernst, E. (ed.) ECOOP 2007. LNCS, vol. 4609, pp. 299–322. Springer, Heidelberg (2007)
29. David, B.: Loveman. Program improvement by source to source transformation. In: POPL 1976, pp. 140–152. ACM Press, New York (1976)
30. Milner, R.: Processes, a mathematical model of computing agents. In: Logic Colloquium, Bristol 1973, pp. 157–174. North Holland, Amsterdam (1975)
31. Milner, R.: Functions as processes. In: Paterson, M. (ed.) ICALP 1990. LNCS, vol. 443, pp. 167–180. Springer, Heidelberg (1990)
32. Morrisett, G., Walker, D., Crary, K., Glew, N.: From System F to typed assembly language. ACM Trans. Program. Lang. Syst. 21(3), 527–568 (1999)
33. Mostrous, D., Yoshida, N., Honda, K.: Global Principal Typing in Partially Commutative Asynchronous Sessions. In: Castagna, G. (ed.) ESOP 2000. LNCS, vol. 5502, pp. 316–332. Springer, Heidelberg (2009)
34. Olukotun, K., Nayfeh, B.A., Hammond, L., Wilson, K., Chang, K.: The case for a single-chip multiprocessor. In: ASPLOS-VII, pp. 2–11. ACM Press, New York (1996)
35. Pham, D., Asano, S., Bolliger, M., Day, M.N., Hofstee, H.P., Johns, C., Kahle, J., Kameyama, A., Keaty, J., Masubuchi, Y., Riley, M., Shippy, D., Stasiak, D., Suzuoki, M., Wang, M., Warnock, J., Weitzel, S., Wendel, D., Yamazaki, T., Yazawa, K.: The design and implementation of a first-generation CELL processor. In: ISSCC 2005, vol. 1, pp. 184–592 (2005)
36. Pollack, F.J.: New microarchitecture challenges in the coming generations of CMOS process technologies. In: MICRO 1999, p. 2. IEEE Computer Society, Los Alamitos (1999)
37. Sancho, J.C., Kerbyson, D.J.: Analysis of Double Buffering on two Different Multicore Architectures: Quad-core Opteron and the Cell-BE. In: IPDPS 2008. IEEE, Los Alamitos (2008)
38. Schneier, B.: Applied Cryptography: Protocols, Algorithms, and Source Code in C. John Wiley & Sons, Inc., Chichester (1993)
39. Spring, J.H., Privat, J., Guerraoui, R., Vitek, J.: StreamFlex: High-Throughput Stream Programming in Java. In: OOPSLA 2007, pp. 211–228. ACM Press, New York (2007)
40. Srinivasan, S., Mycroft, A.: Kilim: Isolation-typed actors for java. In: Vitek, J. (ed.) ECOOP 2008. LNCS, vol. 5142, pp. 104–128. Springer, Heidelberg (2008)
41. Takeuchi, K., Honda, K., Kubo, M.: An interaction-based language and its typing system. In: Halatsis, C., Philokyprou, G., Maritsas, D., Theodoridis, S. (eds.) PARLE 1994. LNCS, vol. 817, pp. 398–413. Springer, Heidelberg (1994)
42. Thies, W., Karczmarek, M., Amarasinghe, S.: Streamit: A language for streaming applications. In: Horspool, R.N. (ed.) CC 2002. LNCS, vol. 2304, pp. 179–196. Springer, Heidelberg (2002)
43. Thies, W., Karczmarek, M., Sermulins, J., Rabbah, R., Amarasinghe, S.: Teleport messaging for distributed stream programs. In: PPoPP 2005, pp. 224–235. ACM Press, New York (2005)

44. Vangal, S.R., Howard, J., Ruhl, G., Dighe, S., Wilson, H., Tschanz, J., Finan, D., Singh, A., Jacob, T., Jain, S., Erraguntla, V., Roberts, C., Hoskote, Y., Borkar, N., Borkar, S.: An 80-Tile Sub-100-W TeraFLOPS Processor in 65-nm CMOS. IEEE Journal of Solid-State Circuits 43(1), 29–41 (2008)
45. Vasconcelos, V.T., Martins, F.: A multithreaded typed assembly language. In: Proceedings of TV 2006 - Multithreading in Hardware and Software: Formal Approaches to Design and Verification (2006)
46. Welch, P.H., Barnes, F.R.M.: Communicating Mobile Processes: introducing occam-pi. In: Abdallah, A.E., Jones, C.B., Sanders, J.W. (eds.) Communicating Sequential Processes. LNCS, vol. 3525, pp. 175–210. Springer, Heidelberg (2005)

Abstract Interpretation of Symbolic Execution with Explicit State Updates[*]

Richard Bubel[1], Reiner Hähnle[1], and Benjamin Weiß[2]

[1] Department of Computer Science and Engineering,
Chalmers University of Technology and Göteborg University
{bubel,reiner}@chalmers.se
[2] Institute for Theoretical Computer Science,
University of Karlsruhe
bweiss@ira.uka.de

Abstract. Systems for deductive software verification model the semantics of their target programming language with full precision. On the other hand, abstraction based approaches work with approximations of the semantics in order to be fully automatic. In this paper we aim at providing a uniform framework for both fully precise and approximate reasoning about programs. We present a sound dynamic logic calculus that integrates abstraction in the sense of abstract interpretation theory. In the second part of the paper, we apply the approach to the analysis of secure information flow.

1 Introduction

Formal verification of software is desirable for many safety- and security-critical applications. Following intense research during the last decade, the reach of formal verification methods has been extended impressively. Different approaches to verification are often categorized as "interactive" versus "automatic" depending on whether they in general require hints from human users or not. Typical interactive systems include generic proof assistants and logical frameworks such as Isabelle [20] as well as deductive verification systems such as KeY [5], KIV [2], Spec# [3], and Why/Krakatoa/Caduceus [10].[1] Typical automated systems include model checkers such as Bogor [21], Java PathFinder [25], Spin [15] and abstract interpreters such as ASTRÉE [8].

Deductive verification systems model the semantics of their target programming language with full precision. This is the source of the need for user interaction, because all interesting properties of Turing-complete programming

---

[*] This work was funded in part by the Information Society Technologies programme of the European Commission, Future and Emerging Technologies under the IST-2005-015905 MOBIUS project. This article reflects only the authors' views and the Community is not liable for any use that may be made of the information contained therein.

[1] We classify systems based on a verification condition generator architecture such as Spec# or Why as interactive, because in general human users have to enrich specifications incrementally until they can be proven.

F.S. de Boer et al. (Eds.): FMCO 2008, LNCS 5751, pp. 247–277, 2009.
© Springer-Verlag Berlin Heidelberg 2009

languages are undecidable. Technically, the necessity of user interaction arises when suitable invariants or induction hypotheses are required that characterize the effect of unbounded loops or recursion.

Automatic verification approaches avoid interaction by working on abstract execution models (and specification languages) that are decidable or even have a finite state space. This allows the full exploration of the state space of a program (as in model checking) or finite fixed point approximation of invariants (as in abstract interpretation).

There are various attempts to combine the advantages of verification systems and abstraction-based approaches, usually, by using the latter to boost the degree of automation of the former (for example, [18,24]). In the present paper we set a more ambitious goal: we want to provide a uniform theoretical basis for fully precise reasoning about programs *and* for abstract interpretation at the same time. The aim is to achieve a deep integration of deductive verification and abstract interpretation. One obvious reason is to be able to re-use the substantial investments and progress made in the context of deductive verification in the past years to improve the precision of abstract interpretation. Another important motivation for this work is the possibility to achieve automation of deductive verification without completely losing precision.

Our starting point is a program logic that allows to cast symbolic program execution as deduction in a sequent calculus. This so-called *dynamic logic* is an extension of first-order logic and is complete relative to arithmetic. The software verification systems KeY [5] and KIV [2] formally model large fragments of the JAVA programming language based on dynamic logic. Our exposition in Sect. 2 is based on a simplified[2] version of the KeY logic [5, Chapter 3].

Section 3 is the core of the paper: we define a calculus for logic-based symbolic execution that allows for any program variable at any time to move from concrete symbolic execution to computation in an abstract domain. The abstract domain is a sound approximation of the program in the sense of abstract interpretation theory [7]. The approach is based on the symbolic state *updates* featured by our logic-based symbolic execution: a very compact language for representing the intermediate results of symbolic computation. It is on these updates that abstraction takes place, not on full target programs. While it is still possible to use the calculus interactively and let the user specify the loop invariants, the abstraction also makes an automatic procedure possible, where loop invariants are derived without interaction by iterating symbolic execution of the loop body until stabilization to a fixed point. The overall approach is illustrated by an extended example in Sect. 4.

One potentially very rewarding area for a program logic with abstraction such as suggested here is the analysis of secure information flow. This problem has received a lot of attention in the past years with many type-based (see [23] for an overview), some deduction-based (for example, [17,4,1,9,6,13]) and a few

---

[2] Ultimately, we aim to cover as much of JAVA as done in the KeY system based on the logic described in this paper, but in order to stay reasonably short and comprehensible we give formal definitions only for a toy programming language.

abstract interpretation-based approaches (for example, [11]). The information flow analysis problem has also been the original motivation for the work undertaken here.

While type-based approaches to information flow analysis are automatic, but suffer from limited precision, most deduction-based approaches recast flow analysis as a general verification problem [4,9,6] that typically requires user interaction to prove it. Other deduction-based approaches provide a logical model of type-based flow analysis [1,13], but this results in rather specialized calculi with limited prospects of re-use of existing verification systems.

In the second part of this paper we extend our symbolic execution/abstract interpretation framework to model secure information flow. It was shown by Hunt & Sands [16] that information flow policies can be expressed as mappings from a program variable to all those locations that may influence its value. This property was exploited in [13] where the symbolic execution machinery and update mechanism of a dynamic logic was used to keep track of the locations that a program variable depends on. By virtue of a simple abstraction rule from a certain point onwards during symbolic execution a program variable x could be made to record dependencies on other variables instead of precise values. Unfortunately, this meant that at this point all information on the symbolic value of x was discarded. It also lead to some non-standard and non-deterministic rules. In the present paper we avoid these disadvantages. In Sect. 5 we extend the semantics of our programming language such that the dependencies of the program variables are tracked explicitly. We give sound modifications of the affected symbolic execution rules with respect to this semantics.

In Sect. 6 we discuss additional related work not mentioned above. In Sect. 7 we give directions for future work and summarize our results.

2   A Dynamic Logic with Updates

In this section, we describe our logic for reasoning about programs. It is a simplified version of the dynamic logic of KeY [5, Chapter 3]. Compared to classical dynamic logic [14] its most important new feature is a new syntactic category called *updates* [22]. Updates are used to describe state changes in an explicit and programming language independent way. Our overview begins with *syntax* in Sect. 2.1, continues with *semantics* in Sect. 2.2, and ends with the *calculus* used for symbolic program execution in Sect. 2.3.

2.1   Syntax

The syntax is based on a (first-order) *signature*:

Definition 1 (Signature). *A signature is a tuple* $\Sigma = (\mathcal{F}, \mathcal{P}, \mathcal{PV}, \mathcal{V})$*, where* $\mathcal{F}$ *is a set of* function symbols, $\mathcal{P}$ *is a set of* predicate symbols, $\mathcal{PV}$ *is a finite set of* program variables, *and where* $\mathcal{V}$ *is a set of (logical)* variables.

Function and predicate symbols have fixed arities. We require that $\mathcal{F}$ *contains infinitely many function symbols of each arity.*

Note that program variables (i.e., variables occurring in programs) and logical variables (i.e., variables that may be quantified over) are separate syntactic categories. For the rest of this paper, we assume a fixed signature Σ. For this reason we drop the signature as a parameter in all subsequent definitions.

Definition 2 (Syntax). *Terms t, formulas φ, updates $\mathcal{U}$ and programs p are defined by the following grammar, where $f \in \mathcal{F}$ ranges over function symbols, $p \in \mathcal{P}$ over predicate symbols, $x \in \mathcal{PV}$ over program variables, and $y \in \mathcal{V}$ over logical variables:*

$$t ::= f(t,\dots,t) \mid x \mid y \mid \mathit{if}(\varphi)\,\mathit{then}(t)\,\mathit{else}(t) \mid \{\mathcal{U}\}t$$
$$\varphi ::= \text{true} \mid \text{false} \mid p(t,\dots,t) \mid \varphi \,\&\, \varphi \mid (\varphi \mid \varphi) \mid \varphi \to \varphi \mid !\varphi \mid$$
$$\forall y.\varphi \mid \exists y.\varphi \mid t \doteq t \mid \{\mathcal{U}\}\varphi \mid [\text{p}]\varphi$$
$$\mathcal{U} ::= (x := t \,\|\, \dots \,\|\, x := t)$$
$$\text{p} ::= x = t \mid \text{p;p} \mid \text{if } (\varphi)\ \{\text{p}\}\ \text{else}\ \{\text{p}\} \mid \text{while } (\varphi)\ \{\text{p}\}$$

Terms $f(t_1,\dots,t_n)$ and formulas $p(t_1,\dots,t_n)$ must respect the arities of the symbols f and p, respectively. Terms and formulas that appear inside programs may not contain any logical variables, quantifiers, updates, or nested programs.

An expression of the form $[\text{p}]\varphi$ is a *program formula*. Intuitively, it denotes partial correctness of the program p with respect to the postcondition φ. The symbol $\doteq$ denotes referential equality. *Updates* are lists of pairs of locations (program variables) and terms. They are used to represent the incremental difference between two states within a computation. In the KeY system [5] updates render symbolic execution efficient. In the present paper updates provide a convenient layer between programs and logic where abstraction takes place.

We allow programs of the form **if** (φ) {p}, i.e., conditionals without an **else**-block. This can be seen as an abbreviation for **if** (φ) {p} **else** {x = x}, where $x \in \mathcal{PV}$ is an arbitrary program variable.

Example 1. Let p denote the following program computing the Gaussian sum for the first i numbers and storing the result in n:

```
n = 0;
while (i>0) {
    i = i-1;
    n = n+i
}
```

We can state partial correctness of this program (with respect to a rather weak postcondition), for example, by $i \geq 0 \to [\text{p}](i \doteq 0 \,\&\, n \geq 0)$.

2.2   Semantics

The semantics of terms, formulas, updates and programs is based on an interpretation I of the function and predicate symbols, a *state s* giving values for the program variables, and a *variable assignment β* assigning values to the logical variables:

Definition 3 (Interpretations, States, Variable Assignments). *Given a universe* D *of values, an* interpretation I *is a function mapping every function symbol* $f \in \mathcal{F}$ *with arity* n *to a function* $I(f) : D^n \to D$ *and every predicate symbol* $p \in \mathcal{P}$ *with arity* n *to a relation* $I(p) \subseteq D^n$. *A* state *is a function* $s : \mathcal{PV} \to D$; *the set of all states is denoted* $\mathcal{S}$. *A* variable assignment *is a function* $\beta : \mathcal{V} \to D$.

Definition 4 (Semantics). *Given a universe* D, *an interpretation* I, *a state* s *and a variable assignment* β, *we evaluate terms* t *to a value* $val_{I,s,\beta}(t) \in D$, *formulas* φ *to a truth value* $val_{I,s,\beta}(\varphi) \in \{tt, f\!f\}$, *updates* $\mathcal{U}$ *to a result state* $val_{I,s,\beta}(\mathcal{U}) \in \mathcal{S}$, *and programs* p *to a set of states* $val_{I,s,\beta}(\mathrm{p}) \in 2^{\mathcal{S}}$, *where the cardinality of* $val_{I,s,\beta}(\mathrm{p})$ *is either* 0 *or* 1. *The evaluation function* $val_{I,s,\beta}$ *is formally defined in App. A.1.*

A formula φ *is called (logically)* valid *iff* $val_{I,s,\beta}(\varphi) = tt$ *for all* interpretations I, *all* states s *and all* variable assignments β.

For terms and formulas without updates and without programs, the evaluation $val_{I,s,\beta}$ is essentially defined as usual in first-order logic. For an *update* $\mathcal{U} = (\mathrm{x}_1 := t_1 \parallel \ldots \parallel \mathrm{x}_n := t_n)$, the result of $val_{I,s,\beta}(\mathcal{U})$ is the state which results from s by assigning the values of the terms t_i to the program variables x_i in parallel. In case of a clash between two sub-updates (i.e., when $\mathrm{x}_i = \mathrm{x}_j$ for $i \neq j$), the rightmost update "wins" and overwrites the effect of the other. The meaning of a term $\{\mathcal{U}\}t$ and of a formula $\{\mathcal{U}\}\varphi$ is that the result state of the update $\mathcal{U}$ should be used for evaluating t and φ, respectively.

A *program* is evaluated to the set of states that it may terminate in when started in s. We only consider deterministic programs, so this set is always either empty (if the program does not terminate) or it consists of exactly one state. The semantics of a program formula $[\mathrm{p}]\varphi$ is that φ should hold in all result states of the program p, which corresponds to partial correctness of p wrt. φ.

2.3 Calculus

We reason about logical validity of dynamic logic formulas via a *sequent calculus*. A *sequent* is an expression of the form $\Gamma \Longrightarrow \Delta$, where Γ (called the *antecedent*) and Δ (called the *succedent*) are finite sets of formulas. The semantics of a sequent is defined as $val_{I,s,\beta}(\Gamma \Longrightarrow \Delta) = val_{I,s,\beta}(\bigwedge \Gamma \to \bigvee \Delta)$. As usual, $\bigwedge \Gamma$ stands for the conjunction (&) and $\bigvee \Delta$ for the disjunction (|) of the formulas in Γ and in Δ, respectively (in an arbitrary order). A sequent calculus *rule* is an inference rule of the form

$$\frac{seq_1 \quad \cdots \quad seq_n}{seq}$$

where $seq_1, \ldots, seq_n$ (called the **premisses** of the rule) and seq (called the **conclusion** of the rule) are sequents. A rule is called *sound* iff logical validity of all the premisses implies logical validity of the conclusion.

A *proof tree* is constructed by starting with some root sequent to be proven, and then applying sequent rules. *Applying* a rule means to find a leaf in the proof tree that is identical to the conclusion of a rule, and to add the rule's premises as new children of the former leaf. Provided that all applied rules are sound, it is guaranteed that at any time during this process, validity of all the leaves implies validity of the root sequent. If one arrives at a tree whose leaves are all obviously valid, one has proven the validity of the original proof obligation.

To achieve finite representation of a calculus, sequent rules are denoted schematically. For example, the following schematic rule is applicable to all sequents where an arbitrary conjunctive formula $\varphi_1 \& \varphi_2$ occurs in the antecedent:

$$\text{andLeft} \ \frac{\Gamma, \varphi_1, \varphi_2 \Rightarrow \Delta}{\Gamma, \varphi_1 \& \varphi_2 \Rightarrow \Delta}$$

We handle formulas with programs in them by transforming them into formulas without programs. This process can be understood as *symbolic execution* of the code: the rules walk through the program in a forward manner, at each step discharging the first statement, until the program has been dealt with completely. For example, an *assignment statement* is handled with the rule below:

$$\text{assignment} \ \frac{\Gamma \Rightarrow \{\mathcal{U}\}\{x := t\}[\ldots]\varphi, \Delta}{\Gamma \Rightarrow \{\mathcal{U}\}[x = t; \ \ldots]\varphi, \Delta}$$

The update $\mathcal{U}$ may have resulted from an assignment symbolically executed earlier. As a border case, this update may be empty and disappear. The notation "…" stands for an arbitrary "trail program" behind the assignment. As another border case, this trail program may be empty; then, the subformula $[\ldots]\varphi$ in the premiss is simply φ without a program attached to it.

The assignment rule transforms a program-level assignment into an equivalent update. This is a useful step because updates are in general easier to reason about than programs; for example, updates always terminate, and they never have implicit side effects. The difference between programs and updates becomes more profound when dealing with a more realistic programming language than the toy language considered in this paper, such as JAVA. In particular, updates are then helpful for a sound handling of the *aliasing* problem, without having to do case splits for every assignment [5, Chapter 3].

A *conditional statement* can be handled by splitting the proof depending on whether the guard is true or false:

$$\text{ifElse} \ \frac{\Gamma, \{\mathcal{U}\}g \Rightarrow \{\mathcal{U}\}[p1; \ \ldots]\varphi, \Delta \qquad \Gamma, \{\mathcal{U}\}!g \Rightarrow \{\mathcal{U}\}[p2; \ \ldots]\varphi, \Delta}{\Gamma \Rightarrow \{\mathcal{U}\}[\text{if } (g) \ \{p1\} \text{ else } \{p2\}; \ \ldots]\varphi, \Delta}$$

For a *loop*, the simplest approach is to *unwind* it:

$$\text{loopUnwind} \ \frac{\Gamma, \{\mathcal{U}\}g \Rightarrow \{\mathcal{U}\}[p; \text{ while } (g) \ \{p\}; \ \ldots]\varphi, \Delta \qquad \Gamma, \{\mathcal{U}\}!g \Rightarrow \{\mathcal{U}\}[\ldots]\varphi, \Delta}{\Gamma \Rightarrow \{\mathcal{U}\}[\text{while } (g) \ \{p\}; \ \ldots]\varphi, \Delta}$$

Obviously, unwinding is sufficient only if an upper bound on the number of loop iterations is known statically. In general, an *invariant* rule is needed. Unlike the other rules described here, such a rule usually cannot be applied automatically, because it relies on the presence of a suitable loop invariant.

Updates can be simplified and applied to terms and formulas using the set of (schematic) rewrite rules provided in App. B.

Example 2. Suppose we want to prove the validity of this sequent:

$$i > 0 \Longrightarrow [\texttt{n=0}; \ \texttt{i=i-1}; \ \texttt{n=n+i}]\texttt{n} \geq 0$$

Applying the assignment rule two times gives us:

$$i > 0 \Longrightarrow \{\texttt{n} := 0\}\{\texttt{i} := i - 1\}[\texttt{n=n+i}]\texttt{n} \geq 0$$

Since the two updates are independent of each other, this can be rewritten to:

$$i > 0 \Longrightarrow \{\texttt{n} := 0 \ \| \ \texttt{i} := i - 1\}[\texttt{n=n+i}]\texttt{n} \geq 0$$

Another application of assignment and another round of update rewriting yields:

$$i > 0 \Longrightarrow \{\texttt{n} := 0 \ \| \ \texttt{i} := i - 1 \ \| \ \texttt{n} := 0 + i - 1\}\texttt{n} \geq 0$$

Note that now, the effect of the sub-update $\texttt{n} := 0$ is overwritten by the rightmost sub-update which also writes to $\texttt{n}$. Since the program has now been dealt with completely, we can syntactically apply the update to the postcondition $\texttt{n} \geq 0$ (also using the rewrite rules in App. B):

$$i > 0 \Longrightarrow 0 + i - 1 \geq 0$$

Proving this sequent is a matter of simple arithmetic reasoning.

3 A Dynamic Logic with Abstraction

The main motivation for incorporating abstraction into a symbolic execution framework is to achieve automation. The core issue is to discover loop invariants automatically instead of relying on a human user. Our main idea is to employ a fixed point algorithm that performs repeated symbolic executions of the loop body, interleaved with abstraction steps, until an invariant is found.

To this end, we first introduce a notion of an *abstract domain* in Sect. 3.1. We expect an abstract domain to be a lattice of "abstract values", each representing a set of possible concrete values. For every abstract value, we introduce a partially interpreted constant symbol into our logic. Partially interpreted in this context means that the interpretation of such a symbol can vary on the concrete value as long as the latter satisfies certain domain restrictions. These constant symbols are used to represent abstract values within our updates. During construction of a proof, abstraction can be performed as an instance of *logical weakening*, for which we define a sound rule in Sect 3.2.

The invariants found by our algorithm can be used to get rid of loops by using the loop invariant rule of Sect. 3.3. Since the invariants we derive are updates instead of formulas, this rule is slightly different from the classical loop invariant rule of dynamic logic. The algorithm itself is described in Sect. 3.4 and Sect. 3.5.

3.1 Abstract Domains

Definition 5 (Abstract Domains). *Given a universe* D *(which we will also call* concrete domain *from now on), an abstract domain is a countable lattice $\mathcal{A}$ with partial order $\sqsubseteq$ and join operator $\sqcup$. We require that $\mathcal{A}$ does not contain any infinite ascending chains. Further, an abstract domain comes with an* abstraction function $\alpha : 2^D \to \mathcal{A}$ *and a* concretization function $\gamma : \mathcal{A} \to 2^D$ *with the following properties (from [7]):*

1. *α and γ are monotone wrt. the partial orders $\subseteq$ and $\sqsubseteq$*
2. *for each $a \in \mathcal{A} : a = \alpha(\gamma(a))$*
3. *for each $c \in 2^D : c \subseteq \gamma(\alpha(c))$*

The second property states that concretizing does not lead to a loss of information, while the third one expresses correctness of the abstraction: no concrete values are lost.

Example 3. As a simple example, our concrete domain may be $D = \mathbb{Z}$, and our abstract domain $\mathcal{A}$ may be the sign lattice depicted in Fig. 1. The abstraction function α and concretization function γ are as usual for this domain. For convenience, γ is given in the right part of Fig. 1.

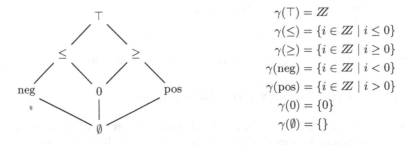

Fig. 1. Abstract domain lattice for sign analysis

Definition 6 (Logical Representation of Abstract Domains). *A signature $\Sigma_\mathcal{A}$ for an abstract domain $\mathcal{A}$ is a signature where*

- *for every $a \in \mathcal{A}$ and every $z \in \mathbb{Z}$, there is a constant symbol $\gamma_{a,z} \in \mathcal{F}$*
- *for every $a \in \mathcal{A}$ there is a unary predicate symbol $\chi_a \in \mathcal{P}$*

For a signature $\Sigma_\mathcal{A}$, we only consider interpretations I satisfying

- *for every $a \in \mathcal{A}$ and every $z \in \mathbb{Z}$: $I(\gamma_{a,z}) \in \gamma(a)$*
- *for every $a \in \mathcal{A}$: $I(\chi_a) = \gamma(a)$*

The constant symbols $\gamma_{a,z}$ are used to represent abstract values in logical formulas, in particular, on the right hand side of updates. For example, using the sign lattice abstract domain from Ex. 3, the update $(\mathtt{n} := \gamma_{\geq,1} \parallel \mathtt{i} := \gamma_{\geq,2})$ sets $\mathtt{n}$ and $\mathtt{i}$ to unknown, not necessarily equal, non-negative values. The predicate symbols

χ_a are used to express membership of a concrete value in the concretization of an abstract value.

For working with the partially interpreted $\gamma_{a,z}$ and χ_a symbols, we need rules for handling them; e.g., we want to be able to prove the validity of a sequent such as $\neg\gamma_{\geq,1} \doteq 0 \Longrightarrow \gamma_{\geq,1} > 0$, which depends on the restriction that $I(\gamma_{\geq,1}) \geq 0$ for every interpretation I. We assume that these rules are provided together with the abstract domain. From now on, we assume a fixed signature Σ_A for an abstract domain $\mathcal{A}$.

3.2   Update Weakening and Abstraction Rule

In this section we extend the classical notion of logical weakening to updates for which we give a weakening rule. Update weakening is used in the loop invariant rule directly and also implicitly during loop invariant computation.

To formulate weakening, respectively, strengthening rules for updates, we need to say what *weaker*, respectively, *stronger* means for updates. We define this ordering here with respect to a given sequent proof P and a set of context formulas (or constraints) C.

Definition 7 ($\triangleleft_{P,C}$-relation on updates). *Let P denote a proof, $\mathcal{U}_1$ and $\mathcal{U}_2$ updates, and C a set of formulas. We call $\mathcal{U}_2$ P,C-weaker than $\mathcal{U}_1$, i.e.,*

$$\mathcal{U}_1 \triangleleft_{P,C} \mathcal{U}_2$$

if for any interpretation I, state s, and variable assignment β, where for all $\psi \in C$ we have $val_{I,s,\beta}(\psi) = tt$, the following holds:

$$val_{I,s,\beta}(\mathcal{U}_1) \in \{val_{I',s,\beta}(\mathcal{U}_2) \mid I \simeq_{P,C} I'\}$$

where $I \simeq_{P,C} I'$ means that I and I' coincide on all function and predicate symbols occurring in P or C.[3] In case of an empty set of context formulas C, we omit C and write P-weaker and $\triangleleft_P$ instead.

Example 4. Assume a proof P consisting of a single sequent

$$c > 0 \Longrightarrow \underbrace{\{\mathtt{i} := \mathtt{i} + 1 \,\|\, \mathtt{j} := c + 3\}}_{\mathcal{U}}\varphi$$

with program variables $\mathtt{i}, \mathtt{j}$ and a constant symbol c.

1. The update $\mathtt{i} := d + 1 \,\|\, \mathtt{j} := e$, where d, e are new constant symbols, is P-weaker than $\mathcal{U}$, because for any I, s, β, we can choose the interpretation $I' \simeq_P I$ with $I'(d) = s(\mathtt{i})$ and $I'(e) = I(c) + 3$.
2. The update $\mathtt{i} := f(1) \,\|\, \mathtt{j} := g(c, 3)$, where f, g are new function symbols, is P-weaker than $\mathcal{U}$, because for any I, s, β we can choose the interpretation $I' \simeq_P I$ with $I'(f)(1) = s(\mathtt{i}) + 1$ and $I'(g)(I(c), 3) = I(c) + 3$.

---

[3] Note that in particular $val_{I',s,\beta}(\psi) = tt$ holds for all $\psi \in C$.

3. The update $i := j \| j := c + 3$ is *not* P-weaker than $\mathcal{U}$, as for any s' with $s'(j) \neq s(i) + 1$ the membership requirement from Def. 7 does not hold.
4. The update $i := \gamma_{\top,0} \| j := \gamma_{pos,0}$, where $\gamma_{\top,0}$ and $\gamma_{pos,0}$ are new, is *not* P-weaker than $\mathcal{U}$, but it is $\{c > 0\}$, P-weaker.

Weakening by replacing the right hand side of an update with a suitable $\gamma_{a,z}$ symbol corresponds to abstracting to the chosen abstract domain. In the following, we restrict ourselves to this form of weakening. The rule weakenUpdate below allows to use it in a sequent proof:

$$\text{weakenUpdate} \quad \frac{\Gamma, \{\mathcal{U}\}(\bar{x} \doteq \bar{c}) \Longrightarrow \exists \bar{\gamma}.\{\mathcal{U}'\}(\bar{x} \doteq \bar{c}), \Delta \quad \Gamma \Longrightarrow \{\mathcal{U}'\}\varphi, \Delta}{\Gamma \Longrightarrow \{\mathcal{U}\}\varphi, \Delta}$$

where

- $\bar{x} = (x_1, \ldots, x_n)$ is a list of all program variables occurring on the left hand side in $\mathcal{U}$ or $\mathcal{U}'$ (duplicate-free, in an arbitrary order)
- $\bar{c} = (c_1, \ldots, c_n)$ is a list of fresh constant symbols of the same length as $\bar{x}$
- $\bar{\gamma} = (\gamma_{a_1,z_1}, \ldots, \gamma_{a_m,z_m})$ is a list of all $\gamma_{a,z}$ symbols introduced freshly in $\mathcal{U}'$
- the notation $\exists \bar{\gamma}.\psi$ is an abbreviation for $\exists \bar{y}.(\chi_{\bar{a}}(\bar{y}) \ \& \ \psi[\bar{\gamma}/\bar{y}])$, where $\bar{y} = (y_1, \ldots, y_m)$ is a list of fresh logical variables of the same length as $\bar{\gamma}$, and where $\psi[\bar{\gamma}/\bar{y}]$ stands for the formula obtained from ψ by replacing all occurrences of a symbol in $\bar{\gamma}$ with its counterpart in $\bar{y}$
- vector notation is used as an abbreviation: $\exists \bar{y}.\psi$ stands for the multiply quantified formula $\exists y_1.\cdots.\exists y_m.\psi$, $\bar{t} \doteq \bar{t}'$ and $\chi_{\bar{a}}(\bar{y})$ stand for the conjunctions $t_1 \doteq t_1' \ \& \ \cdots \ \& \ t_n \doteq t_n'$ resp. $\chi_{a_1}(y_1) \ \& \ \cdots \ \& \ \chi_{a_m}(y_m)$

The first premiss of weakenUpdate guarantees that $\mathcal{U}'$ is $(P, \Gamma \cup !\Delta)$-weaker than $\mathcal{U}$: for any initial I, s, β, it must be possible to choose an interpretation of the newly introduced $\bar{\gamma}$ such that with this interpretation, $\mathcal{U}'$ assigns to all relevant program variables $\bar{x}$ the same value as $\mathcal{U}$. In the second premiss, the proof of φ continues with the weaker update $\mathcal{U}'$ in place of $\mathcal{U}$.

Lemma 1. *The* weakenUpdate *rule is sound: if all of its premises are logically valid, then its conclusion is also logically valid.*

The proof of this lemma is contained in App. C.1.

3.3   An Invariant Rule Based on Updates

Below we define a variation of the classical loop invariant rule, based on updates. The rule makes use of an "invariant update" $\mathcal{U}'$, which must be provided instead of an invariant formula.

$$\text{invariantUpdate} \quad \frac{\begin{array}{c} \Gamma, \{\mathcal{U}\}(\bar{x} \doteq \bar{c}) \Longrightarrow \exists \bar{\gamma}.\{\mathcal{U}'\}(\bar{x} \doteq \bar{c}), \Delta \\ \Gamma, \{\mathcal{U}'\}g, \{\mathcal{U}'\}[\mathtt{p}](\bar{x} \doteq \bar{c}) \Longrightarrow \exists \bar{\gamma}.\{\mathcal{U}'\}(\bar{x} \doteq \bar{c}), \Delta \\ \Gamma, \{\mathcal{U}'\}!g \Longrightarrow \{\mathcal{U}'\}[\ldots]\varphi, \Delta \end{array}}{\Gamma \Longrightarrow \{\mathcal{U}\}[\mathtt{while} \ (g) \ \{\mathtt{p}\}; \ \ldots]\varphi, \Delta}$$

where $\bar{x}$, $\bar{c}$, $\bar{\gamma}$, $\exists \bar{\gamma}.\psi$ and the vector notation are defined as in the weakenUpdate rule.

The first premiss of invariantUpdate is identical to that of weakenUpdate. It ensures that $\mathcal{U}'$ is weaker than $\mathcal{U}$, or in other words, that the initial state for the loop, as produced by $\mathcal{U}$, can also be reached by executing $\mathcal{U}'$ (using some suitable interpretation of the fresh $\bar{\gamma}$ symbols). The second premiss states that $\mathcal{U}'$ is "preserved" by the loop body p: for any state reached by executing first $\mathcal{U}'$ and then p, we can find an interpretation of the $\bar{\gamma}$ such that $\mathcal{U}'$ directly produces this state. Together, the first two premisses establish an inductive argument: any state reachable by an arbitrary number of loop iterations can also be reached directly by $\mathcal{U}'$, for some interpretation of the $\bar{\gamma}$ symbols. The result of this induction is used in the third premiss, where for handling the trail program "..." we only have to consider runs starting in states which can be produced by $\mathcal{U}'$.

Example 5. The following sequent occurs after applying the assignment rule in Ex. 1:

$$i \geq 0 \Longrightarrow \{n := 0\}[\texttt{while (i>0) } \underbrace{\{\texttt{i = i-1; n = n+i}\}}_{\texttt{b}}](i \doteq 0 \ \& \ n \geq 0)$$

An appropriate choice for the "invariant update" is $\mathcal{U}' = (n := \gamma_{\geq,1} \ || \ i := \gamma_{\geq,2})$. We will later see how this update can be found automatically. With this choice, the rule produces the following three sequents:

$i \geq 0, \ \{n := 0\}(n \doteq c_1 \ \& \ i \doteq c_2)$
$\quad \Longrightarrow \exists y_1, y_2.(\chi_{\geq}(y_1) \ \& \ \chi_{\geq}(y_2) \ \& \ \{n := y_1 \ || \ i := y_2\}(n \doteq c_1 \ \& \ i \doteq c_2))$

$i \geq 0, \ \{n := \gamma_{\geq,1} || i := \gamma_{\geq,2}\}(i > 0), \ \{n := \gamma_{\geq,1} || i := \gamma_{\geq,2}\}[b](n \doteq c_1 \ \& \ i \doteq c_2)$
$\quad \Longrightarrow \exists y_1, y_2.(\chi_{\geq}(y_1) \ \& \ \chi_{\geq}(y_2) \ \& \ \{n := y_1 \ || \ i := y_2\}(n \doteq c_1 \ \& \ i \doteq c_2))$

$i \geq 0, \ \{n := \gamma_{\geq,1} \ || \ i := \gamma_{\geq,2}\} \, !(i > 0)$
$\quad \Longrightarrow \{n := \gamma_{\geq,1} \ || \ i := \gamma_{\geq,2}\}(i \doteq 0 \ \& \ n \geq 0)$

All of these sequents are logically valid, and provided that our calculus contains rules covering the semantics of the $\gamma_{\geq,z}$ and $\chi_{\geq}$ symbols, they are proveable. For the first two, one needs to instantiate the existential quantifiers with c_1 and c_2.

Lemma 2. *The* invariantUpdate *rule is sound.*

The proof of this lemma is contained in App. C.2.

3.4   The Proof Search Strategy

In this section we describe the proof search strategy. The proof search strategy implements the fixed point algorithm for handling loops automatically without needing to be provided with loop invariants by a human user.

As our calculus is not proof confluent, defining a *good* search strategy is crucial. In particular, the proof search strategy needs to choose the right degree of abstraction and to maintain normal form-like properties of updates, terms and formulas (this is important, for example, to actually find a fixed point).

Depending on the proof context (e.g., main or side proof to compute the loop invariant) we will employ different proof search strategies.

Assume we intend to prove that after the execution of a program p the formula φ holds:

$$\Gamma \Longrightarrow [\text{p}]\varphi, \Delta$$

The proof search strategy acts now like a symbolic interpreter on p and executes assignments (applying rule assignment) as well as conditional statements (ifElse). Note that these rules are *precise* in the sense that no information on the possible poststate is lost.

The critical point in a proof P occurs when a loop statement is encountered and we are faced with a situation similar to

$$\Gamma \Longrightarrow \{\mathcal{U}\}[\text{while } (g) \ \{b\}; \ \ldots]\varphi, \Delta$$

In abstract-interpretation approaches, loop treatment involves the computation of a safe approximation of the set of states observable after the loop termination. It remains then to show that the formula $[\ldots]\varphi$ holds in all of them. The main idea of our approach is to describe this set in terms of an (abstract) update $\mathcal{U}_a$ such that for each I, β the set $\{s' \mid s' = val_{I',s,\beta}(\mathcal{U}_a)(s), s \in \mathcal{S}, f.a. \ I' \simeq_{P,C} I\}$ is a safe approximation of the post loop states. A higher precision can be achieved by requiring that the considered interpretations I satisfy additional formulas.

To compute abstract (weaker) updates, the proof search strategy spawns side proofs. The purpose of these side proofs is to compute updates that capture the state changes in successive executions of the loop body. The results of the side proofs are later combined after suitable abstraction using the *join* rule. Consequently, in the side proofs we handle the top-level loop by unwinding (loopUnwind) while possible nested loops are treated by rule invariantUpdate. As in the side proofs we are only interested in state changes, all proof branches that do not involve symbolic execution are discarded.

Consider now one unwinding step: the proof search strategy executes the loop body until the loop is about to be re-entered. In general, symbolic execution of the loop body may result in several branches; the proof search continues on these branches until they are either closed or the loop body has been completely symbolically executed and the loop is about to be re-entered. After complete execution of one loop iteration, the proof situation is similar to the one shown in Fig. 2.

At this point the proof search strategy computes a weakened update representing a superset of all possible states reachable after this loop iteration. A new sequent of the form

$$\Gamma' \Longrightarrow \{\mathcal{U}'\}[\text{while } (g) \ \{b\}; \ \ldots]\varphi, \Delta'$$

is created where update $\mathcal{U}'$ is the weakened (by abstraction) update computed by comparing the updates $\mathcal{U}_1, \ldots, \mathcal{U}_m$ from the open branches *and* update $\mathcal{U}$

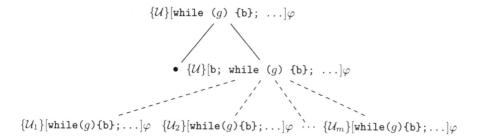

Fig. 2. Invariant computation: side proof after symbolic execution of one loop iteration

representing the symbolic state just before the loop unwinding. Γ' (Δ') are formula sets that are weaker (stronger) than any of the corresponding $\Gamma_1, \ldots, \Gamma_m$ ($\Delta_1, \ldots, \Delta_m$) belonging to the open leaves considered in Fig. 2. In Sect. 3.5 we describe this *join* in detail. The constructed sequent is then appended at one of the open branches. The other branches are closed, i.e. not further taken into consideration.

The proof search strategy stops the side computation if after an application of the join rule a fixed point is detected. A fixed point is reached when update $\mathcal{U}$ taken from immediately before the last loopUnwind rule application is weaker than (or equal to) update $\mathcal{U}'$ resulting from the current join operation.

To detect a fixed point the proof search strategy tries to prove for all program variables $\bar{x}$ that the states represented by update $\mathcal{U}$ subsume those of $\mathcal{U}'$:

$$\forall \bar{y}'.\exists \bar{y}.(Eq(\bar{y}',\bar{y})\ \&\ \chi_{\bar{\gamma}'}(\bar{y}')) -> \chi_{\bar{\gamma}}(\bar{y})\ \&\ \{\mathcal{U}[\bar{\gamma}/\bar{y}]\}\bar{x} \doteq \{\mathcal{U}'[\bar{\gamma}'/\bar{y}']\}\bar{x}) \qquad (1)$$

where

- $\bar{\gamma}, \bar{\gamma}'$ denote sequences of all γ symbols occurring in one of the sequents
- $\bar{y}, \bar{y}'$ are duplicate-free sequences of variables of same length as $\bar{\gamma}$ resp. $\bar{\gamma}'$
- $Eq(\bar{y}',\bar{y}) := \bigwedge_{\substack{y_i \in \bar{y}, y_j' \in \bar{y}', \\ \gamma_{a_i,i} = \gamma_{a_j,j}}} y_i = y_j'$ and $\chi_{\bar{\gamma}}(\bar{y}) := \bigwedge_{\substack{\gamma_{a_i,i} \in \bar{\gamma}, \\ y_i \in \bar{y}}} \chi_{a_i}(y_i)$ (analog. $\chi_{\bar{\gamma}'}$)

To find fixed points earlier the sequent side-formulas $\Gamma, \Delta, \Gamma', \Delta'$ can be used in the proof. The join operation defined in the next section guarantees that if the value of a variable x has been changed in the most recent loop iteration then the abstraction produces an elementary update $x := \gamma_{k,a}$. In combination with a finite abstract domain (1) becomes trivial to prove such that a fixed point is guaranteed to be found.

3.5 Joining Proof Branches

In this section we describe how different execution paths are joined by the proof search strategy in a side proof. The join rule introduced in this section is a combination of a classical weakening and the update weakening rule. Deviating from other rules, it is not a sequent rule but a "meta rule" combining several sequents. Let P denote a proof with several open branches

$$\vdots$$

$$\Gamma_{s_0} \Longrightarrow \{\mathcal{U}_{s_0}\}[\texttt{while } (g)\{\texttt{b}\}]\varphi, \ \Delta_{s_0}$$

$$\vdots$$

$$\Gamma_{s_1} \Longrightarrow \{\mathcal{U}_{s_1}\}[\texttt{while } (g)\{\texttt{b}\}]\varphi, \ \Delta_{s_1} \ \ldots \ \Gamma_{s_m} \Longrightarrow \{\mathcal{U}_{s_m}\}[\texttt{while } (g)\{\texttt{b}\}]\varphi, \ \Delta_{s_m}$$

Applying the join rule closes all except one of these open branches. The open branch that is left is extended by adding the sequent

$$\bigvee_{i=s_0}^{s_m} (\Gamma_{s_i} \ \& \ !\Delta_{s_i}) \Longrightarrow \{(C_{s_0}, \mathcal{U}_{s_0}) \sqcup \ldots \sqcup (C_{s_m}, \mathcal{U}_{s_m})\}[\texttt{while } (g) \ \{\texttt{b}\}]\varphi$$

as a new leaf with

- formula set $C_{s_i} := \Gamma_{s_i} \cup !\Delta_{s_i}$ and
- $(C_1, \mathcal{U}_1) \sqcup (C_2, \mathcal{U}_2)$ is an update join operation as defined below.

Definition 8 (Update Join $\cdot \sqcup \cdot$). *The* update join operation *has the signature*

$$\sqcup : (2^{For} \times Updates) \times (2^{For} \times Updates) \to Updates$$

where 2^{For} denotes the power set of formulas and is defined by the following property:

   Let $\mathcal{U}_1$ and $\mathcal{U}_2$ denote arbitrary updates occurring in a proof P and let C_1, C_2 be formula sets representing constraints on the update values. Then an update $(C_1, \mathcal{U}_1) \sqcup (C_2, \mathcal{U}_2)$ must be $(P, C_{1/2})$-weaker than $\mathcal{U}_1$ resp. $\mathcal{U}_2$, i.e.

$$\mathcal{U}_i \vartriangleleft_{P, C_i} (\mathcal{U}_1, C_1) \sqcup (\mathcal{U}_2, C_2), \ i = 1, 2 \ .$$

Lemma 3. *Rule* join *is sound.*

The join rule, even though sound, is only used within side proofs that compute loop invariants. Its correctness is not strictly necessary as the loop invariant rule checks the invariance property and will reject unsuitable invariants, but increases the likelihood that meaningful fixed points and, hence, loop invariants are found.

   Finally, we describe the concrete realization $\sqcup_{abs}$ of an update join operator for finite abstract domains.

   Let $\mathcal{U}_1, C_1$ and $\mathcal{U}_2, C_2$ denote updates and their value restrictions. The update join $(\mathcal{U}_1, C_1)\sqcup_{abs}(\mathcal{U}_2, C_2)$ computes the update $\mathcal{U}_{res}$ as follows: let x be a program variable occurring on the left side of $\mathcal{U}_1$ or $\mathcal{U}_2$.

1. Try to prove

$$\Longrightarrow \exists y.((C_1 \to (\{\mathcal{U}_1\}\texttt{x}) \doteq y) \ \& \ (C_2 \to (\{\mathcal{U}_2\}\texttt{x}) \doteq y))$$

   if the proof attempt succeeds, then the elementary update $\texttt{x} := t_1$ occurring last in $\mathcal{U}_1$ with x on the left side (resp. $\texttt{x} := t_2$ if x occurred only on the left side of $\mathcal{U}_2$) is added to $\mathcal{U}_{res}$ by parallel composition. Otherwise, if the proof attempt fails (timeout or counterexample found) then continue with the next step.

2. For each pair $(C_i, \mathcal{U}_i)$, $i = 1, 2$, for any abstract domain element a starting with the smallest one, try to prove

$$C_i \Longrightarrow \chi_a(\{\mathcal{U}_i\}\mathbf{x})$$

and stop processing a pair as soon as an a has been found for which the sequent is valid, i.e. a proof has been found (within a given timeout). After termination we are left with two abstract domain elements a_1, a_2 for the resp. pairs for which we compute $a_1 \sqcup a_2$ (or at least an upper bound). Finally, the elementary update $\mathbf{x} := \gamma_{a_1 \sqcup a_2, z}$ is added to update $\mathcal{U}_{res}$ by parallel composition.

Example 6. Given the program variables $\mathbf{i}, \mathbf{n}$ and the update/constraint pairs $(\mathbf{n} := 0, \mathbf{i} \geq 0)$ and $(\mathbf{n} := \mathbf{i} - 1 \| \mathbf{i} := \mathbf{i} - 1, \mathbf{i} > 0)$, the join computation proceeds as follows:

Starting with program variable $\mathbf{n}$, we check first, if $\mathbf{n}$ is evaluated to the same value under both updates in their resp. context. Obviously, that does not hold in a state where $\mathbf{i}$ has, for example, the value 10.

Thus we enter the abstraction phase. Starting with the minimal abstract domain element $\bot$ the proof obligations described in step 2 are attempted to prove. The attempts succeed for

$$\mathbf{i} \geq 0 \Longrightarrow \chi_0(\{\mathbf{n} := 0\}\mathbf{n}) \quad \text{and} \quad \mathbf{i} > 0 \Longrightarrow \chi_{\geq}(\{\mathbf{n} := \mathbf{i} - 1 \,\|\, \mathbf{i} := \mathbf{i} - 1\}\mathbf{n})$$

The join for the abstract domain elements is $(\geq \sqcup 0) = \geq$. Thus, we get as first sub-update $\mathbf{n} := \gamma_{\geq, 0}$. A similar computation for program variable $\mathbf{i}$ gives us finally the complete update

$$\mathbf{n} := \gamma_{\geq, 0} \,\|\, \mathbf{i} := \gamma_{\geq, 1}$$

4 Example

Recall the proof obligation from Ex. 1:

$$\mathbf{i} \geq 0 \Longrightarrow [\mathbf{n} = 0; \texttt{ while (i > 0) i = i-1; n = n+i}](\mathbf{i} \doteq 0 \,\&\, \mathbf{n} \geq 0) \quad (2)$$

In this section, we illustrate our approach by slowly walking through the proof for this sequent. We abbreviate the while-loop with W, the loop body with B and the postcondition with φ. The first step is to apply the **assignment** rule, which produces the following sequent:

$$\mathbf{i} \geq 0 \Longrightarrow \{\mathbf{n} := 0\}[\mathbf{W}]\varphi \quad (3)$$

At this point we open a side computation with this subgoal in order to determine a suitable loop invariant update. After this side computation, we will return to the main proof at sequent (3) and apply the **invariantUpdate** rule using this update.

The side computation starts by applying loopUnwind, which splits the side proof into two branches:

$$i \geq 0, \{n := 0\}(i > 0) \Longrightarrow \{n := 0\}[B;W]\varphi$$

$$i \geq 0, \{n := 0\}\,!(i > 0) \Longrightarrow \{n := 0\}\varphi$$

The second of these branches is uninteresting to us in this side computation, and we simply ignore it. Using update rewriting rules and some arithmetic simplification, the first branch can be simplified to

$$i > 0 \Longrightarrow \{n := 0\}[B;W]\varphi$$

Note that the path condition from the loop guard strengthens the precondition. We continue by symbolically executing the loop body, which (after some update rewriting) yields

$$i > 0 \Longrightarrow \{n := 0 \,\|\, i := i - 1 \,\|\, n := 0 + i - 1\}[W]\varphi \tag{4}$$

Now, we have completed our first iteration: we have unwound the loop once, executed its body, and obtained a sequent where W is the first active statement like in (3). We use the join rule to merge the current state (4) with the previous state (3):

$$i > 0 \,|\, i \geq 0 \Longrightarrow \{n := \gamma_{\geq,1} \,\|\, i := \gamma_{\geq,2}\}[W]\varphi \tag{5}$$

The computation performed by join rule is explained in detail in Ex. 6 in Sect. 3.5. We unwind the loop once more with loopUnwind, which gives us the following for the loop entry branch:

$$i > 0 \,|\, i \geq 0, \{n := \gamma_{\geq,1} \,\|\, i := \gamma_{\geq,2}\}(i > 0) \Longrightarrow \{n := \gamma_{\geq,1} \,\|\, i := \gamma_{\geq,2}\}[B;W]\varphi$$

Update rewriting and arithmetic simplification turns this into:

$$i \geq 0, \gamma_{\geq,2} > 0 \Longrightarrow \{n := \gamma_{\geq,1} \,\|\, i := \gamma_{\geq,2}\}[B;W]\varphi$$

We symbolically execute the body a second time, which produces:

$$i \geq 0, \gamma_{\geq,2} > 0 \tag{6}$$
$$\Longrightarrow \{n := \gamma_{\geq,1} \,\|\, i := \gamma_{\geq,2} \,\|\, i := \gamma_{\geq,2} - 1 \,\|\, n := \gamma_{\geq,1} + \gamma_{\geq,2} - 1\}[W]\varphi$$

This finishes our second iteration. We apply join to combine (6) and (5), which yields:

$$i > 0 \,|\, i \geq 0 \,|\, (i \geq 0 \,\&\, \gamma_{\geq,2} > 0) \Longrightarrow \{n := \gamma_{\geq,3} \,\|\, i := \gamma_{\geq,4}\}[W]\varphi \tag{7}$$

Now, we observe that the update $\mathcal{U} = (n := \gamma_{\geq,3} \,\|\, i := \gamma_{\geq,4})$ of the current sequent (7) "implies" the corresponding update $\mathcal{U}' = (n := \gamma_{\geq,1} \,\|\, i := \gamma_{\geq,2})$ of the previous iteration (5). The fixed point detection formula (1) from Sect. 3.4

$$\forall y_1, y_2. \exists y_1', y_2'. \big(
\chi_{\geq}(y_1) \,\&\, \chi_{\geq}(y_2) \to (\chi_{\geq}(y_1') \,\&\, \chi_{\geq}(y_2') \,\&\,
((\{n := y_1' \,\|\, i := y_2'\}n) \doteq (\{n := y_1 \,\|\, i := y_2\}n) \,\&\,
(\{n := y_1' \,\|\, i := y_2'\}i) \doteq (\{n := y_1' \,\|\, i := y_2'\}i)))$$

becomes then trivial to solve as the existential quantifiers need only to be instantiated with the skolem constant resulting from the enclosing universal quantifier.

Thus, $\mathcal{U}$ (or $\mathcal{U}'$) is a "fixed point". At this point we leave the side computation. We continue the main proof by applying the rule invariantUpdate to (3), which eliminates the loop from our proof obligation, making the remainder of the proof straightforward as shown already in Ex. 5.

In conclusion, we have constructed a proof for the validity of (2). Our use of abstraction allowed us to do so in a completely mechanical process, which did not require any manually supplied loop invariant.

5   Modeling Information Flow

The problem of *information flow security* is about preventing a program from leaking "secret" data to output channels of a "lower security level". Typically, the security levels to be distinguished are defined and ordered in a security lattice. In the simplest case, one distinguishes only between the security levels High and Low.

Example 7. In the following example programs, h and l are program variables, where h has security level High and l security level Low. A program is considered *secure* if an attacker who reads the final values of the Low variables cannot infer any information about the initial values of the High variables.

1. l=h is obviously *insecure*, because information flows directly from h to l.
2. if (h>0) {l=1} else {l=2} is also *insecure*, because information about the sign of the initial value of h flows indirectly to l.
3. if (l>0) {h=1} else {h=2} is *secure*, because the value of l is not touched at all.
4. if (h>0) {l=1} else {l=2}; l=3 is *secure*, because the final value of l is always 3, independently of the initial value of h.
5. h=0;l=h is *secure*, because the final value of l is always 0.
6. if (h>0) {h=1;l=h} is *secure*, because the value of l is not changed.
7. if (h>0) {l=2;h=1} else {l=2;h=2} is *secure*, because the final value of l is always 2.
8. l=h-h is *secure*, because the final value of l is always 0.

The most common technique for a language-based analysis of information flow is to use special type systems. The security levels are then used as types that are assigned to program variables. The analysis ensures via type checking or type inference that no information about the value of a High-labeled variable is leaked to a Low-labeled variable.

Soundness of any approach to information-flow analysis entails that an insecure program will not be classified as secure. To achieve full automation, however, many approaches, in particular type-based ones, classify certain secure programs as insecure. To identify program (4) as secure, the approach under consideration has to be control-flow sensitive. Some, but not all, available analyses have this property. In order to correctly identify programs (5), (6), (7) and (8) as secure, the analysis must be *value-sensitive*. At the moment this is only achieved by some deduction-based systems [9,6,13] that require human interaction.

Information-flow analysis can be restated as an analysis of variable dependencies (see [16]). Here, we want to find for any variable x the set of variables on whose initial values the final value of x can at most depend. In particular, we may ask whether the final value of a Low-labeled variable can depend on the initial value of any High-labeled variable.

In this section we extend our program logic to allow the analysis of variable dependencies in programs. In contrast to [9], where the dependencies of a program variable are implicitly tracked using free logical variables, we use an approach where the dependencies are encoded explicitly into program states. The execution of a program statement directly manipulates these dependencies. This approach allows to apply the abstraction mechanism introduced in this paper also to variable dependencies, which serves to achieve *automation* of our information flow analysis while maintaining a high degree of precision and achieving value-sensitivity in more cases than type-based systems.

We omitted formal correctness statements and proofs in this section which are tedious, but do not offer additional insights.

5.1 Dependencies in Dynamic Logic

Formally, the dependencies of a variable can be defined as follows.

Definition 9 (Variable Dependencies). *Given a program variable x and a program p, the dependencies of x under p form the smallest set $\mathcal{D}(x, p) \subseteq \mathcal{PV}$ of program variables such that the following holds for all interpretations I and all variable assignments β: if $s_1, s_2 \in \mathcal{S}$ are such that for all $y \in \mathcal{D}(x, p)$ we have $s_1(y) = s_2(y)$, then either*

- $val_{I,s_1,\beta}(p) = val_{I,s_2,\beta}(p) = \emptyset$ *(i.e., from both initial states the execution of p does not terminate), or*
- $val_{I,s_1,\beta}(p) = \{s'_1\}$ *and* $val_{I,s_2,\beta}(p) = \{s'_2\}$, *where* $s'_1(x) = s'_2(x)$ *(i.e., from both initial states the execution terminates and yields the same value for x).*

The dependencies formalized in Def. 9 are difficult to reason about: they are based on comparing *all possible runs* of a program p instead of being a local property which is true or false in a given program state. To be able to talk about dependencies in our logical formulas in the same way as about other program properties, we extend our logic and the semantics of programs so that dependencies are stored in states *explicitly*. The main idea is to associate with every program variable x a program variable x^{dep} that records the dependencies of x with respect to the program that has been symbolically executed so far. The variable x^{dep} is updated by the program whenever x itself is changed, such that in any state during program execution, x^{dep} evaluates to a set of program variables which contains all variables on whose initial value the current value of x can depend.

Definition 10 (Logical Representation of Dependencies). *Given a signature* $\Sigma = (\mathcal{F}, \mathcal{P}, \mathcal{PV}, \mathcal{V})$, *the dependency extension of* Σ *is a signature* $\Sigma^{dep} = (\mathcal{F}^{dep}, \mathcal{P}^{dep}, \mathcal{PV}^{dep}, \mathcal{V})$, *where*

- $\mathcal{F}^{dep} = \mathcal{F} \cup \{\{\}, \dot{\cup}\} \cup \{\{x\} \mid x \in \mathcal{PV}\}$, *where* $\{\}$ *is a constant symbol,* $\dot{\cup}$ *is a function symbol with arity 2, and where the* $\{x\}$ *are function symbols with arity 0,*
- $\mathcal{P}^{dep} = \mathcal{P} \cup \{\dot{\subseteq}\}$, *where* $\dot{\subseteq}$ *is a predicate symbol with arity 2, and*
- $\mathcal{PV}^{dep} = \mathcal{PV} \cup \{x^{dep} \mid x \in \mathcal{PV}\}$.

For such a signature Σ^{dep}, *we do not allow the new symbols to occur in programs: programs over a signature* Σ^{dep} *are built only from the symbols defined in the sub-signature* Σ. *We only consider universes* $D \supseteq 2^{\mathcal{PV}}$ *where every set of program variables also occurs as a value in the universe. Finally, we only allow interpretations* I *that fix the meaning of the additional symbols as follows:*

- $I(\{\}) = \emptyset$,
- *for all* $P_1, P_2 \in 2^{\mathcal{PV}}$: $I(\dot{\cup})(P_1, P_2) = P_1 \cup P_2$,
- *for all* $x \in \mathcal{PV}$: $I(\{x\}) = \{x\}$, *and*
- $I(\dot{\subseteq}) = \{(P_1, P_2) \mid P_1 \subseteq P_2 \subseteq \mathcal{PV}\}$.

Definition 11 (Program Semantics with Dependencies). *Given a universe* D, *an interpretation* I, *a state* s *and a variable assignment* β, *we evaluate programs* p *to a set of states* $val'_{I,s,\beta}(p) \in 2^S$ *as defined in App. A.2. As before, our programs are deterministic, so the sets always have at most one element.*

One difference to the program semantics without dependencies is that executing an assignment x = t not only changes x, but also x^{dep}: we assign to it the value of $deps(t)$, where for every term or formula t, $deps(t)$ is a term which over-approximates the precise semantic dependencies of t. For example, $deps(\mathtt{n}+\mathtt{i}) = \mathtt{n}^{dep} \dot{\cup} \mathtt{i}^{dep}$. The formal definition of $deps$ is given in App. A.3.

The second difference is that after executing a conditional statement or a loop iteration with guard g, we add $deps(g)$ to x^{dep} for every program variable x which has been changed in the body of the conditional or loop. This is necessary in order to cover implicit flow of information via control flow (see Ex. 7).

Example 8. Consider program (6) of Ex. 7. We can express security of this program with the sequent

$$\mathtt{h}^{dep} \doteq \{\mathtt{h}\}, \ \mathtt{l}^{dep} \doteq \{\mathtt{l}\} \implies [\texttt{if (h>0) \{h=1;l=h\}}](\mathtt{l}^{dep} \dot{\subseteq} \{\mathtt{l}\})$$

The precondition in the antecedent means that we assume the initial value of every variable to depend exactly on itself. The postcondition demands that after running the program, the final value of l depends at most on the initial value of l (so that in particular, it does not depend on the initial value of h).

Let $s_1 \in S$ be a state satisfying the precondition, i.e., $s_1(\mathtt{h}^{dep}) = \{\mathtt{h}\}$ and $s_1(\mathtt{l}^{dep}) = \{\mathtt{l}\}$. If we execute the assignment h=l in s_1, this will produce a state s_2 with $s_2(\mathtt{h}^{dep}) = s_1(\mathtt{l}^{dep}) = \{\mathtt{l}\}$, reflecting the fact that now the value of h depends on the initial value of l.

Continuing the execution of the program, the assignment l=h yields a state s_3 with $s_3(1^{dep}) = s_2(h^{dep}) = \{1\}$. After the end of the conditional statement, the dependencies of the guard h>0 are injected into all variables changed inside the conditional, yielding a state s_4 where $s_4(1^{dep}) = s_3(1^{dep}) = \{1\}$ (since 1 has the same value in s_3 at the end of the conditional as it had in s_1 before the conditional), and where $s_4(h^{dep}) = s_3(h^{dep}) \cup s_1(h^{dep}) = \{h\}$ (where $s_1(h^{dep})$ are the dependencies of the guard).

Thus, the final state s_4 satisfies $s_4(1^{dep}) = \{1\}$, meaning that the postcondition is satisfied. As this holds for all initial states satisfying the precondition, our sequent is logically valid.

Note that our formalisation of dependencies is control flow- and value-sensitive; it correctly classifies programs (3)–(6) of Ex. 7 as secure. Nevertheless, it is an overapproximation of the semantic dependencies as formalized in Def. 9. For example, it conservatively classifies programs (7) and (8) as insecure, even though they are in fact secure. This is a price we pay for the ability to reason about dependencies in the same way as state properties.

5.2   Dependency Aware Rules

For working with the changed semantics of Def. 11 in our calculus, we need to adapt the symbolic execution rules from Sect. 2.3 and also the update invariant rule from Sect. 3.3 accordingly. The other rules (in particular, weakenUpdate and join) are not affected, because they do not deal with programs. For the assignment rule, we can simply add the update $x^{dep} := deps(t)$:

$$\text{assignment}^{\text{dep}} \quad \frac{\Gamma \Longrightarrow \{\mathcal{U}\}\{x := t \,\|\, x^{dep} := deps(t)\}[\ldots]\varphi, \Delta}{\Gamma \Longrightarrow \{\mathcal{U}\}[x = t; \ \ldots]\varphi, \Delta}$$

For conditional statements, the new semantics introduces an additional state transition after execution of the conditional where the dependencies of the guard are retroactively added to the dependencies of all variables modified inside the conditional. We capture these additional dependencies in the rule by inserting a suitable update $\mathcal{V}$ into our premises:

$$\text{ifElse}^{\text{dep}} \quad \frac{\Gamma, \{\mathcal{U}\}g, \ \{\mathcal{U}\}(\bar{y} \doteq \bar{y}^{pre}) \Longrightarrow \{\mathcal{U}\}[\text{p1}]\{\mathcal{V}\}[\ldots]\varphi, \Delta \qquad \Gamma, \{\mathcal{U}\}!g, \ \{\mathcal{U}\}(\bar{y} \doteq \bar{y}^{pre}) \Longrightarrow \{\mathcal{U}\}[\text{p2}]\{\mathcal{V}\}[\ldots]\varphi, \Delta}{\Gamma \Longrightarrow \{\mathcal{U}\}[\text{if } (g) \ \{\text{p1}\} \text{ else } \{\text{p2}\}; \ \ldots]\varphi, \Delta}$$

where

- $\bar{y} = (y_1, y_1^{dep}, \ldots, y_n, y_n^{dep})$ is a list of all program variables occurring in g, p1 or p2, together with the corresponding dependency variables
- $\bar{y}^{pre} = (y_1^{pre}, y_1^{predep} \ldots, y_n^{pre}, y_n^{predep})$ is a list of fresh constant symbols of the same length as $\bar{y}$
- $\mathcal{V}$ is the update

$$\mathbf{y}_1^{dep} := \mathbf{if}(\mathbf{y}_1 \doteq \mathbf{y}_1^{pre})\,\mathbf{then}(\mathbf{y}_1^{dep})\,\mathbf{else}\,(\mathbf{y}_1^{dep}\,\dot{\cup}\,\{\bar{\mathbf{y}} := \bar{\mathbf{y}}^{pre}\}\,deps(g))$$
$$\|\dots\|$$
$$\mathbf{y}_n^{dep} := \mathbf{if}(\mathbf{y}_n \doteq \mathbf{y}_n^{pre})\,\mathbf{then}(\mathbf{y}_n^{dep})\,\mathbf{else}\,(\mathbf{y}_n^{dep}\,\dot{\cup}\,\{\bar{\mathbf{y}} := \bar{\mathbf{y}}^{pre}\}\,deps(g))$$

The fresh constant symbols $\bar{\mathbf{y}}^{pre}$ are used to store the pre-state values of the program variables $\bar{\mathbf{y}}$. The update $\mathcal{V}$ compares the current values of all (non-dependency) program variables with their pre-state values, and adds $deps(g)$ to variable's dependencies if the value has been changed. A subtle detail is that $deps(g)$ must be evaluated in the pre-state, which is achieved by prefixing it with the update $\bar{\mathbf{y}} := \bar{\mathbf{y}}^{pre}$.

The same idea can be applied to the loopUnwind and invariantUpdate rules (where $\bar{\mathbf{y}}$, $\bar{\mathbf{y}}^{pre}$ and $\mathcal{V}$ are as above):

loopUnwind^{dep}

$$\frac{\Gamma, \{\mathcal{U}\}g,\ \{\mathcal{U}\}(\bar{\mathbf{y}} \doteq \bar{\mathbf{y}}^{pre}) \Longrightarrow \{\mathcal{U}\}[\mathbf{p}]\{\mathcal{V}\}[\texttt{while (t) \{p\};}\ \dots]\varphi, \Delta \qquad \Gamma, \{\mathcal{U}\}!g \Longrightarrow \{\mathcal{U}\}[\dots]\varphi, \Delta}{\Gamma \Longrightarrow \{\mathcal{U}\}[\texttt{while (g) \{p\};}\ \dots]\varphi, \Delta}$$

invariantUpdate^{dep}

$$\frac{\Gamma, \{\mathcal{U}\}(\bar{\mathbf{x}} \doteq \bar{c}) \Longrightarrow \exists\bar{\mathbf{y}}.\{\mathcal{U}'\}(\bar{\mathbf{x}} \doteq \bar{c}), \Delta \qquad \Gamma, \{\mathcal{U}'\}g,\ \{\mathcal{U}'\}(\bar{\mathbf{y}} \doteq \bar{\mathbf{y}}^{pre}),\ \{\mathcal{U}'\}[\mathbf{p}]\{\mathcal{V}\}(\bar{\mathbf{x}} \doteq \bar{c}) \Longrightarrow \exists\bar{\mathbf{y}}.\{\mathcal{U}'\}(\bar{\mathbf{x}} \doteq \bar{c}), \Delta \qquad \Gamma, \{\mathcal{U}'\}!g \Longrightarrow \{\mathcal{U}'\}[\dots]\varphi, \Delta}{\Gamma \Longrightarrow \{\mathcal{U}\}[\texttt{while (g) \{p\};}\ \dots]\varphi, \Delta}$$

5.3 Dependency Aware Abstraction

To apply abstraction in the dependency-aware version of our calculus two abstract domains have to be defined:

1. The abstract domain $\mathcal{A}_{val}$ for the value abstraction of *normal* program variables that carry values. The choice of $\mathcal{A}_{val}$ depends on the application context. An example is the sign domain for integers used for illustration in the previous sections.
2. The abstract domain $\mathcal{A}_{dep}$ for the value abstraction of the *dependency* program variables. Again, the suitable choice depends on the application context. In an information-flow security context, a natural choice for $\mathcal{A}_{dep}$ is suggested by the security lattice.

The proof search strategy remains nearly unchanged from the standard version as defined in Sec. 3.4. When computing an abstraction, the abstract domain $\mathcal{A}_{val}$ is used for normal program variables $\mathbf{x} \in \mathcal{PV}$ and $\mathcal{A}_{dep}$ for dependency program variables $\mathbf{x}^{dep} \in \mathcal{PV}^{dep}$.

Example 9. Assume that we are given a security policy with security levels High and Low for program variables $\mathcal{PV} = \{\texttt{l1}, \texttt{l2}, \texttt{h}\}$.

For regular values, we keep using the sign domain from previous sections as $\mathcal{A}_{val}$. For dependencies, we use $\mathcal{A}_{dep} := \{\emptyset, \mathsf{Low}, \mathsf{High}, \top_{dep}\}$ with $\gamma(\emptyset) = \emptyset$, $\gamma(\mathsf{Low}) = 2^{\{11,12\}}$, $\gamma(\mathsf{High}) = 2^{\{h\}}$, $\gamma(\top_{dep}) = 2^{\mathcal{PV}}$. Consider now the following simple program P:

$$\mathtt{11=0;}\ \mathtt{12=0;}\ \underbrace{\mathbf{while}\ \mathtt{(h<0)\ \{\ 12=12+1;\ h=h+1\ \}}}_{\mathtt{W}};\ \underbrace{\mathbf{if}\ \mathtt{(12<0)\ \{\ 11=1\ \}}}_{\mathtt{C}}$$

To check whether P satisfies the specified security policy for program variable 11, the sequent

$$\mathtt{11}^{dep} \doteq \{\mathtt{11}\},\ \mathtt{12}^{dep} \doteq \{\mathtt{12}\},\ \mathtt{h}^{dep} \doteq \{\mathtt{h}\} \Longrightarrow [\mathtt{P}]\big(\mathtt{11}^{dep} \ \dot{\subseteq}\ \{\mathtt{11}\} \ \dot{\cup}\ \{\mathtt{12}\}\big)$$

needs to be proven. The precondition demands that program variables depend on themselves in the initial state, as in Ex. 8.

Applying rule $\mathsf{assignment}^{dep}$ twice yields an update where 11 and 12 are set to 0 and where all dependencies of 11 and 12 have been erased, i.e. $\mathtt{11}^{dep}$, $\mathtt{12}^{dep}$ are assigned the empty set $\{\}$ $(= deps(0))$. The resulting sequent is:

$$\mathtt{11}^{dep} \doteq \{\mathtt{11}\},\ \mathtt{12}^{dep} \doteq \{\mathtt{12}\},\ \mathtt{h}^{dep} \doteq \{\mathtt{h}\}$$
$$\Longrightarrow \{\mathtt{11} := 0 \,\|\, \mathtt{11}^{dep} := \{\} \,\|\, \mathtt{12} := 0 \,\|\, \mathtt{12}^{dep} := \{\}\}[\mathtt{W;C}]\big(\mathtt{11}^{dep} \ \dot{\subseteq}\ \{\mathtt{11}\} \ \dot{\cup}\ \{\mathtt{12}\}\big)$$

At this point the loop invariant update needs to be computed in a side proof as described in Sect. 3.4, which automatically yields as invariant update $\mathcal{U}_{Inv}$:

$$\mathtt{11} := 0 \,\|\, \mathtt{11}^{dep} := \{\} \,\|\, \mathtt{12} := \gamma_{\geq,0} \,\|\, \mathtt{12}^{dep} := \gamma_{\mathsf{High},0} \,\|\, \mathtt{h} := \gamma_{\top_{val},0} \,\|\, \mathtt{h}^{dep} := \{\mathtt{h}\}$$

Note that we keep the precise value for 11 and $\mathtt{11}^{dep}$, as 11 is not modified by the loop. The other variables may be changed and have to be abstracted. In particular 12 may depend on h due to the implicit information-flow caused by the loop guard, which is reflected in the value for $\mathtt{12}^{dep}$.

Applying now rule $\mathsf{invariantUpdate}^{dep}$ and instantiating $\mathcal{U}'$ with $\mathcal{U}_{Inv}$ creates three new branches. For lack of space we focus on the third branch:

$$\mathtt{11}^{dep} \doteq \{\mathtt{11}\},\ \mathtt{12}^{dep} \doteq \{\mathtt{12}\},\ \mathtt{h}^{dep} \doteq \{\mathtt{h}\},\ \{\mathcal{U}_{Inv}\}!\,\mathtt{h} < 0$$
$$\Longrightarrow \{\mathcal{U}_{Inv}\}[\mathtt{C}]\big(\mathtt{11}^{dep} \ \dot{\subseteq}\ \{\mathtt{11}\} \ \dot{\cup}\ \{\mathtt{12}\}\big)$$

Applying rule ifElse^{dep} results in two branches. As we know that the conditional guard 12<0 under $\mathcal{U}_{Inv}$ is never satisified, we can close the then-branch immediately. We continue on the else-branch and after a few rule applications and simplifications we are left with

$$\mathtt{11}^{dep} \doteq \{\mathtt{11}\},\ \mathtt{12}^{dep} \doteq \{\mathtt{12}\},\ \mathtt{h}^{dep} \doteq \{\mathtt{h}\},\ \gamma_{\top_{val},0} \geq 0 \Longrightarrow \{\} \ \dot{\subseteq}\ \{\mathtt{11}\} \ \dot{\cup}\ \{\mathtt{12}\}$$

This formula is obviously valid, and thus the program does not leak any information on the initial value of h to 11. Note that we would not have been able to prove that fact with a value-insensitive approach as we would then need to consider the possibility of the then branch injecting implicitly a High dependency into $\mathtt{11}^{dep}$ via the conditional's guard. Note also that the security policy does not hold for program variable 12, and that the proof would not close if we had included $\mathtt{12}^{dep} \ \dot{\subseteq}\ \{\mathtt{11}\} \ \dot{\cup}\ \{\mathtt{12}\}$ in our postcondition.

6   Related Work

Several approaches for combining deductive verification and abstract interpretation exist. One example is the "loop invariants on demand" technique [18], where an abstract interpretation system is invoked by a theorem prover to produce invariants for a specific program context. If the generated invariant is too weak, the abstract interpreter is iteratively called again using a more expressive abstract domain. Nevertheless, the theorem prover and the abstract interpreter are separate entities. In [19], a widening operator is built into a theorem prover.

Our goal of deeply integrating abstract interpretation into deductive verification based on dynamic logic is also pursued in [26]. There, the abstraction is done on logical formulas instead of on updates, using the technique of predicate abstraction [12]. The approach of [26] has not been applied to the problem of secure information flow.

For information flow analysis, our approach is more precise than typical security type systems, because it is flow- and value-sensitive. It is also more precise than the abstract interpretation defined in [11]. For example, in our setting not all locations to which a value is assigned in the body of a conditional or loop need depend on the guard (see Ex. 8).

Deductive approaches for reasoning about information-flow have been already listed in Sect. 1. Only some of the approaches focused on automation as one major concern. Papers [6] and [13] aim at the embedding of type-based analyses into program logics. To achieve full automation type-based systems are needed to construct either a certain formula entailing non-interference [6] or a derivation that can be translated into a proof of the program logic [13]. Neither includes a proof search algorithm.

The approach presented in [1] uses a Hoare logic and does not need a theorem prover to generate necessary invariants. On the other hand, it tracks only the independence relationship among variables and is therefore not value-sensitive. In [4] the authors use self-composition of programs to show information-flow security considering a formalisation of non-interference for a Hoare logic and an encoding in CTL. For the first one, automation is not targeted and for the second one model checking would be possible but is restricted to finite state programs.

7   Conclusion and Future Work

In this paper we presented a sound and relatively complete dynamic logic calculus that integrates abstract interpretation and keeps track of variable dependencies. The abstract domain is not fixed and the abstraction can be dynamically changed during symbolic execution. In the first part, we described an algorithm to compute loop invariants by abstraction-on-demand for a classical definition of a program logic. In the second part of the paper we extended the program logic to keep also track of variable dependencies so that information-flow can be modelled in a straightforward manner. We achieve the same degree of automation as type-based approaches while increasing the number of provable programs due to value-sensitivity. The resulting calculus is close to the one used for JAVA in the KeY system [5] and we expect much of the machinery can be re-used.

In the future we want to focus on the followinng aspects: (i) extending the program logic to cover the sequential subset of JAVA; (ii) tracking dependencies even more precisely, e.g. currently an assignment such as l = h-h introduces h in the dependency set of l, even though it is a constant value in each program run and the symbolic execution machinery is in principle able to detect this. We have ideas how to treat such cases by extending our program logic semantics to include a trace semantics; (iii) supporting more sophisticated abstract interpretations involving infinite relational domains such as linear inequations; (iv) implementation and experimental evaluation including a comparison to other approaches.

References

1. Amtoft, T., Banerjee, A.: Information flow analysis in logical form. In: Giacobazzi, R. (ed.) SAS 2004. LNCS, vol. 3148, pp. 100–115. Springer, Heidelberg (2004)
2. Balser, M., Reif, W., Schellhorn, G., Stenzel, K., Thums, A.: Formal system development with KIV. In: Maibaum, T. (ed.) FASE 2000. LNCS, vol. 1783, p. 363–366. Springer, Heidelberg (2000)
3. Barnett, M., Leino, K.R.M., Schulte, W.: The Spec# Programming System: An Overview. In: Barthe, G., Burdy, L., Huisman, M., Lanet, J.-L., Muntean, T. (eds.) CASSIS 2004. LNCS, vol. 3362, pp. 49–69. Springer, Heidelberg (2005)
4. Barthe, G., D'Argenio, P.R., Rezk, T.: Secure information flow by self-composition. In: 17th IEEE Computer Security Foundations Workshop, CSFW-17, Pacific Grove, CA, USA, pp. 100–114. IEEE Computer Society Press, Los Alamitos (2004)
5. Beckert, B., Hähnle, R., Schmitt, P.H. (eds.): Verification of Object-Oriented Software. LNCS (LNAI), vol. 4334. Springer, Heidelberg (2007)
6. Beringer, L., Hofmann, M.: Secure information flow and program logics. In: 20th IEEE Computer Security Foundations Symposium CSF, Venice, Italy, pp. 233–248. IEEE Computer Society, Los Alamitos (2007)
7. Cousot, P., Cousot, R.: Abstract interpretation: A unified lattice model for static analysis of programs by construction or approximation of fixpoints. In: Fourth ACM Symposium on Principles of Programming Languages (POPL), Los Angeles, pp. 238–252. ACM Press, New York (1977)
8. Cousot, P., Cousot, R., Feret, J., Mauborgne, L., Miné, A., Monniaux, D., Rival, X.: The ASTREÉ analyzer. In: Sagiv, M. (ed.) ESOP 2005. LNCS, vol. 3444, pp. 21–30. Springer, Heidelberg (2005)
9. Darvas, Á., Hähnle, R., Sands, D.: A theorem proving approach to analysis of secure information flow. In: Hutter, D., Ullmann, M. (eds.) SPC 2005. LNCS, vol. 3450, pp. 193–209. Springer, Heidelberg (2005)
10. Filliâtre, J.-C., Marché, C.: The Why/Krakatoa/Caduceus platform for deductive program verification. In: Damm, W., Hermanns, H. (eds.) CAV 2007. LNCS, vol. 4590, pp. 173–177. Springer, Heidelberg (2007)
11. De Francesco, N., Martini, L.: Abstract interpretation to check secure information flow in programs with input-output security annotations. In: Dimitrakos, T., Martinelli, F., Ryan, P.Y.A., Schneider, S. (eds.) FAST 2005. LNCS, vol. 3866, pp. 63–80. Springer, Heidelberg (2006)

12. Graf, S., Saïdi, H.: Construction of abstract state graphs with PVS. In: Grumberg, O. (ed.) CAV 1997. LNCS, vol. 1254, pp. 72–83. Springer, Heidelberg (1997)
13. Hähnle, R., Pan, J., Rümmer, P., Walter, D.: Integration of a security type system into a program logic. Theoretical Computer Science 402(2-3), 172–189 (2008)
14. Harel, D., Kozen, D., Tiuryn, J.: Dynamic Logic. Foundations of Computing. MIT Press, Cambridge (2000)
15. Holzmann, G.J.: The SPIN Model Checker. Pearson Education, London (2003)
16. Hunt, S., Sands, D.: On flow-sensitive security types. In: 33rd ACM Symposium on Principles of Programming Languages (POPL), pp. 79–90. ACM Press, New York (2006)
17. Joshi, R., Leino, K.R.M.: A semantic approach to secure information flow. Science of Computer Programming 37(1-3), 113–138 (2000)
18. Leino, K.R.M., Logozzo, F.: Loop invariants on demand. In: Yi, K. (ed.) APLAS 2005. LNCS, vol. 3780, pp. 119–134. Springer, Heidelberg (2005)
19. Leino, K.R.M., Logozzo, F.: Using widenings to infer loop invariants inside an SMT solver, or: A theorem prover as abstract domain. In: Proc. 1st International Workshop on Invariant Generation, WING 2007 (2007)
20. Nipkow, T., Paulson, L.C., Wenzel, M.T.: Isabelle/HOL. LNCS, vol. 2283. Springer, Heidelberg (2002)
21. Robby, M.B.D., Hatcliff, J.: Bogor: A flexible framework for creating software model checkers. In: McMinn, P. (ed.) Testing: Academia and Industry Conference; Practice And Research Techniques (TAIC PART), Windsor, United Kingdom, pp. 3–22. IEEE Computer Society, Los Alamitos (2006)
22. Rümmer, P.: Sequential, parallel, and quantified updates of first-order structures. In: Hermann, M., Voronkov, A. (eds.) LPAR 2006. LNCS (LNAI), vol. 4246, pp. 422–436. Springer, Heidelberg (2006)
23. Sabelfeld, A., Myers, A.C.: Language-based information-flow security. IEEE Journal on Selected Areas in Communications 21(1), 5–19 (2003)
24. Velroyen, H., Rümmer, P.: Non-termination checking for imperative programs. In: Beckert, B., Hähnle, R. (eds.) TAP 2008. LNCS, vol. 4966, pp. 154–170. Springer, Heidelberg (2008)
25. Visser, W., Havelund, K., Brat, G.P., Park, S., Lerda, F.: Model checking programs. Automated Software Engineering 10(2), 203–232 (2003)
26. Weiß, B.: Predicate abstraction in a program logic calculus. In: Leuschel, M., Wehrheim, H. (eds.) IFM 2009. LNCS, vol. 5423, pp. 136–150. Springer, Heidelberg (2009)

A   Formal Semantics

A.1   Basic Semantics

$$val_{I,s,\beta}(f(t_1,\ldots,t_n)) = I(f)(val_{I,s,\beta}(t_1),\ldots,val_{I,s,\beta}(t_n))$$
$$val_{I,s,\beta}(\mathbf{x}) = s(\mathbf{x})$$
$$val_{I,s,\beta}(y) = \beta(y)$$
$$val_{I,s,\beta}(if(\varphi)\,then(t_1)\,else(t_2)) = \begin{cases} val_{I,s,\beta}(t_1) & \text{if } val_{I,s,\beta}(\varphi) = tt \\ val_{I,s,\beta}(t_2) & \text{otherwise} \end{cases}$$
$$val_{I,s,\beta}(\{\mathcal{U}\}t) = val_{I,s',\beta}(t) \qquad \text{where } s' = val_{I,s,\beta}(\mathcal{U})$$

$$val_{I,s,\beta}(\text{true}) = t\!t$$

$$val_{I,s,\beta}(\text{false}) = f\!f$$

$$val_{I,s,\beta}(p(t_1,\ldots,t_n)) = t\!t \quad \text{iff} \quad (val_{I,s,\beta}(t_1),\ldots,val_{I,s,\beta}(t_n)) \in I(p)$$

$$val_{I,s,\beta}(\varphi_1 \,\&\, \varphi_2) = t\!t \quad \text{iff} \quad f\!f \notin \{val_{I,s,\beta}(\varphi_1), val_{I,s,\beta}(\varphi_2)\}$$

$$val_{I,s,\beta}(\varphi_1 \mid \varphi_2) = t\!t \quad \text{iff} \quad t\!t \in \{val_{I,s,\beta}(\varphi_1), val_{I,s,\beta}(\varphi_2)\}$$

$$val_{I,s,\beta}(\varphi_1 \rightarrow \varphi_2) = val_{I,s,\beta}(!\,\varphi_1 \mid \varphi_2)$$

$$val_{I,s,\beta}(!\,\varphi) = t\!t \quad \text{iff} \quad val_{I,s,\beta}(\varphi) = f\!f$$

$$val_{I,s,\beta}(\forall y.\varphi) = t\!t \quad \text{iff} \quad f\!f \notin \{val_{I,s,\beta_y^v}(\varphi) \mid v \in \mathsf{D}\}$$

$$val_{I,s,\beta}(\exists y.\varphi) = t\!t \quad \text{iff} \quad t\!t \in \{val_{I,s,\beta_y^v}(\varphi) \mid v \in \mathsf{D}\}$$

$$val_{I,s,\beta}(t_1 \doteq t_2) = t\!t \quad \text{iff} \quad val_{I,s,\beta}(t_1) = val_{I,s,\beta}(t_2)$$

$$val_{I,s,\beta}(\{\mathcal{U}\}\varphi) = val_{I,s',\beta}(\varphi) \quad \text{where } s' = val_{I,s,\beta}(\mathcal{U})$$

$$val_{I,s,\beta}([\mathtt{p}]\varphi) = t\!t \quad \text{iff} \quad f\!f \notin \{val_{I,s',\beta}(\varphi) \mid s' \in val_{I,s,\beta}(\mathtt{p})\}$$

$$val_{I,s,\beta}(\mathbf{x}_1 := t_1 \,\|\ldots\| \, \mathbf{x}_n := t_n) = \{\mathbf{x} \mapsto s(\mathbf{x}) \mid \mathbf{x} \notin \{\mathbf{x}_1,\ldots,\mathbf{x}_n\}\} \,\cup$$
$$\{\mathbf{x} \mapsto val_{I,s,\beta}(t_k) \mid \mathbf{x} = \mathbf{x}_k \text{ and } \mathbf{x} \notin \{\mathbf{x}_{k+1},\ldots,\mathbf{x}_n\}\}$$

$$val_{I,s,\beta}(\mathbf{x} = t) = \{val_{I,s,\beta}(\mathbf{x} := t)\}$$

$$val_{I,s,\beta}(\mathtt{p1};\mathtt{p2}) = \{val_{I,s',\beta}(\mathtt{p2}) \mid s' \in val_{I,s,\beta}(\mathtt{p1})\}$$

$$val_{I,s,\beta}(\mathtt{if}(g)\{\mathtt{p1}\} \ \mathtt{else} \ \{\mathtt{p2}\}) = \begin{cases} val_{I,s,\beta}(\mathtt{p1}) & \text{if } val_{I,s,\beta}(g) = t\!t \\ val_{I,s,\beta}(\mathtt{p2}) & \text{otherwise} \end{cases}$$

$$val_{I,s,\beta}(\mathtt{while} \ (g) \ \{\mathtt{p}\}) = \begin{cases} \bigcup_{s_1 \in S_1} val_{I,s_1,\beta}(\mathtt{while}(g) \ \mathtt{p}) & \text{if } val_{I,s,\beta}(g) = t\!t \\ \{s\} & \text{otherwise} \end{cases}$$

$$\text{where } S_1 = val_{I,s,\beta}(\mathtt{p})$$

A.2   Semantics Enriched with Dependency Tracking

$$val'_{I,s,\beta}(\mathbf{x} = t) = \{val_{I,s,\beta}(\mathbf{x} := t \,\|\, \mathbf{x}^{dep} := deps(t))\}$$

$$val'_{I,s,\beta}(\mathtt{p1};\mathtt{p2}) = \{val'_{I,s',\beta}(\mathtt{p2}) \mid s' \in val'_{I,s,\beta}(\mathtt{p1})\}$$

$$val'_{I,s,\beta}(\mathtt{if}(g)\{\mathtt{p1}\} \ \mathtt{else} \ \{\mathtt{p2}\}) = \begin{cases} S'_1 & \text{if } val_{I,s,\beta}(g) = t\!t \\ S'_2 & \text{otherwise} \end{cases}$$

$$\text{where } S_1 = val'_{I,s,\beta}(\mathtt{p1}), \, S_2 = val'_{I,s,\beta}(\mathtt{p2}),$$
$$S'_i = \emptyset \text{ iff } S_i = \emptyset, \text{otherwise } S'_i = \{s'_i\} \text{ where}$$

$$s'_i(\mathbf{x}) = \begin{cases} s_i(\mathbf{x}) & \begin{aligned} &\text{if } \mathbf{x} \in \mathcal{PV} \text{ or} \\ &\mathbf{x} = \mathbf{y}^{dep} \text{ and} \\ &s_i(\mathbf{y}) = s(\mathbf{y}) \\ &\text{for } S_i = \{s_i\} \end{aligned} \\ s_i(\mathbf{x}) \cup val_{I,s,\beta}(deps(g)) & \text{otherwise} \end{cases}$$

$$val'_{I,s,\beta}(\mathtt{while} \ (g) \ \{\mathtt{p}\}) = \begin{cases} \bigcup_{s'_1 \in S'_1} val'_{I,s'_1,\beta}(\mathtt{while}(t) \ \mathtt{p}) & \text{if } val_{I,s,\beta}(g) = t\!t \\ \{s\} & \text{otherwise} \end{cases}$$

$$\text{where } S_1 = val'_{I,s,\beta}(\mathtt{p}),$$
$$\text{and where } S'_1 \text{ is derived from } S_1 \text{ as above}$$

A.3   Dependencies of a Term or Formula

This section defines the function *deps* which takes a term or a formula (occurring inside a program) and returns a term that overapproximates the semantic dependencies of the argument. It is used both in the semantics with dependency tracking (App. A.2) and in the dependency-aware calculus rules (Sect. 5.2). Since logical variables, quantifiers, updates, nested programs, and dependency variables $x^{dep} \in \mathcal{PV}^{dep}$ are not allowed to occur in programs, we refrain from providing a definition for these cases.

$$deps(f(t_1,\ldots,t_n)) = deps(t_1)\,\dot\cup\,\ldots\,\dot\cup\,deps(t_n)$$

$$deps(\mathbf{x}) = \mathbf{x}^{dep}$$

$$deps(if(\varphi)then(t_1)else(t_2)) = deps(\varphi)\,\dot\cup\,deps(t_1)\,\dot\cup\,deps(t_2)$$

$$deps(a) = \{\}\qquad\text{where } a \in \{true, false\}$$

$$deps(p(t_1,\ldots,t_n)) = deps(t_1)\,\dot\cup\,\ldots\,\dot\cup\,deps(t_n)$$

$$deps(\varphi_1 * \varphi_2) = deps(\varphi_1)\,\dot\cup\,deps(\varphi_2)\qquad\text{where } * \in \{\&, |, ->\}$$

$$deps(!\,\varphi) = deps(\varphi)$$

$$deps(t_1 \doteq t_2) = deps(t_1)\,\dot\cup\,deps(t_2)$$

B   Update Rewriting Rules

A rewrite rule $a \rightsquigarrow b$ is applicable to any occurrence of a within a sequent, and applying it means to replace that occurrence of a with b.

$$\{\mathcal{U}\}\{x_1 := t_1 \|\ldots\| x_n := t_n\} \rightsquigarrow \{\mathcal{U} \| x_1 := \{\mathcal{U}\}t_1 \|\ldots\| x_n := \{\mathcal{U}\}t_n\}$$

$$\{\mathcal{U}\}f(t_1,\ldots,t_n) \rightsquigarrow f(\{\mathcal{U}\}t_1,\ldots,\{\mathcal{U}\}t_n)$$

$$\{x_1 := t_1 \|\ldots\| x_n := t_n\}x \rightsquigarrow \begin{cases} x & \text{if } x \notin \{x_1,\ldots,x_n\} \\ t_k & \text{if } x = x_k \text{ and } x \notin \{x_{k+1},\ldots,x_n\} \end{cases}$$

$$\{\mathcal{U}\}a \rightsquigarrow a\qquad\text{where } a \in V \cup \{true, false\}$$

$$\{\mathcal{U}\}if(\varphi)then(t_1)else(t_2) \rightsquigarrow if(\{\mathcal{U}\}\varphi)then(\{\mathcal{U}\}t_1)else(\{\mathcal{U}\}t_2)$$

$$\{\mathcal{U}\}p(t_1,\ldots,t_n) \rightsquigarrow p(\{\mathcal{U}\}t_1,\ldots,\{\mathcal{U}\}t_n)$$

$$\{\mathcal{U}\}(\varphi_1 * \varphi_2) \rightsquigarrow \{\mathcal{U}\}\varphi_1 * \{\mathcal{U}\}\varphi_2\qquad\text{where } * \in \{\&, |, ->\}$$

$$\{\mathcal{U}\}!\,\varphi \rightsquigarrow !\{\mathcal{U}\}\varphi$$

$$\{\mathcal{U}\}\mathcal{Q}y.\varphi \rightsquigarrow \mathcal{Q}y.\{\mathcal{U}\}\varphi\qquad\text{where } \mathcal{Q} \in \{\forall, \exists\}, y \notin free(\mathcal{U})$$

$$\{\mathcal{U}\}(t_1 \doteq t_2) \rightsquigarrow \{\mathcal{U}\}t_1 \doteq \{\mathcal{U}\}t_2$$

C   Proofs

C.1   Lemma 1: Soundness of weakenUpdate

Proof. We assume that the following two statements hold for all I, s, β:

$$val_{I,s,\beta}\big(\Gamma, \{\mathcal{U}\}(\bar{x} \doteq \bar{c}) \Longrightarrow \exists \bar{y}.\{\mathcal{U}'\}(\bar{x} \doteq \bar{c}), \Delta\big) = tt \tag{8}$$

$$val_{I,s,\beta}\big(\Gamma \Longrightarrow \{\mathcal{U}'\}\varphi, \Delta\big) = tt \tag{9}$$

Let I_0, s_0, β_0 be an arbitrary interpretation, state, and variable assignment. We need to show that $val_{I_0,s_0,\beta_0}(\Gamma \implies \{\mathcal{U}\}\varphi, \Delta) = tt$. If $val_{I_0,s_0,\beta_0}(\bigwedge \Gamma) = f\!f$ or if $val_{I_0,s_0,\beta_0}(\bigvee \Delta) = tt$, then we are done immediately. Thus, we assume

$$val_{I_0,s_0,\beta_0}\left(\bigwedge(\Gamma \cup !\,\Delta)\right) = tt \tag{10}$$

and aim to prove that $val_{I_0,s_0,\beta_0}(\{\mathcal{U}\}\varphi) = tt$.

Let $s_1 = val_{I_0,s_0,\beta_0}(\mathcal{U})$, i.e., s_1 is the state reached by starting in s_0 and executing $\mathcal{U}$. Our goal is to prove that $val_{I_0,s_1,\beta}(\varphi) = tt$.

Let I_0' be the interpretation which is identical to I_0 except that $I_0'(\bar{c}) = s_1(\bar{x})$, i.e., I_0' interprets the constant symbols $\bar{c}$ like the corresponding program variables $\bar{x}$ are interpreted in s_1. This definition of I_0' implies $val_{I_0',s_0,\beta_0}(\bar{x} \doteq \bar{c}) = tt$, and thus (as the symbols $\bar{c}$ do not occur in $\mathcal{U}$)

$$val_{I_0',s_0,\beta_0}\left(\{\mathcal{U}\}(\bar{x} \doteq \bar{c})\right) = tt \tag{11}$$

Since the symbols $\bar{c}$ occur neither in Γ nor in Δ, and since I_0' is otherwise identical to I_0, we get from (10) that

$$val_{I_0',s_0,\beta_0}\left(\bigwedge(\Gamma \cup !\,\Delta)\right) = tt \tag{12}$$

Combining (12), (11) and the first premiss (8) yields

$$val_{I_0',s_0,\beta_0}\left(\exists \bar{\gamma}.\{\mathcal{U}'\}(\bar{x} \doteq \bar{c})\right) = tt \tag{13}$$

This means that there is an interpretation I_0'' which is identical to I_0' except in the interpretation of the symbols $\bar{\gamma}$, and which satisfies

$$val_{I_0'',s_0,\beta_0}\left(\{\mathcal{U}'\}(\bar{x} \doteq \bar{c})\right) = tt \tag{14}$$

Let $s_1' = val_{I_0'',s_0,\beta_0}(\mathcal{U}')$, i.e., s_1' is the state reached by starting in s_0 and executing $\mathcal{U}'$ under the interpretation I_0''. Equation 14 is equivalent to

$$val_{I_0'',s_1',\beta_0}(\bar{x} \doteq \bar{c}) = tt \tag{15}$$

This means that $s_1'(\bar{x}) = I_0''(\bar{c})$. Also, by definition of I_0'' and I_0', we have $I_0''(\bar{c}) = I_0'(\bar{c}) = s_1(\bar{x})$. Thus, $s_1'(\bar{x}) = s_1(\bar{x})$, i.e., s_1' and s_1 are identical on all program variables $\bar{x}$ which are potentially changed by either $\mathcal{U}$ or $\mathcal{U}'$. Since both s_1 and s_1' are derived from s_0 by executing one of these updates, this implies that $s_1' = s_1$. Inserting the definition of s_1', this reads as

$$val_{I_0'',s_0,\beta_0}(\mathcal{U}') = s_1 \tag{16}$$

Let I_1 be the interpretation identical to I_0'' except that the symbols $\bar{c}$ are interpreted as in I_0. Since the symbols $\bar{c}$ do not occur in $\mathcal{U}'$, we get from (16) that

$$val_{I_1,s_0,\beta_0}(\mathcal{U}') = s_1 \tag{17}$$

Since the $\bar{\gamma}$ do not occur in Γ nor in Δ, (10) tells us that

$$val_{I_1,s_0,\beta_0}\left(\bigwedge(\Gamma \cup !\,\Delta)\right) = tt \tag{18}$$

Combining (18) with the second premiss (9) yields

$$val_{I_1,s_0,\beta_0}\left(\{\mathcal{U}'\}\varphi\right) \tag{19}$$

With (17), this implies

$$val_{I_1,s_1,\beta_0}(\varphi) = tt \tag{20}$$

Since the symbols $\bar{\gamma}$ do not occur in φ, and since I_1 is otherwise identical to I_0, we get

$$val_{I_0,s_1,\beta_0}(\varphi) = tt \tag{21}$$

which is what we had to show. $\square$

C.2   Lemma 2: Soundness of invariantUpdate

Proof. We assume that the following three statements hold for all I, s, β:

$$val_{I,s,\beta}\left(\Gamma, \{\mathcal{U}\}(\bar{x} \doteq \bar{c}) \Longrightarrow \exists \bar{\gamma}.\{\mathcal{U}'\}(\bar{x} \doteq \bar{c}), \Delta\right) = tt \tag{22}$$

$$val_{I,s,\beta}\left(\Gamma, \{\mathcal{U}'\}g, \{\mathcal{U}'\}[\mathrm{p}](\bar{x} \doteq \bar{c}) \Longrightarrow \exists \bar{\gamma}.\{\mathcal{U}'\}(\bar{x} \doteq \bar{c}), \Delta\right) = tt \tag{23}$$

$$val_{I,s,\beta}\left(\Gamma, \{\mathcal{U}'\}\,!\,g \Longrightarrow \{\mathcal{U}'\}[\ldots]\varphi, \Delta\right) = tt \tag{24}$$

Let I_0, s_0, β_0 be an arbitrary interpretation, state, and variable assignment. We need to show that $val_{I_0,s_0,\beta_0}(\Gamma \Longrightarrow \{\mathcal{U}\}[\texttt{while}\ (g)\ \{\mathrm{p}\};\ \ldots]\varphi, \Delta) = tt$. If $val_{I_0,s_0,\beta_0}(\bigwedge \Gamma) = f\!f$ or if $val_{I_0,s_0,\beta_0}(\bigvee \Delta) = tt$, then we are done immediately. Thus, we assume

$$val_{I_0,s_0,\beta_0}\left(\bigwedge(\Gamma \cup !\,\Delta)\right) = tt \tag{25}$$

and aim to prove that $val_{I_0,s_0,\beta_0}\left(\{\mathcal{U}\}[\texttt{while}\ (g)\ \{\mathrm{p}\};\ \ldots]\varphi\right) = tt$.

Let $s_1 = val_{I_0,s_0,\beta_0}(\mathcal{U})$, i.e., s_1 is the state reached by starting in s_0 and executing $\mathcal{U}$. If the loop does not terminate when started in s_1, then our proof goal $val_{I_0,s_0,\beta_0}\left(\{\mathcal{U}\}[\texttt{while}\ (g)\ \{\mathrm{p}\};\ \ldots]\varphi\right) = tt$ holds trivially. Therefore, we assume that the loop terminates. From the programming language semantics, we know that there is a finite sequence of states $s_1, \ldots, s_k$, where

$$val_{I_0,s_i,\beta_0}(\mathrm{p}) = \{s_{i+1}\} \qquad\qquad i \in \{1, \ldots, k-1\} \tag{26}$$

$$val_{I_0,s_i,\beta_0}(g) = tt \qquad\qquad i \in \{1, \ldots, k-1\} \tag{27}$$

$$val_{I_0,s_k,\beta_0}(g) = f\!f \tag{28}$$

Our task is to show that $val_{I_0,s_k,\beta_0}([\ldots]\varphi) = tt$.

We will use induction to prove that for all $i \in \{1, \ldots, k\}$, there is an interpretation I_i which is identical to I_0 except for the interpretation of the symbols $\bar{\gamma}$, and for which $\mathit{val}_{I_i, s_0, \beta_0}(\mathcal{U}') = s_i$. Intuitively, this means we show that for every state s_i of the chain, we can find an interpretation I_i of the symbols $\bar{\gamma}$ such that applying $\mathcal{U}'$ to the initial state s_0 with this interpretation I_i directly produces s_i. Afterwards, we will use this result and the third premiss (24) for showing $\mathit{val}_{I_0, s_k, \beta_0}([\ldots]\varphi) = \mathit{tt}$.

- **Base case** $(i = 1)$. As our first premiss (22) is identical to the first premiss of the weakenUpdate rule (8), we can construct an interpretation I_1 with the desired properties in the same way as we did in the proof of updateWeaken (see (17)). For lack of space, we do not repeat this construction here.
- **Step case** $(i \in \{2, \ldots, k\})$. We assume that the induction hypothesis holds for $i - 1$, i.e., there is an interpretation I_{i-1} identical to I_0 except for the interpretation of the symbols $\bar{\gamma}$, and which satisfies

$$\mathit{val}_{I_{i-1}, s_0, \beta_0}(\mathcal{U}') = s_{i-1} \tag{29}$$

Let I'_{i-1} be the interpretation which is identical to I_{i-1} except that $I'_{i-1}(\bar{c}) = s_i(\bar{x})$. This definition of I'_{i-1} implies $\mathit{val}_{I'_{i-1}, s_i, \beta_0}(\bar{x} \doteq \bar{c}) = \mathit{tt}$. As the symbols $\bar{c}$ do not occur in p, we can combine this with (26) to get

$$\mathit{val}_{I'_{i-1}, s_{i-1}, \beta_0}([p](\bar{x} \doteq \bar{c})) = \mathit{tt} \tag{30}$$

By the induction hypothesis and the definition of I'_{i-1}, I'_{i-1} is identical to I_0 except in the interpretation of the symbols $\bar{\gamma}$ and $\bar{c}$. Since all of these occur neither in Γ nor in Δ, we get from (25) that

$$\mathit{val}_{I'_{i-1}, s_0, \beta_0}\left(\bigwedge(\Gamma \cup !\,\Delta)\right) = \mathit{tt} \tag{31}$$

As the $\bar{c}$ do not occur in $\mathcal{U}'$, and as I'_{i-1} is otherwise identical to I_{i-1}, the induction hypothesis (29) also gives us

$$\mathit{val}_{I'_{i-1}, s_0, \beta_0}(\mathcal{U}') = s_{i-1} \tag{32}$$

Together, (32) and (30) imply

$$\mathit{val}_{I'_{i-1}, s_0, \beta_0}\left(\{\mathcal{U}'\}[p](\bar{x} \doteq \bar{c})\right) = \mathit{tt} \tag{33}$$

Since the symbols $\bar{\gamma}$ and $\bar{c}$ do not occur in g, we can combine (32) with (27) to get

$$\mathit{val}_{I'_{i-1}, s_0, \beta_0}\left(\{\mathcal{U}'\}g\right) = \mathit{tt} \tag{34}$$

Taken together, (31), (34), (33) and the second premiss (23) yield

$$\mathit{val}_{I'_{i-1}, s_0, \beta_0}\left(\exists\bar{\gamma}.\{\mathcal{U}'\}(\bar{x} \doteq \bar{c})\right) = \mathit{tt} \tag{35}$$

This means that there is an interpretation I''_{i-1} which is identical to I'_{i-1} except in the interpretation of the symbols $\bar{\gamma}$, and which satisfies

$$val_{I''_{i-1},s_0,\beta_0}\left(\{\mathcal{U}'\}(\bar{x} \doteq \bar{c})\right) = tt \qquad (36)$$

Let $s'_i = val_{I''_{i-1},s_0,\beta_0}(\mathcal{U}')$, i.e., s_i is the state reached by starting in s_0 and executing $\mathcal{U}'$ under the interpretation I''_{i-1}. Equation (36) is equivalent to

$$val_{I''_{i-1},s'_i,\beta_0}(\bar{x} \doteq \bar{c}) = tt \qquad (37)$$

This means that $s'_i(\bar{x}) = I''_{i-1}(\bar{c})$. Also, by definition of I''_{i-1} we have $I''_{i-1}(\bar{c}) = s_i(\bar{x})$. Thus $s'_i = s_i$. Inserting the definition of s'_i, this reads as

$$val_{I''_{i-1},s_0,\beta_0}(\mathcal{U}') = s_i \qquad (38)$$

Let I_i be the interpretation identical to I''_{i-1} except that the symbols $\bar{c}$ are interpreted as in I_{i-1}. Since the $\bar{c}$ do not occur in $\mathcal{U}'$, we get from (38) that

$$val_{I_i,s_0,\beta_0}(\mathcal{U}') = s_i \qquad (39)$$

Since I_i also differs from I_0 only in the interpretation of the symbols $\bar{\gamma}$, it has both desired properties.

This finishes our induction. We know now that in particular for $i = k$, there is an interpretation I_k which is identical to I_0 except for the interpretation of the symbols $\bar{\gamma}$, and for which

$$val_{I_k,s_0,\beta_0}(\mathcal{U}') = s_k \qquad (40)$$

Since the symbols $\bar{\gamma}$ do not occur in g, we can combine this with (28) to get

$$val_{I_k,s_0,\beta_0}\left(\{\mathcal{U}'\}g\right) = ff \qquad (41)$$

Since the $\bar{\gamma}$ also do not occur in Γ nor Δ, (25) tells us that

$$val_{I_k,s_0,\beta_0}\left(\bigwedge(\Gamma \cup !\Delta)\right) = tt \qquad (42)$$

Combining (42) and (41) with the third premiss (24) yields

$$val_{I_k,s_0,\beta_0}\left(\{\mathcal{U}'\}[\ldots]\varphi\right) \qquad (43)$$

With (40), this implies

$$val_{I_k,s_k,\beta_0}\left([\ldots]\varphi\right) = tt \qquad (44)$$

Since the symbols $\bar{\gamma}$ do not occur in $[\ldots]\varphi$, and since I_k is otherwise identical to I_0, we get

$$val_{I_0,s_k,\beta_0}\left([\ldots]\varphi\right) = tt \qquad (45)$$

which is what we had to show. $\square$

BML and Related Tools*

Jacek Chrząszcz[1], Marieke Huisman[2], and Aleksy Schubert[1]

[1] Institute of Informatics, University of Warsaw, ul. Banacha 2,
02-097 Warsaw, Poland
[2] University of Twente, Faculty EEMCS, P.O. Box 217,
7500 AE Enschede,
The Netherlands

Abstract. The Bytecode Modeling Language (BML) is a specification language for Java bytecode, that provides a high level of abstraction, while not restricting the format of the bytecode. Notably, BML specifications can be stored in class files, so that they can be shipped together with the bytecode. This makes BML particularly suited as property specification language in a proof-carrying code framework. Moreover, BML is designed to be close to the source code level specification language JML, so that specifications (and proofs) developed at — the more intuitive — source code level can be compiled into bytecode level.

This paper describes the BML language and its binary representation. It also discusses the tool set that is available to support BML, containing BMLLib, a library to inspect and edit BML specifications; Umbra, a BML viewer and editor, integrated in Eclipse; JML2BML, a compiler from JML to BML specifications; BML2BPL, a translator from BML to BoogiePL, so that the BoogiePL verification condition generator can be used; and CCT, a tool to store proofs in class files.

1 Introduction

Typically, if formal methods are used in the process of software development, they are applied at source code level [18,24,6]. Modern programming languages introduce a strict structure on the code and provide a layer of abstraction that makes a program quite comprehensive for humans. The use of an appropriate specification language introduces another, even higher, level of abstraction into the software development process. An advantage of this abstraction is that it reduces the difficulty of program construction, in particular when it is supported by tools.

However, sometimes severe restrictions are made on program execution time or resource usage, and to satisfy these demands, code must be optimised. Because

---

* This work was partly supported by Polish government grant 177/6.PR UE/2006/7 and Information Society Technologies programme of the European Commission FET project IST-2005-015905 MOBIUS. This paper reflects only authors' views and the Community is not liable for any use that may be made of the information contained therein.

F.S. de Boer et al. (Eds.): FMCO 2008, LNCS 5751, pp. 278–297, 2009.

of the strict code structure imposed by high-level programming languages, it is often better to fine-tune programs at the lower level of executable code. But if one does this, one still needs to understand why and how the code works. Here a specification language can be useful as well, because it can reintroduce the abstraction that was eliminated by the compilation and optimisation process. Thus, a good specification language for executable code can provide a basis for the development of reliable, highly optimised programs in low-level form.

Moreover, since low-level languages can be the target platform for several different source code languages, a specification formalism for a low-level language can serve as a common ground for understanding software from different sources.

This led to the proposal of a program logic for Java bytecode [5] and, based on this, a specification language for bytecode — the Bytecode Modeling Language (BML) [8]. BML is based on the principle of design-by-contract and it is strongly inspired by the Java Modeling Language (JML) [14,17,18]. JML is the *de facto* Java specification language, supported by a wide range of tools [7].

One of the most promising applications of low-level specification languages such as BML is in the context of proof-carrying code (PCC). In this context, code that is shipped from the code producer to the code consumer comes together with a specification and a correctness proof. Since BML can specify executable code, it seems an appropriate specification language for foundational PCC [2,1], where a relatively small but expressive framework can capture the class of desirable properties of mobile code. Because of its expressiveness, BML specifications can give hints to the prover (e.g., one can supply loop invariants and suggest appropriate lemmas using assert statements), which can ease the automatic construction of proofs. To be able to ship BML specifications together with the code, a BML representation within Java class files is defined.

To be able to use BML in a PCC context, *and* as a specification language on its own, it is designed with the following two goals in mind: (*i*) it should be easy to transform specifications and proofs from the source code level to the bytecode level, and (*ii*) specifications should be comprehensive.

When BML is used in a PCC context, we expect it be used as an intermediate format. People will rather specify and verify their source code, and then translate these into properties and proofs of the executable code. Since Java is our privileged application language, we assume JML will be the source code specification language. Therefore, translation from JML specifications and proofs to BML should be as straightforward as possible. Realising a PCC platform for Java to support this use of BML is one of the goals of the MOBIUS project[1].

Since BML can also be used as a specification language on its own (for example, to ensure that a program optimisation is correct), the specifications should be intelligible. To achieve this, the language reuses many constructs from JML. Since JML is designed in such a way that it is intuitive and easily understandable for common Java programmers, we believe the same should apply to BML. Therefore, we developed a textual representation of bytecode classes augmented

---

[1] See http://mobius.inria.fr for more information.

```
1  public class KeyPool {

      private int[] keyIds;
      //@ invariant keyIds != null;
5     /*@ invariant (\forall int i,j; 0 <= i && i < j && j < keyIds.length;
      @                              keyIds[i] >= keyIds[j]); @*/

      //@ ghost int lastPos;
9     //@ invariant 0 <= lastPos && lastPos < keyIds.length;
      /*@ invariant (\forall int i; lastPos < i && i < keyIds.length;
      @                              keyIds[i] == 0); @*/

13     // ...other methods...

      /*@ requires keyId > 0 && lastPos < keyIds.length − 1;
      @ ensures (\exists int i; 0 <= i && i < lastPos && keyIds[i] = keyId);
17     @*/
      public void insert(int keyId) {
      int i;
      /*@ loop_invariant −1 <= i &&
21     @      (\forall int k; i < k && k < keyIds.length; keyId > keyIds[k]);
      @*/
      for (i = keyIds.length − 2; i >= 0 && keyId > keyIds[i]; i−−) {
          keyIds[i+1] = keyIds[i];
25     }
      keyIds[i+1] = keyId;
      //@ set lastPos = lastPos + 1;
      }
29  }
```

Fig. 1. Source code and JML specifications for class `KeyPool`

with BML that indicate clearly the relation between the specification and the different pieces of the program.

A crucial element for the success of a specification formalism is tool support. Therefore, a set of prototype tools is developed for BML. This tool set contains the following tools:

- BMLLib, a library to represent and manipulate specifications;
- Umbra, a BML editor within Eclipse IDE;
- JML2BML, a compiler from JML specifications to BML;
- BML2BPL, a translator of bytecode enhanced with BML to BoogiePL, a language from which verification conditions can be generated easily; and
- CCT, a tool to store proofs in class files.

A precise description of the BML language is given in the *BML Reference Manual* [10]. The current paper gives a brief overview of BML (Sect. 2) and its two representations (Sect. 3). Then it discusses the tools in the BML tool set (Sect. 4). We conclude the paper in Sect. 5.

Throughout the paper, fragments of a class `KeyPool` are used as example. Figure 1 shows relevant parts of the Java source code and JML specifications of this class. We expect the reader to be able to grasp the intention of this specification.

2   Overview of BML

As motivated above, the design of BML is very similar to its source-code-level counterpart JML: each element of a class file can be annotated with specifications. This section illustrates this by showing how the specifications in Fig. 1 are translated. Figure 2 shows the translation of the Java code, without the specifications. The full definition of BML can be found in [10].

It is important to note that BML covers most of the so-called JML Level 0, i.e., the essential part of JML that is supposed to be supported by *all* JML tools [18, Sect. 2.9]. The missing features are informal descriptions and extended debug statements. Informal descriptions are in fact a special kind of comments, which are impossible to formalise. The JML debug statements can contain arbitrary Java expressions, while BML debug statements allow only variable names, the value of which is supposed to be printed out by tools that execute BML specifications (e.g., a run-time checker). In addition, BML allows one to use pure method calls in specifications (mandated by JML Level 1 — describing features to be supported by *most* tools). Also, the expression language contains a few BML-specific constructs, to denote the size and elements of the operand stack and the size of arrays. Constants and variables are also addressed differently in BML: in the binary representation fields are encoded as an index in the constant pool (to the location where the `FieldRef` structure is stored), while local variables are referenced by a number that denotes their position in the local variable table. This is the same as fields and local variables are addressed in bytecode. For the sake of readability, in the textual representation, those numerical references are shown as appropriate identifiers.

2.1   Class-Level Specifications

Class-level specifications specify behaviour of all instances of a class. The most prominent example of class-level specifications are invariants. An (instance) invariant specifies a property that should hold for all instances of that class, after completion of the constructor and before and after the execution of all methods of the class. Figure 3 shows the BML specification of the invariants and other class-level specification constructs for the class `KeyPool`. Notice that compared to the JML specification, the specifications are more rigid in format: the constructs are given in a fixed order and the receiver object is always mentioned explicitly. In addition, a keyword **length** is used to denote the length of an array.

Another class-level specification is the declaration of a so-called *ghost* field. These are fields that exist only at specification level. To change their value, BML has a special **set** instruction (see also Sect. 2.3). Ghost fields can be used

```
package [default]
// ... Constant pool and Second constant pool omitted ...
public class KeyPool extends java.lang.Object
// ... class-level specifications omitted ...

// ... other methods omitted ...

// ... method specification omitted ...
public void insert(int)
0:    aload_0
1:    getfield        KeyPool.keyIds [I (20)
4:    arraylength
5:    iconst_2
6:    isub
7:    istore_2
//@ loop_specification  ... specification omitted ...
8:    goto            #28
11:   aload_0
12:   getfield        KeyPool.keyIds [I (20)
15:   iload_2
16:   iconst_1
17:   iadd
18:   aload_0
19:   getfield        KeyPool.keyIds [I (20)
22:   iload_2
23:   iaload
24:   iastore
25:   iinc            %2 -1
28:   iload_2
29:   iflt            #42
32:   iload_1
33:   aload_0
34:   getfield        KeyPool.keyIds [I (20)
37:   iload_2
38:   iaload
39:   if_icmpgt       #11
42:   aload_0
43:   getfield        KeyPool.keyIds [I (20)
46:   iload_2
47:   iconst_1
48:   iadd
49:   iload_1
50:   iastore
//@ set ... specification omitted ...
51:   return
```

Fig. 2. Bytecode for class KeyPool

```
/*@ public ghost int lastPos @*/
/*@ invariant keyIds != null @*/
/*@ invariant 0 <= this.lastPos && this.lastPos < \length(this.keyIds) @*/
/*@ invariant \forall int i,j; 0 <= i && i < j && j < \length(this.keyIds)
  @                ==> this.keyIds[i] >= this.keyIds[j]
  @*/
/*@ invariant \forall int i; this.lastPos < i && i < \length(this.keyIds)
  @                ==> this.keyIds[i] == 0)
  @*/
```

Fig. 3. BML class-level specifications for class `KeyPool`

to represent values that are implicit in the actual code, but must be mentioned explicitly in specifications.

In our example, the `lastPos` ghost field represents the position of the last key inserted in the table. The invariants constrain the possible values of the field `keyIds` and the ghost field `lastPos`: `keyIds` cannot be `null`, `lastPos` should be less than the length of the array, the values in the array should be sorted in decreasing order, and all entries of the array to the right of `lastPos` should be 0. The value of `lastPos` is updated by a **set** instruction, placed before instruction label 51 in the bytecode (see Fig. 5).

Apart from invariants and ghost variable declarations, BML class-level specifications can also be static invariants, i.e., invariant properties over static fields; history constraints, that express a relation between two states before and after method calls; and model field declarations to abstract complex expressions (e.g. the sum of all elements in a table).

2.2   Method-Level Specifications

Method-level specifications describe the behaviour of a single method. The basic principle is the use of pre- and postconditions. Preconditions state what is expected about parameters and the state of objects upon method invocation, while postconditions state what the method guarantees upon termination. It is possible to refer to the prestate of the method in the postcondition, using the keyword \old. In addition, BML method-level specifications contain assignable, signals and signals-only clauses. These specify which variables may be modified by a method, which exceptions may be thrown by a method, and under which conditions. Assignable clauses are necessary for sound modular verification. In JML specifications, these clauses are often left implicit, using an appropriate default clause, but in BML they have to be specified explicitly. In addition, BML allows one to flag a method as *pure*, meaning that it does not modify state, and therefore can be used in specifications.

Figure 4 shows the BML specification for method `insert`. The precondition (keyword **requires**) specifies that parameter `keyId` should be strictly positive and ghost variable `lastPos` should be less than the length of the table minus 1, i.e., there should be space for inserting another key. The postcondition (keyword **ensures**) specifies that after completion of the method, one of the elements of

```
/*@ requires keyId > 0 && this.lastPos < \length(this.keyIds) − 1
  @ modifies \everything
  @ ensures (\exists int i; 0 <= i && i < lastPos && this.keyIds[i] == keyId)
  @ signals (java/lang/Exception) true
  @ signals_only \nothing
  @*/
```

Fig. 4. BML method specification for `insert` in class `KeyPool`

the `keyIds` table is the newly inserted `keyId`. Notice that the implicit assignable, signals and signals-only clauses from Fig. 1 are explicit in the BML specification.

2.3 Code-Level Specifications

The last group of BML specifications are those that refer to specific points of the code inside a method body. Such specifications are typically there to help automatic verification procedures. A common code-level specification construct is a loop invariant, specifying a condition that is met every time control is at the beginning of the loop. Loop invariants are necessary to prove partial correctness of a loop.

Figure 5 shows the BML specification of the loop invariant of method `insert` in class `KeyPool`. The loop ranges from label 8 to 39. All instructions before label 8 initialise the loop; the first eight instructions of the loop (labels 8–19) check the loop condition; and the loop body is implemented by the instructions labelled 22–35. The invariant is specified just before the beginning of the loop, i.e., before instruction 8. It states that the loop variable i never is less than -1, and all keys that have been examined, i.e., between i and the length of `keyIds`, are less than `keyId`.

Apart from the loop invariant, a BML loop specification also contains a loop variant, i.e., a non-negative integer expression that is supposed to strictly decrease for each iteration of the loop. The variant is used to prove termination of the loop. In our example it is a meaningless 1, since no variant is given at the source code level. Thus, with this specification, it will not be possible to prove termination of this method.

```
7:     istore_2
/*@ loop_specification
  @ loop_inv −1 <= i && (\forall int k; i < k && k < \length(this.keyIds)
  @              ==> keyId > this.keyIds[k])
  @ decreases 1
  @*/
8:     goto    #28
// ... code omitted ...
50:    iastore
/*@ set this.lastPos = this.lastPos + 1 @*/
51:    return
```

Fig. 5. BML code-level specifications for class `KeyPool`

Other BML code-level specifications include **set** instructions, used to change the value of ghost variables (before label 51 in Fig. 5); **assert** and **assume** annotations, to assert/assume facts about the program; and **debug** annotations, to print out values of a variable in case the program is executed by a BML-aware execution environment.

2.4 Verification of BML Specifications

Work on BML and its semantics was initiated by Mariela Pavlova [25] within the context of JACK (Java Applet Correctness Kit) [4]. Pavlova's work is based on an operational semantics of Java bytecode which covers a representative set of 22 instructions. She gives a semantics for a representative subset of the specification language in the form of a weakest precondition calculus. An overview of the work is presented in [9,8].

Development of the formal underpinning of BML continued in the context of the MOBIUS project (see [22] for more details). The Bicolano specification [26], within the proof assistant Coq, formalises the operational semantics of a considerable subset of bytecode instructions. On top of Bicolano a bytecode logic, called the MOBIUS base logic, is developed and formalised in Coq, following the principles of [5]. A translation from BML specifications into the MOBIUS base logic is defined (where BML predicates are translated using an additional deep embedding layer for assertions in Isabelle).

To make verification of BML specifications more practical, a translation into BoogiePL is necessary. BoogiePL is an intermediate language for program verification [12]. It has procedures and only 5 instructions (including assume and assert). This makes it easy to define a correct verification condition generator for it. The strength of BoogiePL lies in its non-determinism and its use of guards to control the program flow (similar to Dijkstra's guarded commands [13]). A program and its specification are translated into a BoogiePL program; verification conditions are generated from this BoogiePL program.

Lehner and Müller present a translation from bytecode instructions to BoogiePL [19]. Properties are specified in first-order logic. Using a translation that is similar to the one presented by Darvas and Müller for JML0 [11], BML specifications can be translated into first-order logic. In addition, Mallo [21] presents a direct translation for a subset of BML into BoogiePL.

3 Representation of BML Specifications

The bytecode presented in Fig. 2 is of course only a textual representation of the actual binary code. Various tools exist to produce such textual representations from class files, e.g., javap and Umbra (see Sect. 4.3). BML also has two representations: (*i*) a binary form, using non-standard attributes stored inside class files, and (*ii*) a textual representation, as shown in the previous section. This textual representation is very similar to JML, but a bit more rigid, as it must be in correspondence with the binary form. This section discusses the two representations of BML.

```
Invariants_attribute {
  u2 attribute_name_index;
  u4 attribute_length;
  u2 invariants_count;
  { u2 access_flags;
    formula_info invariant;
  } invariants[invariants_count];
}
```

Fig. 6. Structure of the org.bmlspecs.Invariants attribute

3.1   Binary Representation of BML

Several possibilities exist to define a binary format for BML.

A simple approach would be to use standard Java serialisation to dump Java objects representing abstract syntax trees of specifications. However, this choice would force BML tool builders to use Java and our abstract syntax tree definition. Instead, we preferred to define a precise specification of a binary format, that tool builders can freely manipulate.

As said above, BML specifications are stored inside a class file. It would also be possible to store specifications in a separate file, but since specifications refer to elements of the class file, it is most natural to take advantage of the possibility to add information to the class file.

To store additional information in class files, there are currently two different possibilities: attributes and annotations [15]. Attributes are more low-level, they appear in the specification of the Java Virtual Machine since its first version and they are used by the compiler to store the different optional elements of classes, such as the method code, line number tables and local variable tables. Attributes are also used in the initial tools that support BML, in the JACK environment [4].

Java annotations are introduced in Java 5.0 as a mechanism to describe properties of Java methods and classes (metadata). They have become the official standard of annotating Java code with machine checkable information. Support to compile and store them in special attributes inside a class file is available, as well as an API to inspect them at runtime. However, the main benefit of using annotations is at source code level. Inserting annotations in an already compiled class file is a bit contrary to the idea of annotations. Besides, Java annotations cannot be placed inside code[2], specifications would be necessary at least for code-level specifications. In addition, Java annotations are not used in JML, and adopting annotations would practically preclude specifying code written in earlier versions of Java than 5.0.

Taking all these considerations into account, we decided to define a precise binary format for BML specifications, stored as non-standard JVM attributes inside the class file.

---

[2] Even the ongoing development in JSR308 [16] to allow one to use annotations in more places still does not support annotation of instructions.

Encoding of BML Specifications. The structure of Java class files is quite flexible. Some elements are obligatory, e.g., the magic number CAFEBABE[3], header, constant pool, field table and method table, but most elements are optional. All optional elements are stored in so-called *attributes*, which are just blocks of bytes with a name (to distinguish them). Attributes can be stored in different "places" in the class file structure: there are class attributes, field attributes, method attributes, and code attributes. So, for example, the bytecode of a method is stored in a method attribute named `Code`, and inside this `Code` attribute there is also space for code-level attributes, such as `LineNumberTable` and `LocalVariableTable`. Abstract methods simply do not have a `Code` attribute.

BML specifications are stored in appropriately placed JVM attributes: class-level specifications are stored in class attributes, method specifications in method attributes and code-level specifications in code attributes. The names of all BML-related attributes start with a common prefix `org.bmlspecs`. An important class-level attribute is the *second constant pool*. This structure is similar to the standard constant pool, but it is used to stored all constants that are part of the specification only.

All class invariants are stored together in a single class-level attribute named `org.bmlspecs.Invariants`, whose structure is given in Fig. 6. To specify the format of these attributes, we use a C-like structure notation, cf. [20], where each entry is preceded by a special identifier, e.g., `u1`, `u2` and `u4`, that describes the type of the corresponding value. The first two fields of the `org.bmlspecs.Invariants` attribute are `attribute_name_index` and `attribute_length`. These are obligatory for all attributes. They contain an index in the constant pool, where the attribute name (here: `org.bmlspecs.Invariants`) is stored, and the length in bytes of the whole attribute. The next two fields, `invariants_count` and `invariants`, describe the invariants table: the number of invariants and the table containing the invariants themselves. Each entry of the table contains information about an invariant, namely its access flags (`public`, `protected`, `private`, `static`) and its formula.

Formulae and expressions are stored as the prefix traversal sequence of the abstract syntax tree of a given expression, with binary representation of operands. The names of variables and fields are represented as indexes of appropriate string constants in the constant pool (either the original constant pool or the second specification-only constant pool).

As another example, Fig. 7 specifies the binary format for the code-level attribute describing loop specifications. The first two mandatory fields are as before; the attribute name is now `org.bmlspecs.LoopSpecificationTable`. The last two fields describe the length and contents of the loop specification table. Each loop specification in the table is represented by the following elements: `point_pc`, the label of the instruction to which the specification is attached; the `order` entry that specifies the respective order in which code-level specifications should be considered if they are attached to the same instruction; and the

---

[3] See `http://www.artima.com/insidejvm/whyCAFEBABE.html` for more information.

```
LoopSpecificationTable_attribute {
    u2 attribute_name_index;
    u4 attribute_length;
    u2 loops_count;
    { u2 point_pc;
      u2 order;
      formula_info invariant;
      formula_info variant;
    } loops[loops_count];
}
```

Fig. 7. Structure of the `org.bmlspecs.LoopSpecificationTable` attribute

```
PCCClassCert {
    u2 attribute_name_index;
    u4 attribute_length;
    u2 cert_type;
    u1 major_version;
    u1 minor_version;
    u2 imported_certs_count;
    u2 imported_certs[imported_certs_count];
    u4 proofs_section_length;
    u1 proofs_section[proofs_section_length];
}
```

```
PCCMethodCert {
    u2 attribute_name_index;
    u4 attribute_length;
    u2 cert_type;
    u1 cert_major_version;
    u1 cert_minor_version;
    u4 proofs_section_length;
    u1 proofs_section[proofs_section_length];
}
```

(a)   (b)

Fig. 8. Format of PCC certificates in class files

invariant and the variant formulae. The order field is necessary if for example several set annotations are related to the same bytecode instruction: it ensures that the assignments are properly ordered.

Other BML specification constructs are encoded in a similar way. More details can be found in the BML Reference Manual [10].

Representation of Certificates. To support proof-carrying code, besides the attributes that contain specifications, one also needs attributes that can store a proof that an implementation respects its specification. A flexible, generic format in which different kinds of PCC certificates can be encoded is proposed in [23, Sect. 2.5]. In this proposal, the certificates can be divided into two groups: class-level certificates and method-level certificates. The format of these certificates is presented in Fig. 8(a) and Fig. 8(b), respectively. This format allows one to store certificates concerning various properties of bytecode, produced by tools supporting different technologies (e.g., fixpoints for abstract interpretation or type derivations). Note that the actual certification technology may choose not to use both of the certificate levels and to store the complete certificate information in the class-level attribute only or in the method-level attributes only.

To use BML specifications in a PCC context, this generic certificate scheme is instantiated to certificates that encode Coq proofs of the properties expressed in BML. In this case, the type checking engine of Coq, combined with a tool to generate a Coq representation of the program and its BML specifications, is the final certificate checker.

At the client side, the class file, BML specifications and the proofs that are encoded in the certificates are expanded to Coq modules. At class-level these modules include:

- a Coq representation of the class structure (i.e., fields, methods, code of methods etc.) and the BML specifications;
- a representation of properties for each method that express that whenever the method is called in a state in which the method's precondition is satisfied then the method's postcondition holds after the method returns; and
- proofs of the properties above.

The method definitions are generated based on the class file method structures. The method properties combine the BML pre- and postconditions with invariants. The certificates contain the necessary proofs.

In order to conceptually separate proofs of a class's interface properties (like invariants, method specifications, etc.) from the proofs of implementation details (like loop specifications, asserts etc.), the latter are included in separate Coq modules that are constructed from method-level specifications and certificates. These method-level Coq modules contain the following:

- a theorem that states that if the method is called in a state in which the precondition holds then the postcondition holds after a return from the method;
- for each assert, a theorem that states that if the method is called in a state in which the precondition holds then the assert holds in a related program position;
- for each strong invariant (i.e., an invariant that must be maintained by all program steps) and method a theorem that states that if the method is called in a state in which the precondition holds then the invariant holds at each instruction of the method;
- proofs of the theorems above.

3.2 Textual Representation of BML

Since we expect that programmers will read and edit specifications at bytecode level (for example, if one wishes to develop correct code that is more optimal than compilers can generate), we also defined a textual representation of bytecode files augmented with specifications. This ensures that programmers have a file format that is easy to read, exchange, and edit by common textual editors.

There is no standard for textual bytecode representation, but some popular tools (e.g., Sun's javap, Apache's BCEL[4], and ObjectWeb's ASM[5]) print out class files in a textual form to facilitate debugging and understanding of the code. However, these tools do not support parsing of any textual representation of class files (and thus also no editing).

---

[4] Byte Code Engineering Library, available from http://jakarta.apache.org/bcel/
[5] Available from http://asm.objectweb.org/

There are also tools such as Javaa[6] and, more popular, Jasmin[7] that allow one to write classes and methods using Java bytecode mnemonics. However, they are not tuned to program specification and verification, and they require the user to supply much information that is not relevant for specifications. In addition, their source code is only available under a non-standard license, which makes it difficult to integrate them in an open source project such as MOBIUS. Therefore, we decided to develop our own bytecode viewer and editor, described in the next section, that adheres to the textual representation standard of BML.

We assume that programmers work at the same time with class files and textual files. Therefore, we decided not to display certain values such as the bytecode file version number or the contents of foreign attributes. In this way, only the relevant information is presented to the user. Roughly, the format displays in sequence: the package name, the class header with the class name and information about its location in the type hierarchy, the constant pools – including the second constant pool, fields, class-level specifications (such as invariants and constraints) and methods augmented with their method-level specifications and code-level specifications. All other information (e.g., the Line Number Table) is stored in the class file and not shown to the user.

4 Overview of the BML Tools

Just as for a programming language, if a specification language is to be used successfully, it needs good tool support to read, write, and manipulate specifications. Moreover, one needs tools to check that a program respects the properties stated in the specifications.

This section provides an overview of the tools that are developed to support BML. We start with a brief description of JACK, the historical predecessor of the currently existing tools. Then the tools which support the current version of BML are presented: (*i*) BMLLib, a library to represent and manipulate specifications; (*ii*) Umbra, an interactive BML editor integrated into Eclipse IDE; (*iii*) JML2BML, a compiler from JML specifications to BML; (*iv*) BML2BPL, a translator from BML and bytecode to BoogiePL; and (*v*) CCT, a tool to package proofs in class files. Figure 9 shows how the different tools connect with each other.

4.1 JACK

Overview and goals. JACK is a tool that integrates the verification machinery developed for JML with a programming environment, namely Eclipse. Programmers can manipulate Java source code and JML specifications, while the (textual) representation of bytecode specifications is hidden and can be viewed only on demand by expanding the structure of bytecode attributes [9].

---

[6] Available from
    http://tinf2.vub.ac.be/~dvermeir/courses/compilers/javaa/jasm.html
[7] Available from http://jasmin.sourceforge.net/

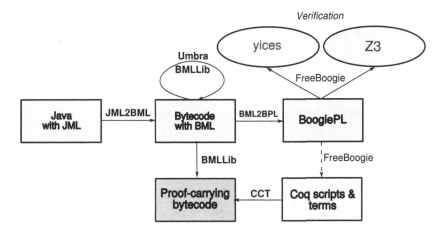

Fig. 9. BML tool set. The tools that are developed especially for BML are written in bold. A dashed line means that the tool is still under development.

Design of the tool. The JACK tool is an Eclipse plugin. It takes JML annotated source code and generates proof obligations expressed in an internal Java/JML Proof Obligation Language. The proof obligations are generated by means of a weakest precondition generator. Then one of the available provers (AtelierB, Simplify, Coq, PVS) can be used to discharge the generated proof obligations. In case the proof obligation cannot be discharged automatically, it can be viewed in the IDE and proved interactively.

Availability. The final release of JACK, both in binary and source form, is available from `http://www-sop.inria.fr/everest/soft/Jack/jack.html`.

4.2   BMLLib: A Library to Manipulate BML Specifications

Overview and goals. The most basic tool support that is needed for BML is parsing and pretty-printing of its textual representation as well as reading and storing of specifications in class files. This functionality is provided by the BMLLib library. In addition, this library provides a Java API to generate and manipulate BML specifications. Most of the tools discussed below depend on BMLLib.

Design of the tool. BMLLib is developed at the University of Warsaw. It uses the BCEL library as the basic library to manipulate class files. BCEL is known to be difficult and non-intuitive in use, but it has the advantage that it is maintained by the Jakarta project[8], which gives confidence in its future existence. BMLLib allows one to store and read BML specifications represented in class files. It defines an abstract syntax tree to represent BML specifications. The classes and methods augmented with specifications are implemented as delegate classes which can either return the specifications or the BCEL representation of the

---

[8] Available from `http://jakarta.apache.org/`

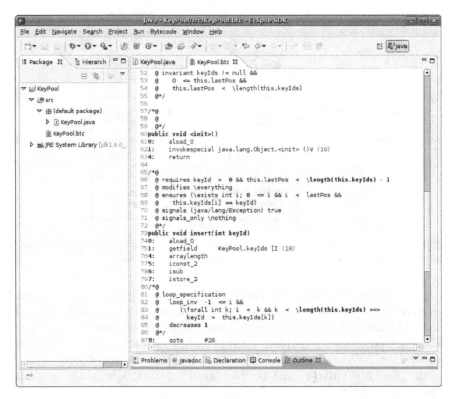

Fig. 10. Bytecode for class KeyPool edited in Umbra

class or method, respectively. The parser of the specifications is written with the
ANTLR parser generator[9], a highly reliable parser generator for Java. A detailed
description of the library is presented in [27].

Additionally, BMLLib provides a translation from the BCEL representation
into ASM representation used in BML2BPL (discussed below). This translation
is necessary to enable the translation into BoogiePL and subsequent generation
of proof obligations with FreeBoogie.

Availability. The alpha version of the library is available from http://www.
mimuw.edu.pl/~alx/umbra/. It is written in Java and tested primarily under
Linux and Windows.

4.3   Umbra: A BML Editor

Overview and goals. Most existing class file editors are developed as a series of
windows that correspond to the layout of the attributes and other structures of
the class file. This design leads to an environment which is not easy to navigate
for a programmer. Instead, we developed Umbra as an Eclipse plugin that allows

---

[9] Available from http://www.antlr.org/

one to view, add, delete and edit BML specifications and bytecode in a textual representation. Moreover, if available, the textual representation is associated with the Java source code. This makes it possible to relate fragments of the source code with fragments of the byte code and the other way round [27]; in particular it allows one to see field and variable names, instead of indexes in the constant pool and local variable table.

Furthermore, Umbra gives programmers the possibility to change not only the specifications, but also the bytecode instructions.

The Umbra plugin also provides a user interface for several of the tools presented below; in particular it has buttons to run the JML2BML compiler, the BML2BPL translator, and the FreeBoogie verification back-end.

Design of the tool. Umbra is developed as an Eclipse plugin that extends the Java editor plugin and adds its own functionality for editing class files. Umbra relies on the representation of class files provided by the BCEL library. The internal representation of BML specifications is provided by BMLLib. Fig. 10 shows the code from Fig. 2 being edited in Umbra.

Availability. The alpha version of the editor is available from http://www. mimuw.edu.pl/~alx/umbra/. It is written in Java and tested primarily under Linux and Windows.

4.4   JML2BML: A Specification Compiler from JML to BML

Overview and goals. The JACK tool contains a compiler of JML annotations to BML. However, this compiler is highly integrated with the tool itself. Therefore, the need for a standalone JML to BML compiler arose.

The JML2BML compiler takes as input a Java source file with JML annotations, together with the corresponding class file and outputs the class file with proper BML annotations inserted. This allows the user to write the specifications at the more comprehensive source code level and then translate them into the bytecode level representation. At bytecode level these specifications can then be combined with specifications written by hand or with specifications coming from other tools. Note that JML2BML does not erase any specifications that are present in the class file, it only adds the specifications translated from the JML specifications.

Currently, the JML2BML compiler focuses on supporting JML Level 0, roughly corresponding to the subset of JML covered by the BML language.

Design of the tool. The compiler uses an enhanced Abstract Syntax Tree (AST) for the Java source code, taken from the OpenJML[10] compiler (a Java compiler with JML checker based upon OpenJDK). The result is stored in the class file, using the BMLLib library [27]. The compilation is described by a set of transformation rules that are one by one applied to the JML AST. This approach makes

---

[10] Available from http://sourceforge.net/projects/jmlspecs

the compiler easily extensible. It is enough to just write a new translation rule to support additional features of the JML language. The JML2BML compiler is intergrated in the Umbra editor as a push-button, but it can also be used as a standalone tool.

Availability. The compiler is available from `http://www.mimuw.edu.pl/~alx/jml2bml/`. It is written in Java and tested primarily under Linux and Windows.

4.5   BML2BPL: A Translation from BML Specifications to BoogiePL

Overview and goals. BoogiePL is an intermediate language designed to alleviate part of the burden of the transformation from the specified source code to proof obligations. The Boogie verifier (which is originally developed to reason about Spec# programs) has the ability to transform BoogiePL code into formulae for various proving back-ends including Simplify, Z3, and HOL/Isabelle [3]. There is also an open source alternative for the environment called FreeBoogie[11].

Lehner and Müller [19] presented a translation from bytecode to BoogiePL. On top of this, one of their students at ETH Zürich, Mallo, developed a tool that transforms BML-annotated bytecode into BoogiePL. This translation is only defined for a subset of the BML language as defined in the BML Reference Manual [10].

Design of the tool. The tool allows one to read class files with BML specifications, and outputs a BoogiePL encoding of the annotated classes. However, BML2BPL uses a non-standard way of representing the BML attributes in classes and it is based on the ASM bytecode library which is different from the one used in other BML-related tools. Therefore a suitable translation is implemented in BMLLib, that provides an interface between the standard representation and BML2BPL (see also Sect. 4.2).

Availability. The translator is available from `https://mobius.ucd.ie/trac/browser/src/BML_BPL_Translator`. It is written in Java and tested primarily under Linux and Windows.

4.6   CCT: A Tool for Packaging Certificates

Overview and goals. The Class Certificate Transformer (CCT) is a modular tool which is able to create and extract certificates from class files [29]. These certificates can for example be typing derivations, information inferred by abstract analysis, or proofs of BML specifications. In addition, CCT allows one to manipulate certificates by adding or removing data. Finally, it also allows one to add plugins which understand the internal structure of certificates and can generate the code which performs the actual verification. For example, one can add a module which retrieves typing information from a certificate and then runs a particular type checker on the program.

---

[11] Available from `http://secure.ucd.ie/products/opensource/FreeBoogie/`

Design of the tool. CCT is built in a highly modular way. One can easily construct plugins for the tool to define the actual PCC certificate verification process. It also allows one to add different libraries that support manipulation of the class file structure so that one is not restricted to using BCEL or ASM for the verification tool.

Availability. The translator is available (in source code format) from `https://mobius.ucd.ie/trac/browser/src/CCT`. It is written in Java and tested primarily under Linux and Windows.

5   Conclusions and Further Work

This paper motivates the development of the specification language BML and its supporting tool set. BML is developed with the proof carrying code paradigm in mind. This motivates part of the design choices: in particular BML is designed to be closely related with the source code level specification language JML, and a binary representation to store BML in class files is defined. However, BML is also intended to be used as a specification language on its own, for example to reason directly about the correctness of low-level program optimisations. Therefore, BML specifications are also designed to be readable and understandable.

An important merit of BML is that it is largely supported by a tool set. The different tools are described in this paper. Currently, the main efforts are focused on filling in the remaining gaps to develop a complete platform for PCC. In particular, we concentrate on the following topics:

- extending the existing verification link through BoogiePL, since it is only defined for a subset of the BML language;
- using the planned extension of FreeBoogie to generate proof obligations in Coq; and
- development of the direct generation of proof obligations for Coq, using the methods of the verification condition generator described in [22, Sect. 5.1].

At the moment, the BML tool set has been tested on small examples only. In the near future, we plan to work on a more realistic case study, that demonstrates the usability of the tools for a non-trivial MIDP application. This case study should demonstrate that the PCC infrastructure works in the environment of the Java Virtual Machine.

In addition to these main goals, we work on a translation from an information-flow type system to BML, based upon the translation described in [28]. This should enable the BML-based verification system to incorporate a mechanism to ensure non-interference.

References

1. Appel, A.W.: Foundational proof-carrying code. In: Halpern, J. (ed.) Logic in Computer Science, p. 247. IEEE Press, Los Alamitos (2001); Invited Talk
2. Appel, A.W., Felty, A.P.: A semantic model of types and machine instructions for proof-carrying code. In: Principles of Programming Languages. ACM Press, New York (2000)

3. Barnett, M., Chang, B.-Y.E., DeLine, R., Jacobs, B., Leino, K.R.M.: Boogie: A modular reusable verifier for object-oriented programs. In: de Boer, F.S., Bonsangue, M.M., Graf, S., de Roever, W.-P. (eds.) FMCO 2005. LNCS, vol. 4111, pp. 364–387. Springer, Heidelberg (2006)

4. Barthe, G., Burdy, L., Charles, J., Grégoire, B., Huisman, M., Lanet, J.-L., Pavlova, M.I., Requet, A.: JACK: A tool for validation of security and behaviour of Java applications. In: de Boer, F.S., Bonsangue, M.M., Graf, S., de Roever, W.-P. (eds.) FMCO 2006. LNCS, vol. 4709, pp. 152–174. Springer, Heidelberg (2007)

5. Beringer, L., Hofmann, M.O.: A bytecode logic for JML and types. In: Kobayashi, N. (ed.) APLAS 2006. LNCS, vol. 4279, pp. 389–405. Springer, Heidelberg (2006)

6. Bjorner, D., Jones, C.B. (eds.): The Vienna Development Method: The Meta-Language. LNCS, vol. 61. Springer, Heidelberg (1978)

7. Burdy, L., Cheon, Y., Cok, D., Ernst, M., Kiniry, J.R., Leavens, G.T., Leino, K.R.M., Poll, E.: An overview of JML tools and applications. In: Workshop on Formal Methods for Industrial Critical Systems. Electronic Notes in Theoretical Computer Science, vol. 80, pp. 73–89. Elsevier, Amsterdam (2003)

8. Burdy, L., Huisman, M., Pavlova, M.I.: Preliminary design of BML: A behavioral interface specification language for java bytecode. In: Dwyer, M.B., Lopes, A. (eds.) FASE 2007. LNCS, vol. 4422, pp. 215–229. Springer, Heidelberg (2007)

9. Burdy, L., Pavlova, M.: Java bytecode specification and verification. In: Symposium on Applied Computing, pp. 1835–1839. ACM Press, New York (2006)

10. Chrząszcz, J., Huisman, M., Schubert, A., Kiniry, J., Pavlova, M., Poll, E.: BML Reference Manual. In: Progress. INRIA and University of Warsaw (December 2008), http://bml.mimuw.edu.pl

11. Darvas, Á., Müller, P.: Formal encoding of JML level 0 specifications in JIVE. Technical report, ETH Zurich, Annual Report of the Chair of Software Engineering (2007)

12. DeLine, R., Leino, K.R.M.: BoogiePL: A typed procedural language for checking object-oriented programs. Technical Report MSR-TR-2005-70, Microsoft Research (2005)

13. Dijkstra, E.W.: Guarded commands, nondeterminacy and formal derivation of programs. Communications of the ACM 18(8), 453–457 (1975)

14. Jacobs, B., Poll, E.: A Logic for the Java Modeling Language JML. In: Hussmann, H. (ed.) FASE 2001. LNCS, vol. 2029, pp. 284–299. Springer, Heidelberg (2001)

15. JSR 175 Expert Group. A metadata facility for the Java programming language. Java Specification Request 175, Java Community Process (September 2004) Final release

16. JSR 308 Expert Group. Annotations on Java types. Java Specification Request 308, Java Community Process (2007) (in progress)

17. Leavens, G.T., Baker, A.L., Ruby, C.: Preliminary design of JML: A behavioral interface specification language for Java. Technical Report TR 98-06y, Iowa State University (1998) (revised since then 2004)

18. Leavens, G.T., Poll, E., Clifton, C., Cheon, Y., Ruby, C., Cok, D.R., Müller, P., Kiniry, J., Chalin, P., Zimmerman, D.: JML Reference Manual, Department of Computer Science, Iowa State University (February 2008), http://www.jmlspecs.org

19. Lehner, H., Müller, P.: Formal translation of bytecode into BoogiePL. In: Huisman, M., Spoto, F. (eds.) Bytecode Semantics, Verification, Analysis and Transformation. ENTCS (2007)

20. Lindholm, T., Yellin, F.: The Java Virtual Machine Specification. Addison-Wesley, Reading (1996)

21. Mallo, O.J.: A translator from BML annotated Java bytecode to BoogiePL. Master's thesis, Software Component Technology Group, ETH Zrich (2007)
22. MOBIUS Consortium. Deliverable 3.1: Bytecode specification language and program logic (2006), http://mobius.inria.fr
23. MOBIUS Consortium. Deliverable 4.2: Certificates (2007), http://mobius.inria.fr
24. Object Management Group. Object Constraint Language. OMG Available Specification, Version 2.0 (May 2006)
25. Pavlova, M.: Java bytecode verification and its applications. Thése de doctorat, spécialité informatique, Université Nice Sophia Antipolis, France (January 2007)
26. Pichardie, D.: Bicolano – Byte Code Language in Coq. In: [22] (2006), http://mobius.inria.fr/bicolano
27. Schubert, A., Chrząszcz, J., Batkiewicz, T., Paszek, J., Wąs, W.: Technical aspects of class specification in the byte code of Java language. In: Bytecode 2008. ENTCS. Elsevier, Amsterdam (2008)
28. Schubert, A., Walukiewicz-Chrząszcz, D.: The non-interference protection in a bytecode program logic (submitted, 2009)
29. Sznuk, T.: Introduction of the proof-carrying code technique to Java class. Master's thesis, Institute of Informatics, The University of Warsaw (2008) (in Polish)

Author Index

Aichernig, Bernhard K.   61
Aldinucci, M.   204
Arbab, Farhad   21

Baier, Christel   82
Blechmann, Tobias   82
Bubel, Richard   247

Cansado, Antonio   180
Chrząszcz, Jacek   278

Danelutto, M.   204
Dustdar, Schahram   1

Griesmayer, Andreas   61

Hähnle, Reiner   247
Hallerstede, Stefan   139
Henrio, Ludovic   159
Honda, Kohei   226
Huisman, Marieke   278

Johnsen, Einar Broch   42, 61

Kammüller, Florian   159
Kilpatrick, P.   204
Klein, Joachim   82

Klüppelholz, Sascha   82
Kokash, Natallia   21
Kyas, Marcel   42

Leuschel, Michael   119

Madelaine, Eric   180
Mayr, Christine   1

Neovius, Mats   102

Paulino, Hervé   226

Rivera, Marcela   159

Schlatte, Rudolf   61
Schubert, Aleksy   278
Sere, Kaisa   102
Stam, Andries   61

Vasconcelos, Vasco   226

Weiß, Benjamin   247

Yoshida, Nobuko   226

Zdun, Uwe   1